Genocide and Settler Society

Studies on War and Genocide
General Editor: Omer Bartov, Brown University

GENOCIDE AND SETTLER SOCIETY

*Frontier Violence and
Stolen Indigenous Children in
Australian History*

Edited by

A. Dirk Moses

Berghahn Books
New York • Oxford

Published in 2004 by
Berghahn Books
© 2004 A. Dirk Moses

First paperback edition published in 2005

Library of Congress Cataloging-in-Publication Data

Genocide and settler society : Frontier violence and stolen indigenous children in Australian
history / edited by A. Dirk Moses.
    p. cm. -- (Studies in war and genocide ; v. 6)
    Includes bibliographical references.
    ISBN 1-57181-410-8 (alk. paper) -- ISBN 1-57181-411-6 (pbk. : alk. paper)
    1. Children, Aboriginal Australian--Relocation. 2. Children, Aboriginal
Australian-Cultural assimilation. 3. Children, Aboriginal Australian--Government policy.
4. Frontier and pioneer life--Australia--History. 5. Aboriginal Australians, Treatment
of--History. 6. Genocide--Australia--History. 7. Australia--Race relations. 8.
Australia--Social policy. 9. Australia--Politics and government. I. Moses, A. Dirk II.
Series.

GN666.G45 2004
305.23'089'9915--dc22   2004046127

British Library Cataloguing in Publication Data

A catalogue record for this book is available
from the British Library.

Printed in the United States on acid-free paper.

Memorial Stone, Myall Creek

On 10 June 1838, twenty-eight Aboriginal men, women, and children were massacred at Myall Creek, in northern NSW, Australia, by a group of armed white stockmen. With the help of local stockmen, the killers were found and identified. Seven men were convicted of the murders, and were hanged in December 1838.

Len Payne, a local resident, first proposed a memorial at the site in 1965. On the suggestion of a descendant of the Aboriginal people who survived the massacre, a conference on reconciliation was held at Myall Creek in 1998. A committee was formed at that conference to develop a permanent memorial. Descendants of the perpetrators, and the Uniting Church, assisted with the planning for the memorial.

One hundred and sixty-two years after the massacre, on 10 June 2000, a memorial walkway and stone were unveiled at the site. There are seven interpretive plaques along the walkway, telling the story of the massacre in both Gumilaroi and English.

The image on the cover of this book is taken from a plaque that also reads:

> Burrulaa Mari gangjibalu
> bawurragu bumaay

> Toward the end of 1837, parties of European stockmen and station hands, encouraged by a punitive expedition of Mounted Police, sent from Sydney, embarked on a bloody rampage throughout the region, hunting down and killing any Aboriginal people they could find. Hundreds of Aboriginal people were slain.

The plaque on the large granite memorial stone at the end of the walkway reads:

In memory of the Wirrayaraay people who were murdered on the slopes of this ridge in an unprovoked but premeditated act in the late afternoon of 10 June 1838.

Erected on 10 June 2000 by a group of Aboriginal and non-Aboriginal Australians in an act of reconciliation, and in acknowledgement of the truth of our shared history.

We remember them. Ngiyani Winangay Ganunga.

Cover image courtesy of Paulette Smith.

CONTENTS

CONTRIBUTORS

PAUL R. BARTROP is a Research Fellow in the Faculty of Arts at Deakin University, Melbourne, Victoria, Australia, and a member of the teaching staff at Bialik College, Melbourne. He has previously been a Scholar-in-Residence at the Martin-Springer Institute for Teaching the Holocaust, Tolerance and Humanitarian Values at Northern Arizona University, and a Visiting Professor at Virginia Commonwealth University. His published works include (with Samuel Totten and Steven Leonard Jacobs), eds., *Teaching about the Holocaust: College Educators* (2004); *Bolt from the Blue: Australia, Britain and the Chanak Crisis* (2002); *Surviving the Camps: Unity in Adversity During the Holocaust* (2000); ed., *False Havens: The British Empire and the Holocaust* (1995); *Australia and the Holocaust, 1933-45* (1994); and, ed., *The Dunera Affair: A Documentary Resource Book* (1990). His current projects include a book entitled *Meanings of Genocide: Essays on a Misunderstood Concept*; and (with Samuel Totten, Steven Leonard Jacobs, and Henry Huttenbach), *A Dictionary of Genocide* (in press). In addition, Dr Bartrop has published numerous scholarly articles in journals and books, as well as being on the editorial committees of a number of periodicals. Dr Bartrop has served on the executive of several Holocaust and genocide studies related organizations in Australia and overseas, and is a Past President of the Australian Association of Jewish Studies. He lives in Melbourne.

RAYMOND EVANS is a Research Associate of History at the University of Queensland, where he taught for many years. He has been working on topics concerning Australian race contact history since the mid-1960s. He has written, cowritten, and edited nine books. His latest book on this subject is *Fighting Words. Writing About Race* (1999). Raymond Evans also publishes widely on convict history, the history of deviance, gender relations, war and society, conflict study, and popular culture.

ANNA HAEBICH is Associate Professor in Australian Studies at Griffith University. Previously she was a Senior Curator of History at the West Australian Museum, where she worked on new galleries of Aboriginal and environmental history. Her most recent publication is *Broken Circles: Fragmenting Indigenous Families 1800-2000* (2001). Other publications include *For Their Own Good: Aborigines and Government in the South West of Western Australia 1900-1940* (1992), and articles on Indigenous history, Australian art, environmental history, women and criminality, and institutionalization.

ISABEL HEINEMANN is a lecturer in the Department of History at Freiburg University in Germany. Her book *'Rasse, Siedlung, deutsches Blut': Das Rasse- und Siedlungshauptamt SS und die rassenpolitische Neuordnung Europas* was published in 2003. She has also written a number of articles in the field, including "'Another Type of Perpetrator': SS Racial Experts and Forced Population Movements in the Occupied Regions," *Holocaust and Genocide Studies* 15 (2001): 387-411; "Towards an 'Ethnic Reconstruction' of Occupied Europe: SS Plans and Racial Policies," *Annali dell Istituto Storico di Trento* XXVII (2001): 493-517; and "'Ethnic Resettlement' and Inter-Agency Cooperation in the Occupied Eastern Territories," in *Networks of Persecution: The Holocaust as Division-of-Labor Based Crime*, ed. Gerald D. Feldman and Wolfgang Seibel (2004). Currently, she is coediting (with Patrick Wagner) a volume called *Wissenschaft, Planung, Praxis: Neuordnungskonzepte und Umsiedlungspolitik im 20. Jahrhundert*.

JAN KOCIUMBAS taught Aboriginal and Pacific History at the University of Sydney between 1985 and 2002. She is the author of two landmark books in Australian history: the *Oxford History of Australia*, Vol. II, *Possessions* (1992), and *Australian Childhood: A History* (1997). Most recently, she edited *Maps, Dreams, History: Race and Representation in Australia* (1998).

ROBERT MANNE, one of Australia's best -known public intellectuals, is Professor of Politics at La Trobe University. He has published extensively in journals and magazines, including the *Journal of Contemporary History* and the *Times Literary Supplement*, and is the author of a number of books including *The Petrov Affair: Pol-*

itics and Espionage (1987), *The Shadow of 1917* (1994), *The Culture of Forgetting* (1996), *The Way We Live Now* (1998), *The Australian Century*, ed. (1999), and *In Denial: The Stolen Generations and the Right* (Black Inc., *Quarterly Essay*, Melbourne, 2001). He is also editor of *Whitewash: On Keith Windschuttle's Fabrication of Aboriginal History* (2003). Robert Manne is currently writing a book on Aboriginal child removal policies in Australia during the twentieth century.

RUSSELL McGREGOR teaches history in the School of Humanities, James Cook University, Townsville, Australia. His publications on the history of white Australian interactions with, and representations of, Aboriginal people include *Imagined Destinies: Aboriginal Australians and the Doomed Race Theory, 1880-1939*, which was awarded the 1998 W.K. Hancock Prize for History. Dr. McGregor is currently working on a study of the connections between shifts in settler Australian understandings of indigenous people and culture, and changing conceptions of Australian nationhood over the course of the twentieth century.

A. DIRK MOSES teaches history at the University of Sydney. He has published articles and book chapters on comparative genocide and German intellectual history.

HENRY REYNOLDS is currently an Australian Research Council Senior Research Fellow and Research Professor at the University of Tasmania. He was for many years attached to the History Department at James Cook University, Townsville, Australia. His major research interest has been the history of European-Aboriginal relations. He has published nine books, which are all still in print. They have won a number of major literary prizes. Some of the better-known books are: *The Other Side of the Frontier* (1982); *Frontier* (1987); *The Law of the Land* (1989); *Aboriginal Sovereignty* (1991); *Fate of a Free People* (1994).

TIM ROWSE is Senior Fellow in the Research School of Social Sciences at the Australian National University. In 2003/2004, he was Visiting Professor of Australian Studies at Harvard University. He is author of nine books since 1978, the latest two being *Indigenous Futures: Choice and Development for Aboriginal and Islander Australia* (2002) and *Nugget: a Reforming Life* (2002).

PAMELA WATSON is an anthropologist and fifth-generation descendant of early British pastoralists who appropriated Aboriginal land in West Australia. Watson's focus has been on the economic and social aspects of drug production and consumption in tribal communities in both the Pacific and Australia, on which she has published journal articles and a monograph. More recently, an interest in drugs in Aboriginal society prior to and immediately following British settlement led her to study a range of early white documents: explorers' journals, archival records, pastoralist memoirs, etc. Horrified by the accounts of brutality towards the indigenous people she encountered in these reports, and the degree to which they contradicted the benign view of white settlement believed by most Anglo-Celtic Australians, she explored these conflicting foundation myths in *Frontier Lands and Pioneer Legends: How Pastoralists Gained Karuwali Land* (1998). The argument Watson makes here for genocide was originally intended for her book, but was omitted from it at the request of the publisher.

JÜRGEN ZIMMERER is currently research fellow at the "Centro de Estudos Interdisciplinares do Século XX," University of Coimbra in Portugal. He is working on transnational European History in the twentieth century, as well as the relationship between colonialism and National Socialism. The second edition of his book, *Deutsche Herrschaft über Afrikaner: Staatlicher Machtanspruch und Wirklichkeit im kolonialen Namibia* appeared in 2002. His edited book (with Joachim Zeller) *Völkermord in Deutsch-Südwestafrika. Der Kolonialkrieg (1904-1908) in Nambia und seine Folgen* appeared in 2003. He has written numerous articles on German colonialism and comparative genocide, and was an editor of the *Newsletter des Arbeitskreises Militärgeschichte*. He currently serves on the editorial team of *Sozial.Geschichte* (formerly 1999) and the online review journal *sehepunkte*.

PREFACE

This book was conceived in early 2000 when I arrived in Australia to take up a post at the University of Sydney. In proposing a new course on comparative genocide, I discovered that I could not prescribe my students a book on genocide in Australia: such a book did not exist (in 2001, Henry Reynolds presented his analysis of the subject in *An Indelible Stain?: The Question of Genocide and Australian History*). At the same time, a lively and at times acrimonious academic and public debate was underway about the topic. Since 1997, it has revolved around past government policies of "removing" Indigenous children of mixed Aboriginal/European descent from their families, ostensibly to "rescue" them from barbarism. In 2000, the genocide controversy turned to frontier conflict in the nineteenth century, which has been the subject of intense research since the 1970s.

Genocide and Settler Society presents recent research on both subjects. The first section, "Conceptual and Historical Determinants," introduces readers unfamiliar with Australian history and genocide studies to the relevant theoretical issues and factual context. The next two sections contain four chapters each on various aspects of frontier violence and stolen Indigenous children, mainly in Australia. Because of the enduring and massive presence of the Holocaust in debates on genocide in Australia and elsewhere, the series editor Omer Bartov thought it appropriate to include a chapter on the relationship between the Holocaust and colonialism, and another on the Nazi policies of removing Slavic children deemed to possess "good Aryan blood" from their families and settling them in Germany. Readers can judge for themselves how relevant these cases are for Australia. At least now they can refer to the latest findings by two outstanding, young German historians.

Genocide studies is a burgeoning field of research. Understandably, it has focused on the enormities of twentieth century totalitarian regimes: Stalin's Soviet Union, Pol Pot's Cambodia, and of course the Holocaust. Or on the internecine legacies of ethnic and civil conflict, like the Turkish-Armenian case, or the all-too-recent instances of Rwanda and Yugoslavia. Now many scholars are beginning to ask after the colonial and imperial roots or dimensions of these conflicts. The inventor of the term "genocide," Raphael Lemkin, certainly conceived of the Nazi project in Europe as colonial. This book aims to contribute to this literature by interrogating the concept of "settler colonialism" in relation to genocide, using Australia as a case study. Each contributor has settled on his or her own definition of genocide—whether that of Lemkin or the narrower formulation of the United Nations—reflecting the open-ended nature of the debate. The book aims to stimulate still more research, rather than provide easy answers.

An editor of any collection accumulates debts in the process of writing and compilation, and this one is no exception. I wish to record my thanks to the following people: to Omer Bartov and Marion Berghahn for intellectual companionship and for enthusiastically supporting the project after Australian publishers had shown a profound lack of interest; to the contributors for their good-humored toleration of my ceaseless demands and unremitting pedantry; to Andrew Beattie for his expert translations; to Caroline Jones and Catherine H. Kirby for their copyediting; to Maria R. Reyes at Berghahn Books for seeing the manuscript through the production process; and to Paulette Smith and Rosemary Hollow for the cover image.

The notion of genocide in relation to the Indigenous peoples of Australia was first conveyed to me in 1996 by a friend, C.L., herself an Indigenous Australian. Hitherto, I had been more or less oblivious to Aboriginal perspectives on Australian history, a regrettable ignorance I can only partially blame on my growing up in the illiberal and racist atmosphere of Brisbane, Queensland, in the 1970s and 1980s. In many ways, the nature of the intellectual journey that I, first and foremost a historian of modern Germany, have been prompted to make since then in order to be able to contribute, in this small way, to scholarly debate and consciousness-raising about this important topic can be attributed to that conversation. I promised her a book then, and here it is.

These chapters have been peer reviewed.

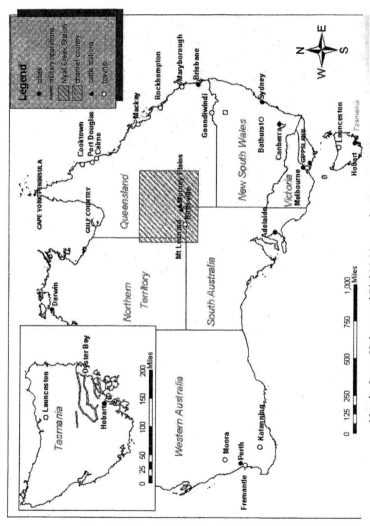

Map by James Hobnen and Phil McManus, the University of Sydney.

– Section I –

CONCEPTUAL AND
HISTORICAL DETERMINANTS

– Chapter 1 –

GENOCIDE AND SETTLER SOCIETY IN AUSTRALIAN HISTORY

A. Dirk Moses

The "Gorgon Effect" and Colonial Genocide

The Gorgon were three mythical sisters, originally beautiful priestesses serving the goddess of wisdom and war, Athena. After the only mortal among them, Medusa, was raped by Poseidon, they vented their anger by torturing men passing Athena's temple. Outraged by such transgressions, Athena turned the sisters into hideous creatures whose image of "Hate, Violence, and Onslaught ... chills the blood."[1] Ever since, the sight of the Gorgon has turned men to stone. Similarly, some have observed, the imagination and will of scholars freezes when they regard the Holocaust. Such is its enormity that conventional categories of analysis fail to apply, and conceptual activity is paralyzed.[2]

Judging by the comparative paucity of publications on colonial genocide, the metaphor of the "Gorgon effect" is equally relevant to this field of inquiry, although it is perhaps less a matter of awed passivity than willful blindness.[3] Consider this observation by a European historian of the Holocaust:

> I think there may have also been a widely-held unspoken assumption that the mass of killing of African or American peoples was a distant

Notes for this section begin on page 37.

and in some senses an "inevitable" part of progress while what was genuinely shocking was the attempt to exterminate an entire people in
Europe. This assumption may rest upon an implicit racism, or simply
upon a failure of historical imagination; it leads, in either case, to the
view that it was specifically with the Holocaust that European civilization—the values of the Enlightenment, a confidence in progress and
modernity—finally betrayed itself. This view claims both too much and
too little. If there had indeed been such a betrayal, had it not occurred
rather earlier, outside Europe?[4]

At least some non-Europeans concur with this suggestion. "From
the standpoint of numerous Asian and Third World scholars,"
wrote one, "the Holocaust, alongside the killings of homosexuals,
gypsies, and the purportedly deranged, visited upon the peoples of
Europe the violence that colonial powers had routinely inflicted on
the 'natives' all over the world for nearly five hundred years."[5]

It is not necessary to join the polemic over the status of the
Holocaust in relation to colonial genocides to recognize that vastly
more scholarly and popular attention has been devoted to the former, and state-sponsored killing in the twentieth century in general,
than to the latter.[6] The "Gorgon effect" here is a product of the
paradox that the largest of the modern empires, Great Britain, was
at once an implacable opponent of totalitarianism and the source of
those settlers who swept aside millions of Indigenous peoples to
establish progressive democracies in North America, New Zealand,
and Australia. Bulwarks of liberty, Britain and its former colonies
also have blood on their hands.

This paradox has issued in two incommensurable responses. In
its extreme incarnation, the first of these condemns European imperialism as a murderous conspiracy against non-Europeans. Typical
is the Native American activist and scholar Ward Churchill, who
regards the English as "global leaders in genocidal activities, both
in terms of overall efficiency — as they consummated the total
extinction of the Tasmanians in 1876 — and a flair for innovation
embodied in their deliberate use of alcohol to effect the dissolution
of many of North America's indigenous peoples."[7] A rival view
lauds Britain as the mildest of Europe's imperial powers: the
"natives" were lucky that the British colonized their country and
not, say, the French or Belgians. Hannah Arendt, for example, was
fascinated by the Anglophone colonies as exceptions to the continental pattern of conquest because they were not "seriously concerned with discrimination against other peoples as lower races, if
only for the reason that the countries they were talking about,
Canada and Australia, were almost empty and had no serious pop-

ulation problem." To be sure, Arendt qualified this extraordinary statement in a footnote that acknowledged "comparatively short periods of cruel liquidation" of the few original inhabitants. Nonetheless, her basic conviction was that British civilization blessed the continents of America and Australia, which, until its arrival, were "without a culture and history of their own."[8] Likely she would have rejected the proposition of Churchill and David E. Stannard that the Native Americans suffered an "American Holocaust," but her naïve paean to British expansion simply repeated contemporary European prejudices about their civilization and non-European barbarism despite the fact that the Holocaust occurred in the heart of Europe.[9]

A closer look at British commentary on Britain's encounter with Indigenous peoples in the nineteenth century reveals that both views are one-sided. Rarely can exterminatory intent be discerned in British authorities, but there was a greater degree of consciousness about the fatal impact of their presence than Arendt was willing to consider. Writing in 1839, for instance, Charles Darwin noted, "Wherever the European has trod, death seems to pursue the aboriginal. ... The varieties of man seem to act on each other; in the same way as different species of animals the stronger always extirpating the weaker."[10] In the same year, the ethnologist James Prichard sounded the tocsin about "the extinction of human races" in *The Edinburgh New Philosophical Journal*: "Wherever Europeans have settled, their arrival has been the harbinger of extermination to the native tribes." Fearful that a further century of colonization would mean "the aboriginal nations of most parts of the world will have ceased to exist," he asked "whether any thing [sic] can be done effectually to prevent the extermination of the aboriginal tribes."[11]

Subsequent instances of Indigenous massacres of settlers and the rise of scientific racism meant that the novelist Anthony Trollope and imperial ideologue Charles Dilke expressed no such anxieties when they wrote about their respective antipodean tours several decades later.[12] The Aborigines were "ineradicably savage," declared the former in 1872; the male possessed the deportment "of a sapient monkey imitating the gait and manners of a do-nothing white dandy," as well as suffering from a "low physiognomy" that rendered him lazy and useless. "It is their fate to be abolished; and they are already vanishing," he concluded without regret or moral scruple. The harshness of Trollope's judgment that the Aborigine "had to go" was hardly mitigated by the wish that they "should perish without unnecessary suffering."[13] Dilke commented in simi-

lar terms in relation to Indigenous population collapse. The "aboriginal Australian blacks ... were so extraordinarily backward a
race as to make it difficult to help them to hold their own." They
were "rapidly dying out, and it is hard to see any other fate could
be expected for them."[14] Many such statements from the period
could be adduced.[15]

Australian Settler Society and its Conscience

Clearly, the British understood the effects of their presence in Australia and other colonies. But this did not mean they took responsibility for the anticipated disappearance of the Indigenous peoples,
despite the obvious connection between colonization and depopulation. Since the nineteenth century, they, and later, Australians,
have engaged in often-acrimonious debate about the causes of the
Aboriginal demographic catastrophe and the apportionment of
blame. As one visitor to New South Wales observed in the early
1840s, colonial society was split between those for whom the Aborigines were "not entitled to be looked upon as fellow creatures,"
and those who viewed "with horror the inroad made into the possessions of the natives."[16] An English settler made the same observation in 1844 when he reported that two friends "argued that it is
morally right for a Christian Nation to extirpate savages from their
native soil in order that it may be peopled with a more intelligent
and civilized race of human beings ... [while] ... (Frederick)
McConnell and myself were of the opposite opinion and argued
that a nation had no moral right to take forcible possession of any
place."[17] The stakes were, and remain, high. Was white Australia
born with the mark of Cain? Or had the settlers built a society
about which they could feel justly proud and that ultimately bene-
fited the Aborigines, at least those prepared to relinquish their
"stone-age" culture for the modern European one? The arguments
fall roughly into the same two camps sketched above: "humanitarian" and "triumphalist."

"That Thin Strand of Humanitarianism"[18]

Australian colonization was triumphant, but its human cost troubled a small minority of Britons. From the 1820s, they believed the
settlers were unjustly treating the original inhabitants and exterminating them when they resisted. Where Aboriginal warriors had
committed "depredations" or "outrages," these critics pointed out,
were they not reacting to white violation of their food supplies and

women? Even if disease carried off the majority of the Aborigines, they continued, had not Indigenous society and its reproductive capacities been fatally smashed by rapacious settlers? Furthermore, it was iniquitous that Aborigines were forbidden from testifying in legal proceedings when they were otherwise regarded formally as British subjects, equal before the law.[19] Expressing the Enlightenment and Christian belief in a universal human nature, they insisted that Aborigines were fully human and children of God, and therefore "civilizable." Such were the assumptions of the colony's first governor, Captain Arthur Phillip, whose orders were to treat the Aborigines well.[20]

In this vein, liberal officials in the Colonial Office in London worried greatly about the frontier struggle transpiring on the other side of the world. In 1837, a Select Committee Inquiry urged the British government to assume moral responsibility for the Indigenous peoples of South Africa, the Australian colonies, and North America lest they become extinct. A year later, Sir George Gipps, Governor of New South Wales, embodied this spirit when he expedited the prosecution and execution of whites who had massacred Aborigines at Myall Creek—one of the very few occasions in the nineteenth century that the law making the murder of Aborigines a capital offence was enforced.[21]

Toward the end of the nineteenth century and early in the next, the humanitarian impulse issued in "protection" legislation for "pacified" Aborigines in the self-governing British colonies (which became the constitutive states of the Commonwealth of Australia in 1901). Such measures, which confined many Aborigines in isolated reserves under oppressive regimes of discriminatory regulation, were designed to afford them security from the exploitation and violence of frontier existence. But these laws also suited the majority of colonists, who were happy to have Aborigines removed from fertile farmland and country towns.[22]

The public, having also applauded the prohibition of non-white immigration into the country (the "White Australia Policy") after Federation in 1901, showed little interest in the "native question" in the two decades of the twentieth century. The question was back on the table, however, after police massacres of Aborigines in northwest and central Australia in 1926 and 1928 scandalized local and international opinion. Small groups of metropolitan Aborigines, as well as white anthropologists, Christians, socialists, and feminists began campaigns to highlight that Aborigines were not in fact a "dying race," as commonly supposed. Their targets were the official policies in the different states in the 1930s that decreed that Aborigines be "absorbed" into the population and eventually disappear as distinct peoples, that their "color" be "bred out" by racial engineering, or that they be strictly segregated until they "died out." By way of resistance, Aboriginal groups and humanitarians lobbied—in vain—for full citizenship rights and policies of "uplift."[23]

During and after the Second World War, however, official policy abandoned racial engineering for "assimilation." The new approach entailed integrating Aborigines into the white community as fellow citizens. Ultimate Indigenous extinction was abandoned as an assumption of governance, although large sections of the public continued to entertain the fantasy of a white Australia. Assimilation, therefore, marked a paradigm change in which the long-standing Enlightenment optimism of the humanitarian position became official policy. And yet, "uplifting" Aborigines entailed the continuity of heavy-handed legal restriction, including the practice of "removing" children of mixed Indigenous-European parentage from their Indigenous mothers. In practice at least, assimilation appeared to some as sharing much with the absorption policies of the 1930s. The anthropologist W.E.H. Stanner (1905-1981) spoke for many when he observed in 1964 that the terms of assimilation were "still fundamentally dictatorial."[24] Aboriginal activists, and humanitarians who formerly had favored "civilizing" Aborigines, now criticized state paternalism in general, advocating not only legal equality, but also self-determination and sovereignty. Because of assimilation's firm commitment to the nation-building project and consequent hostility to any Aboriginal autonomy, it belongs firmly in the triumphalist tradition.

It is important to appreciate that Australians in the 1950s regarded their modernity as unimpeachable, having passed the test of prosperity and viability by generating enormous wealth and fending off Japanese imperial designs. Assimilation was therefore a considered progressive. When Australians thought of racial conflict at all, their eyes turned to South Africa and the American South. Invidious parallels could be made here, so the conservative federal government funded research into Aboriginal culture to showcase its benevolent credentials. As might be expected, the new Australian Institute for Aboriginal Studies, established in Canberra in the early 1960s, was not meant to probe current policy and welfare issues, but to limit itself to apolitical "scientific, cultural and anthropological research."[25]

By the late 1960s, however, the small minority that had rowed against the tide was scoring some successes. This was the time when

Indigenous population recovery meant whites had to "adjust to the idea that Aboriginal Australians are not a dying race after all," as one observer noted at the time.[26] In 1967, after a vigorous campaign, Australians voted to change the constitution to grant the federal government power to make special laws affecting Aborigines (who had been empowered to vote in federal elections in 1962)—hitherto the prerogative of the states—an innovation that promised policy progress and consistency across the country.[27] "Freedom-riders" from the University of Sydney, following in the footsteps of the American civil rights movement, exposed racist practices in rural towns and raised public consciousness about inequality in a country that prided itself on the egalitarian spirit.[28] All the while, the Aboriginal struggle for land rights assumed a higher profile, culminating in a permanent "tent embassy" on the lawns of the federal parliament in Canberra in 1972.[29] The White Australia Policy was also officially abolished in favor of "multiculturalism."

This mood of change was reflected in historical scholarship, although it was two older social scientists who were responsible for coining the terms that became the watchwords of research for a younger generation of historians. W.E.H. Stanner's prestigious Boyer Lectures of 1968, published as *After the Dreaming*, declaimed the "Great Australian Silence" about the Indigenous presence in Australian history, a silence to which he regretted having contributed as a young anthropologist. By way of recompense, he called for a "less ethnocentric social history" that acknowledged "the structure of race relations and the persistent indifference to the fate of the Aborigines." It was also necessary to expose the "apologetic element" in Australian historiography, which "sticks out like a foot from a shallow grave."[30]

The call for a new historical approach was begun in 1964 by the sociologist Charles Rowley (1906-1985), who published a trilogy of works in 1970 and 1971 that established the subdiscipline of Aboriginal History.[31] *The Destruction of Aboriginal Society*, the first continent-wide treatment of the subject, provided the motto for a number of dissertations that aimed to break the great Australian silence.[32] Inspired by post-colonial liberation movements around the globe and appalled by the continuity of popular and institutionalized discrimination in Australia, these young historians began systematic, empirical work on frontier violence and racist traditions, and what they found changed the received view of the peaceful "settlement" of the country. The titles of these books, such as *Exclusion, Exploitation, and Extermination* and *Invasion and Resistance*, captured the new spirit. Their narratives also recast the moral drama of the national history.[33] No longer were Australians to forge a "New Britannia" by carving out a European utopia from the rock of a harsh land. They had to make good the white abuse of Aborigines, non-Anglo immigrants, and the environment. The triumphalist narrative was making way for the humanitarian one.

Journalists and popular writers made use of this "revisionist" scholarship for moral-political purposes. In thrall to the "perpetrator trauma"—the shock of realization at the crimes committed by one's compatriots—such writers urged Australians to face up to their dark past, which they depicted in simplistic terms of good and evil:[34]

> The blood of tens of thousands of Aborigines killed since 1788, and the sense of despair and hopelessness which informs so much modern-day Aboriginal society, is a moral responsibility all white Australians share. Our wealth and lifestyle is a direct consequence of Aboriginal dispossession. We should bow our heads in shame.[35]

The Gorgon Effect—the freezing of the imagination—was evident when they occasionally made wild analogies with Nazi genocide, such as the journalist Phillip Knightley's naïve exclamation:

> It remains one of the mysteries of history that Australia was able to get away with a racist policy that included segregation and dispossession and bordered on slavery and genocide, practices unknown in the civilized world in the first half of the twentieth century until Nazi Germany turned on the Jews.[36]

Scholars, by contrast, have been very circumspect, occasionally drawing some links or parallels between German and Australia history, but without crudely equating the two cases.[37] When one complained in 1987 that the "dispossession-resistance" model of frontier relations had become an "orthodoxy," and suggested supplementing it with the paradigm of "accommodation" between Aborigines and settlers, he was echoing the unease of many historians with such crude popularizations.[38] But this did not mean they abandoned the humanitarian tradition. The "need to decolonise Australian writing" continued.[39]

Indeed, historians applauded the developments in the 1990s when the then Labor Prime Minister, Paul Keating, advocated reconciliation with Indigenous peoples on the basis of a left-liberal perspective of the national past, one strongly influenced by his speechwriter, Don Watson, himself the author of an important book on the frontier.[40] The highest court in the land took much the same view in two key decisions recognizing "native title," Mabo (1992) and Wik (1996), grounded as they were in a generation of revisionist scholarship, especially that of Henry Reynolds, and the tenacity of the Indigenous litigants like Eddie Mabo.[41]

Yet despite such advances, the humanitarian agenda struck only shallow roots in Australian culture. Throughout the 1980s and 1990s, conservatives complained bitterly about the "political correctness" of the Labor Party's shibboleths of multiculturalism and Aboriginal land rights, which they thought criminalized the national past. These positions, they charged, were propounded illegitimately by "elites" who brainwashed the public through their domination of the key institutions of cultural transmission: universities, school curricula, museums, and the national television and radio broadcaster, the Australian Broadcasting Corporation.[42]

A sufficient number of Australians agreed with them in 1996 to elect a conservative federal government determined to replace the "black armband" view of history—as it derided the humanitarian perspective—with pride in settler traditions.[43] To be sure, the government does not advocate renewing the White Australia Policy, although after September 2001 some of its supporters wanted to ban Islamic migrants because of their supposed inability to integrate.[44] In fact, it dines out internationally on the country's "authentically cosmopolitan civic culture of which I for one am very proud,"[45] as one commentator expostulated, while cruelly detaining refugees in camps, pouring scorn on the United Nations' competence to scrutinize its deteriorating human rights record, and denouncing humanitarian dissenters as traitorous fifth columnists.[46]

Yet Indigenous issues gained increasing attention despite official efforts to sweep them under the carpet. In 1997, the *Bringing them Home* report on stolen Aboriginal children—thousands of children of mixed Indigenous/European descent "removed" from their Indigenous mothers by state authorities until the late 1960s—commissioned before the conservative government came to power, hit the headlines. It accused the states of genocide, and was backed by massive public demonstrations across Australia in 2000 for a government apology to the victims.[47] The formal "reconciliation process," initiated after the Royal Commission into Aboriginal Deaths in Custody in 1991, culminated in a controversial "Australian Reconciliation Convention" in 1997 during which the dismay of delegates about the truculently unapologetic Prime Minister John Howard was readily apparent.[48]

These developments, and renewed talk of a treaty between Indigenous and non-Indigenous Australians, were met with sneers by conservatives who exulted when the testimony of some Aboriginal people in *Bringing them Home* was questioned. Not only was the humanitarian "elite" more interested in moral aggrandizement than Aboriginal welfare, they bid us believe, but Indigenous leaders did not represent their constituencies and bullied decent white folk with their ceaseless demands.[49] Most recently, the crusade of conservatives to claw back lost ground has culminated in an ugly campaign to deny that much frontier violence took place at all. The "orthodox" historians, as the humanitarians are categorized, were even accused of fabricating sources, a claim readily accepted by those resentful of "intellectuals" and the "new class."[50] Such was the rhetorical venom that passed for informed debate in the initial years of the twenty-first century, and sadly, most Australians appear to share these views. But there is nothing new about them.

That Hegemonic "Triumphalism"

The triumphalist posture that, except in rare moments, has dominated the policy and cultural agenda of the colonies and nation-state for over 200 years seems as resilient as ever. This is not surprising given that it justifies the European occupation of the continent and dispossession of its inhabitants. To question it is to dispute the moral legitimacy of the Australian nation-state.[51]

The foundations of triumphalist colonization were laid well before the "first fleet" of two warships, six transports of convicts, and three of stores arrived in what is now Sydney in January 1788. European writers like Samuel Pufendorf (1632-1694) had conceived of the historical development of humanity in four stages, the final one being "commercial society"—i.e., "civilization"—of political communities interconnected by trade.[52] English writers of the seventeenth century also ranked societies according to their development in relation to the Europe of their day just as the Scottish Enlightenment proposed a stadial view of human development. Following the natural law arguments of the Salamanca School of Thomist philosophers of the sixteenth century, the English argued that hunter-gatherers stood at the bottom of human social evolution because they did not fulfill their human potential by cultivating the land. One Hobart resident had this idea in mind when he wrote in 1874 of the Indigenous peoples of Tasmania:

> The aboriginal's wants were, indeed, so few, and the country in which it had pleased the Almighty to place him supplied them all in such lavish abundance, that he was not called on for the exercise of much skill or labour in satisfying his requirements. He had no inducement to work and (like all others who are so situated) he did not very greatly exert himself. Necessity, said to be the parent of invention, was known to him only in a limited degree; and in ingenuity was seldom brought into exercise. His faculties were dormant from the mere bounty of providence.[53]

On the basis of these assumptions, the British argued the "natives" had rights only to what they caught and gathered, while uncultivated land belonged to no one *(res nullius)*, and was therefore available to Europeans to settle and exploit.[54]

This agriculturalist argument is well-known—especially as expounded by John Locke (1632-1704) in his *Two Treatises on Government* (1690)—as is James Cook's annexation of the whole east coast of Australia in 1770 on the grounds that it was *terra nullius*, unclaimed waste land.[55] It remains popular in Australia today.[56] What is usually overlooked is that Locke licensed not only such dispossession, but also wars of extermination against Indigenous people if they resisted the loss of their land and customary ways. By breaking natural law in defying the perceived European right to the land and rejecting European entreaties to enter civilization, so the case goes, "natives" rejected "friendship" and "trade," as it was articulated by apologists for English colonists in the seventeenth century. The colonists were justified, therefore, in invoking the theory of just war to defend themselves against the Indigenous attacks on their rightful presence and claims.[57] As Locke put it, such "natives" had

> declared war against all mankind, and therefore may be *destroyed as a lion or tiger, one of those wild savage beasts with whom men can have no society or security*. And upon this is grounded that great law of Nature, 'Whoso sheddeth man's blood by man shall his blood be shed.' Also Cain was so fully convinced that every one had a right to destroy such a criminal, that, after the murder of his brother, he cries out, 'Every one that findeth me shall slay me,' so plain was it writ in the hearts of all mankind.[58]

That Locke could issue warrants for genocide is counterintuitive, because he, and the English generally, condemned the Spanish for violating the natural rights of the Indigenous people and for not attempting to civilize them. By contrast, English colonialism, he wrote, did not proceed by "the sword," respected the property rights of the hunter-gatherers, and sought their uplift.[59] Judging by the furious reaction of British settlers to attacks on their property, however, the presumption that by their presence they were doing the Aborigines a favor only fuelled their indignation and proclivity to take savage reprisals.[60]

Not only was the spirit of revenge rife on the frontier—as several chapters in this volume make plain—the "justice" of crushing Indigenous resistance was as obvious to contemporaries like Trollope in the 1870s as it was to later Australian establishment historians in the 1930s.[61] Grenfell Price of the University of Adelaide, for instance, wrote in the *Cambridge History of the British Empire* that:

> So serious had been the troubles in the Murray area [in southeastern Australia] that settlement virtually ceased until troops were sent to the district, and at the "battle of Pinjarra" [in western Australia] in 1834 *half the males of the Murray tribe were destroyed.* This conflict enabled F.F. Armstrong and others to establish better relations with the natives, although the difficulty was not completely removed for many years.[62]

Two years later, in 1935, the professor of history at the University of Sydney, Stephen H. Roberts, who shortly afterwards would write the critique of Nazi Germany, published an analysis of squatters in colonial Australia that betrayed the same Lockean assumptions. Such grievances as the natives had against the whites "were usually the result of their own ungovernable dispositions and their failure to see any sense in the white man's laws of property." While Roberts was prepared to concede that "Squatting life certainly impinged on native existence," the point was that "the interaction was as between landowner and raiders." Little wonder, he implied, that "Outrage, real or imaginary, was met by outrage, and Europeans killed natives on the slightest pretext."[63]

Roberts' work incarnated other aspects of the triumphalist posture towards Aborigines and colonization. Primary among them was his disapproval of humanitarians, like well-meaning missionaries, whose civilizing aspirations he regarded as naïve. There was no getting around the "nature of the natives."[64] Similarly, Governor Gipps, who tried to guard Indigenous rights, came in for Roberts' hefty criticism. Because of Gipps' leniency, "The natives became unbearably impudent, and no longer were flocks or even human life safe. Seven or eight years of virtual terror set in after 1837." What is more, the governor was hard on the settlers. They were incredulous when seven of them were hanged for massacring a harmless group of Aborigines. "It would be difficult to exaggerate the stir this caused in the squatting ranks, for it changed one of the basic assumptions of life in the bush," noted Roberts. After all, "the colonists had not deemed it possible to try white men for killing natives."[65]

Lampooning the humanitarians in the colonial capitals and London for their ignorance of frontier realities was typical of the colonial press. In 1838, the *Sydney Morning Herald* took aim at James Stephen of the Colonial Office, "being one of those kind-hearted 'Liberals' who bestow so much of their pity on devastating and murderous savages, that they have none to spare for the white people."[66] But such rhetoric also expressed anxiety that the authorities were taking seriously the formal legal equality accorded the Aborigines, and therefore did not side automatically with the settlers. Plainly, such metropolitan "liberals" did not appreciate the "romance" of the great strides being made on the frontier.

"Romance" was a common trope in the memorialization of the frontier, as in the pastoralist Simpson Newland's thinly-veiled memoir of 1893, *Paving the Way: A Romance of the Australian Bush*. It was also the central plot engine of Roberts' first book, *A History of Australian Land Settlement*, which in 460 pages mentions "the natives" once. Instead, he rhapsodizes about "the struggle and the glamour, the *camaraderie* and the fights against uneven odds, the romance of overlanding and mustering, the dirt and droughts and disease."[67] Here, too, was the depiction of the settlers as victims, banished from the British motherland to face an uncertain future in a hostile environment. This self-understanding continues today in conservative memory politics, which urges a narcissistic identification with "our pioneers" and nation-builders like the Anzacs (Australian and New Zealand military forces) in order to gird the communal loins against terrorists, refugees, dissident intellectuals, and other ostensible threats to the Australian way of life.[68]

Another feature of the settler pragmatism that Roberts articulated was the species of racism that regarded Indigenous people as uncivilizable: "It was quite useless to treat them fairly," he opined, "because they were completely ammoral [sic] and usually incapable of sincere and prolonged gratitude."[69] He referred with contempt to Aborigines' supposed "thoughtlessness, ingratitude, debauchery, want of effort, infanticide and outrages." Consequently, he implied, Europeans were not responsible for the eventual passing of the Aborigines; the laws of nature decreed that backward societies gave way before advanced ones. After all, natives "would not work, and only abandoned themselves to fighting and selling their *gins* [women] to shepherds for tobacco or spirits. In the wake of these evils," he averred, "came the inevitable venereal disease, consumption, and an appallingly rapid depopulation."[70] The conclusion to be drawn was that Indigenous society was not destroyed by the Europeans, but collapsed under the weight of its own pathologies. Some anthropologists, as well as a number of local failed academics and credulous journalists, make precisely the same arguments about Indigenous people today, a prejudice they dignify with the jargon of "sick societies."[71]

In marked contrast, firsthand accounts by frontier settlers in the nineteenth century made no bones about their intentions, proclaiming, "let us at once exterminate these useless and obnoxious wretches. It seems that nothing short of extermination will check their animosity to the whites and all that is theirs." And: "Desperate diseases call for strong remedies and while we would regret a war of extermination, we cannot but admit that there exists a stern, though maybe cruel necessity for it."[72] Newland, for example, wrote of "the wiping out process" in Queensland, where the "dispersal" of natives, "put plainly, meant nearly indiscriminate slaughter." With remarkable prescience, he added, "Of course, these stories will be denied."[73]

As already noted, the "doomed race" theory was hegemonic until the Second World War, after which the triumphalists enjoined an authoritarian assimilation, a policy that opposed any notions of "separate development" and self-determination for, or a treaty with, Indigenous peoples. In their symbolic struggles with the humanitarians today, the triumphalists' primary target is the proposition that Aborigines were the victims of genocide because it underwrites anti-assimilationist ideologies and policies.

> the greatest falsification of Australian history is that the nation was born in genocide and oppression and after 200 years remained in what [the historian, Manning] Clark has termed the "age of ruins." You can judge a nation only by reference to contemporary alternatives. So judged, Australia has done well enough to have established our own proven symbols. Regrettably ... this has not been possible, due essentially to the fact that so much of popular history is taught by the alienated and the discontented.[74]

Plainly, the genocide concept is not only a politically-neutral, heuristic device of social science, at least in public discourse. How has it been used in relation to Australia?

The Genocide Concept in Australia

The term genocide is used to refer to two phenomena in Australian history: frontier violence, mainly in the nineteenth century, and the various policies of removing Aboriginal children of mixed descent from their families, mainly in the twentieth century. The structure of this book reflects this division. Both of these phenomena have made for bitter controversies in the "history wars" of the 1990s. But the term has been used for decades in a variety of ways by different people in a variety of contexts.

International consciousness about genocide in Australia has been limited to the case of Tasmania, often cited as a "classical" instance of colonial genocide.[75] Recent Australian scholarship has questioned this view, although no one denies the demographic catastrophe that befell the Aboriginal Tasmanians, who are supposed to have "died out" as "full bloods" in 1876.[76] Of course, the term was not used before it was coined in 1944 and enshrined in international law by the United Nations four years later. Contemporaries spoke instead of "extermination" and "extirpation."[77]

It should come as no surprise that Indigenous peoples have used genocide to name their traumatic experiences because the colonial enterprise is experienced as criminal. "The black extermination drives of the Hawkesbury and Manning Rivers. The genocide of the Tasmanian blacks," declared Aboriginal activist Kevin Gilbert. "These and many, many more were the links in the chain of white inhumanity that lives on in the memories of the southern part-bloods today."[78] In 1963, secretary of the Federal Council for Aboriginal Advancement, Stan Davey, attacked the official policy of assimilation in a pamphlet called *Genesis or Genocide?* Would Australia condone a process of racial elimination by stealth, he asked provocatively, like the Nazis, Czarists, and Russian communists had attempted to solve their national minority problems by outright extermination?[79] Aboriginal leader Mick Dodson continued this line of argument in relation to the Stolen Generations of Aboriginal children:

> the fact is if you look at the government's politics and laws set in place to back them up, their central intention was to destroy the Aboriginality of these kids. I am not equating the Holocaust to the removals, but they fall under the same heading of genocide. They're just a different form of genocide.[80]

As we shall see, conservatives objected vehemently to this proposition, insisting that the United Nations genocide convention did not criminalize "cultural genocide" (cultural rather than physical destruction), but who will gainsay the point of Indigenous jurist Larissa Behrendt that "the political posturing and semantic debates do nothing to dispel the feeling Indigenous people have that this is the word that adequately describes our experience as colonized people"?[81]

Activists on the left throw up their hands in exasperation at the definitional precision demanded by academics because it detracts from ongoing political struggles. "Even if events in Australia don't fit the genocide convention to the letter, is that the point?" one of them asks. "Continuing policies toward Indigenous people continue to result in such serious discrimination and disadvantage that genocide is the only appropriate term to use."[82]

As might be expected, lawyers also insist on exactness when they speak of genocide, but that does not render them immune from ethical considerations. A model of moral clarity was one of the royal commissioners into Aboriginal deaths in custody, J.H. (Hal) Wootten, who in 1989 was shocked by the "foreshadowing of Holocaust languages in the references to the achievements of a 'solution' and of 'finality'" in the reports he read of state protection authorities from 1921. "In its crudest forms," he concluded, "the policy of assimilation fell within this modern definition of genocide, and in particular the attempt to 'solve the Aboriginal problem' by taking away children and merging them into white society fell within that definition."[83]

This viewpoint would cause a national scandal eight years later. Initially, it was played down by the national commissioner who rejected the proposition that, in principle, assimilation amounted to genocide.[84] He in turn was vehemently contradicted by the subsequent *Bringing them Home* report, which focused on Article 2 (e) of the UN Convention on genocide, the section that criminalizes the forcible transfer of children from one group to another with the intention of destroying a racial, ethnic, or religious group. This inquiry was understandably sympathetic to the Indigenous victims, whose shocking stories of abuse and privation received wide publicity for the first time. It concluded with the now famous accusation that postwar assimilation policies had aimed to eliminate Aborigines as a cultural unit, and were therefore genocidal.[85]

Australian historians, by contrast, have been reluctant to invoke genocide despite the fact that the Indigenous population declined from approximately 750,000 in 1788 to 31,000 in 1911. (By way of comparison, the immigrant population rose to 3,825 million by 1901.)[86] Thinking it means total physical destruction, and concerned to stress that Aborigines had survived to make political claims today, these academics were disinclined to use the term.[87] Another reason for this hesitancy was the misconception that genocide entailed the state's intention to exterminate all Australian Aborigines as a single people. "It is not appropriate to refer to the frontier violence as attempted genocide," concluded Richard Broome, "because—despite the desires of individuals—there was no official policy or attempt to eliminate the Aboriginal population."[88]

Writers in the 1970s and 1980s proceeded without much awareness of the UN Convention and its intellectual origins, which was hardly surprising given that the social scientific literature on the subject only began to develop at this time. If historians used the term at all, they did so more or less as a synonym for "extirpation" or "extermination," reflecting the rhetoric of the sources they read.[89] "What *can* be said," affirmed one of them, "is that the spirit of genocide was abroad in eastern Australia from the 1820s until the final 'pacification' of Queensland Aborigines in the first decade of this [the twentieth] century, and that it survived in Western Australia and the Northern Territory until the 1920s."[90]

At the same time, local and regional studies undercut the homogenization of Indigenous peoples into a single entity—"the Aborigines"—by the colonizing perspective. The fact that many of the approximately 600 Indigenous cultural-linguistic groups regarded themselves as separate peoples raised interesting questions about genocide.[91] For adopting their self-understanding in terms of the UN definition can lead to the conclusion that each willed act of extermination by settlers and/or the state of an Aboriginal group could be regarded as genocide. In that case, many genocides took place in Australia, rather than being the site of a single genocidal event.[92]

Most recently, a number of Australian scholars have begun to consider the issue systematically in light of the UN Convention and the now-voluminous literature on comparative genocide.[93] This work is still in progress, but has already met stiff resistance from those for whom genocide is consubstantial with the Holocaust. The Gorgon Effect is most evident in this blanket refusal to consider its meaning in international law and implications for Australian history. The philosopher Raimond Gaita attempted to clear up the confusion about the relationship between genocide and the Holocaust in many articles and in his book, *A Common Humanity*, but the subtleties of his finely-grained analysis were missed by many readers.[94] For instance, Inga Clendinnen, an historian of the Aztecs, complained of the *Bringing them Home* report in the following terms:

> when I see the word "genocide," I still see Gypsies and Jews being herded into trains, into pits, into ravines, and behind them the shadowy figures of Armenian women and children being marched into the desert by armed men. I see deliberate mass murder: innocent people identified by their killers as distinctive entities being done to death by organised authority. I believe that to take the murder out of genocide is to render it vacuous.[95]

Conservative newspaper columnists shared her indignation that the good intentions of white administrators in "rescuing" white-looking black children had been traduced by association with genocide.[96]

To be sure, in the 1930s and early 1940s disturbing parallels between the treatment of Aborigines and that of German Jews were made by some observers. Aboriginal leader William Cooper, for example, pointed to the categorization of Aborigines according to genetic inheritance, their treatment as an "enemy people," and banishment to camps. The Jewish refugee artist Josl Bergner saw matters in much the same terms.[97] But no one equated the Australian case and the Holocaust of European Jewry. Regardless, an editorial in a provincial newspaper in 2001 felt it necessary to complain that "Many Jews and non-Jews familiar with the intrinsic evil and systematic course of the Holocaust in all its extraordinary horror find any notion of parallels with the removal of Aboriginal children utterly offensive."[98] The professor of Jewish Studies at Monash University in Melbourne, Andrew Markus, insisted similarly that genocide not be used in the Australian context because it can only be properly applied to the Holocaust.[99]

The Gorgon Effect is palpable in the doubts that some now entertain about the genocide term. One historian who noted disapprovingly in 1983 that "Such terms as 'invasion' and 'attempted genocide' ... still appear to stick in the typewriters of some historians and others," ate his words eighteen years later, regarding them as dubiously "emotive and arguable."[100] There is a danger that the genocide term will become stuck in the keyboards of historians and social scientists if the confusion over its meaning and relationship to the Holocaust continues to cloud debate.[101]

What is Genocide?

In order to understand the nature of the crime of genocide, it is important to appreciate the intentions of the formulator of the term, the Polish-Jewish jurist Raphael Lemkin (1900-1959). Growing up in multiethnic eastern Poland, where Jews lived as neighbors with Poles and Russians, he became convinced that

the diversity of nations, religious groups and races is essential to civilization because every one of these groups has a mission to fulfill and a contribution to make in terms of culture. To destroy these groups is opposed to the will of the Creator and to disturb the spiritual harmony of mankind.[102]

The "formula of the human cosmos," then, comprised culture-creating human groups, rather than contingent ones like political associations. There were four such groups: national, racial, religious, and ethnic.[103]

Indignant that the perpetrators of the Armenian genocide had largely escaped prosecution, Lemkin, who was a young state prosecutor in Poland, began lobbying in the early 1930s for international law to criminalize the destruction of such groups.[104] Initially, he sought to establish two new crimes: *barbarity* (destruction of national groups), and *vandalism* (destruction of their unique cultural artifacts).[105] Such "acts of extermination directed against the ethnic, religious or social collectivities whatever the motive (political, religious, etc.)," he implored, should be considered "offences against the law of nations by reason of their common feature which is to endanger both the existence of the collectivity concerned and the entire social order."[106] But his lobbying could not overcome the entrenched belief in national sovereignty, and so European peoples had no legal protection in the coming bloodletting unleashed by the German state.[107]

An academic and government advisor in the United States during the Second World War, Lemkin found it almost impossible to convince policy-makers that the Nazis were waging a war of extermination rather than a conventional campaign. To make his case, he compiled the decrees issued by the Germans in the countries they occupied, along with his commentary and a discussion of a new crime, genocide, in his now well-known book, *Axis Rule in Occupied Europe*. Combining barbarism and vandalism into "a generic term," he defined genocide as "the criminal intent to destroy or cripple permanently a human group."[108] It was a new word "to denote an old practice in its modern development."[109] What did it mean? Destruction or crippling did not necessarily entail mass murder: "Generally speaking, genocide does not mean the immediate destruction of a nation, except when accomplished by mass killings of all members of a nation."[110] In fact:

> The end may be accomplished by the forced disintegration of political and social institutions, of the culture of the people, of their language, their national feeling and their religion. It may be accomplished by wiping out all basis of personal security, liberty, health and dignity. When these means fail the machine gun can always be utilized as a last resort.[111]

In elaborating his definition, Lemkin adumbrated eight "techniques of destruction": political, social, cultural, economic, biological, physical, religious, moral. They covered such broad a spectrum of policies because nationhood was constituted by each of these elements according to his conception of ethnogenesis. The capaciousness of his definition of genocide is captured well by his discussion of the attack on a nation's morality:

In order to weaken the spiritual resistance of the national group, the occupant attempts to create an atmosphere of moral debasement within this group. According to this plan, the mental energy of the group should be concentrated upon base instincts and should be diverted from moral and national thinking. It is important for the realization of such a plan that the desire for cheap individual pleasure be substituted for the desire for collective feelings and ideals based upon a higher morality. Therefore, the occupant made an effort in Poland to impose upon the Poles pornographic publications and movies. The consumption of alcohol was encouraged, for while food prices have soared, the Germans have kept down the price of alcohol, and the peasants are compelled by the authorities to take spirits in payment for agricultural produce. The curfew law, enforced very strictly against Poles, is relaxed if they can show the authorities a ticket to one of the gambling houses which the Germans have allowed to come into existence.[112]

Consequently, Lemkin is understood by some to have supported the notion of "cultural genocide," that is, that cultural effacement or assimilation is genocidal.[113] Indeed, a recently released fragment of his autobiography reveals that he strongly supported the retention of an article on cultural genocide in early drafts of the UN's convention on genocide.[114] Judging by his work as a whole, however, it would be safe to infer that he did not equate assimilation with cultural genocide. In fact, using the Nazi example, he took pains to distinguish between genocide and cultural effacement, that is, assimilation. Terms like "denationalization" or "Germanization" of foreign peoples were not synonyms with genocide, he thought, because "they treat mainly the cultural, economic, and social aspects of genocide, *leaving out the biological aspects, such as causing the physical decline and even destruction of the population involved.*"[115] In Lemkin's notion of ethnogenesis, the "biological and physical structure" was elemental, so that policies that attack a group's culture—its morality, for instance—are only genocidal when motivated by the intention to destroy this structure. His unpublished manuscripts confirm this interpretation. The gradual assimilation of a people by processes of "cultural diffusion," even that entailing the incremental disintegration of a culture, was not genocidal; but "premeditated" "surgical operations," and "deliberate assassinations" of them were.[116]

The United Nations Convention on the Prevention and Punishment of Genocide of 1948 omitted cultural genocide from the final version of the drafts it considered, but otherwise remained faithful to Lemkin's intentions.[117] Important to note here is that killing is only one of five techniques of destruction, that the state is not named as the perpetrator, and that the intention to permanently cripple a group is gestured to with the wording that destroying "part" of a group can be genocidal. Genocide is not a synonym for the Holocaust. Article II defines genocide as

> any of the following acts committed with intent to destroy, in whole or in part, a national, ethnical, racial or religious group, as such: (a) Killing members of the group; (b) Causing serious bodily or mental harm to members of the group; (c) Deliberately inflicting on the group conditions of life calculated to bring about its physical destruction in whole or in part; (d) Imposing measures intended to prevent births within the group; (e) Forcibly transferring children of the group to another group.

Rival Paradigms of Genocide

Despite these clear guidelines from Lemkin and the UN, scholars have wrangled with one another over the meaning of genocide, or suggested alternative definitions. Part of the reason for this is that Lemkin's writings are open to rival interpretations. Another is that, as a lawyer, he was concerned above all with criminalizing behavior, rather than accounting for it. Like the UN, his priority was to identify what genocide is, not to explain why it happens. Regrettably, his projected history of genocide, of which a rough draft exists and in which he presents a differentiated analysis of many case studies, was never published. Until this work is made available to the scholars, they must either visit the archives in New York and Cincinnati where it is stored, or limit themselves to his publications. Understandably, they have done the latter—including this writer until recently—and have therefore won the impression that genocide is a massive hate crime based purely on prejudice, rather than on the material, ethnic and other rivalries that usually subtend the escalation of conflict in an exterminatory direction.[118]

Consequently, scholars developed their own definitions of genocide and explanatory frameworks. In general, they have done so in two ways. One paradigm, which I call "intentionalist," regards the Holocaust as the archetypal genocide and therefore emphasizes the official, exterminatory goal of the state to kill groups of people. The other, a reaction to the first, is "structuralist" because it averts the issue of perpetrator agency and intention by highlighting anonymous "genocidal processes" of cultural and physical destruction.[119] Both have important implications for the relationship between genocide and colonialism.

The dominant approach has been the intentionalist one, because until recently genocide studies has been virtually monopolized by North American social scientists. While it rejects the claims of Holocaust uniqueness, intentionalism nonetheless frames the Holocaust as the prototypical genocide. Representative are the Canada-based scholars Frank Chalk and Kurt Jonassohn. In a series of publications in the 1980s, culminating in their widely-used textbook, *The History and Sociology of Genocide*, they attacked the UN Convention and proposed their own influential definition of genocide.[120] The UN's formulation was inadequate, they contended, because it omitted political and social groups as possible targets of genocide, but included nonlethal forms of group destruction. Genocide, they insisted, should be restricted to "one-sided mass killing in which a state or other authority intends to destroy a group, as that group and membership in it are defined by the perpetrator."[121]

Although Lemkin did not support the inclusion of political and social groups, his writings do contain phrases that support the intentionalist viewpoint. With the Nazi plans to reorder the populations of Europe in mind, he wrote that genocide was "a synchronized attack" and "a co-ordinated plan of different actions aiming at the destruction of the essential foundations of life of national groups, with the aim of annihilating the groups themselves." [122] On this reading, the agency of the perpetrator and its exterminatory mens rea is clearly identifiable. Genocide is established when an agent, in particular the modern state, can be determined to possess the requisite genocidal intention.

The intentionalist view has lost ground among genocide scholars, but still suffuses popular imagination.[123] What does it have to say about colonial genocide? Very little. There are three problems with it. The first is that perpetrator agency is often difficult to identify in colonial contexts. As Jürgen Zimmerer points out in this volume, the colonial state was akin to the premodern state, governing via "mediating" powers, and usually not disposing over a monopoly of coercive powers within its claimed borders. Settlers often outstripped the regulatory capacity of the metropolitan authority, which in Australia was anxious to prevent frontier bloodshed. Consequently, in cases where the state wanted to prosecute murders of Aborigines by settlers who refused to cooperate in the legal proceedings, where is one supposed to identify the genocidal perpetrator?[124] Obviously not with the officials. But if genocide is by definition a crime of state, then no one is liable despite the fact many Indigenous groups were wiped out by posses of armed civilians, whose frontier communities protected the killers behind a veil of silence and secrecy.[125]

The second problem with the intentionalist approach is that most Indigenous deaths in colonizing contexts resulted from European diseases, as well as from intensified intra-Indigenous violence that attended the displacement of peoples from their traditional lands.[126] Because these consequences were not an intended result of British colonization or policy, they are not pertinent to the question of genocide. After all, colonization was a complex and unplanned process, as Sir Robert Seeley observed of the British Empire in 1881: "We seem, as it were, to have conquered and peopled half the world in a fit of absence of mind."[127] But does insisting that the catastrophic collapse in Indigenous populations after the arrival of Europeans was an unfortunate accident constitute a satisfactory response?

Thirdly, the intentionalist view of the causes of colonial genocides—if they are considered genocides at all—offers an attenuated account of why they happen. Such scholars are wont to typologize genocides according to motive, distinguishing for example between "developmental" or "utilitarian" genocides of Indigenous peoples, and "ideological" genocides against scapegoated or hostage groups.[128] The motive in imperial contexts is held to be individual and collective "greed." In this vein, nineteenth century settlers would attribute Indigenous deaths to scurrilous whites, such as escaped or former convicts, rather than to the colonization project as a whole. Typical were Adam Smith's observations in his *The Wealth of Nations* of the "dreadful misfortunes" that befell the natives of the East and West Indies. But they

> seem to have arisen rather from accident than from anything in the nature of those events themselves. At the particular time when these discoveries were made, the superiority of force happened to be so great on the side of the Europeans that they were enabled to commit with impunity every sort of injustice in those remote countries.[129]

The problem here, as Stanner pointed out in relation to violent incidents in the first moments of colonization of Australia in 1788, is the blindness to the structural determinants of the colonization: the British "suspected the convicts and to a lesser extent the aborigines, but not themselves or the fact and design of the colony."[130]

The limitations of this approach are readily apparent. It is radically voluntarist and can only "explain" why genocides occur with circular logic by referring to the intentions of the perpetrator: they commit them because they want to. These conceptual problems are not surprising. Such a perspective insulates the state from powerful social forces that push for the expulsion or extermination of native peoples on coveted land by attributing blame to genocide on anti-liberal ideologies that commit mass crimes in the name of utopian fantasies. As a prominent intentionalist Frank Chalk reminds us, "we must never forget that the great genocides of the past have been committed by [state] perpetrators who acted in the name of absolutist or utopian ideologies aimed at cleansing and purifying their worlds."[131] The intentionalist paradigm of genocide is really a species of totalitarianism theory. It is not equipped with the intellectual tools to consider the issues raised by colonialism.

Are we left, then, having to choose "between a pre-meditated and an accidental wrongdoing," the former deemed genocide, the latter trivialized as the unintended consequences of an otherwise benign colonization?[132] A rival school of structuralist scholars has attempted to come to terms with this conundrum. An important contribution is Tony Barta's 1987 intervention, "Relations of Genocide: Land and Lives in the Colonization of Australia."[133] Barta was interested in explaining the "genocidal outcomes" in colonial societies, and he found in the concept of "relations of genocide" a way of obviating the centrality of state policy and premeditation in the hegemonic intentionalist definition of the term:

> Genocide, strictly, cannot be a crime of unintended consequences; we expect it to be acknowledged in consciousness. In real historical relationships, however, unintended consequences are legion, and it is from the consequences, as well as the often muddled consciousness, that we have to deduce the real nature of the relationship.[134]

Barta concluded that all Australians live in objective "relations of genocide" with Aborigines, and that Australia was a "genocidal society," because its original inhabitants were fated to die in enormous numbers by the pressure of settlement, irrespective of the protective efforts of the state and philanthropists. White Australians continued to occupy the land on which Aborigines had once thrived, even if they had no subjective intention to eliminate them. A similar argument has been made recently by Alison Palmer, who shows how colonial genocides are often "society-led" rather than "state-led."[135]

The Australian historians Raymond Evans and Bill Thorpe have continued this line of reasoning, proposing a new term altogether—"indigenocide"—which they distinguish from Holocaust with its concerted, state-driven, bureaucratic, and industrial killing. Although Lemkin does not appear in their footnotes, the concept has clear affinities with his definition:

"Indigenocide" is a means of analysing those circumstances where one, or more peoples, usually immigrants, deliberately set out to supplant a group or groups of other people whom as far as we know, represent the Indigenous, or Aboriginal peoples of the country that the immigrants usurp.[136]

Indigenocide has five elements: the intentional invasion/colonization of land; the conquest of the indigenous peoples; the killing of them to the extent that they can barely reproduce themselves and thereby come close to extinction; their classification as vermin by the invaders; and the attempted destruction of their religious systems. Indigenocide is consistent with the continued existence of indigenous peoples so long as they are classified as a separate caste.[137] Accordingly, not all imperialisms are genocidal. The British occupation of India, for example, was not a project of settlement, and the fact that the colonizers relied on the labor of the locals was an impediment to physical genocide.[138]

Other structuralist scholars like Ann Curthoys and John Docker have pointed to Lemkin's writings that make the link between genocide and colonization.[139] "Genocide has two phases," he wrote:

one, destruction of the national pattern of the oppressed group: the other, the imposition of the national pattern of the oppressor. This imposition, in turn, may be made upon the oppressed population which is allowed to remain, or upon the territory alone, after removal of the population and the colonization of the area by the oppressor's own nationals.

In fact, Lemkin hints that genocide is *intrinsically colonial* and that therefore settler colonialism is *intrinsically genocidal.* The basis of this conclusion is the aim of the colonizer to supplant the original inhabitants of the land. In relation to the Nazis, he thought that the

coordinated German techniques of occupation must lead to the conclusion that the German occupant has embarked upon a gigantic scheme to change, in favor of Germany, the balance of biological forces between it and the captive nations for many years to come. The objective of this scheme is to destroy or to cripple the subjugated people in their development.[140]

Indeed, although he regarded the United States as a refuge and potential agent for the reform of international law to criminalize genocide, Lemkin was under no illusion about the nature of European colonialism. His projected publications on the history of world genocide included the cases of the Indigenous peoples of

South and North America, the Aboriginal Tasmanians, and the Herero of German Southwest Africa.[141] In what follows, I propose to transcend the conceptual tension between intentionalist and structuralist approaches in a manner that, I hope, keeps faith with Lemkin's ecumenical definition of genocide.

Genocide and Settler Society

There are three ways in which the genocide concept and settler society can be brought into a productive relation. One entails considering the nature of intention in colonial contexts, the second reflects on the structure of settler colonialism, and the third isolates processes of radicalization that lead to "genocidal moments."

Rethinking Intention

The current definition of intention—mens rea—means subjectively willing a particular outcome of policy, a definition that favors the intentionalist paradigm of genocide. But this is not the only way to think about the question. In nineteenth century English law, a person was inferred to have intended the "natural consequences" of his or her actions: if the result proscribed was reasonably foreseeable as a likely consequence of his or her actions, the presumption was that the accused had intended the result.[142] Very few genocide scholars have taken seriously this capacious notion of intention. One of them, Roger Smith, however, has seen the implications for colonialism:

> Sometimes ... genocidal consequences precede any conscious decision to destroy innocent groups to satisfy one's aims. This is most often the case in the early phase of colonial domination, where through violence, disease, and relentless pressure indigenous peoples are pushed toward extinction. With the recognition of the consequences of one's acts, however, the issue is changed: to persist is to intend the death of a people. This pattern of pressure, recognition, and persistence is typically what happened in the nineteenth century.[143]

Let us consider the case of the British in nineteenth century Australia in terms of this pattern of recognition and consciousness of consequences in which authorities were implicated. The Colonial Office was constantly warning the settlers—both the governors and the pastoralists—not to exterminate the Aborigines. The Aboriginal population declined drastically because of malnutrition, starvation, disease, frontier violence with whites, increased intra-Aboriginal conflict, and reduced fertility. If we use a differentiated concept of intention, authorities in London cannot escape responsibility for this consequence of British settlement. For while they wrung their hands about the frontier violence and the tribal extinctions, they were unwilling to cease or radically amend the colonization project. The Select Committee Report of 1837, which exhorted greater London supervision, made no impact. Despite admonishing missives from London and occasional colonial compromises, the fatal pattern of events continued to unfold unchanged, such that Colonial Office officials resigned themselves to the inevitable. Wrote one official:

> The causes and the consequences of this state of things are clear and irremediable, nor do I suppose that it is possible to discover any method by which the impending catastrophe, namely, the elimination of the Black Race, can be averted.[144]

Writing soon thereafter, Herman Merivale, a young professor of political economy at Oxford University, prophesied the same conclusion, because of

> the perverse wickedness of those outcasts of society whom the first waves of our colonization are sure to bring along with them. If their violence and avarice cannot be restrained by the arm of power—and it must be confessed that there appears scarcely any feasible mode of accomplishing this—it is impossible but that our progress in the occupation of barbarous countries *must be attended with the infliction of infinite suffering.* ... The history of the European settlements in American, Africa, and Australia presents everywhere the same general features—*a wide and sweeping destruction of native races* by controlled violence of individuals, if not of colonial authorities, followed by tardy attempts on the part of governments to repair the acknowledged crime.[145]

Darwin, too, saw extinction as predictable: "We can see that the cultivation of the land will be fatal in many ways to savages, for they cannot, or will not, change their habits."[146]

Certainly, colonialism in Australia, as elsewhere, could not be halted in the manner of flicking a light switch. The Colonial Office, for example, was only a small part of a massive state apparatus. Nonetheless, the rhetoric of Indigenous decline also served to mask choices open to policy-makers, choices they were not prepared to entertain because they fundamentally approved of the civilizing process in which they were engaged. The fact is that they did not take their own humanitarian convictions seriously enough to implement the radical measures necessary to prevent Indigenous deaths—negotiating over land rights, for instance—whether caused

by massacre and starvation, for these measures would entail relinquishing control of the land and jeopardizing the colonizing mission. Talk of inexorable extinction reflected a racist theodicy as
much as governmental impotence.

The fact is that European colonial powers knew the outcome of
their settlement projects. They were well aware of the choices, and
were prepared to countenance their consequences. This awareness
extended to the mass death caused by diseases like smallpox. Only
an attenuated concept of intention would exculpate the European
powers in these circumstances: after all, the disappearance of many
indigenous peoples from the face of the earth was a natural consequence of their actions, and they knew it on the frontier, in the
colonial capital, and back home at the imperial seat of power.
Where genocide was not consciously willed, then it was implicitly
intended in the sense of the silent condoning, sometimes agonized
acceptance, of a chain of events for which they were co-responsible
and were not prepared to rupture.[147]

Nor did the British colonial states stand by neutrally as the settlers had their way with the Indigenous peoples. They often aided
and abetted their annihilation by disallowing Aboriginal testimony
in legal proceedings or by acting vigorously on their behalf.
Indeed, Aboriginal status as British subjects, equal before the law,
existed more in the breech than the observance, their "criminal"
activity the object of merciless punitive raids that went unpunished by the authorities.[148]

The Deep Structure of Settler Colonialism

Of course, by definition settler societies had emancipated themselves from imperial sovereignty, a fact that historians have regarded as sealing the fate of the Indigenous peoples. "When neither
intervention nor mediation was feasible," wrote one, "victory was
certain to go to the stronger—that is, to the white settlers—as most
of those in London who were officially concerned with the problem
had foreseen with dismay." The Aboriginal defeat was a "tragedy"
and "the almost inevitable result of a conflict between the settlers
and the Aborigines."[149] But why was British "victory"—the meaning is undefined—an inevitable tragedy? Here we touch on an
intrinsic dimension of settler colonialism that has only recently
received explicit recognition in Australian historiography, namely
that, as the historian Patrick Wolfe observed pithily, European
"invasion is a structure not an event."[150] Because of incommensurable modes of production between the Europeans and Aborigines,
settler colonialism entails a "zero-sum contest over land," at least

over land that Europeans coveted. The Europeans wanted Aborigines' land, not their labor, except, ultimately, in various rural industries in northern Australia. "Thus the primary logic of settler colonialism can be characterized as one of elimination."[151]

The objective imperative to eliminate the Aboriginal presence endures apart from the subjectively-held racist beliefs of immigrant Australians. This model does not preclude the granting of reserves for Aborigines or the creative adaptation of Aborigines to European land-use. In the former, where Aborigines were granted reserves on fertile ground in NSW, they were eventually dispossessed in the face of white lobbying. In fact, reserves were conceived, because, as one government official noted in 1905, "Carrying the present policy of Might against Right to a logical conclusion, it would simply mean that, were all the land in the northern areas of the State to be thus leased, all the blacks would be hunted into the sea."[152] In the case of Aboriginal cultural adaptation, the fact remains that the European economic system had supplanted its hunter-gatherer rival. This enduring deep structure thereby undercuts the humanitarians' redemptive hope that harmonious "race relations" would obtain once they had banished subjectively-held racist beliefs.

This fact has been recognized in the past, but not in a systematic way. Clive Turnbull, for example, who in 1948 wrote *Black War* on "the extermination of the Tasmanian Aborigines," was unclear whether the state or society was responsible for the Indigenous disaster. But the either/or nature of this encounter between the British and Aborigines was clear: "No doubt many men were appalled by the atrocities committed upon the natives; but, as the only logical remedy would have been to deny to the invaders all property rights in the island one pious palliative after another was put forward until eventually the aborigines solved the problem in the most convenient way for all by dying." [153]

That the Indigenous peoples as unintegrated, autonomous communities in the body politic would have to be eliminated one way or the other was patent even to humanitarians like Merivale in the 1830s. There were only three paths open for the Aborigines, he told his Oxford audience: their "extermination," training for civilization in isolated reserves, or "amalgamation" with the colonists. Rejecting the first option of the triumphalists, and discounting the second as unfeasible, he advocated the "union of natives with the settlers in the same community," a notion he confessed would appear "wild and chimerical" to his listeners. And yet, he continued, it was "the only possible *Euthanasia* of savage communities," by which he meant their disappearance as peoples by intermarriage and integration into the productive community.[154]

Settler society thereby reveals itself to typify those attributes that the sociologist Zygmunt Bauman regards as inherent to modernity. Borrowing categories from Claude Levi-Strauss, he identifies two strategies by which modern societies deal with alterity:

> One was *anthropophagic:* annihilating the strangers by *devouring* them and then metabolically transforming into a tissue indistinguishable from one's own. This was the strategy of *assimilation:* making the different similar; smothering of cultural and linguistic distinctions; forbidding all traditions and loyalties except those meant to feed the conformity to the new and all-embracing order; promoting and enforcing one and only one measure of conformity. The other strategy was *anthropoemic: vomiting* the strangers, banishing them from the limits of the orderly world and barring them from all communication from those inside. This was the strategy of *exclusion*—confining the strangers within the visible walls of the ghettos or behind the invisible, yet no less tangible, prohibitions of *commensality, connubium and commercium;* "cleansing"—expelling the strangers beyond the frontiers of the managed and manageable territory.[155]

These are compelling terms with which to consider the settler colonial project. A logic of elimination toward Indigenous peoples does indeed constitute its essence. And yet, the historian will want to pose three questions. First, does the term "elimination" obscure as much as it reveals? The American political scientist Daniel J. Goldhagen infamously mounted a case that Germans were possessed by "eliminationist antisemitism," by which he meant both the liberal desire to assimilate Jews *and* the Nazi fantasy to exterminate them. True, public "Jewishness" would be effaced in both cases, but they are also qualitatively different "solutions" to a perceived "Jewish problem": murder cannot be regarded as *simply* a functional equivalent of assimilation.[156] In any event, is assimilation really genocide? Russell McGregor makes a compelling case in his chapter that it is not. The third question would be when and why the various modalities of settler colonialism change. As it stands, the structuralist schema is too static. It needs to be supplemented by an account of how and why the settler-colonial system radicalizes from assimilation to destruction.

Processes of Radicalization as the Generation of "Genocidal Moments"

The deep structure of settler society shows us that the objective and inherent character of the British occupation of the Australian continent necessarily entailed the large-scale attack on Aboriginal society as a culture and vast numbers of Aborigines—their "euthanasia"—even if mass death was not its aim. Triumphalists will point to the benign intentions of policy-makers to excuse them of direct responsibility for the consequences of colonization. Does this mean that we must leave the question of cultural dislocation and mass death that accompanies colonization to the theodicies of the apologists for "economic development"? Not if we can find instances of genocidal policy. To understand how such polices evolve, however, it is necessary to frame them as features of radicalization processes. Colonial decision-makers need to be linked to the structures and contexts in which they were embedded. The intentionalist-structuralist dichotomy can be mediated by embedding subjective genocidal policy development and implementation in the "objective" dimension of the colonial process, highlighted by Barta, Wolfe, and others.[157]

The mechanism of policy radicalization is the intensity of Indigenous resistance. How did authorities respond when Aborigines did not "melt away," and put up sufficient resistance to pastoralists and pastoralism—a key sector of the economy—such as to threaten the viability of one of the colonies? The answer is that governments in the metropolis came under intense pressure from the frontier periphery, and sometimes were prepared to entertain "final solutions" to the "Aboriginal problem." Instead of arguing statically that the colonization of Australia was genocidal *tout court*, or insisting truculently that it was essentially benevolent and progressive, it is analytically more productive to view it as a dynamic process with genocidal potential that could be released in circumstances of crisis. The place to look for genocidal intentions, then, is not in explicit, prior statements of settlers or governments, but in the gradual evolution of European attitudes and policies as they were pushed in an exterminatory direction by the confluence of their underlying ideological assumptions, the acute fear of Aboriginal attack, the demands of the colonial and international economy, their plans for the land, and the resistance to these plans by the Indigenous peoples.

In other words, the British colonization of Australia was *objectively* and *inherently* "ethnocidal" (i.e., the attack of Aboriginal cultures) and fatal for many Aborigines, and potentially genocidal. The destruction of Aboriginal society as a nomadic form of life was an aim of the colonizers after the 1820s in places where British land-use demanded sendentarism; this is what they meant by "civilizing" the Aborigines. But only after the initial illusions of peaceful coexistence had been dispelled with increasing contact between the two sides did the deadly implications *inherent* in the process become apparent to all and, in a particular constellation of circumstances, its *objective implication* become *subjectively located* in the consciousness of the colonial agents themselves. This is the origin of those "genocidal moments" when the triumphalists determine policy.

In their clamor for government protection and the implementation of exterminatory policies, the Europeans on the frontier articulated the logic of the colonization process in its most pure form: driven by international market forces, they seized the land of Aboriginal groups without compensation or negotiation, and excluded them from their sources of food. A struggle for survival ensued in which, from the European perspective at the time, the Aborigines had to be subdued, and, if necessary, exterminated.[158] For if the settlers did not get their way and were forced to abandon the land, the economic system would collapse and with it the colonization project itself. In these circumstances, the structure or objective implication of the process became consciously incarnated in its agents, and this is the moment when we can observe the development of the specific genocidal intention that satisfies the UN definition.

The radicalization of official policy was most intensive where the lobbying by frontier whites was most successful. The variable here is the extent to which the colony was a settler society, that is, an autonomous, self-governing polity free from the supervision of the imperial parent and its humanitarian agenda of Aboriginal legal equality. The Australian colonies that were settled in the first half of the nineteenth century—New South Wales, Tasmania, Victoria, and South Australia—remained under the scrutiny of London and colonial governors. The colony of Queensland, however, which achieved independence from New South Wales in 1859, represented the interest of the squatter—that is, the priorities of the frontier—without the inhibiting factor of control from Sydney or London. It was the purest incarnation of settler priorities and their pragmatist supporters, as Raymond Evans shows in this volume.

The imperial view was certainly that the settlers could not be trusted to treat the Indigenous peoples justly. Merivale, for example, advised that colonial legislatures should not be responsible for "protecting" the natives, nor that settlers have "any share in judicial proceedings against" them.[159] It is with this intuition that one British historian opined recently that "had Australia been an independent republic in the nineteenth century, like the United

States, the genocide [of the Tasmanians] might have been on a continental scale."[160]

This approach towards the genesis of the genocidal moments affords an insight into the character of the colonization process itself. The tendency of historians to isolate the Tasmanian and Queensland cases—Tasmania because "total extinction" is thought to have occurred, and Queensland because it was notoriously violent—from the rest of the colonization experience of Australia and class them as exceptions to the rule of peaceful settlement, can be disposed of by the argument that they were in fact the inevitable consequences of particularly resolute Aboriginal resistance. The extreme measures seen in those cases did not occur to the same extent elsewhere because they did not need to. Invading whites usually were able to clear the land of Aborigines by other, less-systematic methods, or disease and other factors did the work for them. The colonization process was objectively lethal for Aborigines, irrespective of initial intentions of the state and settlers, and where Aborigines did not "fade" or "melt away," the settlers, and where necessary the state, ensured that the process of elimination was continued by consciously expediting its fatal logic.

Conclusion

The traditional settler society model of comparative analysis, which typically traced the different ways in which white male settlers heroically conquered the land and established democracies of one sort or another, has been criticized by post-colonial theorists and anthropologists for ignoring questions of race, ethnicity, and gender.[161] Even in its critical humanitarian incarnation, the settler society paradigm still posits narrative of redemption—a morally clean settlement—once Aborigines have been given native title to land.[162] For these reasons, comparative histories of societies of those European settlements along these lines have gone out of fashion.

And yet, comparative historical analysis is more urgent than ever before, as these societies grapple with questions of Indigenous sovereignty and other legacies of colonization.[163] This book suggests that the settler society paradigm remains a useful way of proceeding when viewed under the aspect of the genocide concept. *Genocide and Settler Society* focuses on Australia—an ignored case in the genocide studies literature—but also considers others, as in the chapters by Jürgen Zimmerer, Paul Bartrop, and Isabel Heinemann. I am not suggesting that the entirety of Australian history can be reduced to genocide. (No one suggests that studying the Holocaust reduces German history to Nazi genocide.) But neither is it possible to regard the country's genocidal moments in the manner of an industrial accident. They are not contingencies, attributable to misguided or wicked men, but intrinsic to the deep structure of settler society. Indeed, the logic of elimination reappears from time to time, as in the hysteria over native title in the 1990s, when certain groups of Aborigines were temporarily granted the right to exercise veto power over mining projects. This impediment to the economic system—in this case represented by mining companies—needed to be eliminated, and so it was, with the so-called easy "extinguishment" of native title legislated by the conservative government in 1997.

The genocide perspective and, in particular, the focus on radicalization offers other advantages. Unlike the alternative approaches of military history or generic frontier violence (especially the preoccupation with massacres), it highlights the complex interplay between settler communities on the frontier and metropolis and the state in its various incarnations.[164] And because it does not insist that total physical extermination take place, and argues that cultural technologies of governance can entail group extinguishments, it draws our attention to the fantasies of racial engineering that policy-makers entertained after the "pacification" on the frontier.

Plainly, more work needs to be done, especially with local and regional analyses.[165] This book does not pretend to provide a conclusive answer to the genocide question in Australian history. Nor does it purport to be a history of Indigenous peoples. It is about the settlers and the society they established. It presents the latest research of scholars in various fields, and by shattering the Gorgon effect in thinking about genocide in settler societies, hopes to stimulate still more research and informed discussion. Through such critical reflection, the authors hope that the potential for genocidal moments inherent in settler societies will disappear.

Acknowledgements

I thank Bain Atwood, Tony Barta, Beth Drenning, Raymond Evans, Andrew Fitzmaurice, Jan Kociumbas, Ben Kiernan, Tim Rowse, and Lyndall Ryan for many helpful suggestions, and Ruth Balint for research assistance on population statistics. The views expressed and any errors committed here, however, remain mine.

Notes

1. *The Iliad*, 5.741.
2. Dan Diner, *Beyond the Inconceivable: Studies on Germany, Nazism, and the Holocaust* (Berkeley, 2000); Saul Friedländer, "The 'Final Solution': On the Unease in Historical Interpretation," *History and Memory* 1 (Fall/Winter 1989): 61-75. Inga Clendinnen uses the term "Gorgon effect" in *Reading the Holocaust* (Cambridge, 1999), 4. She wrote her book to defeat it.
3. Cf. Alison Palmer, "Colonial and Modern Genocides: Explanations and Categories," *Ethnic and Racial Studies* 21, no. 1 (1998): 89-115.
4. Mark Mazower, "After Lemkin: Genocide, the Holocaust and History," *The Jewish Quarterly* (Winter, 1994/5): 8.
5. Vinay Lal, "Genocide, Barbaric Others, and the Violence of Categories: A Response to Omer Bartov," *American Historical Review* 104 (October 1998): 1188.
6. These debates are discussed in: A. Dirk Moses, "Conceptual Blockages and Definitional Dilemmas in the 'Racial Century': Genocides of Indigenous People and the Holocaust," *Patterns of Prejudice* 36, no. 4 (2002): 7-36; Alan S. Rosenbaum, ed., *Is the Holocaust Unique?*, 2nd ed. (Boulder, Colo., 2001); Gavriel D. Rosenfeld, "The Politics of Uniqueness: Reflections on the Recent Turn in Holocaust and Genocide Scholarship," *Holocaust and Genocide Studies* 13, no. 1 (1999): 28-61.
7. Ward Churchill, *A Little Matter of Genocide* (San Francisco, 1997), 405. Churchill is aware that the residue of the Indigenous population was relocated to Flinders Island, noting that "This supposed absolution from allegations of genocide makes about as much sense as to suggest that, had they stopped of their own accord after slaughtering more than 6 million Jews, the World War II nazi extermination program would not have constituted genocide." In this tradition is also Ian Hernon's charge that the extinction of the Aboriginal Tasmanians is "a stain which has never been removed from the banners of the British Empire." See his *The Savage Empire: Forgotten Wars of the 19th Century* (Thrupp, UK, 2000), 62.
8. Hannah Arendt, *The Origins of Totalitarianism*, 2nd ed. (London, 1958), 182, 187n4, 186, cf. 128.
9. David E. Stannard, *American Holocaust: Columbus and the Conquest of the New World* (New York, 1992).
10. F.W. and J.M. Nicholas, *Charles Darwin in Australia* (Cambridge, 1989), 30f.
11. James Pritchard, "On the Extinction of Human Races," *The Edinburgh New Philosophical Journal* (October 1839-April 1840): 169f. On Prichard (not in fact spelled with a 't'), see George W. Stocking's introduction to Prichard, *Researches into the Physical History of Mankind* (Chicago, 1973). I thank Dan Stone for this reference.
12. For Darwinism and Social Darwinism in Australia, see Russell McGregor, *Imagined Destinies: Aboriginal Australians and the Doomed Race Theory, 1880-1939* (Melbourne, 1997); Barry W. Butcher, "Darwin Down Under: Science, Religion, and Evolution in Australia," in *Disseminating Darwin: The Role of Place, Race, Religion, and Gender*, ed. Ronald L. Numbers and John Stenhouse (Cambridge, 1999), 39-60; idem, "Darwinism, Social Darwinism, and the Australian Aborigine: A Re-evaluation," in *Darwin's Laboratory: Evolutionary Theory and Natural History in the Pacific*, ed. Roy MacLeod and Philip F. Rehbock (Honolulu, 1994), 371-94; Mark Francis, "'Social Darwin-

ism' and the Construction of Institutionalised Racism in Australia," *Journal of Australian Studies* nos. 50/51 (1996): 90-105.

13. Anthony Trollope, *Australia* [1872], ed. P.D. Edwards and R.B. Joyce (Brisbane, 1967), 175, 100, 109, 112f.

14. Charles W. Dilke, *Problems of Greater Britain*, 4th rev. ed. (London and New York, 1890), 214.

15. For a catalogue of such quotations, see Patrick Brantlinger, "'Dying Races': Rationalizing Genocide in the Nineteenth Century," in *The Decolonization of Imagination: Culture, Knowledge and Power*, ed. Jan Nedverveen Pieterse and Bhikhu Parekh (London and New Jersey, 1995), 43-56. More generally, see his *Rule of Darkness: British Literature and Imperialism, 1830-1914* (Ithaca, NY, 1988), and Anthony Pagden, *Peoples and Empires* (London, 2001), 150.

16. T. Bartlett, *New Holland etc.* (London, 1843), 65f. cited in Henry Reynolds, "Racial Thought in Early Colonial Australia," *Australian Journal of Politics and History* 20, no. 1 (1974): 45.

17. Cited in Henry Reynolds, "Frontier History After Mabo," *Journal of Australian Studies* no. 49 (1996): 4.

18. Richard Broome, "Historians, Aborigines and Australia: Writing the National Past," in *In the Age of Mabo: History, Aborigines and Australia*, ed. Bain Attwood (Sydney, 1996), 55.

19. Jane Samson, "British Voices and Indigenous Rights: Debating Aboriginal Legal Status in Nineteenth Century Australia and Canada," *Culture of the Commonwealth: Essays and Studies* 2 (Winter 1996-97): 5-16.

20. Henry Reynolds, *This Whispering in our Hearts* (Sydney, 1998), 247.

21. See the discussion of R.H.W. Reece, *Aborigines and Colonists* (Sydney, 1974), 132ff. On the problem of prosecuting white murderers of blacks, see Gary Highland, "Aborigines, Europeans and the Criminal Law," *Aboriginal History* 14 (1990): 182-96.

22. Richard Broome, *Aboriginal Australians*, 2nd ed. (Sydney, 1994), 97ff; Ann McGrath, ed., *Contested Ground: Australian Aborigines under the British Crown* (Sydney, 1995), 73, 135-42, 181-88, 225f., 253f.

23. Bain Attwood, *Rights for Aborigines* (Sydney, 2003), 54-102; Andrew Markus, *Governing Savages* (Sydney, 1990), 158-72; Reynolds, *Whispering*, 216-44.

24. Bain Attwood, "Rights, Racism and Aboriginality: Critics of Assimilation in the 1950s and 1960s," in *Contesting Assimilation*, ed. Tim Rowse (Perth, 2004). For the Stanner quotation, see the Russell McGregor's chapter at 298.

25. Jennifer Clark, "'The Winds of Change' in Australia: Aborigines and the International Politics of Race, 1960-1972," *International History Review* 10, no. 1 (1998): 89-117.

26. John Cawte, "Racial Prejudice and Aboriginal Adjustment," in *Racism: The Australian Experience*, Vol. 2, ed. F.S. Stevens (Sydney, 1972), 45.

27. Bain Attwood and Andrew Markus, *The 1967 Referendum, or, When Aborigines Didn't Get the Vote* (Canberra, 1997).

28. Ann Curthoys, *Freedom Ride: A Freedom Rider Remembers* (Sydney, 2002); idem, "National Narratives, War Commemorations, and Racial Exclusion in a Settler Society," in T.G. Ashplant, Graham Dawson, and Michael Roper, eds., *The Politics of War Memory and Commemoration* (London and New York, 2000), 128-44.

29. Heather Goodall, *From Invasion to Embassy: Land in Aboriginal Politics in New South Wales, 1770-1972* (Sydney, 1996), 335-51; Nicolas Peterson and Marcia Langton, eds., *Aborigines, Land and Land Rights* (Canberra, 1983).

30. W.E.H. Stanner, *After the Dreaming* (Sydney, 1968), 26, and idem, "The History of Indifference thus Begins," *Aboriginal History* 1, no. 1 (1977): 22. This article was drafted in 1963. Good surveys of the literature are Bain Attwood, "Aboriginal History," in *Historical Disciplines in Australasia: Themes, Problems and Debates*, ed. J.A. Moses, Special Issue of the *Australian Journal of Politics and History* 41 (1995): 33-47; Attwood and S.G. Foster, "Introduction," in *Frontier Conflict: The Australian Experience*, ed., Attwood and Foster (Canberra, 2003), 1-30.

31. C.D. Rowley, *The Destruction of Aboriginal Society* (Canberra, 1970); idem, *Outcasts in White Australia* (Canberra, 1971), and idem, *The Remote Aborigines* (Canberra, 1971). See the commentary of Broome, "Historians, Aborigines and Australia," 68. On Rowley, see Elspeth Young, "Charles Rowley – a Fighter for Justice and Equality," *Aboriginal History* 10 (1986): 3-6.

32. For example, Raymond Evans, "European-Aboriginal Relations in Queensland, 1880-1910" (BA Honors Thesis, University of Queensland, 1965); R.W.H. Reece, "The Aborigines and Colonial Society in New South Wales before 1850, with Special Reference to the Period of the Gipps Administration, 1838-1846" (MA Thesis, University of Queensland, 1969); Noel Loos, "Frontier Conflict in the Bowen District, 1861-74" (MA Qual. Thesis, James Cook University, 1970); Ann Curthoys, "Race and Ethnicity: A Study of the Response of British Colonists to Aborigines, Chinese, and Non-British Europeans in New South Wales, 1856-1881" (PhD Thesis, Macquarie University, 1973).

33. Humphrey McQueen, *A New Britannia* (Melbourne, 1970); Raymond Evans, Kay Saunders, Kathryn Cronin, *Exclusion, Exploitation and Extermination: Race Relations in Colonial Queensland* (Brisbane, 1975); Noel Loos, *Invasion and Resistance: Aboriginal-European Relations on the North Queensland frontier 1861-1897* (Canberra, 1982); Henry Reynolds, "Violence, the Aboriginals, and the Australian Historian," *Meanjin* 31, no. 4 (December 1972): 471-77; idem, "The Other Side of the Frontier," *Australian Historical Studies* 17, no. 66 (1976), 50-63; idem, *The Other Side of the Frontier: Aboriginal Resistance to the European Invasion of Australia* (Melbourne, 1981); Michael Christie, *Aborigines in Colonial Victoria, 1835-1886* (Sydney, 1979); Lyndall Ryan, *The Aboriginal Tasmanians*, 2nd ed. (Syndey, 1996).

34. A. Dirk Moses, "Coming to Terms with the Past in Comparative Perspective: Germany and Australia," *Aboriginal History* 25 (2001): 91-115.

35. Bruce Elder, *Blood on the Wattle: Massacres and Maltreatment of Australian Aborigines since 1788* (Sydney, 1988), 200. See also Bernard Smith, *The Spectre of Truganini* (Sydney, 1980); Lorna Lippmann, *Generations of Resistance: The Aboriginal Struggle for Justice* (Melbourne, 1981); Jan Roberts, *From Massacre to Mining: The Colonization of Aboriginal Australia* (Blackburn, Vic., 1981); Michael Cannon, *Who Killed the Koories?* [sic] (Melbourne, 1990), chapter 22; Norman C. Habel, *Reconciliation: Searching for Australia's Soul* (Sydney, 1999), 48-50, 171-73.

36. Phillip Knightly, *Australia: Biography of a Nation* (London, 2000), 107.

37. Mary Kalantzis, "Recognising Diversity," in *Unity and Diversity: A National Conversation*, ed. Helen Irving (Sydney, 2001), 130-148; Tony Barta, "Discourses of Genocide in Germany and Australia: a Linked History," *Aboriginal*

History 25 (2001): 37-56; Simone Gigliotti, "Unspeakable Pasts as Limit Events: the Holocaust, Genocide, and the Stolen Generations," *Australian Journal of Politics and History* 49, no. 2 (2003): 164-81; Paul B. Bartrop, "The Holocaust, the Aborigines, and the Bureaucracy of Destruction," *Journal of Genocide Research* 2 (2001): 75-87.

38. Bob Reece, "Inventing Aborigines," *Aboriginal History* 11 (1987): 16; Marie Fels, *Good Men and True: The Aboriginal Police of the Port Phillip District, 1837-1853* (Melbourne, 1988); Ann McGrath, *'Born in the Cattle': Aborigines in the Cattle Country* (Sydney, 1987). For a criticism of the "accommodation" approach, see Bill Thorpe, "Frontiers of Discourse: Assessing Revisionist Australian Colonial Contact Historiography," *Journal of Australian Studies* 46 (September 1995): 34-45.

39. Reece, "Inventing Aborigines," 22. See also Richard Broome, "Aboriginal Victims and Voyagers, Confronting Frontier Myths," *Journal of Australian History* 42 (September 1994): 70-77.

40. See Don Watson, *Caledonia Australis: Scottish Highlanders on the Frontier of Australia* (Sydney, 1984); idem, *Recollections of a Bleeding Heart: A Portrait of Paul Keating PM* (Sydney, 2002).

41. See the chapters in Bain Attwood, ed., *In the Age of Mabo: History, Aborigines and Australia* (Sydney, 1996); Henry Reynolds, *The Law of the Land*, 2nd ed. (Melbourne, 1992).

42. An excellent analysis of this nationalist anxiety is Ghassan Hage, *White Nation: Fantasies of White Supremacy in a Multicultural Society* (Sydney, 1998).

43. Geoffrey Blainey, "Drawing Up a Balance-Sheet of our History," *Quadrant* (July-August, 1993): 10-15; John Howard, "Confront our Past, Yes, But Let's not be Consumed by it," *The Australian* (19 November 1996).

44. For a critique, see Geoffrey Brahm Levey and A. Dirk Moses, "Debate Should Focus on the Apple, not the Core: Cultural Criteria in Determining Suitable Immigrants are Historically Bankrupt," *The Australian*, 31 December 2001, 11.

45. Inga Clendinnen, *True Stories* (Sydney, 1999), 102. For a critical assessment of Clendinnen's recent neocolonialist turn, see Tony Birch, "'History is Never Bloodless': Getting it Wrong after One Hundred Years of Federation," *Australian Historical Studies* 118 (2002): 42-53.

46. Ghassan Hage, *Against Paranoid Nationalism* (Sydney, 2003).

47. Haydie Gooder and Jane M. Jacobs, "'On the Border of the Unsayable': The Apology in Postcolonizing Australia', *Interventions* 2, no. 2 (2000): 229-47.

48. For the Council of Aboriginal Reconciliation and related Reconciliation Australia, see www.reconciliation.org.au and www.reconciliationaustralia.org.au

49. See the dissection of the arguments by Robert Manne, "In Denial: the Stolen Generations and the Right," *Australian Quarterly Essay* 1 (2001): 1-113.

50. This campaign is evaluated in Robert Manne, ed., *Whitewash: On Keith Windschuttle's Fabrication of Aboriginal History* (Melbourne, 2003). Historical background is given in Stuart Macintrye and Anna Clark, *The History Wars* (Melbourne, 2003).

51. Cf. Moses, "Coming to Terms with the Past in Comparative Perspective."

52. Istvan Hont, "The Language of Sociability and Commerce; Samuel Pufendorf and the Theoretical Foundations of the 'Four States Theory'," in *The Languages of Political Theory in Early-Modern Europe*, ed. Anthony Pagden (Cambridge, 1987), 253-76.

53. J.E. Calder, "Some Account of the Wars of Extirpation and Habits of the Native Tribes of Tasmania," *Journal of the Anthropological Institute of Great Britain and Ireland* 3 (1874): 19.

54. On the English adaptation of this intellectual tradition, see Andrew Fitzmaurice, *Humanism and America: An Intellectual History of English Colonisation, 1500-1625* (Cambridge, 2003), 140f.

55. Alan Frost, "New South Wales as *Terra Nullius:* The British Denial of Aboriginal Land Rights," *Australian Historical Studies* 19 (1981): 512-23. See also Pat Maloney, "Colonisation, Civilisation and Cultivation: Early Victorians' Theories of Property Rights and Sovereignty," in *Land and Freedom: Law, Property Right and the British Diaspora,* ed. A.R. Buck, John McLaren, and Nancy E. Wright (Aldershot, 2001), 39-56.

56. The Lockean tradition is best represented by the celebrated historian Geoffrey Blainey: *A Land Half Won,* rev. ed. (Melbourne, 1983); idem, *Triumph of the Nomads,* rev. ed. (Melbourne, 1983). For trenchant criticisms, see Henry Reynolds, "Blainey on Aboriginal History," in *Surrender Australia? Essays in the Study and Uses of History,* ed. Andrew Markus and M.C. Ricklefs (Sydney, 1985), 82-9, and Tim Rowse, "The Triumph of the Colonists," in *The Fuss that Never Ended,* ed. Deborah Gare et al (Melbourne, 2003) 39-52.

57. Fitzmaurice, *Humanism and America,* 148-56. Germans used the same argument against partisan attacks in occupied eastern Europe in World War II. See Truman Anderson, "Incident at Baranivka: German Reprisals and the Soviet Partisan Movement in Ukraine, October-December 1941," *Journal of Modern History* 71 (September 1999): 585-623.

58. John Locke, *Two Treatises on Civil Government* (London, 1884), 196f. [2:11]. Emphasis added. See the discussion in James Tully, "Placing the 'Two Treatises'," in *Political Discourse in Early Modern Britain,* ed. Nicholas Phillipson and Quentin Skinner (Cambridge, 1993), 264. See also Barbara Arniel, *John Locke and America* (New York, 1996).

59. Bhikhu Parekh, "Liberalism and Colonialism: A Critique of Locke and Mill," in *The Decolonization of Imagination,* Pieterse and Parekh, eds., 88.

60. Henry Reynolds, "The Written Record," in *Frontier Conflict,* ed. Attwood and Foster, 79-87.

61. Trollope, *Australia,* 113.

62. Grenfell Price, "Experiments in Colonisation," *Cambridge History of the British Empire,* Vol. VII, Part 1 (Cambridge, 1933), 209-242. Emphasis added.

63. Stephen Roberts, *The House that Hitler Built* (Sydney, 1938); idem, *The Squatting Age in Australia, 1835-1847* (Melbourne, 1935), 408-11.

64. Roberts, *The Squatting Age in Australia,* 404. His comments are remarkably similar to Trollope's: *Australia,* 107-9.

65. Roberts, *The Squatting Age in Australia,* 404-7.

66. *Sydney Morning Herald* cited in Alan Lester, "British Settler Discourse and the Circuits of Empire," *History Workshop Journal* 54 (2002): 33.

67. Stephen H. Roberts, *History of Australian Land Settlement* (Melbourne, 1924), xiii: "as far back as memory goes, nothing has ever gripped me more than the romance of Australia's squatters—the conquest of an unknown land by a body of adventurers, who spread over hundreds of miles, and who occupied principalities in the face of the Government, the natives, and all manner of natural difficulties."

68. Ann Curthoys, "Expulsion, Exodus and Exile in White Australian Historical Mythology," *Journal of Australian Studies* no. 61 (1999): 2-18. For the historical background to these pathologies, see David Walker, *Anxious Nation: Australia and the Rise of Asia 1850-1939* (Brisbane, 1999).

69. Roberts, *The Squatting Age in Australia*, 407.
70. Roberts, *The Squatting Age in Australia*, 404. Cf. Blainey, *A Land Half Won*, 91f.
71. Robert B. Edgerton, *Sick Societies: Challenging the Myth of Primitive Harmony* (New York, 1992). For an assessment of the debate, see Rosemary Neill, *White Out: How Politics is Killing Black Australia* (Sydney, 2002).
72. Cited in Ian Hughes, "'A State of Open Warfare': Frontier Conflict in the Cooktown Area," in *Lectures on North Queensland*, 2nd Series (Townsville, 1975), 38, 42. Cf. Geoffrey C. Bolton, *A Thousand Miles Away: A History of North Queensland to 1920* (Canberra, 1970), 38, 95; Jan Critchett, *A 'Distant Field of Murder': Western District Frontier, 1834-1848* (Melbourne, 1990), 122-31.
73. Simpson Newland, *Paving the Way: A Romance of the Australian Bush* (Adelaide, 1954), 267f. See Henry Reynolds, *Why Weren't We Told?* (Sydney, 1999), 181f; Tom Griffiths, *Hunters and Collectors* (Cambridge, 1996), 106-115.
74. Gerard Henderson, "Rewriting our History," *The Bulletin* (19 January-5 February 1993): 29.
75. See most recently, David Maybury-Lewis, "Genocide against Indigenous Peoples," and Samuel Totten, Williams S. Parsons and Robert K. Hitchcock, "Confronting Genocide and Ethnocide of Indigenous Peoples," in *Annihilating Difference: The Anthropology of Genocide*, ed. Alexander L. Hinton (Berkeley, 2002), 45, 61f.
76. A. Dirk Moses, "An Antipodean Genocide? The Origins of the Genocidal Moment in the Colonization of Australia," *Journal of Genocide Research* 2, no. 1 (2000): 89-107; Henry Reynolds, *An Indelible Stain? The Question of Genocide in Australia's History* (Sydney, 2001), 49-86. On Tasmania, see Lyndall Ryan, *The Aboriginal Tasmanians*, 2nd ed. (Sydney, 1996).
77. Alan Atkinson, "Historians and Moral Disgust," in *Frontier Conflict*, ed. Attwood and Foster, 117.
78. Kevin Gilbert, *Because a White Man'll Never Do It* (Sydney, 2002, 1973), 4f.
79. S.F. Davey, *Genesis or Genocide? The Aboriginal Assimilation Policy*, Provocative Pamphlet, no. 101, Melbourne (July 1963), 6. I am grateful to Bain Attwood for furnishing me with this source. See his analysis of Davey in *Rights for Aborigines*, 203. On assimilation, see Tim Rowse, *White Flour, White Power; From Rations to Citizenship in Central Australia* (Cambridge, 1998).
80. Cited in Debra Jopson, "Court No Place for Justice: Dodson," *Sydney Morning Herald*, 1 December 2000.
81. Larissa Behrendt, "Genocide: The Distance Between Law and Life," *Aboriginal History* 25 (2001): 132.
82. Ruth Rutcliffe, "Has Henry Reynolds Retreated," *Green Left Weekly*, 20 February 2002 at: www.greenleft.org.au/back/2002/281/481p21/htm
83. Hal Wootten to A. Dirk Moses, personal communication (20 March 2002); J.H. Wootten, *Report of the Inquiry into the Death of Malcolm Charles Smith: Australian Royal Commission into Aboriginal Deaths in Custody* (Canberra, 1989), 77.
84. Elliot Johnston, *Royal Commission into Aboriginal Deaths in Custody: National Report*, Vol. 5 (Canberra, 1991), paras. 36.3.19-20 and 36.3.7.
85. Human Rights and Equal Opportunity Commission, *'Bringing them Home': National Inquiry into the Separation of Aboriginal and Torres Strait Islander Children from their Families* (Canberra, 1997), 272f.

86. *The Encyclopaedia of Aboriginal Australia,* Vol. 2 (Canberra, 1994), 889. In the 1930s, Aboriginal numbers began to grow, and are believed to have reached around 160,196 by the time of the 1976 census. Between 1986 and 1991, the official number of people identifying as Aboriginal and Torres Strait Islanders increased by 37,813, reaching a total of 265,458. By the late 1990s, these numbers had increased to 352,000. Stuart Macintyre, *A Concise History of Australia* (Cambridge, 1999), 261. In 2001, the Australian Bureau of Statistics listed the Aboriginal and Torres Strait Islander population at 410,000. See the detailed treatment by Tim Rowse in this volume.

87. Ryan, *The Aboriginal Tasmanians.*

88. Broome, "Aboriginal Victims and Voyagers," 77.

89. Don Watson wrote of massacres and "black hunts" as "acts of genocide": Watson, *Caledonia Australis,* 169; another historian referred to "local campaigns of genocide": John C. Weaver, "Beyond the Fatal Shore: Pastoral Squatting and the Occupation of Australia, 1826-1852," *American Historical Review* 101 (1996): 1005.

90. R.W.H. Reece, "The Aborigines in Australian Historiography," in *Historical Disciplines and Culture in Australasia,* ed. John A. Moses (Brisbane, 1979), 261.

91. Norman B. Tindale, *Aboriginal Tribes of Australia: Their Terrain, Environmental Controls, Distribution, Limits and Proper Names* (Canberra, 1974).

92. Bob Reece suggested such a local focus in the 1970s but was largely ignored: Reece, "The Aborigines in Australian Historiography," 261; Richard Broome, "The Struggle for Australia: Aboriginal-European Warfare," in *Australia: Two Centuries of War and Peace,* ed. Michael McKernan and Margaret Browne (Canberra, 1988), 116; Moses, "An Antipodean Genocide?," 93; Reynolds, *An Indelible Stain?,* 120; Attwood and Foster, "Introduction," in *Frontier Conflict,* ed. Attwood and Foster, 10.

93. For example, the special issue of *Aboriginal History* 25 (2001) edited by Ann Curthoys and John Docker, and Ann Curthoys, "Cultural History and the Nation," *Cultural History in Australia,* eds. Hsu-Ming Teo and Richard White (Sydney 2003), 22-37. Important, too, is the comparative analysis of the English sociologist, Alison Palmer, *Colonial Genocide* (Adelaide, 2000); Colin Tatz, *With Intent to Destroy* (London, 2003); Reynolds, *An Indelible Stain?.*

94. Raimond Gaita, "Not Right," *Quadrant* (January-February 1997): 46-51; idem, "Genocide and Pedantry," *Quadrant* (July-August 1997): 41-5; idem, "Reply to Kenneth Minogue," *Quadrant* (November 1998): 39-43; idem, *A Common Humanity: Thinking About Love and Truth and Justice* (Melbourne, 1999); idem, "Who Speaks, About What, To Whom, On Whose Behalf, With What Right?" in *Best Australian Essays,* ed. Peter Craven (Sydney, 2000), 162-76; idem, "Why the Impatience? Genocide, 'Ideology' and Practical Reconciliation'," *Australian Book Review* (July 2001): 25-31.

95. Inga Clendinnen, "First Contact," *The Australian's Review of Books* (May 2001): 6-7, 26.

96. Ron Brunton, "Tie to Bury the Genocide Corpse," *Courier Mail* [Brisbane], 18 August 2001; Paul Sheehan, "Saved, Not Stolen: Laying the Genocide Myth to Rest," *Sydney Morning Herald,* 4 July 2001, 22; Michael Duffy, "Who's Sorry Now?" *Courier Mail,* 7 June 2001.

97. Andrew Markus, *Governing Savages* (Sydney, 1990), 189; Smith, *The Spectre of Truganini,* 32.

98. Editorial, "Time to Stop the Real Genocide," *The Courier Mail*, 7 April 2001, 24.
99. Andrew Markus, "Genocide in Australia," *Aboriginal History* 25 (2001): 50-70. In doing so he follows in the footsteps of some Israelis and Americans who insist that the Holocaust be quarantined off as unique and unprecedented. See Steven T. Katz, *The Holocaust in Historical Context*, Vol. 1 (New York, 1994); idem, "The Holocaust: A Very Particular Racism," in *The Holocaust and History*, ed. Michael Berenbaum and Abraham J. Peck (Bloomington and Indiana, 1998), 56-63; Yehuda Bauer, "Comparison of Genocides," in *Studies in Contemporary Genocide*, ed. Levon Chorbajian and George Shirinian (New York, 1999), 33. An excellent analysis of these arguments is Dan Stone, *Constructing the Holocaust* (London, 2003).
100. Peter Read, "'A Rape of the Soul so Profound': Some Reflections of the Dispersal Policy in New South Wales," *Aboriginal History* 7 (1983): 32; idem, Review of Henry Reynolds, *An Indelible Stain?* (Sydney, 2001) in *Aboriginal History* 25 (2001): 297.
101. On this general issue, see A. Dirk Moses, "Genocide and Holocaust Consciousness in Australia," *History Compass* 1 (2003): AU 28, 1-11 at: www.history-compass.com
102. Lemkin cited in Steven L. Jacobs, "Genesis of the Concept of Genocide according to its Author from the Original Sources," *Human Rights Review* (January-March 2002): 102.
103. Lemkin cited in Helen Fein, *Genocide: A Sociological Inquiry* (London, 1993), 11-12.
104. See the account in Samantha Power, *"A Problem from Hell": America and the Age of Genocide* (New York, 2002), chapters one and two.
105. Jacobs, "Genesis of the Concept of Genocide," 99-100; cf. Lawrence J. LeBlanc, *The United States and the Genocide Convention* (Durham, NC, 1991), 16-19.
106. Raphael Lemkin, "Acts Constituting a General (Transnational) Danger Considered as Offences Against the Law of Nations," 1933: http://www.preventgenocide.org/lemkin/madrid1933-english.htm
107. Raphael Lemkin, *Axis Rule in Occupied Europe* (Washington, 1944), 91-2.
108. Lemkin, *Axis Rule*, 80; idem, "Genocide as a Crime under International Law," *American Journal of International Law* 41, no. 1 (1947): 147.
109. Lemkin, *Axis Rule*, 79.
110. Lemkin, *Axis Rule*, xi, 79.
111. Raphael Lemkin, "Genocide - A Modern Crime," *Free World* 9, no. 4 (April 1945): 39-43.
112. Lemkin, *Axis Rule*, 82-90.
113. Churchill, *A Little Matter of Genocide*.
114. Raphael Lemkin, "Totally Unofficial Man," in *Pioneers of Genocide Studies*, ed. Samuel Totten and Steven L. Jacobs (New Brunswick and London, 2002), 393.
115. Lemkin, *Axis Rule*, 80. Emphasis added. Cf. idem, "Genocide – A Modern Crime," 39; Cf. A. Dirk Moses, "The Holocaust and Genocide," in *The Historiography of the Holocaust*, ed. Dan Stone (London, 2004), 533-55.
116. Lemkin, *Axis Rule*, 8f. See the valuable discussion of John Docker who read the Lemkin papers in the New York Public Library: "Are Settler Colonies Inherently Genocidal? Re-Reading Lemkin," in A. Dirk Moses, ed., *Genocide and Colonialism* (New York and Oxford, forthcoming).

117. William A. Schabas, *Genocide in International Law: the Crimes of Crimes* (Cambridge, 2000); Johannes Morsink, "Cultural Genocide, the Universal Declaration, and Minority Rights," *Human Rights Quarterly* 21, no. 4 (1999): 1009-1060; Matthew Lippman, "Drafting of the 1948 Convention on the Prevention and Punishment of Genocide," *Boston University International Law Journal* 3 (1985): 1-65.

118. Lemkin, "Totally Unofficial Man," 371-73.

119. Readers familiar with Holocaust historiography will recognize that I have taken these terms from a prominent debate in that literature. See Ian Kershaw, *The Nazi Dictatorship: Problems and Perspectives of Interpretation*, 2nd ed (London, 1989).

120. Kurt Jonassohn and Frank Chalk, "A Typology of Genocide and Some Implications for the Human Rights Agenda," in *Genocide and the Modern Age*, ed. Isidor Walliman and Michael N. Dobkowski, 2nd ed. (New York, 2000), 3-20; idem, "The History and Sociology of Genocidal Killings," in *Genocide: A Critical Bibliographic Review*, ed. Israel Charny (London, 1988); idem, eds., *The History and Sociology of Genocide* (New Haven, 1990).

121. Chalk and Jonassohn, *History and Sociology of Genocide*, 23.

122. Lemkin, *Axis Rule*, xi, 79.

123. Barbara Harff, "Genocide as State Terrorism," in *Government Violence and Repression*, ed. M. Stohl and G.A. Lopez (New York, 1986), 165f.; Irving Horowitz, *Genocide: State Power and Mass Murder* (New Brunswick, 1976); Lyman H. Legters, "The Soviet Gulag: Is it Genocidal?" in *Toward the Understanding and Prevention of Genocide*, ed. Israel W. Charny (Boulder, Colo., 1988), 60-6; Vahahn N. Dadrian, "A Typology of Genocide," *International Review of Modern Sociology* 5 (1975): 201-12; Christian P. Scherrer, "Towards a Theory of Modern Genocide," *Journal of Genocide Research* 1 (1999): 15.

124. A stellar example of this type of settler-state tension is Heather Goodall, "Authority Under Challenge: Pikampul Land and Queen Victoria's Law During the British Invasion of Australia," in *Empire and Others: British Encounters with Indigenous Peoples, 1600-1850*, ed. Martin Daunton and Rick Halpern (London, 1999), 260-79.

125. Robert Foster, Rick Hosking and Amanda Nettelbeck, *Fatal Collisions: The South Australian Frontier and the Violence of Memory* (Adelaide, 2001), 8.

126. For a regional example, see Beverley Nance, "The Level of Violence: Europeans and Aborigines in Port Phillip, 1835-1850," *Australian Historical Studies* 19, no. 77 (1981): 532-49. On disease in Australia, see Judith Campbell, *Invisible Invaders: Smallpox and Other Diseases in Aboriginal Australia, 1780-1880* (Melbourne, 2002).

127. John R. Seeley, *The Expansion of England* (London, 1883), 8.

128. See the discussion of the various positions in Barbara Harff and Ted Robert Gurr, "Toward Empirical Theory of Genocides and Politicides," *International Studies Quarterly* 32 (1988): 359-371; Helen Fein, "Scenarios of Genocide and Critical Responses," in *Towards the Understanding and Prevention of Genocide*, ed. Israel Charny, 3-31.

129. Adam Smith, *The Wealth of Nations*, Vol. 2 (London, 1910), 122.

130. Stanner, *After the Dreaming*, 7f. This blindness to the insuperable structural determinants of violence is visible, for example, in Inga Clendinnen, *Dancing with Strangers* (Melbourne, 2003). Although she recognizes that the British "wanted land, and they took it," and that "racial frontiers, pushing irresistibly

outwards, would be marked in blood, and many [Indigenous] Australians would die," she concludes nonetheless that the basic problem was "the depth of cultural division" between the peoples (286). Is she proposing that the conflict would not have happened had they been able to understand one another? If not, then the ethnographic method Clendinnen proposes is unable to do the conceptual work she demands of it.

131. Frank Chalk, "Redefining Genocide," in *Genocide: Conceptual and Historical Dimensions*, ed. George Andreopolous (Philadelphia, 1994), 58ff.

132. A sophisticated treatment of the issues is Berel Lang, *The Future of the Holocaust: Between History and Memory* (Ithaca and London, 1999), 25.

133. Tony Barta, "Relations of Genocide: Land and Lives in the Colonization of Australia," in *Genocide and the Modern Age*, ed. Wallimann and Dobkowski, 237-252. The following paragraphs rely on my "Conceptual Blockages and Definitional Dilemmas."

134. Barta, "Relations of Genocide," 239.

135. Alison Palmer, *Colonial Genocide* (Adelaide, 2000), 209.

136. Raymond Evans and Bill Thorpe, "The Massacre of Aboriginal History," *Overland* 163 (September 2001): 36. See also Bill Thorpe, *Colonial Queensland: Perspective on Frontier Society* (Brisbane, 1996).

137. Evans and Thorpe, "Massacre of Aboriginal History," 37.

138. Whether land or labor is the object of the colonial economy is obviously a key variable. For discussions, see Palmer, *Colonial Genocide;* Patrick Wolfe, "Land, Labor, and Difference: Elementary Structures of Race," *American Historical Review* 106, no. 3 (June 2001): 866-904; Michael Freeman, "Genocide, Civilization and Modernity," *British Journal of Sociology* 46, no. 2 (1996): 207-223.

139. Ann Curthoys and John Docker, "Introduction. Genocide: Definitions, Questions, Settler-Colonies," *Aboriginal History* 25 (2001): 1-15.

140. Lemkin, *Axis Rule*, xi.

141. Lemkin, "Totally Unofficial Man," 388, 378 for his positive views of the USA. Various drafts of his work on world genocide are kept by the American Jewish Historical Society, 15 West 16th Street, New York, and by the Jacob Reader Marcus Center of the American Jewish Archives in Cincinnati, Ohio. His paper on Tasmania is located in the New York Public Library, 42nd Street, Manhattan. Special issues of *Patterns of Prejudice* and the *Journal of Genocide Research* in 2005 will make available selections of, and commentary on, Lemkin's unpublished work. It will also be discussed by various authors in Moses, ed., *Genocide and Colonialism*.

142. See the discussion of Lord Diplock in the *Crown v. Lemon*, H.L.(E) (1979): 636. I owe this reference to Lawrence McNamara, Faculty of Law, Macquarie University, Sydney.

143. Roger W. Smith, "Human Destructiveness and Politics: The Twentieth Century as an Age of Genocide," in *Genocide and the Modern Age*, ed. Wallimann and Dobkowski, 23.

144. Reece, *Aborigines and Colonists*, 139.

145. Herman Merivale, *Lectures on Colonization and Colonies* [1861] (Oxford, 1928), 490. Emphasis added.

146. Charles Darwin, *The Descent of Man and Selection in Relation to Sex*, Vol. 1 (London, 1871), 238.

147. Palmer, *Colonial Genocide*, 194. L. Ryan, "Aboriginal Policy in Australia: 1838 – A Watershed?", *Push from the Bush* 8 (December 1980): 14-22.

148. Suzanne Davies, "Aborigines, Murders, and the Criminal Law in early Port Phillip, 1840-1851," *Australian Historical Studies* 22, no. 88 (1987): 313-36; Ben Kiernan, "Australia's Aboriginal Genocide," *Yale Journal of Human Rights* 1, no, 1 (Spring 2001): 49-56. The extent and timing of the acceptance of unsworn Aboriginal testimony varied greatly across the colonies.

149. A.G.L. Shaw, "British Policy Toward the Australian Aborigines, 1830-1850," *Australian Historical Studies* 25, no. 99 (1992): 266.

150. Patrick Wolfe, *Settler Colonialism and the Transformation of Anthropology* (London and New York, 1992), 3.

151. Wolfe, "Land, Labor, and Difference," 867.

152. Walter Roth, *Report of the Royal Commission on the Condition of the Natives* (Perth, 1905), 28. I am grateful to Tim Rowse for this reference.

153. Clive Turnbull, *Black War: The Extermination of the Tasmanian Aborigines* (Melbourne, 1948), 23f.

154. Merivale, *Lectures on Colonization and Colonies*, 511f. Cf. Shaw, "British Policy Toward the Australian Aborigines, 1830-1850," 285. Emphasis added.

155. Zygmunt Bauman, *Postmodernity and its Discontents* (London, 1997), 18f. I thank Peter Beilharz, La Trobe University, Melbourne, for this reference. See his *Zygmunt Bauman: Dialectic of Modernity* (London, 2000), 95.

156. I have discussed this problem in "Structure and Agency in the Holocaust: Daniel J. Goldhagen and his Critics," *History and Theory* 37 (1998): 194-219.

157. The following paragraphs rely on Moses, "An Antipodean Genocide?".

158. Mary Anne Jebb, *Blood, Sweat and Welfare: A History of White Bosses and Aboriginal Pastoral Workers* (Perth, 2002), 36-63 shows how the state backed the Kimberley pastoralists against the Indigenous peoples, such that hundreds of native men were arrested and removed from the area, effectively smashing their communities.

159. Merivale, *Lectures on Colonization and Colonies*, 495, 497.

160. Niall Ferguson, *Empire: How Britain Made the Modern World* (London, 2003), 109-11. A good survey of the historiography is Stuart MacIntyre, "Australia and the Empire," in *The Oxford History of the British Empire*, Vol. 5, *Historiography* (Oxford, 1999), 163-81.

161. Daiva Stasiulis and Nira Yuval-Davis, eds., *Unsettling Settler Societies: Articulations of Gender, Race, Ethnicity and Class* (London, 1995); Udo Krautwurst, "What is Settler Colonialism? An Anthropological Meditation on Frantz Fanon's 'Concerning Violence'," *History and Anthropology* 14, no. 1 (2003): 55-72. See the discussion of the literature in Ian Tyrrell, "Beyond the View from Euro-America," in *Rethinking American History in a Global Age*, ed. Thomas Bender (Berkeley, 2002), 168-91.

162. Paul Patton, "Mabo, Freedom and the Politics of Difference," *Australian Journal of Political Science* (1995): 109-119; Dipesh Chakrabarty, "Reconciliation and its Historiography: Some Preliminary Thoughts," *UTS Review* 7, no. 1 (May 2001): 6-16; Elizabeth A. Povinelli, "Reading Ruptures, Rupturing Readings: Mabo and the Cultural Politics of Activism," *Social Analysis* no. 2 (July 1997): 20-28; idem, The State of Shame: Australian Multiculturalism and the Crisis of Indigenous Citizenship," *Critical Inquiry* 24 (1998): 575-610; Hage, *White Nation;* Gillian Cowlishaw, "The Aboriginal Experience: A Problem of Interpretation," [Review Article], *Ethnic and Racial Studies* 15, no. 2 (1992): 308f.

163. Geoffrey C. Bolton, "Reflections on Comparative Frontier History," in *Frontier Conflict*, ed. Attwood and Foster, 161-68; Deborah Rose, "Aboriginal Life

and Death in Australian Settler Society," *Aboriginal History* 25 (2001): 148-63; Lynette Russell, ed., *Colonial Frontiers: Indigenous-European Encounters in Settler Societies* (Manchester and New York, 2001).

164. Jeffrey Grey, *A Military History of Australia*, rev. ed. (Cambridge, 1999); John Connor, *The Australian Frontier Wars, 1788-1838* (Sydney, 2002); Broome, "The Struggle for Australia" defines war broadly to include unofficial actions against Aborigines; Ian D. Clark, *Scars in the Landscape: A Register of Massacre Sites in Western Victoria, 1803-1859* (Canberra, 1995).

165. Good examples are Mark McKenna, *Looking for Blackfella's Point: An Australian History of Place* (Sydney, 2002), Patrick Collins, *Goodbye Bussamarai: The Mandandanji Land War, Southern Queensland, 1842-1852* (Brisbane, 2002); Cathie Clement, "Historical Notes Relevant to Impact Stories of the East Kimberley," *East Kimberley Working Paper*, no. 29, The Australian National University (Canberra. 1989); idem, "Monotony, Manhunts and Malice: Eastern Kimberley Law Enforcement, 1896-1908," *Early Days: Journal and Proceedings of the Royal Western Australian Historical Society* 10, pt. 1 (1989); R.H. Pilmer, *Northern Patrol: An Australian Saga*, edited and annotated by Cathie Clement and Peter Bridge (Perth, 1996).

– Chapter 2 –

COLONIALISM AND THE HOLOCAUST
Towards an Archeology of Genocide

Jürgen Zimmerer
(trans. by Andrew H. Beattie)

The German war against Poland and the USSR was without doubt the largest colonial war of conquest in history. Never before were so many people and resources mobilized by a conqueror, and never before were war aims so expansive. Unprecedented, too, was the deliberately planned murder of such a large number of people, or at least the willing acceptance of their death. All of this served the goal of conquering "living space" *(Lebensraum)* in the East, a colonial empire to which the Germans were supposedly entitled and that reached far beyond the Ural Mountains.[1]

It was clear to those responsible on the German side, and above all to Hitler, that if there was a historical precedent, then only the history of colonialism could possibly provide an example for their plans:

> The struggle for hegemony in the world is decided for Europe by the possession of Russian territory; it makes Europe the place in the world most secure from blockade. (...) The Slavic peoples on the other hand are not destined for their own life. ... The Russian territory is our India and, just as the English rule India with a handful of people, so will we govern this our colonial territory. We will supply the Ukrainians with headscarves, glass chains as jewelry, and whatever else colonial peoples like. ... My goals are not immoderate; basically these are all areas where

Notes for this section begin on page 69.

Germans (*Germanen*) were previously settled. The German Volk is to
grow into this territory.[2]

Although Hitler thus invoked the British Empire as a model,
the Third Reich and its efforts at expansion are rarely considered
from the perspective of the history of colonialism, either because
colonialism is automatically regarded as applying to regions outside Europe, or because the common understanding of colonialism
is inadequate.

In fact, historical scholarship has largely ignored structural
similarities and has avoided direct references between the two.
Instead, the investigation of the colonial enthusiasm of the National
Socialists has been restricted prematurely to the reacquisition of the
German empire in Africa. And so the literature concludes erro-
neously that Hitler was not particularly interested in a colonial
empire, missing the point that the geographical sphere for a German colonial empire had long since changed from the south to the
east.[3] This move is evident in the meaning of the slogan "Volk without space" *(Volk ohne Raum)*.[4] Hans Grimm's novel of that name
was set in South Africa, but the term was later used for German
attempts to gain territory in Eastern Europe.

Although Hannah Arendt argued as long as half a century ago
that imperialism was the precursor to National Socialism, this idea
was not pursued.[5] Apart from the criticism of her conception of
totalitarianism, the reason for this neglect presumably also lies in
the rapidly expanding scholarship on colonialism and National
Socialism, each of which now fills whole libraries. As a result, our
understanding of both the Third Reich and colonialism has
changed so enormously that comparison is necessary on an entirely
new basis. Furthermore, experts on colonialism have tended not to
be interested in Nazi crimes, preferring to leave them to historians
of Germany and Eastern Europe, while researchers on National
Socialism—used to dealing with large armies, millions of victims
and perpetrators, and warfare between modern states—seem not to
take seriously the colonial conquest of the world. Although there
are plenty of studies that follow the Nazi policy of expansion back
to the German Empire—as exemplified by the Fischer controversy
on German aims in the First World War[6]—or that categorize the
Empire and German colonialism as fascist or proto-fascist,[7] as yet
no one has attempted systematically to portray Nazi expansion and
occupation policy in the East as colonial.[8]

The problem of the connection between colonialism and
National Socialism is highly political and emotional, for the histor-

ical-academic question of the singularity of the Holocaust and the relationship of Nazi crimes to previous or subsequent collective mass murders has long since also taken on a philosophical dimension and is intrinsically linked to identity politics.[9] Whereas supporters of the singularity thesis regard comparisons as a blasphemous mockery of the Holocaust's victims, its opponents—in analogy to the accusation of Holocaust denial—argue that the singularity thesis amounts to the denial of all other genocides.[10]

The question of colonial genocide is disturbing, in part because it increases the number of mass murders regarded as genocide, and in part, too, because it calls into question the Europeanization of the globe as a modernizing project. Where the descendants of perpetrators still comprise the majority or a large proportion of the population, and control political life and public discourse, recognition of colonial genocides is even more difficult, as it undermines the image of the past on which national identity is built. Australian conservatives, for example, have difficulties recognizing the genocide of the Aborigines.[11] Former President Bill Clinton can apologize in Africa for the crimes of slavery—his gesture took place outside the USA—while public commemoration of the destruction of the American Indians continues to be denied.[12] Similarly, former German Federal President Roman Herzog refused to apologize for the genocide of the Herero and Nama peoples during his visit to Namibia in 1998.[13]

Groups of victims and their representatives insist on acknowledging genocide because it is regarded as absolutely the worst human crime. The connection to the Holocaust, with the implicit moral equivalence, is indicated in titles such as *The American Holocaust,*[14] *American Indian Holocaust,*[15] *The Herero Holocaust,*[16] and *The Black Holocaust.*[17] Yet, the inflationary use of the terms "genocide" and "Holocaust" creates problems for the scholarly debate about the history of genocide. Their application to very diverse cases of mass death, where the intentions of the perpetrators vary considerably, and whose contexts, course, and extent are so different, means that the terms lose analytical precision and thus their usefulness for historical analysis. Not every mass death constitutes a case of genocide.

The positions mentioned above—either stressing or denying the singularity of the Holocaust—are reflected in the scholarly debate within Holocaust and genocide studies about the appropriate definition of genocide.[18] Whereas Israel W. Charny defines genocide quite broadly as "the mass killing of substantial numbers of human beings, when not in the course of military forces against an avowed enemy, under conditions of the essential defenselessness and helplessness of the victims,"[19] Steven T. Katz wants the concept limited to the Nazi murder of the Jews, defining it as "the actualization of the intent, however successfully carried out, to murder in its totality any national, ethnic, racial, religious, political, social, gender or economic group, as these groups are defined by the perpetrator."[20] Both definitions are largely useless for a universal-historical consideration because they make sensible comparison difficult. A working definition is needed that neither excludes an event from historical consideration, nor diminishes the horror of the deliberate murder of entire peoples within a general history of mass killings.

The United Nations Convention on Genocide still offers the best and most widely accepted working basis. In 1948, it defined genocide as "any of the following acts committed with the intent to destroy, in whole or in part, a national, ethnic, racial or religious group, as such:

- Killing members of the group;
- Causing serious bodily or mental harm to members of the group;
- Deliberately inflicting on the group conditions of life calculated to bring about its physical destruction in whole or in part;
- Imposing measures intended to prevent births within the group;
- Forcibly transferring children of the group to another group."[21]

Four years earlier, the originator of the term, Raphael Lemkin, defined it inter alia as a "coordinated plan of different actions aiming at the destruction of essential foundations of the life of national groups, with the aim of annihilating the groups themselves."[22] The intentions of the perpetrators are thus central.

If one applies these measures, then many cases of mass death sometimes regarded as genocidal disappear from the list: an intention to annihilate was not evident in the practice of slavery, or in the deaths of millions of indigenous Americans who were above all the victims of diseases brought by Europeans. Nonetheless, cases for genocide can be made in North America, Australia, and southern Africa, and they are considered in the comparative analysis that follows. This is not to suggest that there are not further instances of genocidal massacres. The examples discussed here merely seem to be the most fruitful for an investigation of structural similarities and connections with National Socialism. It is self-evident that, as Stig Förster and Gerhard Hirschfeld formulated recently, "it cannot be about the contrasting of genocides and numbers of victims against each other."[23] Neither is the point to completely equate or deny historical specificities; every case of genocide or mass murder organized socially or by a state is singular in important respects. Rather, the historical roots of the preparedness to resettle whole peoples according to one's own needs, or even to kill them, are explored in the sense of an "archaeology" of the idea of genocide and population economics *(Bevölkerungsökonomik)*. In this regard, European colonialism is an important historical starting point, as it rests on fundamentally similar concepts of space and race to those at the heart of the Nazi policy of expansion and murder. The following section explores the structural similarity in terms of the formulation and the function of the concepts of race and space in the historical phenomena of colonialism and National Socialism, while the second section examines the conditions of genocide in colonialism and National Socialism and addresses their similarities and differences.

Structural Similarity: Space and Race

If one considers Nazi policy in Eastern Europe in its different dimensions—war of annihilation, occupation policy, and genocide—two concepts bind them together.[24] The first is racism, which is the unifying thread in diverging aspects of Nazi ideology and practice;[25] the second is the policy of space, mainly with regard to Eastern Europe and the "economy of destruction" planned for it.[26]

Racism here does not mean simply the ascription of various characteristics to different races and the consequent valuation of races within an assumed ethnic hierarchy, but a conception of the world "that is applied both internally and externally and can be defined as the comprehensive 'biologization [*Biologisierung*] of the social.'"[27] Seen under this aspect, the victims of the forced sterilization policy, of the murder of "life unworthy of life," the Soviet prisoners of war, as well as the Jews were all victims of the same inhumane ideology.[28]

In this racist view of history and society, the Volk is understood as an organic whole, whose preservation and growth was to be ensured under any circumstances. Eugenic measures like breeding and the "purification" of the "body of the Volk" from "impurities" and "sickness" were to guarantee the survival and rise of the German Volk in a struggle for existence understood in Social Darwinian terms.[29] What the Volk, whose viability lay in the number of its "racially healthy" members, lacked above all was "living space." The conception of space was thus directly associated with the racial ideology. It incorporated ideas of economic autarchy as well as the idea of a settlement area for Germans, which was to be found in Poland and Russia where they would find the living space that they supposedly lacked.[30]

Race and space were also at the heart of colonialism. Above all, the settler colonies, like the later German occupation policy in the East, created an economy characterized by the attempt to gain an enormous dependent territory. This was to involve not a partnership of equals, but the subjugation, on occasion even the annihilation, of the original inhabitants. This policy was motivated and justified by racism, i.e., humanity's division into higher races, destined to rule, and lower races, destined to be subjugated. At the lowest end of the scale were groups that were doomed to destruction, or that were to be deliberately murdered.[31]

Of course, European colonialism experienced various stages of development and assumed different forms in its 500-year history. Even the justification for European expansion and rule over the indigenous populations of the newly "discovered" and conquered areas changed. Yet, belief in one's own righteousness or destiny was always the ideological prerequisite for the expansion of power, whether for the missionary conversion of the "heathens," in the "White Man's Burden," or "Manifest Destiny." Social Darwinism, which gained influence in the course of the nineteenth century, directly emphasized a racial hierarchy and competition among the races, which applied to the relationship between the colonizers and the colonized, as well as among the colonial powers themselves. This biological interpretation of world history—the conviction that a Volk needs to secure space in order to survive—is one of the fundamental parallels between colonialism and Nazi expansion policy.[32]

The space won through "discovery" and conquest had then to be developed and "civilized," for in the perception of the colonizers it was wild and dangerous.[33] Particularly in the settler colonies, the land was regarded as "empty of people"[34] and the settlers believed they could transform it according to their own ideas, bringing order to chaos without regard for indigenous communities and economies. Cities were founded; streets and, later, railways were constructed; the land was surveyed and registered.[35]

Similarly, the Nazi conquerors regarded the East as an enormous tabula rasa that could be redesigned according to their own conceptions, and it was an ideal field of operation for regional developers and population economists *(Bevölkerungsökonomen)*, engineers, and economic planners.[36] One only has to think of the gigantic plans for the creation of an Autobahn network to reach deep into Asia, with the new Reich capital *Germania* at its heart. Even in describing what they found, the German conquerors drew on colonial history as a point of reference. For example, a member of the 12th Air Force Regiment reported a few weeks after the attack on the Soviet Union:

> As marvelous as the successes are, as great as the advance. (…) Russia is on the whole still a huge disappointment for the individual. No culture, no paradise (…) the lowest level, filth, a humanity that shows us that we will have a huge task of colonization here.[37]

This conception of "primitiveness, barrenness, and backwardness,"[38] as Christian Gerlach has reconstructed in many examples from White Russia, demanded from the German perspective the comprehensive redesigning and modernization of the whole country without consideration of extant social, political, and economic structures. Precisely this comprehensive redesigning was understood as colonization. The land planner for East Prussia and later for the Reich division of Danzig-West Prussia, Ewald Liedecke, commented on the question of the treatment of local culture and settlements as early as 1939:

> In redesigning German land, we cannot stroll in Polish tracks and make Polish settlements and land divisions the basis of the German settlement landscape. Instead of this partial approach, a total colonizing act is necessary that encompasses the entire area, overturned and settled anew according to German conceptions.[39]

The justification for ruling the conquered lands was provided not just by the underdevelopment of the land but also by the supposed backwardness and immaturity of the inhabitants. According to Hitler, one needed "only to see this primal world *[Urwelt]*" to know "that nothing will happen here if one does not allocate work for the people. The Slav is born a slave crying for a master."[40] Himmler's secretary, Johst, who traveled through Poland with the Reich Leader SS in the winter of 1939 to 1940, presumably reflected his boss's words, too, when he wrote:

> The Poles are not a state-building nation. They lack even the most elementary preconditions for it. I drove alongside the Reichsführer-SS up

and down that country. A country which has so little feeling for systematic settlement, that is not even up to dealing with the style of a village, has no claim to any sort of independent political status within the European area. It is a colonial country![41]

The parallels to colonialism are not limited just to the ideological justification of conquest and domination; they are also evident in the techniques of rule. With the exception of the settler colonies, where the proportion of Europeans to the indigenous population gradually shifted, a small elite of colonial administrators and military ruled a far more numerous local population that was unable to participate in government. Colonizers and colonized were ruled by different legal systems, and this "dual legal system" rested on racial criteria.

Advantages for Europeans in this "racially privileged society" *(rassische Privilegiengesellschaft)*, however, were not limited to formal law.[42] The *situation coloniale* penetrated all spheres of social interaction between colonizers and colonized. The former were always privileged in every respect. They had their own schools and kindergartens, their own counters at post offices and other government agencies. This constant symbolic subordination was evident, for example, in German Southwest Africa, where Africans were obliged to salute whites, and forbidden from riding horses and using the sidewalk. In occupied Poland, too, Poles had to display appropriate humility before the Germans by making way for them on sidewalks, removing their hats, and saluting. They were prohibited from attending cinemas, concerts, exhibitions, libraries, museums, and theatres, and from owning bicycles, cameras, and radios.[43] To be sure, this everyday discrimination pales in significance in comparison with the contemporaneous mass murders, but it nevertheless provides an indication of an often-overlooked line of tradition of German policy in the occupied territories. The ideal of the "racially privileged society" is also the basis for the following statement by Hitler: "Our Germans—that is the main thing—must form a closed community like a fortress, outside the centers the lowest horse boy must stand above any of the natives."[44] Of course, this only applied to that part of the local population whose right to life was recognized at all.

Not only was the separate treatment of Germans and non-Germans, or whites and nonwhites, prescribed legally and in everyday life in both colonialism and National Socialism, but active steps were taken to avoid any "mixing" of the two populations. The problem of maintaining the separation of the privileged upper and the non-privileged lower strata was particularly acute in the settler colonies where there was a relatively large number of European residents. So-called people of "mixed-blood" *(Mischlinge)*, who blurred the boundaries between the races, were seen as a potential threat. Thus attempts were made to prevent such occurrences and, beginning in the English colonies in North America, "mixed marriages" were forbidden. For example, in German Southwest Africa transgressions against the prohibition of sexual relations were branded as "sinning against racial consciousness," as the Protestant missionary Wandres put it.[45] It is not hard to recognize a parallel with the "racial shame" and the racial laws in the Third Reich, where the Nuremberg Laws of 1935 forbade marriages between Germans and Jews and "extramarital intercourse between Jews and citizens of German or related blood."[46]

The notion of the free design of the colonized space corresponded to the disenfranchisement of the indigenous population and its degradation to a group that stood at the disposal of the colonial masters and could be used according to the latter's interests. This manifested itself in two ways: the forced recruitment of labor and the arbitrary resettlement of the native population. Recruitment for labor assumed different forms. In the Congo, for instance, there were outright hunts for men capable of working, women and children were taken as hostages to force the men to come out of hiding, and whole villages were destroyed if they failed to meet quotas for the provision of workers.[47] In Southwest Africa, by contrast, recruitment was ensured after 1907 through the introduction of native ordinances. With the aid of a system of surveillance probably unique in the history of colonialism, the Africans were supposed to be completely integrated as workers in the colonial economy.[48] Even if this constituted a "semi-free labor market" rather than a system of forced labor, behind this practice stood the notion of the indigenous population completely at the disposal of the colonial state.[49] This was even taken to the extent that larger African settlements were forbidden in order to ensure the even distribution of laborers across the whole country. The National Socialist economy also recruited forced laborers in every occupied country and transported them to Germany.[50] The German armaments industry rested to a considerable extent on an economy of slavery, and the recruitment of workers in the east assumed forms that are familiar from reports from the Congo.[51]

The claim to utter disposability of the indigenous population according to the colonial masters' economic and security requirements had been evident even earlier in other colonies in the readiness to resettle the native population according to economic needs, to cram them into reserves, or to expel them completely from the colonial territory. Whether in the Indian reservations in North America or the reserves in German Southwest Africa, the common thread was that people deemed superfluous to the new colonial society were simply physically removed. Not surprisingly, the land to which they were to be resettled was almost without exception unusable. That the economic and social decline that all too often ensued in such cases was intended or at least willingly accepted, suggests preexisting genocidal tendencies. The German plans, naturally on a much larger scale, for the resettlement of populations in Eastern Europe and the cramming together of Jews in "reserves" may have borrowed from these experiences. At the very least, the fact that the reserve policy was regarded as "normal" practice in handling indigenous populations meant that it was not perceived as being criminal.[52]

Genocides: similarities and differences

The most radical consequence of a policy of conquest and settlement based on the conceptions of "race" and "space" was genocide. This section attempts to explore the connections between the genocidal moments in colonialism and National Socialism. It shows how genocidal tendencies developed at the colonial frontier and how their degree of organization and the responsible groups of perpetrators in many ways resembled the state crimes of modern bureaucratic genocide. However, it is necessary first to differentiate between how colonial and Nazi genocides are to be understood.

In the Third Reich, genocidal policy arose in such a concentrated fashion and was directed against so many different groups in such a short period that the genocides can justifiably be seen as one, if not the main characteristic of National Socialism. Although they were the product of the same policy aimed at achieving a racial utopia, the Nazi genocides can be differentiated according to the motives and methods used for destroying the various groups of victims. Such a differentiation is necessary particularly for the sake of comparison with genocides committed in colonial contexts.

Because the Jews occupied the lowest position in the Nazis' new "racial hierarchy" and were to be accorded no place in the racial utopia of the future, they were to be completely eradicated. They supposedly posed a worldwide threat that had to be fought everywhere, and they were regarded as "parasites" in the body of the Volk that had to be destroyed.[53] By contrast, the Sinti and

Roma, "a-socials," and the disabled were also regarded as parasites to be destroyed, but were not seen as a global threat and were not deemed to be involved in a worldwide conspiracy.[54]

Nonetheless, the methods of destruction were shared by all victim groups. In accordance with their intended radical and systematic annihilation, the genocide of the Jews was bureaucratically organized and carried out in a quasi-industrial manner with techniques adopted from the so-called "euthanasia campaign." It was also applied to homosexuals and Sinti and Roma. As this feature—in the form of the universally-known gas chambers and crematoria—has shaped our understanding of Nazi crimes generally, it is necessary to emphasize that many Jewish victims, as well as Sinti and Roma, were also killed in mass shootings and in summary executions associated with the campaign against "partisans."[55] Murder through gas was the culmination of a process that began with arbitrary shootings and local killings; and many murders, as Christian Gerlach has also shown since the shooting of Jews in White Russia in the summer of 1941, also had economic motives. Like Poles and Russians, Jews were deliberately killed in order to ensure the supply of provisions for the German Army in the occupied territories. To create a surplus for the German troops, the consumption of the local population had to be lowered.

Moreover, in the "greatest murder plan in history," the Nazis intended to allow up to thirty million Russians to starve in order to use the food that would thus be saved to supply the German Army and the Reich.[56] At the same time, the number of people in the occupied territories was to be reduced by expelling local inhabitants to the east, and the future area of German settlement was to be protected by a "burnt strip" *(Brandstreifen)*. All foodstuffs were to be transported out of this area, which was to lie east of the border of the German settlement area along the line Bakuto—Stalingrad—Moscow—Leningrad, and anyone living there was to be destroyed.[57]

The mass murders were also related to the general settlement policy. In a Europe-wide attempt at "ethnic disentanglement" *(Ethnischer Entflechtung)*, the Germans to be settled in those occupied territories were to come from areas such as South Tyrol, Bessarabia, or the Bukovina, where they comprised ethnic minorities. In a "policy of ethnic dominos," these people were to be allocated areas from which Polish farmers, for example, had been expelled while they in turn would take the place of Jews who were to be deported to the margins of the German area of rule. As this was ultimately impossible due to the military situation, and none of the German governors wanted to keep the Jews in their dominions, the readiness to kill them grew.[58]

Aside from the concentration camps, mass murders were also committed in prisoner of war camps, ghettos, and settlements in the occupied territories. The fate of Russian prisoners of war constitutes an intermediate point between industrial annihilation and genocidal massacres. They were interned and subjected to bureaucratic authority, and then killed through intentional neglect, a policy that was also genocidal, as the victims were left to die because of their Russian descent.[59] There was no such policy in camps with British, French, or American prisoners of war.

In addition to this bureaucratically-organized form of murdering millions of people, there were also genocidal massacres. These included both mass shootings carried out on orders from above, as well as, killings in the context of fighting partisans.[60] The killing of partisans should be seen as genocidal because whole areas of land were to be cleansed, and children and old people were deliberately murdered, indicating the connection of these measures with broader demographic objectives.[61]

In contrast to National Socialism, the individual cases of genocide in the history of European colonialism are more difficult to identify despite the fact that mass deaths accompanied the paths of Europeans into America, Africa, Asia, and Australia, and indigenous states and peoples were destroyed. In all probability, no other period in human history saw the destruction of so many cultures as did the sixteenth and seventeenth centuries. The overwhelming majority of deaths resulted from imported diseases, while many people died performing slave labor or were put to the sword during Christianization. The victims' suffering was certainly just as great as in cases of intentional annihilation, and yet one cannot speak of genocide in these colonial cases, as the destruction of entire peoples was not intended. In fact, the colonial economy needed the indigenous population for exploitative purposes.[62] The same is true of slavery, which does not constitute genocide, despite the fact that it affected an estimated twenty-four million African men and women, of whom about half were transported to America and the Caribbean where they had to perform forced labor, often in the most inhumane conditions.[63] After all, the intention to exploit Africans' labor was inconsistent with their physical destruction, even if working them to death was willingly accepted in some cases. These conclusions apply to the other continents as well.[64]

Nonetheless, there were genocidal moments in the process when the tendency to declare the original inhabitants of a country to be "subhuman creatures" *(Untermenschen)* and to eliminate them rather than simply dispossessing them prevailed. Such cases mainly concern North America, Australia, New Zealand, and southern Africa. It is no coincidence that these were places that became settler colonies or were intended as such, for the genocidal idea could assume relevance where the replacement of the indigenous population with another was possible or seemed desirable. Following Raphael Lemkin,[65] Ann Curthoys and John Docker have recently postulated that the combination of murder and settlement is a constant factor in genocides. Whereas they, like Lemkin, conceive of genocide as a two-step process, whereby new settlement follows murder,[66] I see the relation of cause and consequence working in a circular manner: a genocidal dynamic can develop from the process of settlement, while space for settlement can also be created by the mass murder of the original inhabitants.

The ideological basis for such events was provided by worldly or millennial utopian thinking. The dream of the promised land, of the white settler colony, of the unpopulated tabula rasa that was to be developed anew according to one's understanding of civilization, or the identification of one's own life with a Godly, historical, or civilizing mission, could create the readiness to commit mass murder if necessary.[67] The combination of a highly developed sense of calling, the conviction of one's own predestination, as expressed, for example, in the doctrine of the "Manifest Destiny," with the proclivity to see Indians as heathens, or even as rats and mice, is characteristic of this genocidal impetus and can already be found among the Puritans in New England. Captain Wait Winthrop prophesied as early as 1675 in "Some Meditations" that God would help them destroy the Narragansett Indians who had just fought the New England militia in the "Great Swamps."[68] Sir Jeffrey Amherst, commander of the British troops in North America, stood in the same tradition when he initiated biological warfare against the Delaware Indians by having his officers give them blankets contaminated with smallpox: "You will do well to try to innoculate *[sic]* the Indians by means of blankets as well as try every other method that can serve to extirpate this exorable race."[69]

In the nineteenth century, the religious justification for one's destined role was gradually replaced by a Social Darwinian racial-biological view of history. For General Lieutenant von Trotha, commander of the German troops in the war against the Herero and Nama in Southwest Africa (1904–1908), the man responsible for the first German genocide, the destruction of the enemy was absolutely essential in a racial struggle that supposedly could only end with the demise of one party. In Trotha's opinion, the Africans would "only give in to violence," so he wanted to employ it "with crass terrorism and even with cruelty" and destroy "the rebellious tribes with streams of blood,"[70] because after all, a war in Africa could not be waged "according to the laws of the Geneva Convention."[71] Von Trotha also clearly articulated the connection between the settlement colony and genocide. When the long-serving Governor Leutwein attempted to dissuade the newly-arrived general from mass murder by arguing that Herero laborers were needed, von Trotha answered that Southwest Africa was the colony "in which the European himself can work in order to support his family."[72]

Whether the indigenous population's heathenism was emphasized, they were equated with rats and mice, or they were credited with inhuman fighting practices, scare propaganda prepared the ground for genocide. The racism evident in each case placed the indigenous population outside the "universe of obligation" that is an essential precondition for genocide by making mass murderers out of otherwise normal people.[73] How this dehumanization of the indigenes affected individual perpetrators is indicated by the "practice shooting" of Aborigines in Australia, of which an eyewitness reported in 1889: "There are instances when the young men of the station have employed the Sunday in hunting the blacks, not only for some definite purpose, but also for the sake of the sport."[74] And this was only possible because the Aborigines, including women and children, were not regarded as belonging to human society. From this position it is not a large step to the murder of women and children, especially if one can justify the act with the protection of one's own property, as an Australian squatter did, of whom it was reported in 1889:

> He shot all the men he discovered on his run, because they were cattle killers; the women, because they gave birth to cattle killers; and the children, because they would in time become cattle killers.[75]

Justifications of the murder of women and children in order to interrupt the biological reproductive process are also found in North America. H.L. Hall, a well-known murderer of Indians, justified the slaughtering of babies with the saying known since King Philip's War (1675–1676) that "a nit would make a louse." The slogan was popularized by Colonel John Milton Chivington who claimed that "My intention is to kill all Indians I may come across."[76]

Some scholars argue that individual intention to exterminate a population does not constitute genocide unless it becomes state policy.[77] The UN Convention leaves open the questions of who and how many people must belong to the group of perpetrators. What is important here is that the question of the role of the state points to a significant difference between colonial and Nazi genocides. For whereas the murder of Jews, Sinti and Roma, Poles, and Russians was centrally run and carried out by state organs, this type of state involvement was rarer in the colonial context. Particularly on the frontier, private actions at a local level were predominant as this was the mixed zone where contact between new arrivals and indigenes occurred, where the whites were at least initially not yet in the majority, and where state structures were lacking.[78] This is the reason why in most cases the planned murder of Indians and Aborigines cannot be traced back to the highest state representatives in the colonies, let alone to London or later, in the American case, to Washington. Often, local army or militia commanders or bands of settlers took matters into their own hands. Hence, different situations obtained from town to town and from colony to colony, and hence, too, orders for the protection of the "natives" often went unheeded. The colonial states lacked the power and the means to control the behavior of their citizens. Even in the case of the murder of Herero and Nama in German Southwest Africa (1904–1908) where there was an order for elimination, it was not the product of the highest state representatives such as the Kaiser or the Chancellor. Its initiator was General von Trotha, the local military commander.[79]

Yet, does it make sense in a historical comparison of mass murders to conceive of the state as the bureaucratic and centralized institution in the particularly highly developed form that it was in the Third Reich? Is it rather not essential to historicize our conception of the state?[80] If one applies a concept of the state appropriate for colonial contexts, then the differences between colonial and Nazi genocides do not appear so great. The colonial state was by and large a premodern and incompletely bureaucratized state that relied heavily on the influence of intermediary powers. The heads of local communities, parish priests, and local military commanders represented the state at the grass roots and had the symbolic power to legitimize actions on its behalf. Even if their words or actions were not legally binding, perpetrators could feel justified in their actions or even duty bound to perform them on the basis of what these local leaders did. To constitute a state crime in the colonial context, the chain of command does not have to reach back to the colonial center or even to the central colonial office in Europe.

Accordingly, the biological attack on the Delaware Indians mentioned above was legitimized by the state through Amherst's order, while in this sense the murder of the Herero and Nama was officially committed in Germany's name. The significance of inter-mediary powers has also been confirmed in recent research into National Socialism. Detailed analysis of the decision-making processes in German-occupied Eastern Europe has questioned the notion of a chain of command from above down, emphasizing instead the importance of local initiative.[81]

The question of the state's role in the execution of genocide is, however, of considerable significance with respect to the forms of mass murder: genocidal massacres do not require a large degree of organization, whereas the quasi-industrial extermination in camps is predicated on a modern, centralized, and bureaucratized state. As argued above, both massacres and camps are found in National Socialism, whereas in the colonial context massacres or other strategies with relatively low organizational requirements clearly dominated.

The most common form of killing was the genocidal massacre. Whether in the Pequot War in New England or in the fight against the Round Valley Indians, or at the Sand Creek Massacre, examples of the butchering of men, women, and children by bands of settlers and local militia can be readily found. Acts of reprisals by settlers for actual or alleged attacks by Aborigines also belong in this cate-gory, such as were reported by *The Queenslander* in 1867:

> There is not much more in the present system by which blacks are shot down most ruthlessly for weeks and months after a case of murder or theft has been reported, and when many innocent are either killed in order that the guilty party may be included in the number or so hunted about that the spirit of revenge is aroused in them.[82]

Over time, army and police units were established for this pur-pose. The "Third Colorado Cavalry," responsible for the massacre of the Cheyennes at Sand Creek, was assembled especially for the fight against the Indians.[83] The "Native Police of Queensland" were also state units, in this case employing Aborigines from other parts of the country under white officers. As "mobile death squads aimed at eradicating Aborigines," they attempted to "cleanse" the frontier in Queensland of the local indigenes in order to make room for an increasing number of settlers and their livestock.[84]

A heightened form of these campaigns of annihilation was genocidal war of conquest and pacification, a larger military action requiring a correspondingly higher level of organization. The most important example of this was the war waged by German imperial troops against the Herero and Nama in German Southwest Africa between 1904 and 1908, which constituted an important connection between colonial genocide and the crimes of the Nazis.

Sparked in January 1904 by an attack by the Herero, this conflict soon went beyond the bounds of previous warlike conflicts in the German colony.[85] This was in part due to the extraordinary success of the Herero, who in a few days almost brought German rule to collapse, and in part to the German reaction. The General Staff in Berlin sent an expeditionary corps and removed the long-serving governor, Theodor Leutwein, replacing him with General von Trotha, who pursued a genocidal policy from the outset. This culminated on 2 October 1904 in the infamous order to shoot. Von Trotha ordered a chain of posts to seal off the Herero in the Omaheke desert, where they had fled following the only large battle of the war at Waterberg:

> The Hereros are no longer German subjects.
>
> They have murdered and stolen, have cut off the ears and noses and other body parts from wounded soldiers, and in cowardice no longer want to fight. I say to the people: Everyone, who brings one of the captains to one of my stations as prisoners, will receive 1,000 marks, whoever brings Samuel Maharero will receive 5,000 marks. However, the Herero people must leave the country. If the people does not do that, then I will force it to with the Groot Rohr [big cannon].
>
> Within the German border every Herero, armed or not, with cattle or without, will be shot, I will not take up any more women or children, will drive them back to their people or let them be shot at.

In an order of the day, he clarified that for the maintenance of the good reputation of German soldiers the instruction to "shoot at women and children" meant "that shots are to be fired above them, to force them to run." He said that he assumed that his decree would lead to "no more male prisoners [being] taken, but not to cruelty against women and children." They would "already run away, when shots [are] twice fired above them."[86] The only place to which they could run, though, was the desert, where thousands died of thirst as a result of this order.

The official historical depiction of the war reads as follows: "Like a wild animal half hunted to death," the enemy was "driven from one source of water to the next, until, his will gone, he finally became a victim of the nature of his own land." Thus the "waterless Omaheke" was to "complete what German weapons had begun: the destruction of the Herero people."[87] The intention to destroy an entire people and the official acknowledgement of its execution can hardly be expressed more clearly. The strategy was ordered from above, and the perpetrator was the army, even if the

number of those killed directly by the Germans was significantly
less than that of those who died of thirst.

The German strategy, though, was not limited to the now
proverbial practice of "driving them into the desert," the order for
which was soon lifted as impracticable. In the second phase of the
war, the opponents' food and particularly their sources of water
were actively destroyed: watering holes were poisoned, and
ambushes were set at wells. The Nama, for their part, waged a
guerilla war that almost defeated the German Empire militarily.
Even if no "order to shoot" has been found for the war against the
Nama,[88] the genocidal intention can be seen in the method of waging war. The Germans pursued a campaign of annihilation that also
targeted women and children.

In addition to deaths in battle, expulsion into the waterless
Omaheke desert, and the destruction of the means of life, the Germans also used camps to deliberately exterminate the indigenous
population. Prisoners-of-war camps were established across the
country between 1904 and 1908 where, after the lifting of the
order to shoot, Herero and Nama men, women, and children were
interned. Massive numbers of people died in these "concentration
camps," as they were called at the time,[89] the most notorious of
which were in Swakopmund and on Shark Island near Lüderitz.[90]
In total, between October 1904 and March 1907, between 30 and
50 percent of the camp population died —7,682 prisoners.[91] While
disease and weakness caused by the privations of war were certainly a factor in this mass death, deliberate neglect was also significant. The responsible commander, Deimling, refused to
improve the state of the Shark Island camp by moving it to the
mainland. For as long as he was in command, he said, no African
was to leave the island alive. Even the need for forced laborers,
which would have required improving the prisoners' nutrition, did
not alter his position. Instead, building projects already begun at
Lüderitz were stopped.[92]

A superficial consideration suggests that the tank battles and
sweeping bombing campaigns of the Second World War have nothing in common with this sort of colonial war. And yet, on closer
inspection, the war against the Herero and Nama reveals clear parallels with the "war of destruction" of 1941–1945 in the East.
These parallels deserve closer consideration, for the two wars are
separated by only forty years, and it is possible to speak of a certain
military tradition of "war of racial extermination" *(Rassen und
Vernichtungskrieg)*.[93] Although the war against the Soviet Union
was formally a "normal" war between European powers, the Ger-

mans did not fight it as such, waging instead a war of exploitation from the beginning that in its conscious neglect of the laws of warfare more resembled a colonial war. In the conventional European war, the status of the enemy as a legitimate opponent of equal value is recognized; some basic rights are accorded to him even in defeat and captivity. In the colonial war, however, this status is denied, and prisoners are left to perish or are directly murdered on the basis of their race. The massacres in the "fight against partisans" resemble the common colonial warfare practice of fighting guerillas with punitive expeditions. Himmler's order of the day of 1 August 1941, in which he ordered the massacre of the Pripjet marshes, could almost have come from von Trotha: "All the Jewish men must be shot, all the Jewish women driven into the marshes."[94] There, it was intended, they would meet their demise just like the women and children of the Herero in the Omaheke, without a German soldier having to fire a shot in anger. That Hitler was also familiar with the colonial "driving them into the desert" is clear from his comment in October 1941, when—in relation to his prophesied eradication of the Jews—he protested against the possibility that someone might suggest moderation: "But we cannot send them into the swamp!"[95]

Conclusion

The structural similarity between colonialism and National Socialism went beyond the continuity from the Herero war. With its central concepts of "race" and "space," the Nazi policy of expansion and annihilation stood firmly in the tradition of European colonialism, a tradition also recognizable in the Nazi genocides. Yet, it would be wrong to see the Third Reich's murderous policies in the East merely as a copy of the conquests of the Americas, Australia, or Southern Africa; they constituted instead an extremely radicalized variant. Particularly with regard to its readiness to wipe out whole peoples, European colonialism stood at the beginning of a development of particular notions of space and race that found its culmination in the "hunger plan" of 1941, the genocidal massacres in the context of combating partisans, and the utilization of gas for organized suffocation.

Colonial genocides did not constitute a fundamentally different category from the Nazi genocides. They were merely less-organized, centralized, and bureaucratized forms of genocide. Ultimately, the various colonial manifestations of genocide could also be found in the Nazis' murderous policies, exemplified by genocidal massacres of partisans and the practice of eradication through deliberate neglect. The main difference between the two lay in the different roles played by the state. Thus the Nazis' bureaucratized and state-organized murder was less a fundamental structural departure than a gradual variation dependent upon the degree of development of the state. While massacres by settlers and militia corresponded to the weakly developed state of the New England frontier, the instruments of genocide expanded to include arms of the state itself, such as the army or the Native Police, with an increasing establishment of the state in Queensland or North America. In modern administrative states, as found in initial stages in Southwest Africa, concentration camps were utilized as the site of extermination, and although there was no active "industrial" murder there, murder through neglect was already in evidence.

To be sure, the crimes of the National Socialists cannot be traced back monocausally to the tradition of European colonialism. The Nazi ideology and policy were far too complex and eclectic for such a straightforward reduction. Yet, in the sense of an archeology of the idea of population economy and genocidal thinking, colonialism provided important precedents. Even the murder of the Jews, which was distinguished by the notion of eradicating a worldwide conspiracy, would probably not have been thinkable and possible if the idea that ethnicities can simply be wiped out had not already existed and had not already been put into action. What is more, colonialism occupied such a prominent position in this tradition of genocidal thought because the "discovery," conquest, development, and settlement of the new world was positively connoted and enjoyed popular support. The parallels with colonialism also help to explain why the expulsion and resettlement of Jews and Slavs, and ultimately their murder, were not perceived as breaking a taboo. At the very least, colonial history offered the Nazi perpetrators the possibility of exculpating themselves and obscuring the enormity of their own actions.

Notes

1. I would like to thank John Docker, Clara Ervedosa, Jan-Bart Gewald, Christian Gerlach, Christoph Marx, A. Dirk Moses, Armin Nolzen, and Eric D. Weitz for their constructive criticism and valuable advice. For an overview of the enormous literature on the German war against the USSR, see Rolf-Dieter Müller and Gerd Überschär, *Hitlers Krieg im Osten 1941–1945: Ein Forschungsbericht* (Darmstadt, 2000).

2. Hitler, 17 September 1941, in Adolf Hitler, *Monologe im Führerhauptquartier,* ed. Werner Jochmann (Hamburg, 1980), 60–64.

3. See Klaus Hildebrand, *Vom Reich zum Weltreich: Hitler, NSDAP und koloniale Frage 1919–1945* (Munich, 1969); Jan Esche, *Koloniales Anspruchsdenken in Deutschland im Ersten Weltkrieg, während der Versailler Friedensverhandlungen und in der Weimarer Republik (1914 bis 1933),* (Hamburg, 1989). For an exaggerated view of Africa's importance to Hitler, see Alexandre Kum'a N'dumbe III, *Was wollte Hitler in Afrika? NS-Planungen für eine faschistische Neugestaltung Afrikas* (Frankfurt, 1993).

4. Hans Grimm, *Volk ohne Raum* (Munich, 1926).

5. Hannah Arendt, *The Origins of Totalitarianism* (New York, 1951).

6. Fritz Fischer, *From Kaiserreich to Third Reich* (London, 1986); idem, *Germany's aims in the First World War* (New York, 1967); idem, *War of illusions: German Policies from 1911 to 1914* (London, 1975). On the controversy surrounding his thesis, see John A. Moses, *The Politics of Illusion* (London, 1975).

7. Peter Schmidt-Egner, *Kolonialismus und Faschismus: Eine Studie zur historischen und begrifflichen Genesis faschistischer Bewußtseinsformen am deutschen Beispiel* (Gießen, 1975).

8. Mark Mazower's plea for a close examination of the colonial roots of Nazi policy seems to have gone unheard. See his "After Lemkin: Genocide, the Holocaust and History," *The Jewish Quarterly* 5 (Winter 1995): 5–8. In his *Dark Continent: Europe's Twentieth Century* (London, 1998), Mazower suggests that European outrage over the Nazis was so great because they treated Europeans like aboriginals, but he does not discuss the connection systematically. The best-known consideration of the connection between colonial mass murders and the Holocaust is that by Sven Lindqvist. As his understanding of European colonialism and of the German policy of annihilation in the East does not go beyond simplistic descriptions, the questions he poses are more significant than his answers: *"Exterminate all the Brutes"* (London, 1997). Much the same applies to Ward Churchill, who speaks of the National Socialists imitating the colonial conquest of North America in *A Little Matter of Genocide: Holocaust and Denial in the Americas, 1492–Present* (San Francisco, 1997); Richard L. Rubinstein has also touched on the idea in "Afterword: Genocide and Civilization," in *Genocide and the Modern Age: Etiology and Case Studies of Mass Death,* ed. Isidor Wallimann and Michael N. Dobkowski, 2nd ed. (Syracuse, 2000), 283–98, 288.

9. Norman G. Finkelstein, *The Holocaust Industry* (London, 2000); Peter Novick, *The Holocaust in American Life* (Boston, 1999); Daniel Levy and Natan Sznaider, *Erinnerung im globalen Zeitalter: Der Holocaust* (Frankfurt, 2001).

10. See Lilian Friedberg, "Dare to Compare: Americanizing the Holocaust," *American Indian Quarterly* 24, no. 3 (2000): 353–80; David E. Stannard, "Unique-

ness as Denial: The Politics of Genocide Scholarship," in *Is the Holocaust Unique? Perspectives on Comparative Genocide*, ed. Alan S. Rosenbaum (Oxford, 1996), 163–208; See the discussion in A. Dirk Moses, "Conceptual Blockages and Definitional Dilemmas in the Racial Century: Genocide of Indigenous Peoples and the Holocaust," *Patterns of Prejudice* 36, no. 4 (2002): 6–37; Jürgen Zimmerer, "Kolonialer Genozid? Möglichkeiten und Grenzen einer historischen Kategorie," in *Enteignet-Vertrieben-Ermordet. Beiträge zur Genozidforschung*, ed. Dominik J. Schaller, et al. (Zürich, 2004).

11. See A. Dirk Moses, "Coming to Terms with Genocidal Pasts in Comparative Perspective: Germany and Australia," *Aboriginal History* 25 (2001): 91–115.

12. See Stannard, "Uniqueness as Denial"; Churchill, *A Little Matter of Genocide*. For the blank spots in American commemorative culture generally, see James W. Loewen, *Lies across America: What our Historic Sites Get Wrong* (New York, 2000).

13. "Kein Pardon für Herero-Morde," *Die tageszeitung*, 5 March 1998. Also see, "Herzog lobt die Beziehungen zu Namibia," *Frankfurter Allgemeine Zeitung*, 5 March 1998; "Herzog will Deutsch in Namibia stärken," *Süddeutsche Zeitung*, 7 March 1998. German Foreign Minister Joschka Fischer repeated this position during his visit in Windhoek in October 2003: "Keine Entschuldigung, keine Entschädigung," *Die tageszeitung*, 10/11 January 2004.

14. David E. Stannard, *American Holocaust: The Conquest of the New World* (Oxford, 1992).

15. Russell Thornton, *American Indian Holocaust and Survival: A Population History since 1492* (London, 1987).

16. Jeremy Silvester, Werner H. Illebrecht and Casper Erichsen, "The Herero Holocaust? The Disputed History of the 1904 Genocide," *The Namibian Weekender*, 20 August 2001.

17. *Slavery: An Introduction to the African Holocaust, with Special Reference to Liverpool, "Capital of the Slave Trade,"* ed. Black History Resource Working Group in conjunction with the Race Equality Management team, 2nd ed. (1997); Thomas Mordekhai, *Vessels of Evil: American Slavery and the Holocaust* (Philadelphia, 1993). There are now also museums and societies for the memory of the Black Holocaust, such as "America's Black Holocaust Museum" and "The Black Holocaust Society" in Milwaukee, Wisconsin. See www.blackwallstreet.freeservers.com.

18. For a brief overview of the phases of genocide scholarship, see Frank Chalk and Kurt Jonassohn, "Genozid: Ein historischer Überblick," in *Genozid und Moderne*, vol. 1: *Strukturen kollektiver Gewalt im 20. Jahrhundert*, ed. Mihran Dabag and Kristin Platt (Opladen, 1998), 294–308. Also see Myriam Gessler, *Die Singularität des Holocaust und die vergleichende Genozidforschung: Empirische und theoretische Untersuchung zu einem aktuellen Thema der Geschichtswissenschaft* (unpublished MA thesis, University of Bern, Switzerland, 2000).

19. Cited in Helen Fein, "Definition and Discontent: Labelling, Detecting and Explaining Genocide in the Twentieth Century," in *Genozid in der modernen Geschichte (Jahrbuch für Historische Friedensforschung* 7), ed. Stig Förster and Gerhard Hirschfeld (Münster, 1997), 11–21, 17.

20. Steven T. Katz, *The Holocaust in Historical Perspective*, vol. 1: *The Holocaust and Mass Death before the Modern Age* (Oxford, 1994), 131.

21. Article 2, United Nations "Convention on the Prevention and Punishment of the Crime of Genocide," 9 December 1948, reproduced in Frank Chalk and

Kurt Jonassohn, *The History and Sociology of Genocide: Analyses and Case Studies* (New Haven, 1990), 44–49.

22. Raphel Lemkin, *Axis Rule in Occupied Europe: Law of Occupation, Analysis of Government, Proposals for Redress* (Washington, 1944), 79. Helen Fein calls it a "sustained purposeful action by a perpetrator to physically destroy a collectivity directly or indirectly." See Helen Fein, "Genocide: A Sociological Perspective," *Current Sociology* 38 (1990): 24.

23. Stig Förster and Gerhard Hirschfeld, "Einleitung," in *Genozid in der modernen Geschichte*, eds. Förster and Hirschfeld, 5–10, 7.

24. Among the enormous amount of literature, see the following more recent works which deal with relevant issues: Ulrich Herbert, ed., *National Socialist Extermination Policies: Contemporary German Perspectives and Controversies* (New York, 2000); Götz Aly and Susanne Heim, *"Vordenker der Vernichtung": Auschwitz und die deutschen Pläne für eine neue europäische Ordnung* (Hamburg, 1991); Götz Aly, *"Final Solution": Nazi Population Policy and the Murder of the European Jews* (London and New York, 1999); Christian Gerlach, *Kalkulierte Morde: Die deutsche Wirtschafts und Vernichtungspolitik in Weißrußland, 1941–1944* (Hamburg, 1999); Christian Gerlach, *Krieg, Ernährung, Völkermord: Forschungen zur deutschen Vernichtungspoltik im Zweiten Weltkrieg* (Hamburg, 1998); Dieter Pohl, *Nationalsozialistische Judenverfolgung in Ostgalizien, 1941–1944: Organisation und Durchführung eines staatlichen Massenverbrechens* (Munich, 1996); Thomas Sandkühler, *"Endlösung" in Galizien: Der Judenmord in Ostpolen und die Rettungsinitiativen von Berhold Beitz* (Bonn, 1996).

25. See Michael Burleigh and Wolfgang Wippermann, *The Racial State: Germany, 1933–1945* (Cambridge, 1991).

26. See Aly and Heim, *"Vordenker der Vernichtung"*; Aly, *"Final Solution."*

27. Ulrich Herbert, "Traditionen des Rassismus," in Ulrich Herbert, *Arbeit, Volkstum, Weltanschauung: Über Fremde und Deutsche im 20. Jahrhundert* (Frankfurt, 1995), 11–29, 13.

28. This is clearly evident in the fact that the practice of "euthanasia" was first applied to "a-socials" and the disabled, then used in concentration camps, and its practitioners were later used by Himmler when the mass murder of the Jews began. Michael Burleigh, *The Third Reich: A New History* (London, 2000), 345–81.

29. There is a relatively large literature on this question. See Michael Burleigh, *Death and Deliverance: Euthanasia in Germany c. 1900–1945* (Cambridge, 1994); Peter Weingart, Jürgen Kroll and Kurt Bayertz, *Rasse, Blut und Gene: Geschichte der Eugenik in Deutschland* (Frankfurt, 1988). On the international context, see Stefan Kühl, *Die Internationale der Rassisten: Aufstieg und Niedergang der internationalen Bewegung für Eugenik und Rassenhygiene im 20. Jahrhundert* (Frankfurt, 1997); idem, *The Nazi Connection: Eugenics, American Racism, and German National Socialism* (New York, 1994).

30. For a striking example of the settlement policy, see Wendy Lower's interesting article on the Hegewalt project, Himmler's model for an active SS settlement policy. Lower uses the term "colonial" more or less synonymously for settlement: "A New Ordering of Space and Race: Nazi Colonial Dreams in Zhytomry, Ukraine, 1941–1944," *German Studies Review* 25 (2002): 227–54.

31. See for example Russell McGregor, *Imagined Destinies: Aboriginal Australians and the Doomed Race Theory, 1880–1939* (Melbourne, 1997); Saul Dubow, *Scientific Racism in Modern South Africa* (Cambridge, 1995). For a compari-

son of eugenic and racist discourses in Australia and Germany, even if direct
influence is not proven, see Tony Barta, "Discourses of Genocide in Germany
and Australia: A Linked History," *Aboriginal History* 25 (2001): 37–56.

32. Woodruff Smith comes to the same conclusion: *The Ideological Origins of
    Nazi Imperialism* (Oxford, 1986). See also Charles Reynolds, *Modes of Impe-
    rialism* (Oxford, 1981), 124–71.

33. See, for example, Albert Wirz, "Missionare im Urwald, verängstigt und hilflos:
    Zur symbolischen Topografie des kolonialen Christentums," in *Kolonien und
    Missionen*, ed. Wilfried Wagner (Hamburg, 1994), 39–56; Johannes Fabian,
    Out of Our Minds: Reason and Madness in the Exploration of Central Africa
    (Los Angeles, 2000).

34. For example, John Noyes, *Colonial Space: Spatiality in the Discourse of Ger-
    man South West Africa, 1884–1915* (Chur, 1992).

35. On the surveying of the American West which was perceived as an undifferen-
    tiated mass that required order, see Stefan Kaufmann, "Naturale Grenzfelder
    des Sozialen: Landschaft und Körper," in *Grenzgänger zwischen Kulturen*, eds.
    Monika Fludernik and Hans-Joachim Gehrke (Würzburg, 1999), 121–36. On
    the tradition of developing the earth, see Dirk van Laak, *Imperiale Infrastruk-
    tur: Deutsche Planungen für eine Erschließung Afrikas, 1880 bis 1960* (forth-
    coming 2003).

36. A vigorous debate has arisen in recent years on the participation of scientists
    and experts generally in Nazi crimes. See Franz-Rutker Hausmann, *"Deutsche
    Geisteswissenschaft" im Zweiten Weltkrieg: Die "Aktion Ritterbusch"
    (1940–1945)*, (Dresden, 1998); Michael Fahlbusch, *Wissenschaft im Dienst
    der nationalsozialistischen Politik? Die "Volksdeutschen Forschungsgemein-
    schaften" von 1931–1945* (Baden-Baden, 1999); Winfried Schulze and Otto
    Gerhard Oexle, eds., *Deutsche Historiker im Nationalsozialismus* (Frankfurt,
    1999). On the question of scholarship on, and planning for, the East, see Bruno
    Wasser, *Himmlers Raumplanung im Osten* (Basel, 1993); Mechthild Rössler,
    *"Wissenschaft und Lebensraum": Geographische Ostforschung im National-
    sozialismus, Ein Beitrag zur Disziplingeschichte der Geographie* (Berlin, 1990);
    Michael Burleigh, *Germany turns Eastwards: A Study of Ostforschung in the
    Third Reich* (Cambridge, 1988); Mechthild Rössler and Sabine Schleierma-
    cher, eds., *Der "Generalplan Ost"* (Berlin, 1993); Czeslaw Madajczyk, ed.,
    Vom Generalplan Ost zum Generalsiedlungsplan (Munich, 1994); Aly and
    Heim, *"Vordenker der Vernichtung"*; Aly, *"Final Solution"*. Specifically on the
    scholarly continuity between colonialism and National Socialism, see Jürgen
    Zimmerer, "Wissenschaft und Kolonialismus: Das Geographische Institut der
    Friedrich-Wilhelms-Universität vom Kaiserreich zum Dritten Reich," in *Kolo-
    nialmetropole Berlin: Eine Spurensuche*, ed. Ulrich van der Heyden and
    Joachim Zeller (Berlin, 2002), 125–30; Jürgen Zimmerer, "Im Dienste des
    Imperiums. Die Geographen der Berliner Universität zwischen Kolonialwis-
    senschaften und Ostforschung, " *Jahrbuch für Universitätsgeschichte* 7 (2004):
    73-100.

37. A soldier of the 12th Air Force Regiment, 20 July 1941, cited by Gerlach,
    Kalkulierte Morde, 102.

38. Gerlach, *Kalkulierte Morde*, 102.

39. Liedecke, "Kolonisatorische Aufgaben der Raum-Ordnung im Nordosten des
    Deutschen Reiches," Königsberg, 1 September 1939, cited by Michael A.
    Hartenstein, *Neue Dorflandschaften: Nationalsozialistische Siedlungsplanung
    in den "eingegliederten Ostgebieten", 1939–1944* (Berlin, 1998), 79.

40. Hitler, 17 September 1941, in Hitler, *Monologe*, 63.
41. Hanns Johst, *Ruf des Reiches: Echo des Volkes!* (Munich, 1940), cited by Burleigh, *The Third Reich*, 447.
42. On this concept, see Jürgen Zimmerer, *Deutsche Herrschaft über Afrikaner: Staatlicher Machtanspruch und Wirklichkeit im kolonialen Namibia* (Hamburg, 2001), 94–109.
43. Burleigh, *The Third Reich*, 450f.
44. Hitler, 17 September 1941, in Hitler, *Monologe*, 62–63.
45. Missionary Wandres in a memorandum "Bemerkungen über Mischehen und Mischlinge aus der Praxis für die Praxis" (1912), Namibian National Archives in Windhoek, F.IV.R.1., 143b–145b. For the example of German South-West Africa, see Zimmerer, *Deutsche Herrschaft über Afrikaner*, 94–109.
46. "Law for the Protection of German Blood and of German Honor," 15 September 1935, reproduced in *Der Nationalsozialismus: Dokumente, 1933–1945*, ed Walther Hofer, revised ed. (Frankfurt, 1982), 285. Also see Saul Friedländer, *Nazi Germany and the Jews, vol. 1: The Years of Persecution, 1933–1939* (New York, 1997), 145–64; Anegret Ehmann, "From Colonial Racism to Nazi Population Policy: The Role of the so-called Mischlinge," in *The Holocaust and History: The Known, the Unknown, the Disputed, and the Reexamined*, ed. Michael Berenbaum and Abraham J. Peck (Washington, 1998), 115–33; Cornelia Essner, *Die 'Nürnberger Gesetze' oder die Verwaltung des Rassenwahns 1933-1945* (Paderborn, 2002).
47. Adam Hochschild, *Schatten über dem Kongo: Die Geschichte eines der großen fast vergessenen Menschheitsverbrechen* (Stuttgart, 2000), 165–99; Samuel Henry Nelson, *Colonialism in the Congo Basin, 1880-1940* (Athens, Ohio, 1994).
48. Jürgen Zimmerer, "Der totale Überwachungsstaat? Recht und Verwaltung in Deutsch-Südwestafrika," in *Das deutsche Kolonialrecht als Vorstufe einer globalen "Kolonialisierung" von Recht und Verwaltung*, ed. Rüdiger Voigt (Baden-Baden, 2001), 175–98.
49. On this concept, see Jürgen Zimmerer. "Der Wahn der Planbarkeit. Unfreie Arbeit, Zwangsmigration und Genozid als Elemente der Bevölkerungsökonomie in Deutsch-Südwestafrika," *Comparativ* 13 no. 4 (2003): 96-113; Zimmerer, *Deutsche Herrschaft über Afrikaner*, 126–75.
50. Gerlach, *Kalkulierte Morde*, 449–502. Also see the classic study of Ulrich Herbert, *Hitler's Foreign Workers: Enforced Foreign Labor in Germany under the Third Reich* (Cambridge and New York, 1997).
51. For examples of this sort of forced recruitment see Michael Burleigh, *The Third Reich*, 551–54.
52. Similarly, Gerlach argues that the so-called territorial plans made the civilization break a gradual one. See Christian Gerlach, *Krieg, Ernährung, Völkermord*, 262.
53. See Friedländer, *Nazi Germany and the Jews:* vol. 1, 73–112.
54. On the individual groups, see Michael Zimmermann, *Rassenutopie und Genozid: Die nationalsozialistische "Lösung der Zigeunerfrage"* (Hamburg, 1996); Burleigh, *Death and Deliverance*; Wolfgang Ayaß, *"Asoziale" im Nationalsozialismus* (Stuttgart, 1995); Ernst Klee, *"Euthanasie" im NS-Staat: Die "Vernichtung lebensunwerten Lebens"* (Frankfurt, 1983); Hans-Walter Schmuhl, *Rassenhygiene, Nationalsozialismus, Euthanasie* (Göttingen, 1987).
55. See, for example, Ruth Bettina Birn, "Zweierlei Wirklichkeit? Fallbeispiele zur Partisanenbekämpfung," in *Zwei Wege nach Moskau: Vom Hitler-Stalin Pakt*

zum "Unternehmen Barbarossa," ed. Bernd Wegner (Munich, 1991), 275–90. For the German anti-partisan warfare in general, see Philip Warren Blood, "*Bandenbekämpfung*: Nazi Occupation Security in Eastern Europe and Soviet Russia 1942-45" (Ph.D. Thesis, Cranfield University, 2001).

56. Christian Gerlach, "Deutsche Wirtschaftsinteressen, Besatzungspolitik und der Mord an den Juden in Weißrußland, 1941–1943," in *Nationalsozialistische Vernichtungspolitik*, ed. Herbert, 263–91, 268.

57. Christian Gerlach, *Kalkulierte Morde*, 53.

58. Götz Aly, "'Jewish Resettlement': Reflections on the Political Prehistory of the Holocaust," in *National Socialist Extermination Policies*, ed. Herbert, 53–83; Aly, "*Final Solution.*"

59. See the classic study on prisoners of war: Christian Streit, *Keine Kameraden: Die Wehrmacht und die sowjetischen Kriegsgefangenen, 1941–1945* (Stuttgart, 1978).

60. Gerlach, *Kalkulierte Morde*, 859–1,054.

61. It should be pointed out that supporters of the singularity thesis reject the collective consideration of several groups of victims under the term "genocide." For Steven T. Katz, the Sinti and Roma were not the victims of genocide, but were suffocated with gas in Auschwitz because they had typhoid. See Helen Fein, "Definition and Discontent," 15. This is also true of Yehuda Bauer, who accepts the category "genocide" but uses the expression "Holocaust" as a special category for the murder of the Jews: "The conclusion to draw is that one ought to differentiate between the intent to destroy a group in a context of selective mass murder and the intent to annihilate every person of the group. To make this as simple as possible, I would suggest retaining the term *genocide* for 'partial' murder and the term *Holocaust* for total destruction" (emphasis in original). See Yehuda Bauer, *Rethinking the Holocaust* (New Haven, 2001), 10–11. In this view, "total destruction" was until then only intended for the Jews, and the Holocaust was thus "unprecedented."

62. Cf. Gründer, who rejects the notion of colonial genocide, even if he does not deny that in some situations there were genocidal orders, massacres, or consequences. Horst Gründer, "Genozid oder Zwangsmodernisierung? Der moderne Kolonialismus in universalgeschichtlicher Perspektive," in *Genozid und Moderne* vol. 1, eds. Dabag and Platt, 135–51.

63. Seymour Drescher, "The Atlantic Slave Trade and the Holocaust: A Comparative Analysis," in *Is the Holocaust Unique?* ed. Rosenbaum, 65–86, 66–67.

64. For the opposite position regarding Australia and America, see Churchill, *A Little Matter of Genocide*; Stannard, *American Holocaust*; Tony Barta, "Relations of Genocide: Land and Lives in the Colonization of Australia," in *Genocide and the Modern Age*, ed. Wallimann and Dobkowski, 237–51.

65. Lemkin talks of colonization but uses the term as a synonym for settlement. See Lemkin, *Axis Rule in Occupied Europe*.

66. Ann Curthoys and John Docker, "Genocide: Definitions, Questions, Settler-Colonies," *Aboriginal History* 25 (2001): 1–15.

67. On the significance for genocide of utopian conceptions of the re-creation of the world and of mankind, see Omar Bartov, "Utopie und Gewalt: Neugeburt und Vernichtung der Menschen," in *Wege in die Gewalt: Die modernen politischen Religionen*, ed. Hans Maier (Frankfurt, 2000), 92–120.

68. Cited by Chalk and Jonassohn, *The History and Sociology of Genocide*, 194.

69. Cited by Chalk and Jonassohn, *The History and Sociology of Genocide*, 177. See also the discussion of Jan Kociumbas in her chapter in this volume.

70. Trotha to Leutwein, 5 November 1904, *cited* by Horst Drechsler, *Südwestafrika unter deutscher Kolonialherrschaft: Der Kampf der Herero und Nama gegen den deutschen Imperialismus, 1884–1915*, 2nd ed. (Berlin, 1984), 156.

71. "Politik und Kriegsführung," *Der Deutschen Zeitung*, 3 February 1909, cited by Gerhard Pool, *Samuel Maharero* (Windhoek, 1991), 293.

72. Trotha's diary, cited by Pool, *Samuel Maharero*, 265.

73. Helen Fein, "Definition and Discontent," 20.

74. Cited by Alison Palmer, *Colonial Genocide* (Adelaide, 2000), 44f. See the chapters of Raymond Evans in this volume for details of exterminatory rhetoric and practice on the colonial frontier.

75. Cited by Palmer, *Colonial Genocide*, 43.

76. Churchill, *A Little Matter of Genocide*, 229; Stannard, *American Holocaust*, 131, fn. 123.

77. Helen Fein, "Genozid als Staatsverbrechen: Beispiele aus Rwanda und Bosnien," *Zeitschrift für Genozidforschung* 1 (1999): 36–45; Chalk and Jonassohn, *The History and Sociology of Genocide*, 23.

78. For a compelling description of the frontier as a stateless realm, see Stefan Kaufmann, "Der Siedler," in *Grenzverletzer*, ed. Eva Horn, Stefan Kaufmann and Ulrich Bröckling (Berlin, 2002), 176–201.

79. Jürgen Zimmerer, "Kriegsgefangene im Kolonialkrieg: Der Krieg gegen die Herero und Nama in Deutsch Südwestafrika (1904–1907)," in *In der Hand des Feindes: Kriegsgefangenschaft von der Antike bis zum Zweiten Weltkrieg*, ed. Rüdiger Overmans (Cologne, 1999), 277–94.

80. On the development of the modern state as it originated in Europe and spread throughout the world, see Wolfgang Reinhard, *Geschichte der Staatsgewalt: Eine vergleichende Verfassungsgeschichte Europas von den Anfängen bis zur Gegenwart* (Munich, 1999).

81. See Herbert, *National Socialist Extermination Policies*; Gerlach, *Kalkulierte Morde*.

82. Cited by Palmer, *Colonial Genocide*, 43.

83. Chalk and Jonassohn, *The History and Sociology of Genocide*, 199–201. The background was a conflict between Indians and settlers, who managed to involve the state in their struggle. The regiment deployed consisted of volunteers who were temporarily engaged. The force they used was thus legitimized by the state.

84. Palmer, *Colonial Genocide*; A. Dirk Moses, "An Antipodean Genocide? The Origins of the Genocidal Moment in the Colonization of Australia," *Journal of Genocide Research* 2 (2000): 89–106, 102.

85. Various aspects of the war and its outcome are covered in *Völkermord in Deutsch-Südwestafrika. Der Kolonialkrieg (1904-1908) und seine Folgen*, ed. Jürgen Zimmerer and Joachim Zeller (Berlin, 2003). On the war, see also Zimmerer, *Deutsche Herrschaft über Afrikaner*, 31–55; Jan-Bart Gewald, *Towards Redemption: A Socio-Political History of the Herero of Namibia between 1890 and 1923* (Leiden, 1996), 178–240; Helmut Walser Smith, "The Logic of Colonial Violence: Germany in Southwest Africa (1904–1907); the United States in the Philippines (1899–1902)," in *German and American Nationalism: A Comparative Perspective*, ed. Hartmut Lehmann and Hermann Wellenreuther (Oxford, 1999), 205–31; Tilman Dedering, "The German-Herero War of 1904: Revisionism of Genocide or Imaginary Historiography?" *Journal of Southern African Studies* 19 (1993): 80–88; idem, "'A Certain Rigorous Treatment of All Parts of the Nation': The Annihilation of the Herero in German

South West Africa, 1904," in *The Massacre in History*, ed. Mark Levene and Penny Roberts (New York, 1999), 205–22; Gesine Krüger, *Kriegsbewältigung und Geschichtsbewußtsein: Realität, Deutung und Verarbeitung des deutschen Kolonialkriegs in Namibia 1904 bis 1907* (Göttingen, 1999); Henrik Lundtofte, "'I believe that the nation as such must be annihilated ...'—The Radicalization of the German Suppression of the Herero Rising in 1904," in *Genocide: Cases, Comparisons and Contemporary Debates*, ed. Steven L.B. Jensen (Copenhagen, 2003), 15–53.

86. Proclamation by Trotha, Osombo-Windhuk (copy), 2 October 1904, Bundesarchiv Berlin-Lichterfelde (German Federal Archive, Berlin Lichterfelde), R 1001/2089, 7f. I have discussed the meaning of this proclamation and the genocidal German policy in general in: Jürgen Zimmerer, "Das Deutsche Reich und der Genozid. Überlegungen zum historischen Ort des Völkermordes an den Herero und Nama, " in *100 Jahre geteilte namibisch-deutsche Geschichte: Kolonialkrieg – Genozid – Erinnerungskulturen*, ed. Larissa Förster and Dag Henrichsen (Cologne, 2004).

87. *Die Kämpfe der deutschen Truppen in Südwestafrika* (Auf Grund amtlichen Materials bearbeitet von der Kriegsgeschichtlichen Abteilung I des Großen Generalstabes), 2 vols. (Berlin, 1906/07), vol. 1, 211.

88. In his proclamation from 22 April 1905, von Trotha threatened the Nama with the same destiny as the Herero should they not surrender. Published in: *Kämpfe deutschen Truppen*, vol. 2, 186.

89. The term concentration camp was first used by the Spanish during their campaign in Cuba in 1896, later by the Americans in the Philippines, the British in South Africa, and the Germans in South-West Africa. See Andrzej J. Kaminski, *Konzentrationslager 1896 bis heute: Geschichte-Funktion-Typologie* (Munich, 1996); Joël Kotek and Pierre Rigoulet, *Le siècle des camps* (Paris, 2000).

90. Zimmerer, "Kriegsgefangene im Kolonialkrieg."

91. These are the numbers provided by the army. See Drechsler, *Südwestafrika unter deutscher Kolonialherrschaft*, 213.

92. Zimmerer, "Kriegsgefangene im Kolonialkrieg," 291–92.

93. My current research project "From Windhoek to Warsaw" is dealing with this question in detail. My initial thoughts are in Jürgen Zimmerer, "Die Geburt des 'Ostlandes' aus dem Geiste des Kolonialismus. Die nationalsozialistischer Eroberungs- und Beherrschungspolitik in (post-)kolonialer Perspektive," *Sozial.Geschichte. Zeitschrift für historische Analyse des 20. und 21. Jahrhunderts* (formerly *1999. Zeitschrift für historische Analyse des 20. und 21. Jahrhunderts*) 18 (2004). Various aspects of the continuity between German colonialism in Southwest Africa and the Third Reich have been touched upon by Drechsler, *Südwestafrika unter deutscher Kolonialherrschaft*; Helmut Bley, *Kolonialherrschaft und Sozialstruktur in Deutsch-Südwestafrika 1894-1914* (Hamburg, 1968); Henning Melber, "Kontinuitäten totaler Herrschaft. Völkermord und Apartheid in Deutsch-Südwestafrika," *Jahrbuch für Antisemitismusforschung* 1 (1992): 91-116.

94. Cited by Gerlach, "Deutsche Wirtschaftsinteressen," 278.

95. Hitler, 25 October 1941, in Hitler, *Monologe*, 106.

Chapter 3

GENOCIDE AND MODERNITY IN COLONIAL AUSTRALIA, 1788-1850

Jan Kociumbas

Could the invasions of the New World in the eighteenth and nineteenth centuries have been the most genocidal? The very suggestion seems preposterous for, notwithstanding the influence of post-colonialism, modernity is still often associated with progressive forces of moral and scientific improvement, forged in some cases by war and revolution, but inexorably taking people all around the globe towards a happier, healthier, and more egalitarian future.

Nowhere are such ideas more entrenched than in Australia. Claimed and settled in the wake of the Enlightenment, this land has long been painted by its historians as the "quiet continent," its indigenes dreamily awaiting discovery by the civilized British, then luckily protected by colonists who were natural heirs to liberalism's enlightened fruits. "Born modern," such a nation could have no equivalent of Cortes, who in 1520 reduced the sophisticated, 250,000-strong city of Tenochtitlan to ruins, or De Soto, who in 1539 permitted the slaying of up to 11,000 "Indians" in a single encounter.

Yet arguably what has distinguished modern colonizing practices is not that they were less genocidal than prior ones, but that both intent and effect have been far less honestly addressed. This applies whether one conceives of genocide as deliberate physical or biological extermination, or includes such "bloodless" activities, such as destruction of health, standards of living, language, faith, and cultural identity. Abstruse "scientific" studies of indigenous people have largely supplanted the frank (if smug) admissions of past conquerors, as lengthy, self-serving debates about the supposed medical, sociological, psychological, and cultural causes of demographic decline became the rule. Modern, democratic imperialism even has used the visibility of savage, lethal acts by earlier colonizers to distract attention from its own more clandestine and morally ambivalent tactics, so that progressive views of civilization continue to cast a positive glow over genocidal incidents, events varying from face-to-face killing to state processes of concealment and studied neglect.

 In Australia, though race relations have been no more violent than elsewhere, disinclination to address past injustices has been extreme. Lofty and often legalistic debates about assimilation, protection, unfree labor, population, Christianization, health, and most recently, historiography, have combined to obscure mass death and trauma, while also helping to silence or erase indigenous perspectives on these issues.

The obfuscation of genocide was and is to a large extent inherited from the ideology of liberal reform already in train when Australia was settled in the late eighteenth century. In Britain, the loss of the American colonies brought an especially reformist edge to concurrent attacks both on slavery and on the old mercantilist system of colonization and trade. Spanish imperialism was already stereotyped as the epitome of past errors, violent, extortionate, priest-driven, and tyrannical, not only inefficient but causing massive human misery and costly wars.[1] Yet neither the British nor the French were strangers to the politics of economic, physical, and cultural annihilation that the expansion of Europe imposed on the New World. Though relatively new players in this process, and sometimes expressing pithy sentiments about the supposed nobility of the "savage," both were recipients of at least three centuries of Western knowledge about how to colonize neighboring lands, pacify and exploit their inhabitants, and deal with each other's claims to "new" territories. Both were also deeply implicated in commercial and technological processes that demanded continued imperial expansion virtually at any human cost. Similarly, the fledgling American state was already moving to acquire the "Indian" lands ceded by the retreating British, and all three nations had learned much from the recent American wars.

In terms of colonizing knowledge, Britain's "First Fleet" was particularly well equipped, since it carried not only 1,000 white people, but the latest scientific and technological information necessary to establish a colony in such a faraway land. Moreover, this was a new departure in colonization as a blueprint for exploiting and recycling convict labor by transforming hopeless felons into enterprising colonists. Certainly, preparations for this testing experiment in social engineering were hastily made in order to dispose of convicts who, from 1776, were no longer accepted by the American colonies.[2] Nevertheless, the ships were dispatched under the eye of an Admiralty long experienced in fitting out large human cargoes of marines and slaves, and able to launch this little flotilla into an unfamiliar landscape without the loss of a single ship.

In addition, there was the palpable influence of Joseph Banks. An ambitious savant, he had been to the South Seas and back with James Cook, and was keen to examine any human or botanical exhibit proffered to him from the New World. Banks, on his voyage to Oceania, had carried with him not only a large personal staff to record and store information, but the latest chemicals able to operate new, electrical instruments, a technology he occasionally tested on humans, playfully administering electric shocks.[3] Rocketed to a scientific stature that eclipsed that of Cook, Banks went on to become a major adviser to the British both in their decision to colonize New South Wales and in its later development as a major supplier of wool for British manufacturers. He could ensure that the Fleet carried with it the latest colonizing equipment, from maps to medicine, and that this was not made available to either the convict cargo or Britain's rivals on the high seas. Thus, both ideologically and scientifically the stage was set for brutal but much more modern and covert forms of colonization than benevolent and benign official accounts and legal statutes tender.

Biological Warfare in Early New South Wales

Prominent in this knowledge of modern colonization was the growing understanding of the aetiology of certain infectious diseases, how they could be both prevented and unleashed. Knowledge of smallpox, in particular, was increasing, and the ravages of this virus on indigenous populations were well understood. It had contributed, after all, to the destruction of Tenochtitlan and more recently caused the deaths of numerous New World peoples brought to Europe, from Pocahontus in 1617, to the small party of Eskimos transported from Labrador by a fur trapper and presented before Joseph Banks in 1773. During the Seven Years' War (1756–

1763), this fatal epidemic appeared many times among Native Americans allied to the French. In 1762, it shattered Pontiac's war of resistance against British commander Sir Jeffrey Amherst, thus allowing British settlements to push westward into the vacuum created by the departure of the French. During the War of Independence, documents show clearly that in 1763 at Fort Pitt, Amherst recommended deliberately spreading smallpox among the Native Americans allied to the Americans. There is also evidence that military officials in the field were of the same mind. They had in fact already distributed blankets and handkerchiefs infected with variola by the time Amherst's approval arrived.[4]

In April 1789, the new British settlement at Sydney, New South Wales, was in a desperate situation. Notwithstanding British colonizing skills, this lonely outpost had suffered a series of misfortunes by the end of its first year, creating a situation propitious for a genocidal response. Crops had failed, livestock had been lost, and by the first winter both the settlers and the Aboriginal people were hungry, the newcomers having quickly exhausted local resources of fish and game. No vessels to reinforce the settlement's food and equipment had as yet arrived, and of the two ships remaining in the colony one had been dispatched to the Cape of Good Hope for emergency food and medical supplies. Far too many convict men had succumbed to scurvy, been hanged for theft of stores, or been picked off by Aboriginal spears, while convicts on Norfolk Island had risen in revolt.[5] It was a crisis not unlike that faced in 1622 by the British at Chesapeake Bay when, having lost a quarter of their numbers at the hands of the Powhatan Confederacy, the settlers were advised by the British authorities to resort to a policy of extermination.[6]

At Port Jackson, no such directive was ever issued. Instead, the problem was conveniently solved by the outbreak of a deadly disease. Resembling smallpox, this fatal pestilence caused the deaths of an unknown number of Aboriginal men, women, and children not only in the immediate vicinity of the settlement, but far inland where it traveled via indigenous gift-exchange networks and social relationships. Making food-gathering impossible and eroding faith in traditional medicine and cosmology, the illness also destroyed morale among survivors, the more so since it visibly attacked none of the white settlers. The British had at their disposal "variolus matter in bottles",[7] but though written accounts from the period describe with wonder and sometimes horror the number of corpses strewn around the harbor, none mention the use of the variola, even for the purposes of inoculating the newly-born white children who, though particularly susceptible to the disease, nevertheless appeared to have survived.[8]

The causes of the 1789 epidemic have been the subject of a long and continuing debate among Australian historians. Most writers remain adamant that the disease was not unleashed deliberately by the surgeons or officials. Certainly, it is known that variola had been brought with the Fleet,[9] and understanding of variola's role in both preventing and unleashing the disease was readily available to both the medical fraternity and the officer class.[10] Both Collins and Major Robert Ross had been junior officers under General Gage, the officer who actually signed the docket to convey the infected blankets and handkerchiefs from the hospital to the Delawares and Shawnee.[11] In New South Wales, however, no release or theft of this substance from the medical stores is recorded, nor is it even known precisely who brought the variola to the colony, for it was not listed among the medical supplies that accompanied the ships from England. We would not even know of its existence in the little garrison town were it not for a casual footnote in the records of First Fleet Aboriginal sympathizer, Captain Tench.[12] Indeed, the whole issue of the variola is shrouded in mystery, for no officials left written discussion of either its use or non use. By contrast, in 1804 the threat of a similar epidemic resulted in the vaccination of 400 white children as a matter of course.[13] To this day, the absence of all medical records pertaining to treatment of the sick at the time of the outbreak is not remarked upon, neither the gaps in the journals of Surgeon White,[14] nor in those of such a detailed narrator as Ralph Clark, whose diaries are missing for the relevant period in 1789.[15] The hidden hand of advisers like Banks has not been seriously considered, even though that gentleman was particularly well-situated to assist the Admiralty with knowledge of all aspects of this disease. In 1774, he had personally attended the inoculation of Omai, a man from the Society Islands whom Furneaux brought to England in 1774.[16] Banks remained at the cutting edge of this technology. Edward Jenner, who in 1798 would publish his "discovery" of the benefits of the alternative procedure known as vaccination, was actually employed by Banks to help catalogue his Pacific specimens.[17]

In terms of race relations in Australia, the smallpox epidemic of 1789 provides important insights both on genocide and its denial. Neither contemporary chroniclers nor most later historians sought to deny that this epidemic had occurred, but most sought to excuse it as a tragic sideline in the overall theme of the humanity and liberalism of British colonial policy.[18] Most searched for some "natural" or non-British cause, arguing for instance that the virus was already present in Aboriginal Australia, a notion strongly put by First Fleet Judge-Advocate, David Collins.[19] Other scapegoats included the convict riff-raff or the French navigator, La Perouse, who to the consternation of the British, had sailed into Botany Bay within days of their own arrival. Later apologists focused on Macassan fishermen, who from the mid-eighteenth century regularly visited the continent's northern coastline.[20] One recent historian has even resorted to inferring that infectious disease in general was brought by such natural processes as migratory birds.[21] The refusal to raise the obvious question continues.[22]

The epidemic also paved the way for a cluster of rationalizing stereotypes. These were and are based on the fact that by dwelling on smallpox and other infectious diseases as faceless killers, colonists and historians directed attention away from more overtly murderous acts such as shooting and poisoning. In particular, the 1789 epidemic laid the foundation for the notion that Aboriginal people were not killed outright, but owing to their own personal weaknesses and cultural flaws, sadly just "faded away." It was as if smallpox was nothing more than the first stage in the tragic but necessary workings of evolutionary law, annihilating all species slow to "adapt." Coupled with emphasis on intertribal killings, alcoholism, unhygienic living conditions and, more recently, deaths in police custody, the result has been to blame the victims for their own demise.

Demography and "The Land That Waited"

Stereotypes derived from the initial smallpox epidemic also included long-standing allegations of the insubstantial nature of the Aboriginal population in 1788. These too have been of immense ideological significance, contributing to the notion that any intentional killing by settlers was so infrequent as to be statistically and therefore morally insignificant. These demographic theories in turn fed into nationalistic discourses created in the lead-up to Federation in 1901. They also laid the basis for a bevy of sexual and sociological theories in which Malthusian assumptions played a substantial role.

Colonial settlers and explorers, venturing well into the inland from around 1815, frequently came upon pockmarked survivors of earlier epidemics. This was clear evidence of the spread of the disease, but most nevertheless concluded that the entire preinvasion indigenous population had always been small. Though by the 1880s it was feared that people of mixed descent might be increasing, colonists remained adamant that there could not have been more than 150,000 people originally occupying the entire continent, a total that, it was thought, had since been halved.[23] These estimates were rationalized by sexual stereotypes that western men had long projected onto New World peoples and that Malthus, relying heavily on Collins, had used to explain low indigenous populations, such as female promiscuity, abortion, and infanticide, and, in the case of males, effeminacy, lack of sexual ardour and prowess, and brutal enslavement of women.[24]

Yet, before the smallpox outbreak, the Port Jackson officials had by no means thought that Aboriginal numbers were few. Certainly Banks, along with earlier Dutch visitors, had reported that the population appeared insignificant and the eople timorous, but this was an issue that the civil, army, and medical officers at Sydney were quick to dispute. Surprised by the sheer number of Aboriginal people with whom they had to contend, the first governor, Arthur Phillip, began to fear that there were at least 1,500 people in the immediate vicinity of the settlement, and no one knew how many might be found in the hinterland.[25]

Nevertheless, in 1930, the comforting illusion that the land had always been virtually empty was apparently confirmed by a University of Sydney anthropologist, A.R. Radcliffe-Brown. Though doubling existing estimates to 300,000 for the whole continent, with survivors of full descent numbering perhaps one quarter of the original, this was a poorly-informed yet enormously influential guess, making the Australian record of race relations relatively acceptable by world standards until recently.[26] Radcliffe-Brown's estimate also both rationalized and endorsed the tightening of colonial legislation that from the 1880s had ensured Aboriginal populations were hidden away, classified, and contained in missions and reserves. To the white administrators, however, whose brief was to manage such "remnant" populations on missions and reserves, Radcliffe-Brown's figures justified such "protective" action as kindly, propping up a people soon to be extinct, as well as confirming the concept of the continent as originally and for all practical purposes, vacant and void.

The application of modern demographic science was further endorsed in the Australian nationalist ideology that relied more heavily on Malthusian assumptions than is sometimes realized. Actively constructed from the 1880s, this patriotic sentiment made much of the inland or "Bush" as freely available to the white man

and his sons, as if bereft of indigenous people with any claims upon
it. These larger-than-life white frontiersmen closely resembled
Malthus's 1798 vision of expansionist male colonists, daring
"young scions" pushed out from the parent stock to explore fresh
regions, animated with the spirit of enterprise, "inured to hardship," "delighting in war," and formidable adversaries to all who
opposed them.[27] Whereas in most settler ideologies, these men of
action won their right to pillage, conquer, and rule out of a primal
clash with warlike, barbarous heathens, in Australian nationalist
iconography, it was alleged, Aboriginal people were too primitive
and apathetic to have fought for their land.[28] Accordingly, the primal battle by which the pioneer male established both his mas-
culinity and land rights was less with the demonized savage than
with the land itself, which was invested with many of the bizarre
characteristics elsewhere applied to the treacherous native.[29]

So entrenched was the alliance of Malthusian and nationalist
mythology that only in the 1970s did a number of archaeological
studies begin to find evidence of local population densities that cast
doubt on Radcliffe-Brown's population estimate.[30] Then, in 1983,
historical demographer Noel Butlin argued that the 1789 smallpox
epidemic, when considered in conjunction with follow-ups in 1829
to 1831 and again in the 1860s, plus venereal disease (also introduced by the British), meant that there were probably 250,000 people in New South Wales and Victoria alone. Butlin also mentioned
Jeffery Amherst's infamous approval of biological warfare at Fort
Pitt in 1763, suggesting that the 1789 colonists might have "deliberately opened Pandora's Box."[31] Paradoxically, these latter claims
detracted attention from the population question, though most
writers now argue that 750,000 or even a million is a more likely
figure. Still, the vital nexus between a low population and the legal
foundations on which white settlement of Australia was based is
still to some extent overlooked.[32]

Kings, Chiefs, and Treaties

The fact that initially there seemed to be no individualistic kings,
queens, priests, warriors, or chiefs with whom the British might
negotiate, also helped to create an environment that could support
both genocide and its denial. Combined with the absence of foreign
nations to dispute British claims, this produced a dangerous scenario where the possibility of pretending that the continent was
empty of people was particularly tempting.

This is not to say that the early governors automatically or immediately thought of the continent as "terra nullius" and therefore disregarded the need to conciliate and treat, but such matters were considered of importance only insofar as they might affect Britain's ability to hold its claim (initially to the entire eastern coastline charted by Cook) against competing claims of rival commercial powers; for example, by citing rights by conquest or prior discovery. Even Vattel declared that European nations were justified in punishing and even exterminating "barbarians," such as the Mongols and Turks.[33]

Phillip's instructions to treat the local people with amity reflected pragmatic realities, rather than any erudite consideration of Aboriginal rights. European experience had established the rule that initial landing-parties were likely to be heavily outnumbered, so it was vital to keep the peace while ascertaining as much as possible about indigenous social and political organization in order to form an alliance with the most powerful leader or clan. Anthropological reconnaissance was also a necessary prelude for the standard colonialist tactic of exploiting intertribal divisions. Moreover, without peaceful overtures accompanied by data collection, it might not be possible to preempt rival European powers from forming an alliance with other, hostile indigenous groups, or even worse, supplying them with weapons or even armies to use against the settlers. At Port Jackson, Governor Phillip's capture of Arabanoo (December 1788), followed by Bennelong and Colebee (November 1789), conformed to these unwritten rules, for even if these men proved to be powerless to effect a treaty or unwilling to supply information, they might still be of enormous utility as hostages. Arabanoo died of smallpox, Colebee escaped, and Bennelong played a double game until, having survived being paraded in England, he eventually succumbed to alcohol. The dismal results of this experiment were taken to confirm growing allegations that Aboriginal "kings" were too short-lived, weak-willed, and politically impotent to be honorable and effective allies.[34]

In addition to the apparent absence of autocratic leaders or priests, the other factor that distinguished race-relations policy in early Australia was the fact that none of Britain's trading rivals, the Spanish, Dutch, and French, were in a position to enforce prior claims on the continent at that time. Already in 1804, when Van Diemen's Land was being settled, the British were reasonably confident they could proceed without conciliation or treaties. Certainly, the French were known to be looking for a new base east of Mauritius to support further Pacific exploration. Van Diemen's Land, "discovered" by Tasman in 1642, had been visited by Du Fresne in 1772, while the southwest corner of the continent had been claimed by St Allouarn in 1772. More recently, it was the fact that first D'Entrecasteaux and then Baudin inspected and allotted French names to the continent's southern coastlines that had prompted the inception of British settlements there. But the French formed no alliance with coastal people (though Baudin did brazenly send a letter to Governor King provocatively accusing him of dispossessing the native Tasmanians from their soil).[35] At Hobart, Van Diemen's Land, in May 1804, the settlers did not hesitate to use a cannon to cut down the first party of Aboriginal people who approached the infant settlement.[36]

Though charismatic Aboriginal leaders did arise, in settler chronicles and later histories these people tended to be treated as criminals or bushrangers rather than as a military or political threat—outlaws, usually with a price on their heads. This tradition began in 1790, after Pemulwuy speared Phillip's gamekeeper and thereby triggered the colony's first "punitive expedition." Pemulwuy went on to organize a series of daring attacks, terrorizing the early settlements from Sydney west to Parramatta, where many of the ex-convicts who had chosen to stay in the colony were struggling to farm small thirty-acre grants. Eventually shot by settlers in 1802, Pemulwuy's head was dispatched to the ubiquitous Joseph Banks.[37] Yet so convinced were historians that Aboriginal warriors or prophets were of little account that Pemulwuy's story was soon forgotten or erased. Deemed insufficiently evil or romantic to be of interest, he was rendered just as invisible as the Botany Bay "nation" of which he was a part.

Even so, the authorities' search for dominant kings or queens to conciliate or take hostage, as circumstances might dictate, was pursued as late as the 1820s. In New South Wales, Augustus Earle's painting of Bungaree, clad in a Nelson-like hat and with a breastplate proclaiming him "King of the Blacks," may be read as a comment on this practice. A man from the lands immediately north of Sydney, Bungaree had assisted Flinders and P.P. King in their detailed charting of the continent's coastlines, and was a prominent figure around Sydney until his death in 1830. His breastplate, presented by Governor Macquarie in 1815, was copied by many pastoral settlers who awarded similar regalia to selected "Kings" and "Queens."[38] Macquarie's annual feast at Parramatta (fourteen miles west of Sydney Harbor) may be seen as a more concrete effort to attract or create leaders, pursued in the hope that a regular display of vice-regal generosity might yet produce some form of truce or treaty to facilitate land annexation. This annual ritual was recognized by some Aboriginal leaders in this light.[39] On the whole, however, the absence of hierarchical social systems and professional warriors permanently organized for aggressive conflict helped to render the whole population invisible, an attitude eventually confirmed in law when the extreme land annexations of the 1820s and 1830s made clarification of Aboriginal people's legal position mandatory.

The Irish Model

Another distinctive feature of early British colonization experience was the ongoing application of knowledge acquired in the colonization of the Irish. This acted to prevent any alliance between these "savages" and Aboriginal people, while also providing a ready-made model for the repression of both.

From the sixteenth century in Ireland, enormous confiscations of land, campaigns of extermination, proscriptions on intermarriage, transplantation of an English oligarchy, and restrictions on trade meant that Ireland was of lesser status than even a plantation colony, while its Catholic majority were reduced to servitude by a savage penal code. The treatment of these people and their priests was not different in kind from policies pursued by the Spanish in Mexico and Peru, as even historians sympathetic to modern British imperialism concede.[40] In early Sydney, where the first convict vessels launched directly from Ireland arrived from 1791, and where there were over a thousand Irish convicts by 1800, the presence of the Irish served further to draw attention away from Aboriginal resistance, both at the time and since.[41] It was they rather than Aborigines who were seen as *the* foreign enemy, and since they were thought far more likely to be reinforced by the French, they were perceived as many times more dangerous.

In 1804, a major convict rebellion, thought to have been inspired by that in Ireland in 1798, coincided with new Aboriginal resistance as settlement reached the Hawkesbury (northwest of Sydney), a major river artery and rich source of food for all concerned. Yet like the ongoing threat of the French, this uprising, like later minor outbreaks that followed, was of no assistance to Aboriginal opposition. Governments had sufficient military power to send in the troops almost simultaneously against convict and Aboriginal rebels, the more so as they successfully enlisted the aid of the ex-convict farmers. Clamoring for action against Aboriginal "depredations," these people were in effect permitted to take the law into their own hands. When in 1799 five Hawkesbury settlers savagely killed two Aboriginal boys to avenge the death of one of their own, the court referred the matter to London for advice while the perpetrators went free, an action that was eventually ratified by the British authorities in 1802.[42] Judge-Advocate Richard Atkins, when belatedly called upon to comment on the legal status of Aboriginal people in 1805, declared that they were too ignorant of moral and religious ties to be permitted to enter a plea or testify. He therefore could see no problem with allowing the settlers to pursue and punish Aboriginal people harassing their farms.[43]

Settler Armies and Native Police

The sheer speed and scale of land annexation as British settlement moved into the pastoral phase was another factor helping to create a climate where the sheer scale of destruction could be effectively blurred, rationalized, or denied. Unlike America, Australia had few broad navigable rivers whereby rival maritime powers might be swept into the heartlands, thus joining hands with Aboriginal resistance; but British technology and military prowess had been advanced rapidly by the land wars against Napoleon, which included experience in guerilla warfare. Prior to 1810, all the early governors had been naval captains, their main field of expertise being defense of waterways, ships, and shipping, and the governance of marines, human cargoes, and crew. Beginning with Macquarie, however, colonial governors and many land-takers were army veterans with knowledge of road and bridge-making, surveying, and supply, all vital to moving settlement quickly into the interior. They were also familiar with military weapons and tactics. This special expertise was graphically demonstrated in the new colony of Swan River, Western Australia, where in 1834 a party comprising the governor and leading landholders expertly trapped a family group containing Calyute and other suspected troublemakers in the Murray River at Pinjarra, shooting an unknown number in crossfire and jocularly celebrating and parodying the event as comparable with Waterloo.[44]

Pastoral expansion was most rapid in the two eastern convict colonies, where from 1825 till 1831 a new wave of free settlers, arriving after 1815, had the advantage of cheap convict labor as well as special access to capital necessary for the purchase of stock and supplies. Reflecting the fact that Britain, with no more major European wars to fight until the Crimea, was focusing on wholesale imperial expansion, settlers who were military and naval officers could exchange their commissions for large parcels of Aboriginal land. In 1825, changes to land regulations also facilitated expansion, ending the original practice of small grants of farmland to ex-convicts, and giving preference to gentleman settlers who might acquire generous holdings for nothing or by purchase on very liberal terms.[45] Most soon took up additional sections "further out," where stock was depastured either illegally or for very cheap rental. Large parcels were also alienated on behalf of British absentee investors. As well, there were the earlier free settlers who, along with former military men and traders from India, had reaped a fortune from maritime trade, and now participated in the rush to imitate the British gentry in colonial pastoral pursuits. By the early 1840s, most of the well-watered land in the southeast of the continent was occupied by sheep, cattle, and convict or ex-convict stockmen, spreading out well in advance of survey and policing, and creating a situation where race relations reflecting Atkins's judgment of 1805 prevailed.[46]

The sheer speed of these changes left little time for inland Aboriginal people to form alliances or make other adjustments preparing them for the white man's presence. Certainly, they employed their superior knowledge of the country to delay invasion, attacking bullock-drays, isolated stockmen, and the flocks and herds. All this had to be achieved without widespread use of the white man's horse, though most did rapidly acquire his hunting dogs and adapt glass and metal to their weapons and tools. Aboriginal opportunities for resistance thus must be contrasted to those of the Plains Indians, who had much more time to master and exploit the horses that, brought by Columbus, were widely dispersed from 1680.[47] Even guns, which underwent rapid improvement in accuracy, portability, and range by mid-century, were not widely acquired by Aboriginal people, though there were exceptions.[48]

This was not only because of the dearth of foreign powers and fur-traders who might have supplied weapons, but also because of official prohibitions.[49] The speed of the land invasion meant that in white minds, there was no time for a strong consciousness of Aboriginal dispossession to be registered among urban settlers. The Sydney people were scattered and few by the 1820s; the Tasmanians by the 1840s. In Port Phillip, an Aboriginal population almost certainly underestimated at 11,000 to 15,000 people in 1834, had been reduced to less than 2,000 within a generation, while the white population boosted by gold rushes had leapt from 77,000 in 1851 to 540,000 within a decade.[50]

In these conditions, it was not difficult for pastoralists to deny that large-scale killings were occurring, or to represent them as mere skirmishes or justifiable paybacks to unprovoked violence on the part of the "Blacks." The widespread use of Aboriginal trackers to bring in convict absconders continued to discourage alliances between these two groups, though the Mounted Police, a permanent, trained militia, was created (New South Wales, 1825) to deal both with Aboriginal and convict resistance in border districts. Similarly, in Port Phillip, the specially trained and mounted Native Police (1837–1853), which combined Aboriginal bushcraft with military discipline, was used against the last phases of Aboriginal "depredations" in that colony, as well as to control the disorder brought by gold. On occasions, when it was acknowledged that militia, pastoralists, or convicts had slain Aboriginal people, it became customary to find the cause in the convict presence or mentality, a strategy increasingly employed as the whole system of transportation came under increasing attack. It would prove perhaps the most effective tool of all in denying that nationwide genocide had occurred.

Liberalism, Labor, and Genocide

By the early 1830s, this system of laissez-faire genocide began to be questioned by growing liberal and humanitarian reformers both in the colonies and in Britain. This development was the climax of the long debate on slavery, but was far less altruistic than much current white Australian historiography has tended to assume. Anti-slave rhetoric, though undoubtedly humanitarian, also reflected pragmatic political and economic realities. For instance, the emerging industrialized economies required more mobile, literate, and consumption-motivated workers, preferably white adult males, their emerging class-consciousness divided by racism and their wages kept low by oversupply.

The Australian colonies, founded at the onset of these debates, inevitably figured as a test case, with forced convict labor in private service projected as morally indefensible, corrupting both master and man. Moreover, the dialogue during which these principles were formulated soon extended to more efficient ways to "manage" colonization so as to make it more godly, liberal, profitable, and populous, hopefully introducing the sexual division of labor and avoiding prodigious waste of "native" life. Again, the convict colonies provided graphic examples, having produced a demographic shortage of white women, who were needed to boost population and consumerism.

These various themes were synthesized in 1837, when the British abolition of slavery throughout the empire produced a particularly dramatic enquiry into the convict system. Critics dwelt luridly on the sexual evils of assignment to declare that the resultant preponderance of males had led not only to unspeakable vice and loathsome disease, but to skirmishes between convicts and Aboriginal men over access to Aboriginal women. Preferring to find fault with settler and especially convict morality than with general European investment in dispossession, they depicted this as a major cause of the frontier conflict that was occurring.[51]

This reformist dialogue has usefully lent weight to recent statutory revision of the concept of "terra nullius." Nevertheless, at the time, the anti-slave debate served only to make killings more secretive, with poisoning becoming a preferred method of eliminating whole families.[52] Anti-slave rhetoric also produced stereotypes indicating that if depopulation continued to occur, it must be caused by the alleged moral debasement of Aboriginal people themselves.

Rapid modification of current land, labor, and missionary policies along liberal lines fostered such assumptions. Already on the west coast, the Swan River colony had been founded with contract labor instead of convicts (though a system of penal transportation was introduced to boost the economy in 1850 to 1867). In the eastern colonies, the use of convict laborers in private service was replaced by various combinations of penal incarceration followed by "probationary" labor. This was accompanied by further changes to land policy, introduced by British reformers in 1831. Henceforth, all land was to be sold in much smaller parcels and at a very high price, the funds deployed to assist the immigration of free white laborers, especially pauper women. Thus would tidy, civilizing villages, each with its own church and school, replace the present sprawling stations (ranches) with their preponderance of males. Anarchy, godlessness, violence, venereal disease, homosexuality, and waste of Aboriginal life were all to be terminated by simple changes in the allocation of colonial labor and land.[53]

For Aboriginal people, these innovations brought little change. To be sure, the reformers' idea that slavery was illiberal, inefficient, and cruel meant that, unlike in early indigenous America, Aboriginal people were never officially captured and sold as slaves. Nevertheless, the fact that throughout the peak years of pastoral expansion in the south, the land-takers were provided with their own captive labor force meant that in terms of the labor market,

Aboriginal people were regarded as dispensable, or at best a labor reserve. Moreover, as early visitors like Banks had noted with disdain, Aboriginal people displayed little interest in trade or private property, which meant that as consumers, too, they were seen as quite expendable.

Indeed, in the absence of rich mines and manufactures, the settlers had never wanted much from Aboriginal people except their women and their land. State-assisted free "pauper" immigration, introduced from 1832, followed by the importation of "coolies" in the 1840s, assured that the labor market continued to be well supplied. By the time convict immigration to the eastern colonies was terminated altogether in 1852, the white free working population had been swelled by the inception of the gold rushes (1851) which, though causing temporary labor shortages, in the long run ensured a surfeit of disappointed diggers. By the 1860s in Queensland, the importation of South Seas Island people further relieved labor demands.

The importation of labor did not mean that Aboriginal people performed no work. Indeed, young children were in such demand for housework and harvesting that they were frequently kidnapped or "adopted."[54] Aboriginal workers were largely restricted to onerous and unskilled fields, and were always poorly paid, or more often not paid at all. Furthermore, a stereotype developed that Aboriginal people were so nomadic, lazy, and unreliable that they were unemployable, an allegation that further fed the notion of a small population condemned to extinction by virtue of its own innate deficiencies. Though further embellished during the heyday of pastoral expansion, the idea of an ungovernable instinct to "go walkabout" owed much to the failure of the Native Institution (1814–1833), the first school for Aboriginal "orphans," and especially to the opinions of Reverend Samuel Marsden, the colonies' second clergyman. By the 1820s, he publicized both his criticisms of the Aboriginal school and his own lack of success in turning various children into tractable house-workers. He and other missionaries also popularized the idea that Maori children, whom Marsden brought to Sydney from his trading ventures in the Pacific, were more robust, clever, and honest.[55] It was a view that arguably also began the tendency for white Australians to romanticize "Maoriland" rather than Aboriginal Australia whenever they felt inclined to address the prior existence of exotic indigenes, a whim that further contributed to Aboriginal invisibility.[56]

Liberalism and Legalism

Liberal-humanitarian rhetoric on free labor not only failed to halt ongoing processes of genocide; it was also integral to the development of the concept of Aboriginal people as a child-race, in need of state-sponsored, protective custody, and re-education. Though ostensibly a rescue mission, intended to prevent exploitation and death, "protection" was a complex and often contradictory cluster of assimilationist policies, statutes, and debates. Casting a long shadow, it would usher in more than a century of various legally-condoned methods of erasing cultural identity and excusing death.

This subtle and sinister side of "protection" is best illustrated in the trial and hanging of seven white convicts and ex-convicts in 1838 for the massacre of some thirty men, women, and children at Myall Creek. Though often hailed by historians as marking a new determination by liberals to offer Aboriginal people legal protection, clarifying that they were British citizens under the protection of British law, this was arguably a show-trial, staged by urban-based liberals concerned to streamline and modernize the process of colonization by preventing further private land "treaties" on the model pioneered by John Batman in 1835.[57]

Negotiated at Port Phillip near the present site of Melbourne by a group of land-hungry settlers from Van Diemen's Land, this treaty was in effect a modern contract for the sale of land as real property, skillfully devised so as to evade having to purchase land under the new rules. In Batman's view, the deal meant that the Aboriginal people had ceded 600,000 acres of land in return for a quantity of scissors, handkerchiefs, mirrors, shirts and jackets, flour, blankets, tomahawks, and knives. As had been the case in America after the Revolution, when the new republican administration sent out commissioners to "buy" the land prior to resale at government profit to colonists, so in Australia colonial reformers moved rapidly to disallow the treaty and give the Crown sole rights to process land allocation. At the same time, they limited but did not disallow the existing system of informal occupation of outstations (by then known as "squatting"), merely insisting on a more efficient system of leasehold ensuring the collection of rent. Border Police (1839) were sent both to settle disputes between these various "squatters" and to put down protest from Aboriginal people.[58]

While establishing that henceforth it was the Crown alone that had the initial right to acquire Aboriginal land, these responses did not quite resolve the related issues of Aboriginal sovereignty and the status of Aboriginal law. Supreme Court case-notes on the trial of Jack Congo Morrell (1836), followed by the Myall Creek hangings, were taken to establish that Aboriginal people had actually ceded sovereignty by means of the legal fiction of "terra nullius," held to be operative from 1788. Following these legal debates, it became gradually less common for colonists to speak of Aboriginal people as a foreign foe, as some had done for instance at the height of the "Black War" in Van Diemen's Land.[59] In 1835, liberal governor Bourke abolished the Parramatta feast; in 1844 his successor Gipps discontinued the annual distribution of blankets that had formerly been a government gesture of recognition and compensation. With leaders who attacked out-stations classified as lawbreakers, not generals, and the business of "dispersal" officially relegated to the less visible activities of the police, legal attention moved on to determining the practicalities of "protection," focusing on preferred issues such as the inadmissibility of Aboriginal evidence in court.

Of particular interest was the liberal principle that as British subjects, Aboriginal people must accept the punishments as well as the protection of the law. Any offence they committed was now to be brought to court, and penalties were to be consistent with those handed out to white lawbreakers. Nor were Aboriginal people any longer to evade legal scrutiny when they punished each other according to the dictates of Aboriginal law. As Judge Burton, liberal hero of the Myall Creek hearings, explained, such simpleminded folk had no law, only "lewd practices and irrational superstitions, contrary to Divine Law and consistent only with the grossest darkness."[60]

Complicity of Missionary Ideology

Missionaries have traditionally played a significant role in colonization, being both agents of assimilation and a check on some of imperialism's extremes. The British settlement at Port Jackson, however, occurred at a particularly secular moment. The first clergyman, Richard Johnson, boarded the First Fleet almost as an afterthought, and both he and Marsden were more concerned with convict morality than with Aboriginal issues. As late as the 1820s, missionaries were few in number and unlike the Spanish Jesuits, never in the front line.

By the 1830s, however, rising evangelical influence in Britain provided increased personnel and funds and many liberal social reformers began to see missionary endeavor as a useful branch of their plans to make colonization more profitable and efficient, paving the way for consensual dispossession and preventing costly frontier wars. Darling, arriving in 1825, was the first governor specifically instructed to Christianize Aboriginal people, and by the 1830s, influential individuals such as L.E. Threlkeld, whose mission was at the gateway to the Hunter region (north of Sydney), and G.A. Robinson in Van Diemen's Land, were projecting themselves as experts in the field and key advisers to the liberal, protectionist state.

Even at this time of maximum British support and funding, the speed of land annexations was such that most missionaries were mere reserve managers and suppliers of rations, powerless to mitigate the violence of colonization and the ambitions of investors, both local and British, who coveted mission land. Most could offer no protection against female abduction, starvation, and disease, so that for Aboriginal people life within these self-styled sanctuaries could be as impoverished and dangerous as anywhere outside. With dwindling inmates and few conversions achieved, most missionaries blamed what they saw as an exceptionally primitive people, destined to disappear. Some invented or refined coercive processes of acculturation, where indigenous religion was condemned as slavery, lechery, and worse, and therefore was to be eliminated entirely. Even in the days of the Native Institution it came to be considered necessary to separate children from parents, a policy further developed by Reverend Watson at Wellington Valley mission (1832).[61]

Robinson in particular had much to answer for, personally traveling round the island colony (1829–1834) to persuade Tasmanian resistance leaders to relocate to mission land that was temporarily provided for them in Bass Strait. This strategy was hailed as more successful and humane than Arthur's declaration of martial law (1828–1832), in spite of the fact that most of the inmates died. It also had an indelible influence on both short and long-term protection policies. At Port Phillip, under the terms of an official "Protectorate," established in 1838, no less than four missionaries, directed by Robinson himself, were appointed to repeat the Tasmanian experiment. Moving out in advance of land alienation, and traveling with the tribes, it was hoped they would persuade these people to remove themselves, like the Cherokees in 1838, onto special reserves gazetted by the state.

Like other liberal reformers, missionaries had much to say about the immorality of depriving innocent savages of their hunting grounds, but it was mainly of the sprawling pastoral industry that they were thinking, along with its preference for cheap, captive labor. As with their secular allies, they did not believe that "primitive" and "godless" folk should be permitted to occupy huge wastes.[62] All Aboriginal people, therefore, were to be ushered into missions, and there, safe from the influence of evil white men, persuaded to exchange their lands for the priceless gift of Christianity that everyone soon decided was compensation enough.[63]

The failure of the Port Phillip Protectorate marked the withdrawal of state funding from missionary endeavor and its relocation to other, more secular liberal initiatives, such as a new branch of the Native Police. For Threlkeld, ensuring that Aboriginal men who committed offences *inter se* suffered the full penalty of British law became almost as important as tracking down white offenders. He interpreted in court for the accused whether or not he understood the language, and congratulated himself on conversions achieved at the foot of the gallows. Meanwhile the notion of concentrating survivors in remote areas from which escape was difficult became a long-accepted state and missionary ideal. Though missionaries and their supporters did succeed in sustaining various systems of reserves, killings continued to occur on mission land itself, while the enforced Anglicization, poor diet, removal of children, and growing management by the state, often offset Aboriginal attempts to transform missions into self-managed centers of resistance and reforging of identity.

Racial Science

The fact that Australia's indigenous people very early became seen as raw material for the construction of modern racial science was likewise a dangerous development, helping to rationalize and obscure inhuman policies. Noting the apparent absence of permanent villages and cities, religious observance, along with built monuments, cultivated crops, domesticated animals, pottery and metals, early observers concluded that these people exhibited extreme social failings.

The concurrent rise of Darwinist theory added new, dehumanizing elements. By the 1830s, when brutal dispossession of the better-watered lands in the eastern parts of the continent was at its peak, such views were developed further by theories that indigenous survivors were not really people at all. Could they be "the connecting link between man and the monkey tribe?" speculated convict-ship surgeon turned Hunter River pastoralist Peter Cunningham in 1827. Like many such observers, he reserved a special invective for older women, alleging that they only required "a tail to complete the identity."[64] Aboriginal women were widely blamed by pastoralists for spreading venereal disease among their workers, rather than the other way round, and far from being abducted, were said to be willing partners, either eagerly seeking such liaisons or delivered into them by shameless, indolent Aboriginal men, a view endorsed by most missionaries.[65] As killings escalated west of Bathurst in the 1820s, land-taker William Lawson admitted frankly that the aim was to "exterminate." William Cox allegedly suggested that as "breeders," it was Aboriginal women on whom the guns should be trained, and that the best thing to be done with the race would be to use its carcasses to fertilize the ground.[66]

In fact, carnage from the massacres in this and other regions was exploited for more scientific purposes. Beginning with the dispatch of Pemulwuy's head, a strong demand developed throughout the medical schools and scientific societies of Europe for Aboriginal remains. Skeletal parts from the Bathurst massacre sites were supplied to phrenologists, and visiting European collectors such as Bougainville (1825) were readily supplied with both living and dead specimens for perusal.[67] By then, the failure of the missionaries to protect and convert their charges prompted these people also to become major stakeholders in the growing ethnological debates. Some believed in the theory of separate creation of black and white; others believed Aboriginal people were actually traveling backwards down the line of progress, being now unable to produce paintings of the quality of their imagined forebears.[68] Most alleged that Aboriginal people were so sunk in depravity as to make civilization impossible, the only hope lying with the children, who thus must be taken from their families while very young.

Though some like Threlkeld deplored the trade in body parts, others had no such reservations. Archdeacon Scott was provided with skulls by Alexander Berry, whose Shoalhaven estate included an Aboriginal burial ground and who used the demand for such material to advance his own affairs. On Flinders Island, Robinson supplied human remains of dead inmates to such eminent collectors as Sir John and Lady Franklin.[69] Elsewhere missionaries, though drawing the line at grave-robbing and body-snatching, continued the catalogue of dehumanizing practices begun by Collins, adding colorful allegations of cannibalism and vile superstition to existing emphasis on savage rites, polygamy, gang rape, infanticide, and vicious, intertribal war, the more so as they failed to achieve conversions and faced the withdrawal of funds.[70]

As elsewhere in the West, white working people became increasingly receptive to such theories, as the attack on slavery, plus employer efforts to circumvent it, brought white and "colored" labor into direct competition.[71] State-funded elementary education, based on the Irish model, was introduced in the convict colonies as early as the 1830s, where it was seen as vital to offset the supposed vices of convict parents. Growing in tandem with the use of ideologically-charged material in education, and the separation of Aboriginal children into mission schools, formal education ensured that the "rising generations" grew up imbued with the view that Aboriginal people were a lesser species.

The fact that Australia's indigenous people were so extensively dismembered and exhibited as scientific freaks made for a particularly virulent form of racism, which rendered it increasingly impossible for even model, educated Aboriginal people to find acceptance in settler society. Men became extremely vulnerable to capital conviction of rape against white women, though white men continued to rape Aboriginal women virtually as a right.[72] Moreover, liberal and missionary aversion to miscegenation was widely expressed as early as the 1830s, a development that helped deny visibility and acceptance to families of mixed descent.

Conclusion

The issue of genocide in Australian history remains a contested issue today. Radical "black armband" writers are taken to task either for overemphasizing the cruelty and greed of Western colonizers, or for conveniently omitting documentary evidence that does not fit their damning hypotheses.[73] While making valid points regarding the need for historians to be more alert to the absence of eyewitnesses in reportage of massacres, as well as the agenda of those who reported atrocities, these critics have not abided by their own rules. Among other problems, these writers disregard the law's own dismissal or discrediting of Aboriginal testimony, along with other problems of applying white man's law to Aboriginal people, such as the reluctance of relatives to mention the names of the dead. Indeed, these critics' assumption that white law could uncover "the whole truth" gives them much in common with the missionaries and humanitarians of whom they are otherwise so suspicious. Both groups assume it was and is both appropriate and necessary to contain Aboriginal experience and Aboriginal law within modern Western systems of law, history, and cosmology.

These most recent denials of genocide thus have much in common with those of the past. What is unique about genocide in Australia is not its violence, but its apparent legality and above all its modernity. It was modern technology that made possible the pace and effectiveness of the killing, and modern law that provided the judicial niceties that condoned it. This in turn enabled minimal state involvement via visible, military action, and gave carte blanche to changing groups of helpers claiming expertise in managing surviving populations where extreme surveillance did not preclude starvation, the absence of medical services, and utter neglect. Similarly, it was modernity that created the "surplus" and "free" populations to overwhelm the surviving indigenous ones, and it was modern education, not colonial ignorance, that helped create the conditions where official silence and legally-sanctioned cover-ups could prevail. A broader comparative study of genocide, including the draconian repression and relocation of suspect populations within Britain itself, will provide a much-needed, wider perspective on these issues and events.

Notes

1. See, for instance, T.R. Malthus, *An Essay on the Principle of Population* [1798], ed. E.A. Wrigley and D. Souden in *The Works of Thomas Robert Malthus* (London, 1986), 39.
2. Reasons for the British settlement in New South Wales have been much debated. For a summary see, *The Founding of Australia*, ed. G. Martin (Sydney, 1978); A. Frost, *Botany Bay Mirages* (Melbourne, 1995), 2–8.
3. *The Endeavour Journal of Joseph Banks*, ed. J.C. Beaglehole, 2 vols. (Sydney, 1962), vol. 1, 160, vol. 2, 276–78; J. Gascoigne, *Science in the Service of the Empire: Joseph Banks, the British State and the Uses of Science in the Age of Revolution* (Cambridge, 1998).
4. A.M. Josephy, *Five Hundred Nations* (London, 1995), 257–58; E.A. Fenn, "Biological Warfare in Eighteenth-Century North America," *Journal of American History* 86, no. 4 (2000): 552–58.
5. For a day-by-day summary of the early settlement, see J. Cobley's series of volumes commencing with *Sydney Cove, 1788* (London, 1963).
6. Cf. P. Bartrop, "The Powhatans of Virginia and the English Invasion of America: Destruction without Genocide," in *Genocide Perspectives*, ed. C. Tatz (Sydney, 1997), 66–105.
7. W. Tench, *A Complete Account of the Settlement at Port Jackson* [1793], in *Sydney's First Four Years*, ed. L.F. Fitzhardinge (Sydney, 1979), 146.
8. N.G. Butlin, *Our Original Aggression* (Sydney, 1983) remains the seminal work. See also, J. Cobley, *Sydney Cove, 1789–1790* (Sydney, 1963), 4–41; K. Willey, *When the Sky Fell Down* (Sydney, 1985), 58–78, 106–7.

9. Tench, *Complete Account*, 146.

10. Fenn, "Biological Warfare," 1,567–81.

11. H. Reynolds, *An Indelible Stain?* (Melbourne, 2001).

12. Tench, *Complete Account*, 146–49, 305–6.

13. It appears that inoculation was also attempted. See *Historical Records of New South Wales* (*HRNSW*) V, 115, 429, 552, 740.

14. The only extant MS. is that which White sent to London in November 1788 and which was published in 1790. See *Journal of a Voyage to New South Wales*, ed. A.H. Chisholm (Sydney, 1962).

15. The second of Clark's three notebooks (11 March 1788 to 14 February 1790) has been lost. See *Journal and Letters of Lt. Ralph Clark, 1787–1792*, ed. P.J. Fidlon & R.J. Ryan (Sydney, 1981).

16. P. O'Brian, *Joseph Banks* (London, 1987), 179–84, 190–91.

17. O'Brian, *Banks*, 170.

18. Exceptions include those who argue that the disease may have been chicken pox. See for instance, P. Curson, *Times of Crisis* (Sydney, 1985), 43; Frost, *Botany Bay Mirages*, 205.

19. D. Collins, *An Account of the English Colony in New South Wales* [1802], ed. B.H. Fletcher (Sydney, 1975), vol. 1, 53, 496.

20. Macassans were expelled from the area in 1906 as part of the new federal government's White Australia policy. See D.J. Mulvaney, *Encounters in Place* (Brisbane, Qld., 1989), 22–28.

21. G. Blainey, *Triumph of the Nomads* (Melbourne, 1983), 103–4.

22. Frost, *Botany Bay Mirages*, 190–210; J. Campbell, *Invisible Invaders: Smallpox and Other Diseases in Aboriginal Australia, 1780–1880* (Melbourne, 2002).

23. Butlin, *Our Original Aggression*, 4.

24. T.R. Malthus, *An Essay on the Principle of Population* [1803], (London, 1948), 21–25.

25. HRNSW I, i, 133, 153, 177, 191–92.

26. Butlin, *Our Original Aggression*, 4, 6, 119–30.

27. Malthus, *An Essay* [1798], 21, 40.

28. W.E.H. Stanner, "The Aborigines," in *Some Australians Take Stock*, ed. J. Kevis (London, 1939), 8–9.

29. The classic study of rural mythology was R. Ward, *The Australian Legend* (Melbourne, 1958). Influential critiques include S. Magarey et al., eds., *Debutante Nation* (Sydney, 1993); and K. Schaffer, *Women and the Bush* (Melbourne, 1988).

30. See for instance, H. Lourandos, "Aboriginal Spatial Organization and Population: South-Western Victoria Reconsidered," *Archaeology and Physical Anthropology in Oceania* 12, no. 3 (1977): 202–25.

31. Butlin, *Aggression*, ix, 17, 22, 146–47, 175.

32. See for instance "Dramatic Revision of 1788 Aboriginal population to 750,000," *University of Sydney News*, 24 February 1987, 15; and D.J. Mulvaney and J. Peter White, "How Many People?" in *Australians to 1788* (Sydney, 1987), 116–17.

33. E. de Vattel, *The Law of Nations* [1758], (New York, 1964), 246. Cf. Frost, *Botany Bay Mirages*, 176–89.

34. *ADB*, vol. 1, 84–85.

35. L. Marchant, *France Australe* (Perth 1982); L. Ryan, *The Aboriginal Tasmanians* (Brisbane, 1982), 64.

36. *HRA* III, i, 237–38; *The Diary of the Reverend Robert Knopwood,* ed. M. Nicolls (Hobart, 1977), 51.

37. *HRNSW* IV, 784; E. Willmot, *Pemulwuy: The Rainbow Warrior* (Sydney, 1987); Willey, *When the Sky Fell Down,* 122–23, 164–68.

38. R. Reece, "Feasts and Blankets: The History of Some Early Attempts to Establish Relations with the Aborigines of New South Wales," *Archaelogy and Physical Anthropology in Oceania* 2, no. 3 (1967): 190–206; T. Cleary, "The History of Breastplates and their Distribution," *Poignant Regalia* (Sydney, 1993).

39. See for instance, M. Coe, *Windradyne: A Wiradjuri Koorie* (Sydney, 1986), 44.

40. V.T. Harlow, *The Founding of the Second British Empire* (London, 1952), 502–3.

41. P. O'Farrell, *The Irish in Australia* (Sydney, 1987), 23–39.

42. *HRNSW* V, 1–7, 639, 640, 795.

43. *HRNSW* V, 653.

44. G.F. Moore, *Diary of Ten Years Eventful Life of an Early Settler in Western Australia* (London, 1884), 239–43; F. Goldsmith, "The Battle of Pinjarra," *Journal of the Royal Australian Historical Society* (JRAHS), 37, no. 6 (1951): 344–50; A. Hasluck, "The Battle of Pinjarra," *Australia's Heritage* 2, no. 29 (1970): 695; N. Green, "Aborigines and White Settlers in the Nineteenth Century," *A New History of Western Australia,* ed. C.T. Stannage (Perth, 1981), 83–85.

45. *HRA* I, xii, 113–25.

46. See footnote 43.

47. Josephy, 358.

48. *HRV* IIb, 528, 538, 545, 550, 723–34; *HRA* I, xxi, 208–9; L. Robson, *A History of Tasmania* (Melbourne, 1983), 215–16, 218, 219, 242–45.

49. In 1816, Macquarie attempted to prohibit Aborigines near settlements even from carrying clubs and spears; see *HRA* I, ix, 142–44. In 1839, Gipps attempted to prohibit supplying them with arms; see *HRA* I, xxi, 485.

50. M. Christie, *Aborigines in Colonial Victoria* (Sydney, 1979), 78–79, 136, 206–7.

51. For a useful summary, see J. Hirst, *Convict Society and its Enemies* (Sydney, 1983), 9–27.

52. R. Reece, *Aborigines and Colonists* (Sydney, 1974), 49–50.

53. These debates have a large British and Australian literature. The classic study was R.C. Mills, *The Colonization of Australia, 1829–42* [1915] (Sydney, 1974).

54. See Henry Reynolds' chapter in this volume.

55. "Reverend Samuel Marsden's Report to Archdeacon Scott on the Aborigines of N.S.W. (2 December 1826)" in *Australian Reminiscences and Papers of L.E. Threlkeld,* ed. N. Gunson (Canberra, 1974), 347–49; J.J. Fletcher, *Documents in the History of Aboriginal Education in New South Wales* (Carlton, NSW, 1989), 26–35; J. Brook and J.L. Kohen, *The Parramatta Native Institution and the Black Town* (Sydney, 1991), 227.

56. For instance, where Asian men were banned from the Australian Workers' Union, and Aboriginal membership was tenuous, Maoris were unconditionally included (Ward, *Australian Legend,* 122); and where nationalist journalism vilified Aboriginal culture, Maori "traditional" activities were reported with interest. See for instance, "Some Quaint Maori Customs," *Lone Hand,* 14 February 1920, 35.

57. A. Castles, *An Australian Legal History* (Sydney, 1982), 515–42.
58. *HRA* I, xviii, 379.
59. See, for instance, *Jorgen Jorgenson and the Aborigines of Van Diemen's Land*, ed. N.J.B. Plomley (Hobart, 1991), 47, 51.
60. B. Bridges, "The Extension of English Law to the Aborigines for Offences Committed *Inter Se*, 1829–1842," *JRAHS* 59, no. 4 (1973): 244–49.
61. NSW LC V&P, 1824–37, pt. 2, Report of Wellington Valley Mission, 1833, 164; NSW LC V&P, 1843, Report of Wellington Valley Mission, 1841, 483–84.
62. For example, *BPP*, Report from the Select Committee on Aborigines, 1836, I, i, 202–3 (Rev. W. Yate); 515–16 (Rev. J. Beecham); *HRA* I, xxvi, 225–26 (Grey to Fitzroy, 11 February 1848).
63. C.M.H. Clark, *History of Australia*, vol. 3 (Melbourne, 1973), 42–61.
64. P.M. Cunningham, *Two Years in New South Wales* (London, 1827), 46.
65. *Sydney Herald*, 19 Sept. 1838; *Historical Records of Victoria* (*HRV*) IIb, 695, 698, 712; *BPP*, Select Committee on Aborigines, 1836, 487–89 (Rev. W. Watson).
66. A. MacSween, "Some Lawson Letters, 1819–1824," *JRAHS* 50, no. 2 (1964): 239; Gunson, *Threlkeld*, 49.
67. Gunson, *Threlkeld*, 49, 66, 78, 186, 307.
68. Reece, *Aborigines*, 75–77, 81–102.
69. E. Brenchley, "The Enlightenment in Australia: Attitudes of Alexander Berry towards Aboriginals," (BA Honors Thesis, Macquarie University, 1982), 18, 59–60, 94; V. Rae-Ellis, *Black Robinson* (Melbourne, 1988), 131.
70. *HRV* IIa, 84–85, 107, 115, 117, 141; IIb, 574, 610.
71. M. Daunton and R. Halpern, "Introduction," in *Empire and Others*, ed. M. Daunton and R. Halpern (London, 1999), 13.
72. See, for example, P. McGonigal, "The Role of Law in the Foundation and Settlement of New South Wales prior to 1828," (LLM Thesis, University of Sydney, 1976) (execution of "Daniel"); E. Mumewa and D. Fesl, *Conned* (St. Lucia, 1993), 60–61.
73. R. Moran, *Massacre Myth* (Perth, 1998); K. Windschuttle, *The Fabrication of Aboriginal History* (Sydney, 2002).

Chapter 4

"PIGMENTIA"
Racial Fears and White Australia

Raymond Evans

There are times when it seems so useless, hopeless—all this prodigious preparation to kill or be killed. But after all it is based on the one truth, which is true beyond question ... that there are worse things than dying; that, if it comes to that pass, life which would have to be lived not as you think right, but as some Asiatic thinks right, is not worth living at all.

C.E.W. Bean, With the Flagship in the South

"White Australia" as both an ideal and a colonial project long preceded its implementation as national policy in 1901.[1] Its origins are obscure, yet arguably begin with the enfolding process of Aboriginal dispossession from 1788. Its first articulation, inter alia, was probably by James Stephen, permanent British Under Secretary for the Colonies, when he floated the intention in 1841 of preserving the Australian continent "as a place where the English race shall be spread from sea to sea unmixed by any lower caste."[2] The sense of ethnic exclusivity embodied in this hope seems unambiguous, as does its explicit Anglo thrust. Yet there have been certain suggestions that mid-nineteenth century colonial society exhibited a relatively more inclusive, liberal ethos in relation to racial issues; and that the situation became restrictively tougher in the century's closing decades.[3]

Notes for this section begin on page 120.

Although it is clear that exclusivist mobilizations by colonists grew more single-minded and encompassing as time passed, the impression of a tolerant, mid-century "golden era" should be resisted. Certainly a concerted trawling of newspaper files has uncovered statements to the effect that "Englishmen are ever ready to receive foreigners as brethren with open arms"[4]; but cheek-by-jowl with these, one can also discover press columns, as early as 1851, declaiming against Chinese migrants as "filthy-eating" and "beastly strangers," swarming into the colonies and introducing "disastrous and debasing practices."[5] The latter assertions appear more representative of the prevailing colonial mood. Outcries against the introduction of Melanesian and Indian bonded laborers begin in New South Wales during the 1840s, and reverberate in concert with anti-convict transportation campaigns. A correspondent to the Sydney *Weekly Dispatch* thundered in 1847:

> Our firm resolve is this—Let any hell-born squatter kidnap or import Coolies or Cannibals, the result will be
> 1st   That ships will blaze
> 2nd   That houses shall blaze
> 3rd   That [pastoral] stations shall be laid desolate ...
> I challenge any squatter to import and introduce Cannibals and Coolies. Try it.[6]

Anti-Asian disturbances begin in 1851, preceding the large Chinese influxes onto Australian goldfields by several years; while those influxes themselves would be met by waves of rioting in Victoria and New South Wales that mark the 1850s and 1860s off as perhaps Australia's severest decades of race conflict.[7] Between 1855 and 1877, consequently, Victoria, South Australia, New South Wales, and Queensland would all introduce proscriptive, discriminatory legislation against Chinese migrants. By 1888, a pan-colonial nexus to end Chinese immigration to Australia was securely in place.[8]

At the same time, on the frontiers of white settlement, the mid-century decades from 1840 to 1870 encompass a dramatic retreat from the Exeter Hall-driven, humanitarian thrust of Aboriginal relations policies in the 1830s; an increasingly destructive deployment of Native Mounted Police against indigenes; the local circumvention by pastoralists of British attempts to impose dual rights to land usage for colonists and Aborigines alike; and a general hardening of white attitudes towards Aboriginal peoples as both "subhuman" and predestined towards "extinction."[9] Finally, the substantial military role played by the Australian colonies in the

New Zealand Maori Wars of the 1860s encouraged a mid-century flowering of anti-Maori rhetoric that would actually diminish with time, as Maoris were later quarantined from the exclusionary campaigns being waged by the 1880s and 1890s against Melanesians, Indians, Malays, Afghans, Chinese, and Japanese.[10] These spirited and often violent forays to oust non-European minorities, however numerically minute, may be visualized as "the heat lightning that portends a gathering storm," as, in delineating the character of the new Australian nation, the legislative and administrative hands of the Commonwealth fell heavily upon virtually all "nonwhites" from 1901.[11]

Another difficult problem for historians studying the White Australia Policy is that it was never enunciated as a bounded official package of procedures. Its contours are elusive and controversial. Arguably, it can be suggested that its effective domain spreads far beyond the racially restrictive migration regime embodied in the *Immigration Restriction Act* of December 1901. For it also incorporated legislation with the power to deport those of certain ethnicity *(Pacific Island Labourers Act 1901)*; to deny naturalization and citizenship rights to others *(Naturalization Act 1903)*; and to withhold the vote *(Franchise Act 1902)*. Beginning with the *Invalid and Old Age Pensions Act* and *Maternity Allowance Act,* both of 1912, health and welfare rights were also systematically denied to any "Aboriginal native of Asia, Africa or the Pacific, excepting New Zealand"; while, throughout the various states of the Commonwealth, racial discrimination was incorporated into rafts of legislation dealing with employment opportunities, working conditions, land ownership, and mining licenses.[12] In Queensland alone there were more than thirty such Acts targeting occupational choice, most of which embodied a notoriously bogus "dictation test," applied selectively to resident non-Europeans to ensure their ineligibility in the same way as it was utilized under the *Immigration Restriction Act* to deny "nonwhites" entry into Australia.[13]

Arguably, too, well into the years of World War One, "White Australia" was also the clarion call driving the fledgling defense policies of the new Commonwealth. Even though, by 1901, "almost the entire Asian region was under direct colonial rule or subject to western imperialist hegemony," the fear of some form of Asian military invasion burgeoned. Pre-Federation alarm over China's demographic immensity gave way in the early twentieth century to an increasingly feverish focus upon Japan, the only genuinely independent nation remaining in Asia, even though Japan's territorial ambitions were directed against China and Korea rather than southward. Potential Asian anger over the White Australia Policy was ironically converted into a cause for boosting that Policy further, by adding the necessity, as Senator George Pearce commented, of "rifles to back it up."[14]

From a fringe minority of political alarmists in the late nineteenth century, "Yellow Peril" advocates and "Pacific race war" forecasters grew numerically in the space of a decade to dominate Australian parliamentary thought, almost without dissent. Fears and forecasts were transmuted into material force by a five-fold increase in defense spending before World War One; the establishment of an Australian Navy between 1911 and 1913; the unique introduction in a modern, English-speaking nation of compulsory military training for its male white youth from 1909; as well as an officer-training college at Duntroon and an embryo flying school at Port Phillip in 1914.[15] All such developments were constituted to secure "Anglo-Saxon dominance in the Pacific"; and to this project, the power of the United States was enjoined, when in its visiting naval capacity as the Great White Fleet ("sixteen battleships painted white and yellow") it was tumultuously welcomed into Sydney and Melbourne in 1908 by larger and more enthusiastic crowds than those that had celebrated Federation in 1901.[16]

During the nineteenth century, the Australian colonies had been replete with war alarms and invasion scares, directed against not only Asia but also various "enemies of the Empire"—France, Russia, and Germany. The military historian Robert Hyslop identified almost two hundred of such scares among Australian colonials between 1788 and 1901, accelerating in their profusion during the later nineteenth century.[17] Yet potent as these were for the evolution of public opinion and policy, they invariably addressed a phantom threat. Not so the internal struggle to attain white dominance and security, however, as political theorist Anthony Burke comments of early New South Wales:

> [T]he colony's first strategic threats and its first attempts to arrest a strategic control of space and economic resources, were made and encountered within a struggle for the nation's interior—in a simultaneously material, economic and ontological sense. Aboriginal peoples could never be allowed to inhabit (or disrupt) that interior, in the form of the juridical and psychological unity of the state, its hold on the soil, or its economic progress.[18]

Although many White Australians have obdurately packaged the story of their colonial settlement within a myth of peaceful penetration, the reality is otherwise. The foundation years of convict

settlement and white incursion into Aboriginal lands were thoroughly military in nature. Violent skirmishes, sorties, and massacres became commonplace, escalating in their vehemence as the
century advanced, migration increased, and western weapons technology expanded. Aboriginal resistance fighters were met first by
regular British garrisons and then by the more furtive and successful strategy of mounted "flying columns"—border police, roving
parties and punitive bands of settler vigilantes mounted on horseback, culminating in the formation of Native Mounted Police
forces. Thus, a combination of European "irregulars" and co-opted
Aboriginal troopers, operating as cavalry and/or mounted infantry,
fighting from the saddle or on foot with increasingly sophisticated
repeating rifles, outmaneuvered and outgunned Aboriginal defenders, resisting on foot with spears, clubs, and firebrands.

Casualty rates were high and arguably, in certain times and
contexts, genocidal. The historian David Day, writing in 1996,
disputes the often-quoted professional guess of 20,000 Aborigines
killed as straining "credulity to its limits." "A more reasonable,
even conservative 'guestimate' would be somewhat more than
50,000 Aborigines killed during 150 years of sporadic conflict,"
he concludes.[19] Additionally, two to three thousand colonists had
perished as, in hundreds of separate incidents, thousands more on
both sides were injured and massive damage done to European
property and Aboriginal lifeways. As in most historical incidences
of war and conquest, vastly more indigenes died from introduced
European diseases, sometimes unavoidably spread, sometimes
knowingly inflicted.

The impact of the overall invasion catastrophe upon the character of the White Australia policy is difficult to overestimate. In
the heart of the nation's secret history, a massive human culling had
occurred. From a pre-contact high point of over one million Aboriginal peoples, numbers had crumbled to only 60,000 by 1888
and possibly as low as 31,000 by 1911.[20] To begin with, the
fortress of white denial, constructed from the late nineteenth century to surround this tragedy, was buttressed with projections of
white unease in a debatably won continent. The European "title
deed" to Australia was quite insecure, argued the ailing radical
journalist Francis Adams in the Brisbane *Boomerang* of 1888.[21] Its
tenure and ownership entitlement, based upon forcible seizure, was
feeble and unconvincing. Just as Robert Wolter's Chinese invasion
scenario for California in 1882 compared the Europeans' routing
of the Red Indian with their own coming displacement by the
"alien Mongolian," so too contemporary speculation in Australia

worried that "rampant 'Asia' might 'Aboriginalise' the Australian people."[22] As David Walker asserts:

> [T]he invocation of an Asian future required Australians to consider what dispossession might mean. ... The Aborigines were commonly depicted as a timorous, unprepared people who had been displaced and humiliated by the more powerful and determined British. Would the newly awakened East brush aside white Australia's small city-based populations with the same contemptuous ease?[23]

Thus, although reference to the Aboriginal predicament figured only sparingly in the parliamentary debates that framed the passage of the *Immigration Restriction Act,* an anxiety (at times verging on paranoia) that the faltering folk memory of their displacement invoked seemed ever-present. It would be most dramatically conjured by future wartime Prime Minister William Morris Hughes at the inauguration of the national capital, Canberra, in March 1913 when he candidly observed that Australia and the United States were two nations "destined to have our own way from the beginning"—for they had "killed everybody to get it!" As testament, he observed how this "first historic event *[sic]* in the history of the Commonwealth" was unfolding "without the slightest trace of that race we have banished from the face of the earth"— that is, the Aboriginal people. "We should not be too proud lest we should, too, in time disappear," he intoned: "We must take steps to safeguard the foothold we now have."[24]

Such stunning verbal juggernauts were rare; but an adjunct to the White Australia project also involved administratively deciding upon what was to become of the depleted Aboriginal survivors of white dispossession. Even though they had not been entirely "banished from the face of the earth," the landscape of most white Australian minds (and probably consciences) had already been cleared of them by the belief that they were, in any case, "a doomed race," decreed by Western science to "vanish," whatever remedies the settlers might now attempt.[25] As Attorney General Alfred Deakin sanctimoniously intoned during the White Australia debates, he hoped that the "dying race ... in their last hours" would be able "to recognise, not simply the justice, but the generosity of the treatment which the white race, who are dispossessing them and entering into their heritage are according them."[26]

Talk of justice and generosity, however, was merely ideological bunting, behind which a further exclusionary drama was unraveling. During 1897, Federation Conventions in the south-eastern colonies were ratifying a draft constitution for the future Com-

monwealth, while in London colonial premiers, gathered to celebrate Queen Victoria's Jubilee, were receiving from Joseph Chamberlain, the Secretary of State for the Colonies, a migration formula
for effecting racial exclusion that the British Empire could live with,
in the form of the Natal Dictation Test.[27] At the same time, in
Queensland, the colony that had hosted Australia's most violent
frontier excesses, an experiment was underway that would transform Aboriginal policy throughout the nation in the twentieth century. Beginning in February, fringe-dwelling Aboriginal people,
subsisting upon the outskirts of various urban centers were being
removed, usually under police escort, to a central holding area on
Fraser Island in Harvey Bay, southern Queensland. By December,
when legislation to ratify the expulsions retrospectively was passed
*(The Aboriginal Protection and Restriction of the Sale of Opium
Act)*, Aborigines from ten widely scattered areas were sequestered
upon an isolated, swampy region of that island; and, by Federation
in 1901, people from some thirty-five separate localities had been
forcibly removed there.[28]

Prior to this, Aboriginal survivors of the various frontier clearances had been subjected to a wide range of micro- and mezzo-seg-
regative restrictions: in schools, hospitals, and public entertainment
venues, and upon public transport; as well as having their movements curtailed by curfews, police supervision, and the imposition
of restricted occupational and residential settings.[29] The state
enforcement of macro-segregation in 1897 superseded and concentrated these processes towards the potential outcome of geographic
banishment and confinement. Viewed from one perspective, it was
a logical endpoint of the preceding frontier land clearances—what
germs, lead, or poison had not dispatched, the colonial state would
now sequester. From another angle, segregative intervention operated as a sanitary "mopping-up" exercise. Aborigines who were fit
and gainfully employed by white pastoralists, farmers, and others
were passed over, while those conceived as hygienic or moral dangers were targeted. Calls by white settlers for Aboriginal removals
bear eloquent testimony to this. Petitions emphasize their troublesome and "dangerous" nature. Sometimes a contagion threat to
Europeans from sick Aborigines, variously described as "stinking
wretches," "almost rotten with VD," "a menace to peace and
health", or "polluting water" is the hallmark of the complaint. In
other appeals, the Aborigines' "alarming immorality," "propensity
for thieving," affronting white women, or "walking about town
without trousers" is the highlight, attesting to a fin-de-siècle emphasis upon public order, sexual panic, and bourgeois respectability.[30]

The Fraser Island experiment, located at Bogimbah Creek, ended tragically after a seven-year trial period with a vast deathrate among the Aboriginal inmates from disease, malnutrition, and neglect. In short, it formed a local genocide module. Yet its processes—interventionist, authoritarian, and pitiless—were to shadow Aboriginal lives in Queensland for most of the twentieth century, as a wide range of restrictive reserve and mission enclaves were established state-wide "under the Act." In 1905, Western Australia adopted much of the Queensland model of "native affairs" under its *Aborigines Act,* with the Northern Territory and South Australia following suit in 1910 and 1911 respectively. Again in 1918, in the Northern Territory (by then under Commonwealth control), the *Aboriginal Ordinance* was passed, embodying, as in Queensland, "a policy of segregation and control under the guise of protection, implemented through restrictions on Aboriginal employment, mobility and family and personal matters."[31] These four political zones contained most of the Aboriginal people remaining in Australia in the early twentieth century.

It is a convention of mainstream Australian historiography to present contact history and the Aborigines' subsequent fate as discretely apart from the story of migration restriction and the preoccupations of external defense. But these are, in reality, all interlocking parts of the one story—the single-minded drive to create in Australia a mono-racial continental community, via the processes of displacement, exclusion, deportation, and segregation, targeted against nonwhite indigenes, outsiders or incomers, viewed comprehensively as an unwanted, tainted mélange of alien "others." Its ideological underpinnings tell us as much about white self-perceptions and self-serving policies as they do about the beliefs, attitudes, and plans of Westerners concerning "nonwhite" peoples. For racist perceptions gaze simultaneously and provocatively in opposite but complementary directions, boosting the human worth of the signifiers at the same time as they denigrate the human worth of the signified.

White Australians at the time of Federation present, through their self-perceptions and forecasts, a fascinating study. On the one hand, they appear as an acutely insecure, uncertain people, haunted by their past, uneasy about their present, and worried about their future. From their past they carried a "Botany Bay complex"—a sense of convict "taint" that they struggled to disavow—as well as a less publicized disquiet about their multiple acts of violent dispossession.[32] Their settler history too was slim, and it bequeathed to their present a sense of almost paper-thin cultural worth; in comparison with the historical depth and contemporary splendor of the British Empire. Many nursed a debilitating sense of cultural inferiority—a pronounced "cultural cringe"—as it would come to be termed; and, in relation to their future prospects, their forecasts were often gloomy and dystopian.[33] In her study of 211 examples of Western futuristic writing at the turn of the twentieth century, the cultural historian Nan Albinski concludes that in Britain and America, optimistic forecasts outweighed pessimistic ones. Not so in Australia, however, where dystopian themes of warfare, internal revolt, national downfall, and, in particular, race invasion outnumber positive, utopian themes by a ratio of two to one.[34]

On the other hand, however, such anxieties were often overlaid by a vaunting, boastful sense of superior worth. If white Australian origins were shifty, then its British heritage was empowering. And if Britons, by virtue of technological and cultural achievements as well as their global span, were undoubtedly great, then white Australians, by virtue of their bloodstock, enhanced by the advantages of a superior soil and environment, were destined to be even greater. The Australian, it was trumpeted, represented "a new Southern race"—the Coming Twentieth Century Man.[35] The Sydney *Bulletin*, as Walker comments, "wanted the declining energies of the Anglo-Saxon race to flower again in the unique conditions of a new continent."[36] Australia could become "the home of a brilliant new race, a new breed of adventurers." As the poet Bernard O'Dowd lavishly described them—"a coming Sun-God's race."[37] Yet securing Australia as the site for the "full flowering of the Caucasian mind" depended vitally upon manning its foreshores against inferior racial incursions, preserving race purity, and maintaining vigilance against race suicide or racial decay. "A racially 'clean,' radiant Australia" as nativist journalist Randolph Bedford depicted it was predicated upon "Anglo-Saxon Rule in the Southern Hemisphere."[38] Its downfall lay in such impediments as Asian engulfment, rampant miscegenation, birthrate-decline, or tropical enervation.

Thus racial bravado and racial angst, though logically opposed, operated viscerally together to produce a profound sense of racial purpose. Australia had been handed "a sacred duty, the breeding of a pure race in a clean continent," Bedford intoned in 1911.[39] Furthermore, it was reiterated, Australia was "the last part of the world in which the higher races can live and increase freely, for the higher civilization."[40] Thus as "the last great continental space available for race renewal," its glorious destiny was to serve, the *Bulletin* predicted, as "the model white tropical State of the globe and of history."[41] It was, concluded novelist Arthur Adams, former editor of the defense-boosting *Lone Hand* "the largest-sized and the most tremendous experiment ever tried in race building."[42]

It is therefore reductionist and erroneous to view the White Australia Policy as simply a narrowly economic strategy for maintaining working class conditions, rights, and wages. For decades, Australian historians exoneratively presented it as such, ignoring the point that this strategy rested upon the invalid racist assumption that nonwhites were, as workers, intrinsically worth less than white ones, as well as being irrevocably servile. Furthermore, the thesis is belied by the fact that contemporaries often themselves asserted that economic rivalries were of less concern in the race struggle than eugenic, sexual, moral, or hygienic ones.[43] Labour journalist Robert Ross wrote in the Brisbane *Worker* in April 1899 that economic competition with "Chinese, Kanakas and Japanese" was of little consideration, compared with the dangers they posed to "public health and morals." The "economic loss of cheap labour" was endurable, editorialized the Charters Towers *Eagle*, co-owned by Queensland Labor premier Anderson Dawson, compared with "the irreparable damage ... done by ... intercourse with these bestially vital semi-savages, these diseased and immoral low-caste brutes ... Protest with a pick-handle if necessary."[44] In Federal Parliament, the Labor leader, John Watson, agreed that although "industrial" concerns existed, "the larger, more important question" involved racial purity: "The question is whether we would desire our sisters and brothers to be married into any of these races to which we object."[45]

Yet it is vital to understand that economic considerations did lie close to the heart of racist campaigns, though not in the manner that such campaigns alleged. At the core of anti-Aboriginal antipathies lay the economic struggle for land and the utilization, for social growth and material profit, of its resources. The colonists' land-taking campaign was one of strict monopolization, as no prior land-holding rights whatever were recognized and no treaties were signed with the indigenes. It was the maintenance of this resource monopoly in white hands that drove the exclusionary campaigns to oust Chinese and other nonwhite miners from colonial mineral rushes. In a racially and ethnically segmented labor market, non-European workers had only been tolerated insofar as they provided opportunities for super-exploitation by Australian capitalists, invariably in occupations that white workers usually avoided (e.g., plantation field labor; deep-sea diving; droving and rouseabout work on distant cattle stations). Yet the severe depression years of the 1890s and the massive unemployment figures they created popularized the Australian working class cry that all jobs, more or less, should become an exclusive white preserve, converting this campaign by Federation into an irresistible tide.[46]

This entitlement to economic monopoly and exclusivity was expressed within a context of ideas appealing to "race and blood in [their] most raw and virulent form, excluding from the blood-bond all those with pigmented skin."[47] When the Federation compact is examined comprehensively, paying attention not only to what non-whites were denied but also to what whites were given, the stark contrasts of negation and privilege are arrestingly revealed. From 1901, white Australians were granted citizenship rights—particularly political and social ones—substantially in advance of citizens in other contemporary Western nations. The reforms introduced prior to World War One, especially in the areas of social welfare, workplace relations and conditions, as well as health and education, brought Australia briefly to the global forefront as a "social laboratory" for the enhancement of national efficiency and citizen well-being.[48] Average living standards approached the best in the world, and the infant mortality rate was around half of Great Britain's at the time. In the *Franchise Act* of 1902, white Australian women received the vote nationally, decades ahead of their British counterparts, and were enfranchised in all States by 1908. "In no other Western nation at the time," writes historian Bob Birrell, "was there any parallel to the extent of this reform."[49]

Yet whereas white men and women were being afforded access to leading world standards of social well-being as Australian citizens, nonwhites were being denied residency or citizenship rights more stringently than in other Western nations. Not only had Aboriginal peoples uniquely been refused all land rights, the segregative processes introduced from 1897 also removed from them all semblance of civil, social, and political rights as well. The same legislation that enfranchised white women in 1902 effectively disenfranchised them.[50]

As an ideological adjunct to all of this, even in respectable intellectual, political and scientific quarters, Aborigines were regarded as either one of the lowest races of humanity or distinctly subhuman.[51] Early in 1901, the Assistant Private Secretary to the Duke and Duchess of Cornwall and York noted in his diary, after the Royal Party had witnessed a Brisbane Aboriginal display in their honor: "Of the fauna ... we notice one genus which was conspicuous by its absence in Melbourne—the aboriginal population ... on this occasion ... used for decorative purposes."[52] In the Federal Parliament, the American-born Labor politician King O'Malley argued, without objection, that there was no scientific evidence to link Aborigines with humanity whatsoever.[53] Such utter denial of normal human claims, British philosopher Jonathan Glover points out, strips its target group of respect and dignity and maximizes their vulnerability to barbaric treatment, which may then escalate towards genocidal outcomes without normal restraints.[54]

In the same way as Aborigines were being socially and institutionally afforded one of the worst deals of any indigenous minority in a white settler society, so too nonwhite migrants were being denied residency by what was then, administratively speaking, the most stringent migration legislation based upon race in the world.[55] Australia was the first modern nation to place a blanket ban upon the entrance of virtually all non-European communities.[56] Its utilization of the Natal "dictation test" to do so was more severely applied than the same formula was in Natal itself. There the intending migrant was merely expected to fill out a simple form in any European language. In the Australian case, a fifty-word dictation test was stipulated and applied "with such stringency as to place its sufficiency beyond doubt."[57] As Prime Minister Alfred Deakin admitted in November 1905, "the object of applying the language test is not to allow persons to enter the Commonwealth, but to keep them out."[58] Several years earlier, the Commonwealth Government began deporting Melanesians who had worked within the northern New South Wales and Queensland sugar industries. Thus 7,262 Pacific Islanders were "repatriated" under the *Pacific Island Labourers Act* of 1901 between 1904 and 1914, amid often tragic scenes of separation. Some 2,000 or so remained behind under various exemptions or by stealth, but these were mostly males who were expected to "dwindle in number and die out."[59]

Thus, whereas white citizenship rights in the 1900s were at the forefront of global democratic reform, nonwhites conversely were having their rights withheld and denied more comprehensively than in any other white-settler society. It is a challenge to find another contemporary Western example for a contrast in social and political treatment that is so stark. What it represents is, arguably, the quintessence of racism: the bountiful over-privileging of one group and the bleakest disadvantaging of others upon the stated criteria of their ethnicity or race.[60]

The ideological underpinnings for these institutional prescriptions were provided by a range of thinkers and writers—intellectuals, novelists, poets, dramatists, cartoonists, journalists, and filmmakers. This cultural industry of producers impacted upon different areas of Australian consciousness—the academic, the scientific, the imaginative, and the popular—to create a composite, exonerative, almost hermetically-sealed world view of racial hierarchy and contestation. Much of this revolved around themes of the infection, pollution, degradation, and inundation that would inevitably accompany race mixing, contrasted against images of the health, purity, decency, and breathing space that reflected the advantages of a racially unitary society.

Foremost among these writers was Charles Henry Pearson, former Oxford Don and leading Australian progressive, whose gloomily prophetic *National Life and Character: A Forecast* captured the Western imagination "from St. Petersburg to Tennessee" in 1893.[61] Pearson believed that although "evanescent races" like Aborigines and Melanesians were passing inevitably into extinction, other "lower" races "who should be looked down on as servile" were poised to expand demographically "into what were now colonial areas."[62] "No-one, of course, assumes that the Aryan race ... can stamp out or starve out all their rivals on the face of the earth," he reasoned:

> It is self-evident that the Chinese, the Japanese, the Hindoos ... and the African Negro are too numerous and too sturdy to be extirpated.

Extermination, too, was no longer "sanctified by religion." Thus, the "black and yellow races," in a "continuous zone" circling the globe, would eventually "swamp" the "higher races of man," humiliating their pride and undermining "the highest forms of civilization."[63]

Pearson's study met with a mixed reception, yet the debate that ensued never questioned the inevitability of a massive racial struggle. Rather, it revolved around whether the Aryan or Nordic peoples possessed sufficient race-strength to win it. In Britain, William Gladstone lauded the book; while in Germany, Kaiser Wilhelm coined the term "yellow peril" upon reading it.[64] In the United States, the historian Henry Adams agreed with Pearson that "the dark races are gaining on us," but Theodore Roosevelt in a twenty-six-page article in the *Sewanee Review* refused to accept such melancholy predictions. Just as insurrectionary movements by African-Americans or Indian outbreaks on the frontier were met by greater suppression from whites acting "as if they were crusaders," he wrote to Pearson, so too "race war ... on a much bigger scale" would result in "inferior races" being mercilessly "exterminated or dispossessed bodily by the superior."[65]

Yet both Pearson and Roosevelt agreed that a White Australia would have a vital role to play in the coming struggle. It was "the last Aryan homeland, a land where white races could breed, regenerate and marshal their forces."[66] After Pearson's book was republished in the United States in 1913, it strongly influenced the nativist and anti-Semite Madison Grant in the writing of *The Passing of the Great Race* (1916). While cosmopolitan migration was gradually converting America into "a freak show of 'racial hybrids,'" Grant wrote, Australia and New Zealand remained as "important 'communities of pure Nordic blood,' which could be called upon to help regenerate the once great Nordic race." In the 1920s, a politically ambitious Adolf Hitler wrote to Grant that he regarded *The Passing of the Great Race* as "his Bible."[67]

Elite opinion in Australia was equally stimulated by Pearson's work. Alfred Deakin carried a copy of his friend and mentor's *National Life and Character* into the parliamentary chamber and quoted from it during the *Immigration Restriction Act* debates.[68] Yet probably of more impact socially was the stream of cruder and more sensational invasion scare literature, appearing in novel form and increasingly pervading the popular journalism of such periodicals as the *Boomerang*, the *Bulletin*, the *Worker, The Call*, and the *Lone Hand* from the late 1880s. Invasion narratives begin in Australia with such titles as George Rankin's *The Invasion* (1877) and the anonymous *The Battle of the Yarra* (1883), both depicting a Russian military attack on major colonial cities.[69] From this point, however, the "Slavic peril" fades and nonwhites become the major aggressors. In 1885, *The Fall of Melbourne* described a French attack, but the focus of outrage was upon the Arab horsemen utilized in the assault.[70] By 1888, the anonymous novella *The Battle of Mordialloc or How We Lost Australia* and the racist labor polemicist William Lane's serialized novel *White or Yellow? A Story of the Race War of A.D. 1908* featured a rampant Chinese foe.[71]

What is striking in retrospect is the violent candor of these accounts, their "paranoid, masculine" construction and the sense of vulnerability they display towards Asian marauders, pouring in like "masses of mindless automata," as numerous and indistinguishable as "the grains of yellow sand on the sea shore."[72] In *The Yellow Wave: A Romance of the Asiatic Invasion of Australia* (1895), New South Wales parliamentarian Kenneth Mackay's magnum opus of racial outrage, a Russian-backed "Mongol" assault upon Queensland results in inconceivable mayhem. For instance, through the gaze of his hero-protagonist, Hatten, Mackay describes the scene at Hughenden railway station, as panic-stricken whites attempt to escape from the Chinese army, thus:

For a moment his eyes took in the whole fearful scene: the screaming women pushed back by frantic men only to fall on the bloody bayonets of their foes: the children tossed from point to point in wonton devilry. Then his ears caught the shriek of the whistle and the fearful cries of those who were being ground to death between the wheels and the bloody pavement, and over all rang the yells of the Mongols as they thrust their bayonets into the passing trucks and dragged back struggling women by their hair from the still open doors ...

Tearing his eyes away from the awful picture, Hatten saw a crowd of Mongols and coolies running towards them. "Thank God, here are some devils to kill!" he muttered grimly as he drew his sabre.[73]

Such hyperbolic escalation of horror upon horror was stock-in-trade of invasion scare literature. So too was the solution to engulfment provided by the literary device of bands of Aryan brotherhood, hardened and skilled by bush living to resist Asian encroachment, after effete city-dwellers, untrustworthy politicians, or fickle white women had encouraged such intrusions. Dick Hatten's mounted marauders in *The Yellow Wave*, the White League in Lane's *White or Yellow?*, and the White Guard in C.H. Kirmess's *Australian Crisis (1908–1909)* are all "men from the borderlands of civilization who provide the manly vigor necessary to enforce the nation's boundaries."[74] "A finer body of men never took the field to do battle for Aryan ideals," Kirmess comments:

It was composed of the sturdy sons of the Australian bush ... they felt that nothing less was expected of them than the extermination of the invaders.[75]

Racial commentary, from Pearson's high-flown speculations to the most lurid of the colonies' and new nation's muck-raking journalism, was replete with talk of racial antipathy, race war, and extermination. Particularly in the radical and labour press, the invective was furious and unrestrained. For instance, a columnist in the *Worker,* H.J. McCooey, fulminated in August 1900:

I'm ineffably disgusted with the kanaka [i.e. Melanesian] and regard his introduction to Queensland as pre-eminently the worst of the innumerable curses (not excepting leprosy and bubonic plague) that ever befell Australia. The black-hided, filthy, foul-smelling ... hypocrite crowns his infamy by being a servile cringling ... In Heaven's name when are we Australians going to arise as one man and wipe this odious, smelliferous species of human vermin from the face of this unfortunate country. [It] ... makes one yearn for a meat-ax to split him down with! ... If this state of things continue only a few short years longer blood will be spilt—black blood, the blood of the kanaka and all other colors.[76]

Such hysteria was fuelled by largely male anxieties over sexual violation, moral debasement, miscegenation, hybridity, and "mongrelization" that "race mixing," it was believed, must bring.[77] Regions of northern Australia were consistently referred to as "Mongrelia," "Leper-land," or "Piebald Land" due to their mixed -race populations.[78] Male protagonists in invasion scenarios declare that female companions or relatives must die at their hands rather than be ceded to intimacies with debased Asians or Blacks.[79] Bob Flynn, one of Lane's heroes in *White or Yellow?* states of his fiancée:

> Cissie can die as well. She is Australian too. And I'd sooner kill her with my own hands than have her live to raise a brood of coloured curs.[80]

White Australian "mentalities" therefore fixed disproportionately upon the necessity for racial purity and a "paranoid fear of the hybrid."[81] The *Bulletin* of May 1901 speculated that:

> if Australia is to be a country fit for our children ... we must KEEP THE BREED PURE. The half caste usually inherits the vices of both races and the virtues of neither. Do we want Australia to be a community of mongrels? ... Brutal whites fall as low as brutal Asiatics; but Asiatics have not white possibilities. Whatever our failings, we are the heirs of European civilization, and we cannot merge our nationality in a barbarism or in an alien civilization to which European ideals are incomprehensible. ... The vital thing is to stop the coming flood.[82]

Reiterating the primacy of eugenic over economic concerns, the journal editorialized several years later:

> Not the loss of a job, but the loss of racial purity is at the bottom of the demand for a White Australia. "So petty, so unnecessary," the perplexed Briton says. "So petty" to struggle against degeneration into a decadent race of half-breeds? "So unnecessary" to strive to cultivate a race which shall have pride of birth?[83]

The writings of Adams, Bedford, Pearson, Lane, Mackay, Kirmess, and a host of others—either fearfully or exultantly—play upon themes of purity of blood, race warfare, and sexuality similar to those expounded in European racial theorizing of this era. As the historian, George L. Mosse comments:

> Blood, war and sex form a triad which is constantly repeated in twentieth century racism ... Nationality and race focused on the male ideal-type. In the words of a Nazi journal, where Aryan man is the sun, all others are moon-people.[84]

In Australia, speculative writings on race similarly focus upon Aryan or Nordic manhood—muscular, dedicated, sun-blessed, and racially fit—as the purveyors of racial superiority and national excellence. Alfred Deakin in 1900 eulogized them as "a stalwart, sun-browned, rough-hewn race of adventurers and toilers engaged in conquering a continent."[85] Through determined struggle to keep the bloodlines unpolluted, this "blue-gold rosy race"—as Australian composer Percy Grainger dubbed Nordic peoples[86]—would create upon an isolated island continent a "pure race" society—a distinct biological community, extolling its excellence within a single, defensible geographic zone.[87] Reflecting Madison Grant, who in turn had paraphrased Charles Pearson's writings of a generation earlier, Harvard's Lothrop Stoddard predicted in 1921 that Australia was destined to play a crucial part in the coming race struggle by acting as "a racial blood-donor ... to help maintain an unpolluted stream of 'clean, virile, genius-bearing blood'."[88]

How little removed were these ideas, we might ask, from those of that array of racist thinkers, pamphleteers, and polemicists who laid the intellectual foundations in the early twentieth century for the emergence of National Socialism in Nazi Germany: those occult-fringe race theorists, Jorg Lanz von Liebenfels and Guido von List, for instance, whose pamphlets influenced a young Adolf Hitler in Vienna from 1908; and who both wrote of racial mixing and "mongrelization" as "the crime of crimes," positing "the creation of a racially pure state which would battle to the death the inferior races";[89] or composer Richard Wagner, obsessed by "the Aryan blood strain";[90] or Otto Weininger, who "constructed an Aryan ideal-type on the basis of sex and race" in his influential *Sex and Character* (1903);[91] or Houston Stuart Chamberlain, who wrote mystically of the triumph of an "Aryan race-soul" in "a race war—a fight to the finish between two principles of life."[92] Such *völkisch* thought, clearly, seems barely distinguishable from White Australian mindsets at Federation and beyond, transfixed as they were upon race war, race purity, racial cleanliness, and the creation of a pristine racial state, quarantined invitingly "for Whites only" in the sparkling Pacific.[93]

In his illuminating cultural history, *Anxious Nation*, David Walker gently chides any who would look judgmentally upon those white Australians of the 1900s, uncritically championing such concepts, when he writes:

> Australians today, backed by a larger, more widely traveled and better-educated population, should hesitate before accusing the four million

insecurely established and predominantly Anglo-Celtic settlers of 1900 of developing an irrational fear of Asia and especially so at a time when the basic structures of national life were still in their infancy. The idea that Australia was a continent under threat seems all too rational for those who saw the world as a place in which the strong preyed upon and eliminated the weak.[94]

Such empathetic awareness is crucial. Yet it is equally important that historical empathy should not simply follow along Eurocentric lines. The anxious outlook of a small, isolated white population activated policies that impacted detrimentally upon other contemporary populations of different cultures and darker pigmentations. Under this aegis, Aborigines were decimated, exiled, and segregated; Pacific Islanders were exploited and then deported en masse back into societies that had long ago closed behind them; and unwary "non-European" migrants were refused entry, confined, and repatriated. Those "nonwhites" resident in Australia, meanwhile, led parlous, impoverished lives through the imposition of racially discriminatory policies. Thus, in the study of White Australia, it is important to examine relations of power as well as the interplay of sentiment. Anglo-Celtic Australia's sense of superiority and entitlement, undercut by its profound insecurities, carried an enduring legacy of trauma and suffering into the lives of others. The pretensions and insecurities were largely illusory; the sufferings imposed were real. In establishing the integrity of its own "place in the sun," White Australia, across much of the twentieth century, was to cast a long, dark, uneven shadow.

Notes

1. My thanks to Andrew Bonnell, Greg Picker, and Jahara Rhiannon for help with this chapter.
2. A. Markus, *Australian Race Relations, 1788–1993* (Sydney, 1994), 59–60.
3. A. Markus, *Fear and Hatred: Purifying Australia and California, 1850–1901* (Sydney, 1979), 18–21; Markus, *Race Relations*, 60–61.
4. Markus, *Fear and Hatred*, 20.
5. R. Evans, "Keeping Australia Clean White" in *A People's History of Australia since 1788*, vol. 1: *A Most Valuable Acquisition* ed. V. Burgmann and J. Lee (Melbourne, 1988), 178.
6. *Weekly Despatch*, 7 August 1847.

7. K. Cronin, *Colonial Casualties: Chinese in Early Victoria* (Melbourne, 1982), 41–62; C.A. Price, *The Great White Walls Are Built: Restrictive Immigration to North America and Australia, 1836–1888* (Canberra, 1974), 82–85.

8. R. Evans, "The White Australia Policy" in *The Australian People: An Encyclopedia of the Nation, its People and their Origins,* ed. J. Jupp (Cambridge, 2001), 45.

9. H. Reynolds, *Aboriginal Sovereignty: Reflections on Race, State and Nation* (Sydney, 1996), passim; R. Evans et al., *Race Relations in Colonial Queensland: A History of Exclusion, Exploitation and Extermination* (Brisbane, 1993), 67–84.

10. G. Hopkins-Weise, "The Australian Colonies and the Maori Wars," unpublished MS.; J. Donegan and R. Evans, "Running Amok: The Normanton Race Riots of 1888 and the Genesis of White Australia," *Journal of Australian Studies* 71 (2001): 83–98, 164–66; Markus, *Fear and Hatred,* 200–233.

11. R. Senechal, *The Sociogenesis of a Race Riot: Springfield, Illinois, in 1908* (Urbana, 1990), 199.

12. D. Dutton, "A British Outpost in the Pacific" in *Facing North: A Century of Australian Engagement with Asia,* ed. D. Goldsworthy (Melbourne, 2001), 38–39.

13. Evans, "The White Australia Policy," 48.

14. Dutton, "A British Outpost," 39–43.

15. D. Walker, *Anxious Nation: Australia and the Rise of Asia, 1850–1939* (Brisbane, 1999), 108; Dutton, "A British Outpost," 44–45.

16. N. Meaney, *The Search for Security in the Pacific, 1901–14* (Sydney, 1976), 163–75; Walker, *Anxious Nation,* 93–97.

17. R. Hyslop, "War Scares in Australia in the 19th Century," *The Victorian Historical Journal* 47, no. 1 (1976): 23–44.

18. A. Burke, *In Fear of Security: Australia's Invasion Anxiety* (Sydney, 2001), 9–10.

19. D. Day, *Claiming a Continent: A New History of Australia* (Sydney, 1996), 130.

20. Day, *Claiming a Continent,* 130; C. Tatz, *Genocide in Australia* (Canberra, 1999), 9.

21. F. Adams, *The Boomerang,* 1 February 1888, quoted in Walker, *Anxious Nation,* 40–41.

22. R. Wolter, *A Short and Truthful History of the Taking of California and Oregon by the Chinese in the Year AD 1899* (San Francisco, 1882), quoted in ibid., 101.

23. Walker, *Anxious Nation,* 7–9.

24. *Sydney Morning Herald,* 13 March 1913, quoted in Meaney, *Search for Security,* 241.

25. R. Evans, *Fighting Words: Writing About Race* (Brisbane, 1999), 124–25; R. McGregor, *Imagined Destinies: Aboriginal Australians and the Doomed Race Theory, 1880–1939* (Melbourne, 1997), 48–59.

26. R. Hall, *Black Armband Days* (Sydney, 1998), 136.

27. R. Huttenback, *Racism and Empire: White Settlers and Colored Immigrants in British Self-Governing Colonies, 1830–1910* (Ithaca, 1976), 162–64.

28. Evans, *Fighting Words,* 123–46.

29. Evans et al., *Race Relations in Colonial Queensland,* 118–21.

30. Evans, *Fighting Words,* 136–37.

31. A. Haebich, *Broken Circles: Fragmenting Indigenous Families, 1800–2000* (Fremantle, 2000) 18, 197–99.
32. Noel McLachlan, *Waiting For the Revolution: A History of Australian Nationalism* (Melbourne, 1989), 5–7.
33. A.A. Phillips, *The Australian Tradition: Studies in a Colonial Culture* (Melbourne, 1958).
34. N. Albinski, "Visions of the Nineties," *Journal of Australian Studies* No. 20 (1987): 12–22.
35. J. Webb and A. Enstice, *Aliens and Savages: Fiction, Politics and Prejudice in Australia* (Sydney, 1998), 12.
36. Walker, *Anxious Nation*, 91.
37. W. Murdoch, ed., *The Poems of Bernard O'Dowd* (Melbourne, 1944) 35; V. Kennedy and N. Palmer, *Bernard O'Dowd* (Melbourne, 1954), 105–6, quoted in Walker, *Anxious Nation*, 91.
38. R. Bedford, "White, Yellow or Brown," *Lone Hand*, 1 July 1911; Walker, *Anxious Nation*, 73.
39. Bedford, "White, Yellow or Brown."
40. J. Tregenza, *Professor of Democracy, The Life of Charles Henry Pearson, 1830–1894: Oxford Don and Australian Radical* (Melbourne, 1968), 234.
41. R. Laurie, "'Not a Matter of Taste but a Healthy Racial Instinct'– Race Relations in Australia in the 1920s: Racial Ideology and the Popular Press" (MA Thesis, Griffith University 1989), 51.
42. A. Adams, *The Australians* (London, 1920), 30, quoted in Walker, *Anxious Nation*, 150.
43. Evans et al., *Race Relations*, 300, 359–62.
44. R. Evans, "The Politics of Leprosy: Race, Disease and the Rise of Labor" in *The World's First Labor Government*, ed. J. Scott and K. Saunders (Brisbane, 2001), 41.
45. Hall, *Black Armband*, 139.
46. Evans, "Keeping Australia Clean White," 172–73.
47. D. Cole, "The Crimson Thread of Kinship: Ethnic Ideas in Australia, 1870–1914," *Historical Studies of Australia and New Zealand* 14, no. 56 (1971): 511.
48. J. Roe, ed., *Social Policy in Australia: Some Perspectives, 1901–1975* (Sydney, 1977), 3–23.
49. B. Birrell, *Federation: The Secret Story* (Sydney, 2001), 25–27, 222–57.
50. R. Evans, "White Citizenship: Nationhood and Race at Federation," *Memories of the Queensland Museum, Cultural Heritage Series* 2 (2002): 6–7.
51. Evans, et al., *Race Relations*, 74–76.
52. D.M. Wallace, *The Web of Empire: A Diary of the Imperial Tour of their Royal Highnesses, The Duke and Duchess of Cornwall and York in 1901* (London, 1908), 45.
53. J. La Nauze, *The Making of the Australian Constitution* (Melbourne, 1972), 326.
54. J. Glover, *Humanity: A Moral History of the Twentieth Century* (London, 2001), 337–39.
55. Markus, *Australian Race Relations*, 110–15.
56. K. Rivett, ed., *Australia and the Non-White Migrant* (Melbourne, 1975), 14–22; Huttenback, *Racism*, 279–316.
57. Huttenback, *Racism*, 153; Evans, "White Australia," 46–47.
58. Huttenback, *Racism*, 310.

59. C. Moore, "Australia in the World: Nation, Community and Identity," in R. Evans et al., *1901 – Our Future's Past: Documenting Australia's Federation* (Sydney, 1997), 217-20.
60. Evans, "White Citizenship," 8.
61. C.H. Pearson, *National Life and Character: A Forecast* (London, 1894); Tregenza, *Professor*, 238.
62. Pearson, *National Life*, 84-85; Hall, *Black Armband*, 115, 119; Tregenza, *Professor*, 227-29.
63. Hall, *Black Armband*, 117; Walker, *Anxious Nation*, 45; Pearson, *National Life*, 37.
64. Tregenza, *Professor*, 231; Walker, *Anxious Nation*, 3.
65. Tregenza, *Professor*, 232.
66. Walker, *Anxious Nation*, 46.
67. Tregenza, *Professor*, 233; Walker, *Anxious Nation*, 182; E. Black, "Hitler's Race Hate Debt to America," *Guardian Weekly*, 12-18 February 2004, 24.
68. Tregenza, *Professor*, 230; Hall, *Black Armband*, 142-43.
69. Robert Dixon, *Writing the Colonial Adventure: Gender, Race, and Nation in Anglo-Australian Popular Fiction, 1875-1914* (Cambridge, 1995), 136; Walker, *Anxious Nation*, 136.
70. Webb and Enstice, *Aliens*, 144.
71. Anon., *The Battle of Mordialloc, or How We Lost Australia* (Melbourne, 1988); Walker, *Anxious Nation*, 41-44; Webb and Enstice, *Aliens*, 150-59; Evans, *Fighting Words*, 79-82.
72. Dixon, *Writing the Colonial Adventure*, 135; Walker, *Anxious Nation*, 36, 101.
73. K. Mackay, *The Yellow Wave: A Romance of the Asiatic Invasion of Australia* (London, 1895), 274.
74. Dixon, *Writing the Colonial Adventure*, 146-47; Webb and Enstice, *Aliens*, 123, 153, 165; Walker, *Anxious Nation*, 121.
75. Dixon, *Writing the Colonial Adventure*, 147.
76. H.J. McCooey, "McCooey and the Kanakas," *The Worker*, 25 August 1900.
77. Evans et al., *Race Relations*, 293-99, 355-64.
78. Hall, *Black Armband*, 32, 71-72; Evans, "Politics of Leprosy," 40-48.
79. H. McQueen, *A New Britannia: An Argument Concerning the Social Origins of Australian Radicalism and Nationalism* (Harmondsworth, 1970), 112; Webb and Enstice, *Aliens*, 141; Walker, *Anxious Nation*, 102-3, 129.
80. Walker, *Anxious Nation*, 103.
81. Dixon, *Writing the Colonial Adventure*, 139.
82. *The Bulletin*, 25 May 1901.
83. *The Bulletin*, 12 May 1904.
84. G.L. Mosse, *Toward the Final Solution: A History of European Racism* (London, 1978), 101, 110.
85. Tregenza, *Professor*, 239.
86. Walker, *Anxious Nation*, 182.
87. Evans, "White Australia," 49.
88. Walker, *Anxious Nation*, 170.
89. Mosse, *Toward the Final Solution*, 98-100; R.G.L. Waite, *The Psychopathic God: Adolf Hitler* (New York, 1977), 91-93; See also N. Goodrick-Clarke, *The Occult Root of Nazism – Secret Aryan Cults and their Influence on Nazi Ideology: The Ariosophists of Austria and Germany, 1890-1935* (New York, 1992) and B. Hanann, *Hitler's Vienna: A Dictator's Apprenticeship* (New York, 1999).

90. Mosse, *Toward the Final Solution*, 101–5; Waite, *Psychopathic God*, 99–113.
91. Mosse, *Toward the Final Solution*, 108–11.
92. Mosse, *Toward the Final Solution*, 105–8. For a summation of this thought, see G.L. Mosse, *The Crisis of German Ideology: Intellectual Origins of the Third Reich* (London, 1966).
93. Webb and Enstice, *Aliens*, 157–58; Hall, *Black Armband*, 129.
94. Walker, *Anxious Nation*, 231–32.

– Section II –

FRONTIER VIOLENCE

Chapter 5

GENOCIDE IN TASMANIA?

Henry Reynolds

Tasmania, or Van Diemen's Land as it was called until 1855, was so remote from anywhere that mattered. It was the antipodes; an ideal place to get rid of criminals forever and to dispatch unwanted characters in novels and stage plays. Its isolation and dramatic scenery suggested that it could be the setting for violent and unusual behavior. Its role for the first fifty years of British settlement as a large open prison for tens of thousands of convicts confirmed its evil reputation. It seemed to be the sort of place where genocide could occur. Much of the literature on the subject suggests strongly that it did.

A True Genocide

In his best-selling history of the convict system entitled *The Fatal Shore*, the celebrated art critic Robert Hughes declared that the Tasmanian Aborigines were "shot like kangaroos and poisoned like dogs." What happened to them was "the only true genocide in English colonial history."[1] A few years later, Australia's premier economic historian, N.G. Butlin, argued that in the late 1820s and early 1830s genocide "directed and organized by the government substantially eliminated the indigenous population."[2]

Few international genocide scholars would have faulted these condign judgments. Many of them have named Tasmania in their lists of legitimate case studies, although their usually slight grasp of island history might have counseled caution. Raphael Lemkin considered Tasmania as the site of one of the world's clear cases of genocide,[3] and in one of the first major works on the subject, published in 1981, Leo Kuper referred to the "systematic annihilation" of Aborigines in Tasmania.[4] In 1986, Ward Churchill, seeking to craft a functional definition of genocide, referred to those cases in which the intention was to destroy the whole population of specific groups "such as Tasmania and Cambodia."[5] The prominent biologist Jared Diamond contributed his opinion in 1985, contrasting those situations where people have died en masse as a result of callous actions not designed specifically to kill them, with well-planned genocides including that of the Tasmanians, the Armenians by the Turks during the First World War, and the Jews by the Nazis during the Second.[6] A similar assessment and comparison was made by Florence Mazian in her 1990 book *Why Genocide?* The crime, she concluded, was not always as blatantly practiced as it was with the Nazis, nor with as much ruthlessness as in the case of the British in Tasmania or the Dutch in South Africa.[7]

In an article in the *New York Review of Books* in 1995, Bernard Bailyn contrasted the Tasmanian experience with the Indian wars of the early United States, declaring that in the British colony the goal of policy was extermination.[8] Three years later D.C. Watt, the Professor of International History at the London School of Economics, contributed his perception of Tasmanian history to the ongoing, informal international colloquium in a review in the *Times Literary Supplement*. The two greatest pre-twentieth-century examples of racial elimination, he declared, were the destruction of the Indians of Patagonia and the "aboriginal inhabitants of Tasmania."[9] In a follow-up letter, he set out to define what he meant by genocide and in the process referred again to Tasmanian history. He wrote:

> What distinguishes murder from manslaughter and accidental death is the motive of the killer. This is equally true of genocide—in two ways. For an individual German to kill a Jew or a Gypsy, just because of the race of the victim, is an act of genocide. But to accuse the machinery of State under which such killings took place as an act of policy requires proof that this is their aim. There is ample proof that this was the aim of the "Final Solution." Jews were to be killed because they were not human, just as the Tasmanian Aborigines were hunted to death for the same reason.[10]

It is an impressive lineup of authorities, and others supportive of the same position could be cited. If the near unanimity of critical opinion is to be questioned, several things need to be done. Some assessment must be made of why the Tasmanian experience seems to be so well known and then, at greater length, the detail of the history needs to be carefully examined.

A Distinctive History

The relations between Tasmanian Aborigines and British settlers were meticulously recorded by the administration of Governor George Arthur, which was relatively large and efficient and inured to meticulous paperwork, as might be expected in a prison colony. Many of those records were published in Britain in a series of House of Commons papers between 1829 and 1837 and reached a much wider audience than was the case with colonies like Queensland, where frontier conflict occurred in an era of internal self-government. The Aboriginal population of the Island was small, perhaps five thousand at the time of first contact with the Europeans, and the last so-called "full blood" Aborigine, Truganini, died amidst widespread public recognition in 1876. At the time—and for many years after—the Tasmanians were thought to be a unique race of people. So Truganini's death attracted far greater attention than the deaths of many old men and women in similar circumstances all over southeastern Australia in the last quarter of the nineteenth century. They could be seen as "the last of their tribe" but not "the last of the race."

Another feature of Tasmanian history, pertinent to the present discussion, is that by Australian standards the island is quite small and in the period in question only about a quarter of the land was occupied by the settlers. The colonial government both aspired to maintain firm control over the island and its largely convict workforce, and was able to do so. Relations with the Aborigines were principally controlled by the government, something that became less and less common on mainland Australia as the settlers and their flocks and herds struck out in a vast and usually lawless hinterland. Events that were recorded in Tasmania usually passed unnoticed in the rest of Australia. Governor Arthur's administration, therefore, has been judged on the basis of its own well-kept records.

But what of the history itself? It will be necessary to consider a number of issues—the Governor himself, the problems that confronted him, the attitudes of the politically influential free settlers, and the policies of the imperial government. All the major events usually considered when referring to genocide—the warfare in the bush, the Black Line and the establishment of settlement on Flinders Island in Bass Strait—all took place during Arthur's administration during the years 1824 to 1836. So what of the man himself?

The Governor Arrives

Arthur arrived in Tasmania in 1824 predisposed to humanitarian policies towards the Aborigines. He was an evangelical Christian, an acquaintance of leading antislavery activists with a reputation for defending the rights of indigenous people. He had attempted to free enslaved Indians when he was Superintendent of British Honduras between 1814 and 1822, in the face of strong opposition from the local oligarchy.[11]

Arthur's first public statements about the Aborigines were aglow with good intentions. A proclamation was sent to all the magistrates with instructions to give it wide publicity, "enjoining the utmost attention to the full intent and meaning of it." It was an important document and deserves to be quoted in full:

> Whereas it has been represented to his Honour the Lieutenant-Governor, that several Settlers and others are in the habit of maliciously and wantonly firing at, injuring and destroying the defenceless Natives and Aborigines of this island.
>
> And whereas it is commanded by His Majesty's Government, and strictly enjoined by his Excellency the Governor-in-Chief, that the Natives of the Colony and its dependencies shall be considered under British government and protection.
>
> These instructions render it no less the duty than it is the disposition of his Honour the Lieutenant-Governor to support and encourage all measures which may tend to conciliate and civilize the Natives of the island, and to forbid and prevent, and, when perpetrated, to punish, any ill-treatment towards them.
>
> The Natives of this island being under the protection of the same laws which protect the settlers; every violation of those laws in the persons or property of the natives shall be visited with the same punishment as though committed on the person or property of any settler. His Honour the Lieutenant-Governor therefore declares his determination thus publicly, that if after the promulgation of this proclamation, any person or persons shall be charged with firing at, killing, or committing any act of outrage or aggression on the native people, they shall be prosecuted for the same before the Supreme Court.
>
> All magistrates and peace officers, and other of His Majesty's subjects in this colony, are hereby strictly required to observe and enforce the provisions of this proclamation, and to make them known more

especially to stock-keepers in their several districts, enjoining them not only to avoid all aggression, but to exercise the utmost forbearance towards the Aborigines, treating them on all occasions with the utmost kindness and compassion.[12]

But Arthur was constrained in many ways despite his authoritarian power and administrative zeal. The Colonial Office was a long way away, but he had to follow policy guidelines and attempt to trim his sails to shifting winds from London. He had to maintain the penal system, assist the expansion of the economy, and keep as many of the powerful free settlers on side as his other objectives allowed. Like other early Australian governors, he had to deal with quite contradictory Imperial policies relating to the Aborigines. They were theoretically British subjects, to be treated with amity and kindness, but there was no recognition of either their sovereignty or their land tenure. The Colonial Office counseled peace, but sanctioned the use of military force and the declaration of martial law when the tribes resisted the incursion of the settlers and their flocks and herds.

The instructions given to both Governor Arthur and Governor Darling of New South Wales (1825–1831) illustrated the problem. The governors were encouraged to promote religion and education among the indigenous subjects, and to:

> Especially take care to protect them in their persons, and in the full enjoyment of their possessions, and that you do by all lawful means prevent and restrain all violence and injustice which may in any manner be practised against them.[13]

But the realities of frontier life and the endemic conflict on the outer fringes of settlement called forth much harsher instructions concerning the "manner in which the Native Inhabitants" were to be treated when making "hostile incursions for the purpose of plunder." Darling and Arthur were informed by the Secretary of State, Lord Bathurst, in 1825:

> [Y]ou will understand it to be your duty, when such disturbances cannot be prevented or allayed by less vigorous measure, to oppose force by force, and to repel such Aggressions in the same manner, as if they proceeded from the subjects of an accredited State.[14]

Arthur was handed these instructions in person by Darling, who landed in Hobart in November 1825 on his way from England to New South Wales. Arthur clearly saw them as an authoritative guide to action, and read them to his officials at critical moments during the campaign against the Aborigines, to which we must now turn.

War in the Bush

Unfortunately for the Governor, benign intentions could not survive the brutal realities of life in the bush as the settlers took up the best land. Aboriginal resistance intensified from the spring of 1826. Having put down the wave of bushranging during 1825 and 1826, Arthur was faced with a far more dangerous guerrilla war that raged across the so-called settled districts in the river valleys of central Tasmania between Hobart and Launceston. In November 1826, he issued a public statement condemning the series of outrages that had been "perpetrated by the Aborigines of the colony" and setting out six conditions that could justify settler violence or, as it was phrased, action, "in the execution of the justifiable measures to which they may have recourse." They were:

1st. If it should be apparent that there is a determination on the part of one or more of the native tribes to attack, rob, or murder the white inhabitants generally, any person may arm, and, joining themselves to the military, drive them by force to a safe distance, treating them as open enemies.

2nd. If they are found actually attempting to commit a felony, they may be resisted by any person in like manner.

3rd. Where they appear assembled in unusual numbers, or with unusual arms, or, although neither be unusual, if they evidently indicate such intention of employing force as is calculated to excite fear, for the purpose of doing harm, short of felony, to the persons and property of any one, they may be treated as rioters, and resisted if they persist in their attempt.

4th. If they be found merely assembled for such purpose, the neighbours and soldiers armed may, with a peace officer or magistrate, endeavour to apprehend them; and if resisted, use force.

5th. If any of the Natives have actually committed felonies, the magistrates should make such diligent inquiries as may lead to certainty of the persons of the principals, or any of them (whether this consists in knowledge of their names, or any particular marks or characteristics by which these persons may be distinguished), and issue warrants for the apprehension of such principals. The officer executing a warrant may take to his assistance such persons as he may think necessary; and if the offenders cannot otherwise be taken, the officer and his assistants will be justified in resorting to force, both against the principals and any others who may, by any acts of violence, or even of intimidation, endeavour to prevent the arrest of the principals.

6th. When a felony has been committed, any person who witnesses it may immediately raise his neighbours and pursue the felons, and the pursuers may justify the use of all such means as a constable might use. If they overtake the parties, they should bid or signify to them to surrender; if they resist, or attempt to resist, the persons pursuing may use such force as is necessary; and if the pursued fly, and cannot otherwise be taken, the pursuers may then use similar means.[15]

To investigate further the policy and intention of the colonial government, it is necessary to examine the three steps taken between April 1828 and October 1830 that aimed to intensify the pressure on the Aborigines: firstly, the decision in April 1828 to demand that the tribes "remove" from, or be driven out of, the settled districts; secondly, the declaration of martial law later that year over the same area to enforce the earlier injunction; and thirdly, the organization of the Black Line in October and November 1830, when 2,200 well-armed men tramped across Tasmania from north to south making for the peninsulas in the far southeastern corner.

Decisive Measures

The Governor was convinced by the end of 1827 that he had to do something, given the number of settlers killed in the spring of that year. In a dispatch to the Colonial Office in January 1828, he explained that the insurgent tribes had "latterly assumed so formidable an appearance, and perpetrated such repeated outrages," that he had been "pressingly called upon by the settlers" to free them from these "troublesome assailants." He still hoped to achieve a negotiated settlement that would allow him to provide the Aborigines with "some remote corner of the island, which would be strictly reserved for them." He realized that such a plan faced great difficulties, but believed that it was:

but justice, to make the attempt, for notwithstanding the clamour and urgent appeals which are now made to me for the adoption of harsh measures, I cannot divest myself of the consideration that all aggression originated with the white inhabitants, and that therefore much ought to be endured in return before the blacks are treated as an open and accredited enemy of the government.[16]

His language was tougher in internal memos written to his officials. In one, dated 30 November 1827, he wrote that it had become a "measure of indispensable necessity" to drive the "black savages" from the settled districts, and he indicated that more troops would be sent into the country to enforce the policy.[17]

But the problem still perplexed him. There were no easy answers "unless a war of extirpation is sanctioned," which nothing, he emphasized, other than "absolute and inescapable necessity will induce me to authorize or sanction."[18]

When writing to his superiors in Downing Street of his decision to force the tribes out of the settled districts, Arthur spent more time explaining his motivation. He referred to the "painful necessity" of adopting some "decided measures to suppress the increasing spirit of resentment" manifested by the "coloured inhabitants of this colony" and the difficulty he felt in determining the measures it would be most advisable to pursue. He continued:

> It gives me great concern to state that the animosity of these wretched people is in no degree abated, and that their increasing predatory incursions upon the settled districts, which are accompanied with the perpetration of frequent barbarous murders, have overcome my reluctance to proceed to any coercive measures against them.
>
> The subject has undergone several days' anxious deliberation and discussion in the Executive Council; and having examined all such persons as are competent to give information, I am at length convinced of the absolute necessity of separating the Aborigines altogether from the white inhabitants, and of removing the former entirely from the settled districts, until their habits shall become more civilized.
>
> The proclamation which I have issued, with the unanimous advice of the Council, fully explains the origin and progress of the unhappy feeling which exists, and the measures directed for the purpose of averting its further fatal consequences.
>
> It is a subject most painful under every consideration; we are undoubtedly the first aggressors, and the desperate characters amongst the prisoner population, who have from time to time absconded into the woods, have no doubt committed the greatest outrages upon the natives, and these ignorant beings, incapable of discrimination, are now filled with enmity and revenge against the whole body of white inhabitants. It is perhaps at this time in vain to trace the cause of the evil which exists; my duty is plainly to remove its effects; and there does not appear any practicable method of accomplishing this measure, short of entirely prohibiting the Aborigines from entering the settled districts, a measure, however, which you may be assured shall be carried into execution without the least avoidable harshness.
>
> I have long indulged the expectation that kindness and forbearance would have brought about something like a reconciliation, but the repeated murders which have been committed have so greatly inflamed the passions of the settlers, that petitions and complaints have been presented from every part of the Colony, and the feeling of resentment now runs so high that further forbearance would be totally indefensible.
>
> My intention was to have given up one district to the Natives from their favourite haunts, but, beyond this, there is no occasion that His

Majesty's Government should be apprehensive, and I do not even yet resign all hope of pacifying those angry feelings which are at present but too evident on both sides.

His Majesty's instructions command that every measure shall be resorted to for the instruction and civilization of the Natives; may I therefore beg to be honoured with your commands, whether, in promoting this attempt, I am to consider myself authorized to afford some temporary relief in food and clothing, which I fear affords the only prospect of quieting a tribe of savages, and may perhaps be absolutely necessary for their support beyond the settled districts.[19]

Martial Law

The policy adopted in April 1828 had little effect. Violence escalated during the year, leading to the decision to declare martial law over the settled district. This, the solicitor-general explained, placed the Aborigines "within the prescribed limits on the footing of open enemies of the king, in state of actual warfare against him."[20]

In justifying this decision, Arthur referred to the instructions he had received from Darling in 1825 concerning the need to "oppose force by force." He read them to his Executive Council on the eve of the decision to declare martial law, and he quoted them again in his next dispatch to the Colonial Office.[21] The council agreed that the measure was the only means of affording to the King's subjects protection against the atrocities of the Aborigines. It was hoped that it would be the means of "putting a speedy stop, without much bloodshed, to the lawless warfare" between the Aborigines and the frontier settlers.[22] The council felt the "deepest regret in advising these measures," but members found themselves compelled to do so by "an inevitable necessity." "To inspire them with terror," the councilors declared, "will be found the only effectual means of security for the future."[23]

At the same time, the Government spoke of restraint. In his official proclamation, Arthur urged on his troops and their civilian auxiliaries in a measured response, declaring:

> But I do, nevertheless, hereby strictly order, enjoin and command, that the actual use of arms be in no case resorted to if the Natives can by other means be induced or compelled to retire into the places and portions of this island hereinbefore excepted from the operation of martial law; that bloodshed be checked as much as possible; that any tribes which may surrender themselves up shall be treated with every degree of humanity; and that defenceless women and children be invariably spared.[24]

The Proclamation was a public document prepared for a wide audience, and may therefore be viewed with suspicion. However, similar sentiments were expressed in the confidential instruction delivered to the military officers out in the field, who were told:

> You will understand that the Government puts forth its strength on this occasion by no means whatever with a view of seeking the destruction of the Aborigines; on the contrary, it is hoped, by energetic and decisive measures, and by punishing the leaders in the atrocities which have been perpetrated, that an end will be put to that lawless and cruel warfare which is now carrying on, and which must terminate in the annihilation of the Natives.

The officers were urged to see the necessity of conducting all proceedings in their respective districts "with moderation and humanity" and to provide the Governor with weekly reports of operations that should include "very *minutely*" what steps had been taken for "opening a conciliatory intercourse and arrangements with the tribes."[25]

The Black Line

But neither terror nor conciliatory intercourse had much effect on the level of violence. Thus the third and most dramatic policy decision was made: to organize a massive armed sweep across the center of the colony. The Black Line has loomed so large in accounts of Tasmanian genocide that it is necessary to consider it in detail.

In the relevant dispatch to London, Arthur emphasized that his primary objective was not to kill the Aborigines, despite the size of the well-armed force. It was the government's earnest desire "rather to capture the savages, and place them in some situation of security, where they can neither receive nor inflict injury, than destroy their lives." The Line was designed to capture them with the least possible destruction of life, or to drive them into Tasman's Peninsula.[26]

Given the humanitarian views of the Colonial Office, it is only to be expected that Arthur would emphasize in his dispatch his earnest desire to avoid bloodshed. A better idea of the Governor's intentions emerges from the private correspondence sent out to magistrates and military officers. In a Government Order issued on 9 September, Burnett observed that should success crown the contemplated measure, the Governor earnestly enjoined that "the utmost tenderness and humanity may be manifested towards whatever Natives may be captured."[27] On 22 September when the final plans were being put in place, Arthur took the opportunity:

of again enjoining the whole community to bear in mind, that the object in view is not to injure or destroy the unhappy savages, against whom these movements will be directed, but to capture and raise them in the scale of civilization, by placing them under the immediate control of a competent establishment, from whence they will not have it in their power to escape and where they themselves will no longer be subject to the miseries of perpetual warfare, or to the privations which the extension of the settlement would progressively entail upon them ... [28]

More detail about policy emerges from the letters sent out to minor officials and prominent settlers in the countryside. The police magistrate at Oatlands, Thomas Anstey, wrote to James Cox of *Clarendon* that while "one or two parties may fall in with the Tribes and destroy some of them," experience had shown that nothing but "a very large force is capable of *capturing* them which is the object everyone must have most at heart."[29] Burnett wrote to the police magistrate in Launceston, urging that nothing should be omitted "to cultivate and promote a good understanding with the friendly natives" north of the town who were to be by no means injured or in any way molested.[30] In a memo to the magistrates, Burnett explained that much depended on them to enjoin the assigned servants to be orderly and sober and to point out to them that the object "is to capture and civilize the wretched Natives and not destroy them."[31]

There is little in Arthur's public or private papers to indicate what he was thinking as the Line moved slowly towards the southeast corner of the Colony. The closest we can come to an understanding of the personal views of the senior officials is in the letters written by Burnett to Arthur while he was out in the field directing operations between 15 October and 16 November 1830. A striking aspect of the letters is Burnett's obvious anxiety about the outcome of the Line and his uncertainty as to how it would turn out.

"We are all here as you may well believe," he wrote on 15 October, "on the tip-toe for intelligence from the 'seat of war.'" As nothing of an authentic nature had reached Hobart, "a thousand vague and absurd reports of Battles fought and captives taken" were in circulation.[32] The surface anxiety reflected a deep ambivalence on Burnett's part about the policy, the outcome of the Line, or the Aborigines themselves, who were described variously in letters written only days apart as "unfortunate natives," "poor savages," and "wretched savages." His swirling emotions were expressed in a letter of 18 October, thanking Arthur for the first news from the Line and the proceedings:

against the unfortunate Natives, for whom I must ever entertain sentiments of commiseration, and hence arises the intense interest which I take
in the present operations, the final result I look for with such anxiety. [33]

On 20 October, Burnett referred to "this most desirable object,"
the reconciliation of "these unfortunate beings" to the white inhabitants.[34] Three days later he told Arthur that in Hobart every person "seems to take the greatest interest in, and to feel the most
intense anxiety respecting the present operation." He was happy to
hear that there was still a good chance of succeeding in the capture
of the most "daring and inveterate Tribe of Aborigines."[35] By 4
November, he observed that the feeling of intense interest and anxiety for the success of the venture was universal in the town. It had
naturally increased as the operation appeared to be drawing to a
crisis. "God grant," he wrote, "that your Excellency's exertions to
drive these unfortunate and wretched beings" across Tasmania
would prove successful and that "you may be spared the lamenta-
ble and dreadful alternative of putting them to death."[36]

A week later, Burnett reported a conversation with the tough
frontiersman John Batman, who shocked the studious civil servant
with stories about the boldness of the Aborigines and their knowledge of firearms. The exchange led him to fear that:

> Should the present enterprise fail ... the only chance of safety or secu-
> rity to the Settlers and white inhabitants will arise from the utter exter-
> mination of these wretched savages, who I greatly fear in that event will
> be hunted on all sides like Wild Beasts; an alternative too dreadful to be
> thought of, and whence I pray God in his infinite Mercy, will yet inter-
> pose to avert. But self-preservation is certainly the first law of nature,
> and it can hardly be expected that the white inhabitants of this Fine
> Island will much longer patiently endure the aggressions of these unfor-
> tunate people, and in that case, they will most assuredly be picked off
> one by one, till not a vestige of the original owners and occupiers of the
> Soil will remain.[37]

Arthur himself reflected on the outcome of the Line on 20
November when success appeared unlikely. He wrote to Sir George
Murray that:

> I cannot ... say that I am sanguine of success, since their cunning and
> intelligence are remarkable; but whilst I hope His Majesty's Government
> will approve of my having omitted no measures which had a tendency to
> conciliate, or to preserve the lives of these savages, I am sure it will
> always be a matter of consolation to the Government of the Colony, and
> to its respectable inhabitants, that we have made every effort in our
> power to save the aboriginal race from being exterminated ... [38]

Whatever the real intentions of Arthur and his senior officials actually were, the Black Line failed to capture the Aborigines apart from an old man and a boy, despite the great expenditure of money and the full mobilization of the Colony's resources. But there is a need to look again at the attitude of the Colonial Office that had ultimate responsibility for what happened in the antipodes. Only then can we come closer to the question of genocide.

The Colonial Office Responds

When faced with the rising tempo of violence, the Colonial Office accepted Arthur's explanations and sanctioned his actions while continually counseling restraint. Responding in May 1828 to Arthur's desire to force the Aborigines away from the settled districts, Secretary of State Huskisson observed that it was difficult to conciliate and civilize "these unfortunate beings," while their "restless Character would seem to render it extremely difficult to confine them to any particular limits within the Colony." But Arthur was urged to proceed with caution "in the spirit of utmost kindness" in order to contain Aboriginal hostility.[39]

Nine months later, when responding to the Governor's proclamation declaring that the Aborigines should leave the settled district, Huskisson's successor, Sir George Murray, was supportive. He indicated that he appreciated the difficulty of convincing the Aborigines to "acknowledge any authority short of absolute power," particularly when they were "possessed with the idea which they appear to entertain in regard to their own rights over the country" in comparison with those of the colonists. But Arthur was cautioned about going too far, Murray writing:

> I cannot, however, omit to impress upon you my earnest desire that no unnecessary harshness may be exercised in order to confine the Coloured Inhabitants within the boundaries you have fixed.[40]

In August 1829, Murray approved, in retrospect, the declaration of martial law the previous November, but it was with "extreme regret" and the hope that the measure would both "secure the lives and properties of the settlers and benefit the Natives themselves."[41]

In November 1830, Murray refused to accept the suggestion made by the official Aborigines Committee that Aboriginal aggression proceeded from a "wanton and savage spirit inherent in them." With lofty disdain, he observed that in order to accept this opinion it would be necessary to establish that aggressions "had not begun with the new settlers."[42] Surveying the troubled relations between settlers and Aborigines, he wrote:

> Although it is greatly to be feared that much time and pains will be requisite to alter the footing upon which the British Settler and the Aborigines of the colony unfortunately stand towards one another, I cannot conclude this Dispatch without urging upon you, in the strongest manner, to continue to use your utmost endeavour to give to the intercourse between them a less hostile character than it now has; and to employ every means which kindness, humanity and justice can suggest, to reclaim the Natives from their original savage life, and render them sensible to the advantages which would ultimately result to themselves, and to their descendants, from the introduction amongst them of the religion and the civilization of those whom it must be difficult for them to regard at present in any other light than as formidable intruders. With this object in view, the utmost forbearance will be requisite on the part of the settlers, in every case in which a Native may fall in their way, and I hope you will be able by degrees, to prevail upon the settlers to believe that such a line of conduct, both on their own part, and on that of their assigned servants, will not only be the most proper and becoming, but will also prove, in the end, to be the most conducive to their interests and their security.[43]

In June 1831, when the failure of the Black Line became known in London, Viscount Goderich observed that Arthur's strategy had been well calculated to afford security to the colonists for their lives and property "with the least possible injury to the unhappy beings you were forced to treat as enemies." He complimented Arthur on his humanity "towards a race entitled by the wrongs which they have suffered to much forbearance, even while it was necessary to repel their attacks."[44]

The most compelling and relevant piece of evidence regarding the decline of the Aboriginal population was provided by Sir George Murray in his letter to Arthur in November 1830. He directed his attention to the main question at issue, writing:

> The great decrease which has of late years taken place in the amount of the aboriginal Population, renders it not unreasonable to apprehend that the whole race of these people may, at no distant period, become extinct. But with whatever feelings such an event may be looked forward to by those of the Settlers who have been sufferers by the Collisions which have taken place, it is impossible not to contemplate such a result of our occupation of the Island, as one very difficult to be reconciled with feelings of humanity or even with principles of justice and of sound policy: and the adoption of any line of conduct having for its avowed or for its secret object, the extinction of the native race, could not fail to leave an indelible stain upon the character of the British Government.[45]

This was an extraordinary dispatch. Was it an attempt to avoid responsibility for an impending disaster? Did the Colonial Office suspect that Arthur had sinister but hidden ambitions? Were officials in Downing Street informed by people returning from Tasmania? Were they referring to the attitudes of the colonists and warning Arthur against them?

The Extirpationists

The leading scholar of the history of Tasmanian Aborigines, N.J.B. Plomley, believed that in the 1820s most colonists were "extirpationists at heart," and there is no doubt that at the time, genocide was openly talked about—or rather what was termed extermination or extirpation.[46]

Many examples of these views could be adduced. William Barnes, a justice of the peace, landowner, and brewer, wrote to Governor Arthur in March 1830 expressing his alarm about continuing Aboriginal hostility. If acts of mutual vengeance did not cease, he remarked, "then the dreadful alternative only remains of a general extermination by some means or other."[47]

Rural landowner George Espie informed the official government committee set up to deal with the Aboriginal question that in his view the country must either belong to the Black or the White, and that he could see "no other remedy but their speedy capture or extermination."[48] Temple Pearson, another prominent settler, gave similar advice to the Colonial Secretary in June 1830, arguing that:

> Total extermination however severe the measure, I much fear will be the only means left to the Government to protect the Whites.[49]

The Director of the Van Diemen's Land Company, Edward Curr, added his voice to the brutal clamor, outlining what he saw as the dilemma faced by the government:

> If they [the settlers] do not abandon the Island [and will not] submit to see the white inhabitants murdered one after another ... they must undertake a war of extermination on principles of which many will be disposed to question ...

He believed the matter would end, "as all such matters have ended in other parts of the world, by the extermination of the weaker race" although he shuddered at the idea of "butchering the poor natives in the mass"; it was "dreadful to contemplate the necessity of exterminating the aboriginal tribes."[50]

The colonial newspapers regularly reported on conflict in the interior, and called at times for the destruction of the tribes. In 1826, after reporting several murders of frontier shepherds, the editor of the *Colonial Times* declared:

> We make no pompous display of Philanthropy—we say unequivocally, SELF DEFENCE IS THE FIRST LAW OF NATURE—THE GOVERNMENT MUST REMOVE THE NATIVES—IF NOT, THEY WILL BE HUNTED DOWN LIKE WILD BEASTS AND DESTROYED.[51]

In February 1830, the editor of the *Tasmanian* remarked that the Aborigines were displaying a determination to destroy all before them. "Extermination," he declared, "seems to be the only remedy."[52]

The *Independent* reported in September 1831 that following the spearing of a prominent settler, Captain Thomas, several correspondents had written in arguing that "nothing but a *war of extermination* now remains to be applied."[53] A fortnight later, the editor himself looked forward with foreboding to the return of spring and the prospect of renewed Aboriginal attacks. "Even their warmest advocates," he wrote:

> must, we fear, admit that unless something forthwith be done by the government, the end will be, horrible as the idea is, EXTERMINATION, as the only means of securing our settlers from their cruel and indiscriminate attacks.[54]

These views tell us little about the intentions or the policies of the Colonial government. But the private and the public came close together in a speech of Solicitor General Alfred Stephen, delivered to a large public meeting held in Hobart on the eve of the Black Line. Stephen declared that:

> as they have waged such a war upon the settlers, you are bound to put them down. I say that you are bound to do, in reference to the class of individuals who have been involuntarily sent here [the convicts], and compelled to be in the most advanced positions, where they are exposed to the hourly loss of their lives. I say, sir, [Mr. Stephens here spoke with much animation] that you are bound upon every principle of justice and humanity, to protect this particular class of individuals, and if you cannot do so without extermination, then I say boldly and broadly exterminate! I trust I have as much humanity as any man who hears me, but I declare openly, that if I was engaged in the pursuit of the blacks, and that I could not capture them, which I would endeavour to do by every

means in my power, I would fire upon them. ... I expose myself, I am aware, thereby to attack on the grounds of humanity, but I am satisfied that we are bound to afford all possible protection to those who are exposed to the attacks of the blacks, and therefore I am of the opinion—capture them if you can, but if you cannot, destroy them.[55]

Stephen insisted on several occasions that he spoke as a private citizen and not as a spokesman for government, yet he apparently showed no fear of censure or dismissal.

An Indelible Stain?

So what of Governor Arthur and his administration? Did it pursue policies with the avowed or secret objective of "the extinction of the native race"? Were the officials guilty of what we now call genocide—the intention to destroy the Tasmanian Aborigines as a people?

Arthur was a professional soldier. He believed he was engaged in warfare, in a war "of the most dreadful kind" that presented enormous difficulties to the government.[56] The Aborigines were elusive; they were experts in the bush who could attack isolated Europeans and disappear into the mountains before they could be pursued, making it impossible even to find any large body of tribesmen to attack and defeat. There were no forts to besiege, villages to attack, crops to burn, or wells to poison. Nor did there appear to be any chiefs or leaders with whom to negotiate. If Arthur and his military officers could not create conditions where they could employ their great superiority in both manpower and firepower to inflict a decisive defeat on the enemy, they would endeavor to drive them away from the contested territory. In many ways, Arthur's response to the Aboriginal insurgency was more measured and gradual than his ruthless and decisive crushing of the bushranging gangs that roamed the colony during 1825 and 1826.

How far was Arthur willing to go to defeat the enemy? Ideally, he would have sought his ends without bloodshed. He wrote many official instructions urging his subordinates to attempt to conciliate and persuade. However, there is no doubt he intended to use whatever force was required to crush the indigenous insurgency. In November 1827, he explained that he would not authorize "a war of extirpation" unless there was a situation of "absolute and inescapable necessity." So we know from his own words that Arthur had at least contemplated such a war—but did "absolute and inescapable necessity" ever confront him?

We must remember that a year after this statement, the Secretary of State sternly warned him that any plan that sought the extinction of the native race would leave an indelible stain on the British government (and, no doubt, on the record of the culpable official). The warning must have alerted Arthur to the growing strength of humanitarian ideas in Britain in the late 1820s and the need to take heed of them. He was an able and ambitious official who was keenly aware of the importance of maintaining his reputation in Downing Street. Even so, the Black Line could have ended in bloodshed. Presumably, Arthur was willing to accept that risk—although the very size of the operation was probably designed to overawe the Aborigines and thereby lessen the likelihood of conflict. Arthur may well have seen the situation in the same way as Burnett, who hoped the Line would drive the tribes across Tasmania and avoid direct confrontation.

In his own justification, Arthur argued that given the intensity of the conflict in the late 1820s and the deep hatred generated, the settlers would eventually wipe out the Aborigines of central Tasmania. He returned to the same argument when justifying the Black Line, which he said was launched to impose a peace, put down insurgency, and "save the Aboriginal race from being exterminated."[57]

Members of the executive council made similar observations on the eve of the Black Line. The relevant minute read:

> [The Council] hopes and believes that if a sufficient force can be thus collected, the expulsion of the Natives may be effected at the expense of little bloodshed; and even if it should cost more lives than the Council anticipates, it is a measure dictated not less by humanity than by necessity, since it is calculated to bring to a decisive issue a state of warfare which there seems no hope of ending by other means, and which, if much longer continued, the Council feels will become a war of annihilation.[58]

The official Aborigines Committee took the view that without Government action the colonists would "individually or in small bodies take violent steps against the Aborigines." It was an eventuality that committee members could not "contemplate the possibility *[sic]* without horror," but at the same time they were convinced that many colonists welcomed the prospect of a genocidal campaign.[59]

Whatever one makes of these justifications by the Governor and senior members of his administration, there is no doubt that, left to themselves, the settlers would have eventually wiped out the tribes of central Tasmania. By the late 1820s, they outnumbered the Aborigines by twenty to one, and rapidly expanding settlement was increasing the pressure on land and resources. By the time the Black Line advanced across the colony Aboriginal numbers were greatly reduced. One of the reasons for the spectacular failure of the Line—only two Aborigines were captured—was that there were so few people left. In 1831, when the remnant of the much-feared Big River and Oyster Bay tribes surrendered to the government negotiator, George Robinson, there were only twenty-six of them left—sixteen men, nine women and one child.

A distinctive feature of the Tasmanian experience was the central role played by the government, which appears to modern scholars to bring it within the range of systematic and well-planned genocides. But an often-overlooked aspect of Tasmanian history is that Arthur was always acutely aware of the fact that he governed a penal colony and that most of the workforce in the rural areas was made up of assigned servants still under sentence. He dreaded the prospect of armed convicts engaging in uncontrolled skirmishing with the Aborigines. He was unwilling to let the frontier shepherds and stockmen fight it out with their tribal adversaries: convicts with guns in their hands could easily cohere into bushranging gangs.

So if conflict was inevitable, it was essential to keep control of it and ensure that military officers, magistrates, and prominent settlers managed all local operations and continued "to enforce a due degree of subordination on the Convicts."[60] In a circular to his magistrates in November 1828, Arthur observed:

> You will, therefore, see the necessity of regulating all proceedings in your district, as far as possible, by principles of moderation and humanity; and you will perceive the advantage and propriety of consultation and frequent communication with all the magistrates and respectable inhabitants, so as to form a combined plan of operation, and to leave nothing that is avoidable in the hands of undirected convicts, or other unauthorized persons.[61]

Whatever is said about the Black Line, the fact is that it failed. It did not effect the removal of the tribes from central Tasmania; nor did it bring an end to conflict. But the events of 1828 to 1830 do provide material for a reconsideration of some of the main themes found in the contemporary literature on genocide and related phenomena.

The attempt, by various means, to sweep the settled districts clear of the resident Aboriginal tribes has similarities with the modern practice of forced removal of peoples and ethnic cleansing recently defined as "the deliberate removal from a certain territory

of an undesirable population distinguished by one or more characteristics such as ethnicity, religion, race, class, or sexual prefer-
ences."[62] But it is important to emphasize that the Line was only
directed against the tribes in the central districts and not those in
the northwest, northeast, west, and far south of the colony.

Was It Genocide?

What of genocide? Perhaps the most relevant area of study to pursue is the relationship between genocide and warfare. One problem
with much of the international literature concerning Tasmania is
that most writers appear to be unaware that at the critical period in
question, the colony was immersed in fierce guerrilla warfare.
Lacking this essential information, the writers cannot understand
the actions of the colonial government beyond assuming there was
a brutal but generalized desire to get rid of the Aborigines. Linked
to this failure to understand settler motivation is an entirely patron-
izing view of the Aborigines as helpless but pathetic victims of the
colonists' murderous impulses or the violence of psychologically
disturbed or even psychopathic convicts.

The reality was quite different. For five years the Colony was
seriously disrupted by Aboriginal aggression. As Arthur explained
in a dispatch to London, the guerrilla war was a "heavy calamity
upon the Colony"; it was a subject that, he explained, "wholly
engrosses and fills my mind with painful anxiety."[63] The settlers in
the countryside lived in high anxiety for years on end. The Aborigines Committee reported in March 1830:

> They continue to occupy and ravage, beyond the reach of control, and
> in defiance of the orders and efforts of Government. ... Since the com-
> mencement of the present year an unparalleled series of devastations
> has marked their passage through the country.[64]

After listing all the recent attacks, committee members had no
hesitation in expressing their belief:

> that a sentiment of alarm pervades the minds of the settlers throughout
> the Island, and that the total ruin of every establishment is but too cer-
> tainly to be apprehended, unless immediate means can be devised for
> suppressing the system of aggression under which so many are at this
> time suffering, and of which all are in dread that they may themselves
> become the victims.[65]

The Tasmanian government was at war with the local Aborigines during the late 1820s and early 1830s, operating under official instructions that permitted the authorities to oppose force with force. Many settlers undoubtedly were extirpationists at heart, but it is not clear if this was true of the officials and military officers. Whether Governor Arthur strayed over the unmarked border between warfare to genocide cannot be answered with any certainty. As always, it depends on what is meant by genocide. It is clear he was determined to defeat the Aborigines and secure the permanent expropriation of their land, but there is little evidence to suggest that he wanted to reach beyond that objective and destroy the Tasmanian race in whole or in part. After all, he had been specifically warned against such action by his superiors in London, and carrying it out would serve no particular purpose. He was above all a measured man who was willing to use force, but only as much as appeared necessary. He was not consumed with malice—with *dolus specialis*. In retrospect, he was remorseful about what had happened to the Tasmanians and pressed on the Colonial Office the need to begin any further colonizing ventures with a treaty. Indeed, he had a considerable influence on the decision to negotiate what became the Treaty of Waitangi in New Zealand in 1840.

Notes

1. R. Hughes, *The Fatal Shore* (London, 1987), 120.
2. N.G. Butlin, *Economics and the Dreamtime* (Melbourne, 1993), 134.
3. H. Fein, *Genocide; A Sociological Perspective* (London, 1990), 13.
4. L. Kuper, *Genocide* (Harmondsworth, 1981), 40.
5. W. Churchill, "Genocide: towards a Functional Definition," *Alternatives* 11 (1986): 421.
6. J. Diamond, "In Black and White," *Natural History* (October 1988): 257.
7. F. Mazian, *Why Genocide?* (Des Moines, 1990).
8. B. Bailyn, "An American Tragedy," *New York Review of Books*, 5 October 1995.
9. D. Cameron Watt, "Genocide," *Times Literary Supplement*, 20 February 1998.
10. *Times Literary Supplement*, 10 April 1998.
11. For the most recent biography of Arthur, see A.G.L. Shaw, *Sir George Arthur, 1784–1854* (Melbourne, 1980).
12. A.G.L. Shaw, ed., *Van Diemen's Land* (Hobart, 1971), 75.
13. *Historical Records of Australia*, series 1, vol., 12, 125.

14. Ibid., 21.
15. Shaw, *Van Diemen's Land*, 21–22.
16. Shaw, *Van Diemen's Land*, 3.
17. See Arthur's Minute, 3 Nov. 1827, Colonial Secretary's Files, Tasmanian State Archives, CSO/1/170–4072, 21.
18. Memo to Captain Clark, 3 Nov. 1827, Colonial Secretary's Files, Tasmanian State Archives, CSO/1/170–4072, 24.
19. Arthur to Huskisson, 17 Apr. 1828, Colonial Secretary's Files, Tasmanian State Archives, CSO/1/170–4072, 5.
20. Governor's Office papers, TSA, G.O. 33/7, 901.
21. See H. Reynolds, *Fate of a Free People* (Melbourne, 1995), 110.
22. Arthur to Murray, 4 Nov. 1828, in Shaw, *Van Diemen's Land*, 9.
23. Executive Council Minutes, 31 Oct. 1828, TSA, A.O./E.P., 11.
24. Shaw, *Van Diemen's Land*, 12.
25. Shaw, *Van Diemen's Land*, 12.
26. Arthur to Murray, 20 Nov. 1830, in Shaw, *Van Diemen's Land*, 58–59.
27. Shaw, *Van Diemen's Land*, 66.
28. Shaw, *Van Diemen's Land*, 70.
29. Anstey to Cox, 13 Oct. 1830, Colonial Secretary's Files, TSA, CSO/1/329, 23.
30. Burnett to Lyttleton, 17 Sept. 1830, Colonial Secretary's Files, TSA, CSO 1/317.
31. Colonial Secretary's Files, TSA, CSO/1/329, 23.
32. Burnett to Arthur, 15 Oct. 1830, J. Burnett Letters, 1826–1834, TSA, FM4/3673, 15/2175.
33. Ibid., 18 Oct. 1830.
34. Ibid., 20 Oct. 1830.
35. Ibid., 23 Oct. 1830.
36. Ibid., 4 Nov. 1830.
37. Ibid., 11 Nov. 1830.
38. Shaw, *Van Diemen's Land*, 60.
39. Huskisson to Arthur, 6 May 1828, Inward Dispatches, TSA 60/1/7, vol. 2, 109.
40. Murray to Arthur, 20 Feb. 1829, Inward Dispatches, TSA 60/1/9, 1829, 141.
41. Murray to Arthur, 25 Aug. 1829, ibid., 233.
42. Murray to Arthur, 5 Nov. 1830, Inward Dispatches, TSA 60/1/11, vol. 16, 421.
43. Ibid.
44. Goderich to Arthur, 17 June 1831 in Shaw, *Van Diemen's Land*, 75.
45. Murray to Arthur, 5 Nov. 1830, Inward Dispatches, TSA 60/1/11, vol. 16, 421.
46. N. J. B. Plomley, ed., *Friendly Mission* (Hobart, 1966), 435.
47. Colonial Secretary: In Letters, TSA, COL/1/323, 303.
48. Aborigines Committee Records, TSA, CBE/1, 7.
49. Colonial Secretary: In Letters, TSA, CSO 1/323, 380.
50. Ibid., 373.
51. 1 Dec. 1826.
52. 26 Feb. 1830.
53. 10 Sept. 1831.
54. 24 Sept. 1831.
55. *Colonial Times*, 24 Sept. 1830.
56. Arthur to Murray, 4 Nov. 1828, in Shaw, *Van Diemen's Land*, 9.
57. Executive Council Minutes, 31 Oct. 1828, TSA, A.O./E.P., 11.
58. Shaw, *Van Diemen's Land*, 12.
59. Shaw, *Van Diemen's Land*, 12.

60. Colonial Secretary's Files, TSA, CSO/1/317, 73.
61. Shaw, *Van Diemen's Land*, 28.
62. A. Bell-Fialkoff, *Ethnic Cleansing* (New York, 1996), 3.
63. Arthur to Murray, 20 Nov. 1830, in Shaw, *Van Diemen's Land*, 60.
64. Aborigines Committee Minutes, 19 March 1830, TSA, CBE/1, 41.
65. Ibid., 42.

Chapter 6

"PLENTY SHOOT 'EM"
The Destruction of Aboriginal Societies along the Queensland Frontier

Raymond Evans

Frontier Historiography

Australian frontiers have remained uneasy sites of contestation. Long after the physical conflicts there had ended, interpretive and semantic struggle over the extent and meaning of their violence has persisted.[1] While serious academic consideration of Australian history was barely emerging in the 1930s, frontier relations in certain remote corners of the continent were coming to a painful close. Yet from the interwar years until the 1970s there existed a pervasive intellectual reticence about discussing such matters.[2] Of the few historians who broke ranks to examine the destructive interaction between Aborigines and colonists, one was G.V. Portus of Adelaide University, who in 1935 admitted in a school history-text that:

> the story of Queensland is sad reading. The relations between the blacks and whites were marked by bitter ferocity ... spearings and murders by the blacks were met by organized hunting and shooting parties of whites. And, worse still, there are fiendish stories of poisoned food being offered to natives under the cloak of friendship. Not until the whites were settled in such numbers as to make their eventual conquest certain did their hostility to the blacks diminish.

Notes for this section begin on page 168.

He went on to typify Tasmanian frontier relations as "war to the knife," an impression fleshed out in 1948 by journalist-historian Clive Turnbull in his book *Black War*, which argued that interracial violence was the principal cause of what was then believed to be the utter extermination of the Tasmanian Aborigines.[3] But such candor was rare. More in keeping with mainstream interpretation was the avoidance practiced in Australia's first volume of social history, edited by Gordon Greenwood in 1955. Aborigines rated no mention in the book's large index, and rarely appeared in the text. Economic historian R.M. Hartwell, in his chapter on the pastoral advance, argued that colonial Australia possessed "some of the features of the American frontier," but only insofar as life there for colonists meant "a harsh struggle" against environmental odds; for this antipodean frontier apparently faced no contesting societies. Instead, Hartwell maintained:

> Australia had large tracts of empty grazing country awaiting occupation ... the settlement was relatively uncomplicated: the continent was empty, for the unfortunate aborigines offered no serious cultural or economic opposition.[4]

Even application of the word "frontier" to the pattern of non-Aboriginal settlement appeared semantically novel. America had a frontier, it was contended; Australia merely had an "outback." And the latter term carried a sense of a boundary-less void—a spatial and historical desert around the ridges of which a "sand-castle civilization" had been fashioned, its sense of past struggles constantly obliterated by present and future tides.[5] Writing in 1962 in the *Texas Quarterly*, Mary Durack, herself a descendant of one of the great pastoral dynasties, found the concept of a local frontier somewhat risible. Her article, "In Search of an Australian Frontier," carried no hint of racial struggle. "[N]either my father nor those to whom he wrote would, in their right minds, have traveled or slept without a firearm in the bush," she observed,

> [t]hey were simply "stockmen" or "bushmen" and the country they pioneered the "back blocks" or "back o' beyond" if you like, but nothing as "high falutin'" as a "frontier." While their American counterparts galloped the prairies with swinging lariats, these men rode on in obscurity, performing feats of bushmanship and triumphs of endurance. ... A newcomer looking for frontiers ... will amuse Australians. ... They never concede a destination—only a horizon.[6]

Three years later, the leftist cultural historian Russell Ward virtually divested Durack's bushmen even of their firearms in his seminal general history, *Australia* (1965). Reflecting Hartwell's analysis, Ward contended that Aborigines were so "primitive and peaceable," and their reaction to invasion was "so sporadic and ineffectual, that men *[sic]* seldom had to go armed on the Australian frontier." From earliest colonial times, he wrote, governments were "much more concerned with protecting the Aborigines than with fighting them." Frontier relations, moreover, had provided a powerful moral imperative for the nation-to-be, for the pacifistic tenor of white settlement had contributed to the production of a society where social violence had remained at a low ebb, producing citizens who were "remarkably slow to kill *each other*"![7]

Ward wrote upon the brink of a historical revolution in Australian frontier studies. Beginning with a group of history theses researched from hitherto neglected or cautiously avoided archival, manuscript, and other primary sources in the mid–1960s, and branching into a range of more substantial published works by the early to mid–1970s, concerted analysis began to plot the forbidding contours of conflict, resistance, and dispossession. Significantly, it was anthropologists such as N.J.B. Plomley and W.E.H. Stanner, and a sociologist, Charles Rowley, who led the way with this publishing surge, rather than historians, many of whom continued to regard frontier studies as disreputable.[8] Yet, by the early 1980s, a new paradigm had emerged that located frontier violence across the Australian mainland and its offshore islands, including Tasmania, at the center of race contact history. A dramatic indication of the interpretive sea change that had occurred in the space of little more than a decade may be gleaned from an Introduction written by Russell Ward himself to amateur historian Geoffrey Blomfield's *Baal Belbora: The End of the Dancing* in 1981. It marks the most dramatic intellectual volte-face to be found in Ward's numerous publications. Based on Blomfield's discovery of more than a score of documented Aboriginal massacres in a small triangle of territory, composing the "Falls Country" on the southwestern edge of the New England Tableland in northern New South Wales, Ward contended that private colonists and officials:

> certainly butchered, in the aggregate, scores of thousands of black men, women and babies but ... tacitly conspired to say ... and to write nothing of these deeds. So succeeding generations of white Australians are easily able to believe that actual slaughter of the Aborigines occurred rarely if at all.

If Blomfield's findings of more than 1,200 Aborigines perishing violently in "this single quite small district of Australia" were projected nationwide, Ward concluded, then "genocide of one third of the black people" might be "about the right figure for the continent as a whole."[9] Here Ward, the 1960s "denialist," had ironically staked out a more extravagant claim than other race conflict historians were prepared to make. "Genocide" was then a term rarely used in the Australian context; and Henry Reynolds's conservative, widely accepted figure of 20,000 Aborigines killed by frontier violence represented only around one-fiftieth—rather than one-third—of the projected one million pre-contact indigenes.[10]

From the mid–1980s, an interpretive countermovement began in a series of studies that, although not denying violence, ceased to investigate or foreground it. Emphasis shifted to examining cooperative activities and patterns of conciliation between Aborigines and Europeans. Aboriginal "agency" was stressed: not resistance but their choice, adaptation, survival, and opportunity. As one of these historians noted in 1995:

> In recent years another school of interpretation has become more evident in academic historiography, one which challenges the emphasis on conflict and resistance. Scholars such as Diane Barwick, Bob Reece, Ann McGrath, Marie Fels and myself [Bain Attwood] have contended that in the history of relations between Aborigines and Europeans relationships of cohesion and cooperation have been as important as those of confrontation.[11]

In the wake of this drive to allow equal time to images of both hostility and appeasement, a more confronting challenge to conflict study emerged at the beginning of the new century in a series of articles appearing in the right-wing journal *Quadrant*, principally written by media studies critic Keith Windschuttle. Windschuttle argues that much of the evidence presented concerning "massacres, terrorism and genocide" is "very poorly founded … seriously mistaken," and "designed to serve highly politicized ends." A good deal of it, he goes so far as to claim, is "outright fabrication"—the civilized background, Christian beliefs, respect for "the rule of law," and the essential Britishness of the settlers would not allow frontier excesses to occur systematically.[12] His basic thesis that Britishness and brutishness are somehow incommensurable appears ahistorical, even naïve, and tends to turn back the historiographical tide to its low 1950s watermark. For this reason, his theses have gained favor in the Australian media and among the non-Aboriginal public that is tiring of the attention given to Aboriginal suffering, and is happy to be relieved of any sense of collective moral burden for the "sins of the past." What the media have been eager

to call the "History Wars" is really only one persistent warrior
obstinately marching to a different drummer than every other professional researcher in the field.

Significantly, both the consensual histories of the late 1980s
and *Quadrant's* denialist thrust, to the present, avoid analysis of
the Queensland frontier. By contrast, many of the researchers em-
phasizing the ubiquity of frontier conflict—such as Henry Reynolds,
Noel Loos, Maurice French, Lorna McDonald, Gordon Reid,
Denis Cryle, Bill Thorpe, Jan Walker, Clive Moore, Kay Saunders,
Ross Johnston, Rod Fisher, Alan Hillier, Timothy Bottoms, Bruce
Breslin, Les Skinner, Ross Fitzgerald, Ros Kidd, Robert Armstrong,
Bill Rosser, A. Dirk Moses, Alison Palmer, Patrick Collins, Michael
Slack, Mark Copland, Jonathan Richards, Pamela Watson,
Rebekah Crow, and myself—have been motivated specifically by a
connection with Queensland's racial history in pursuing such
analyses. Queensland's frontier historiography thus tends to trace
a relatively unbroken line of conflict study from its modest begin-
nings in the early observations of G.V. Portus, and, more specifically, in the pioneering research of Winifred Cowin, a history
honors graduate at the University of Queensland in 1950, up to the
present day.[13]

What follows is a *reconnoiter* across the Queensland frontier
that explores its essentially volatile and conflictual nature. It is
viewed here largely through the eyes of white participants,
observers, and commentators. Were a comparable archive of Aboriginal record available to match this white worldview, it is likely
that the account would be transformed into a considerably more
sanguine and tragic one.

Frontier Impressions

Traveling through Central Queensland in early 1862, a French representative of the Geographical Society of Geneva, Edouard
Marcet, described himself and his party as *"armé jusqu'aux dents,"*
that is, "armed to the teeth" with carbines, pistols, and knives
against the threat of Aboriginal attack. On a journey from Logan
Downs to the coast, he was wary of lighting campfires for fear of
attracting hostile attention, and kept a gun at hand on all occasions. Stumbling upon a group of Aborigines for the first time while
circumventing a bushfire, his first reaction was to gallop his horse
into their midst, firing off six shots from his "pistolet and scatter-
ing them in panic in all directions."[14]

A decade later, a British migrant, Augustus Cutlack, recalled how his first encounter with an Aborigine on the outskirts of Brisbane had terminated with his drawing a "long sheath knife" on the man after the latter had remonstrated with him for matches. In late 1873, Cutlack joined an expedition of surveyors, government officials, police, and navvies sent to open the port of Cooktown for the Palmer gold rush into the Cape hinterland. Four months later, there were sixty vessels riding at anchor in the Endeavour River, disgorging miners and supplies. Cutlack wrote:

> Many were the shooting parties formed and as there was no game to kill, it consisted of making repeated attacks on the blacks. Each day a shooting party was out somewhere and all armed to the teeth.[15]
> All *"armé jusqu'aux dents"*!

Both the Frenchman in 1862 and the Englishman in 1873 found themselves upon frontiers that, from both sides, bristled with weaponry. The passions of fear, anxiety, and vengeance were running high in these regions, and European attitudes towards Aborigines as the hated and despised "Other" were intense. "The aboriginals," Cutlack wrote, "are a low, savage, treacherous looking race of people. ... [They] are the most degraded race on the face of the earth. They are dirty, lazy ... specimens of human beings."[16] Both frontiers were suffused with acts of violence and terror—a consequence of single-minded dispossession and spirited indigenous defense.

In 1862, as Lorna McDonald has commented, Central Queensland was arguably the center of Australian "pioneer warfare."[17] Beginning with the Mt. Larcom tragedy in December 1855 where six station workers were killed by the Darumbal; leading into the Hornet Bank killings of October 1857 where eleven whites had perished at the hands of the Jiman; on to the rape and murder of Fanny Briggs, a former Sydney barmaid, in Rockhampton by Native Policemen in November 1859; the slaughter of two parties of Europeans at Castle Creek and Clematis Creek in the lower and upper Dawson respectively in early 1860; and culminating in the unprecedented massacre of 19 settlers out of a party of 22 by the Kairi at Cullin-La-Ringo, south of Emerald in October 1861, Central Queensland in this period represented, as Gordon Reid observes, "a very violent place."[18] In four of these six incidents, white women had perished as well as men; and in three of them, the women were also raped.[19] European retaliation was incendiary and ungovernable. In payback campaigns of mass destruction involving white vigilantes and Native Police, following the loss of some forty

European lives, "untold hundreds" of Aborigines perished. Perhaps 500 or more were killed in total and the Jiman, Wadja, Kairi, and Darumbal peoples were eventually reduced to remnant groups.[20]

Mass killings of Aborigines in Central Queensland persisted through the 1860s. Darumbal people, gathering together for ceremonial purposes in the vicinity of Samuel Birkbeck's Glenmore Station, a mere ten kilometers from Rockhampton, were set upon by a Native Police detachment in July 1865 after the white family had panicked over the Aboriginal presence. Birkbeck's three sons witnessed eighteen Darumbal shot and their corpses incinerated.[21] Later in the decade, a much larger slaughter occurred in the Goulbolba Hills, near the Nogoa River. An eyewitness (and probable participant) later recalled how a settler army of one hundred white males, again accompanied by Native Police, flushed Darumbal men, women and children from their hiding places in the caves and crevices of the hills. McDonald writes:

> An estimated three hundred Aboriginals were shot or drowned in the [adjacent] lake. For about thirty years their skulls and bones lay scattered on the hillside or beside the water until most were destroyed in a fierce bushfire in 1898.

The settler action was in reprisal for the spearing and mutilation of a single white shepherd.[22]

By the early 1870s, when Augustus Cutlack traveled north, the scene of major carnage had shifted to the Cape York region; and especially to the coastline and hinterland between Cardwell and the Endeavour River. Violent reprisals seem to have become particularly intense following the wreck of the *Maria* on Bramble Reef, when a dozen or so shipwrecked New Guinea gold-seekers were killed by the Djiri in late February 1872. Reprisal raids by Native Police, marines, local settlers, and vigilantes from Sydney continued for many months.[23] Scores of vengeance-seeking whites, many armed with new Winchester rifles, and a dozen members of the Native Police took part in the protracted onslaught. Historian, Alan Hillier, comments:

> The effects ... on the Rockingham Bay tribes were never recorded. Every camp fifty miles north of Cardwell was raided and destroyed. Many dispersals took place ... and the death toll ... must have been high.[24]

Charles Heydon, who had come north on the *Governor Black-all* to search for or to avenge the missing men, was sickened by what he observed. In early 1874, he wrote to the *Sydney Morning Herald:*

I heard white men talk openly of the share they had taken in slaughtering whole camps, not only of men, but of women and children. They said that the gins were as bad as the men, and that the picaninnies, all their tribe being killed, would die of starvation if not also put out of the way.[25]

Heydon wrote, however, specifically to protest at activities then occurring on the Endeavour River, to which Augustus Cutlack was also witness. "Private persons go out to kill blacks and call it 'snipe-shooting,'" Heydon alleged:

Awkward words are always avoided you will notice. "Shooting a snipe" sounds better than "murdering a man." But the blacks are never called men and women and children; "myalls" and "niggers" and "gins" and "picaninnies" seem further removed from humanity. ... What right have "myalls" to exist at all—mischievous vermin with their ignorance, and their barbarism, and their degradation and their black skins?[26]

Heydon later became a New South Wales Supreme Court Judge and Attorney General in the 1890s, chosen to consolidate that colony's statute law.[27] Writing in support of his son's charges, Jabez Heydon, former Editor of Sydney's Roman Catholic *Freeman's Journal*, asserted to F.W. Chesson of the Aborigines Protection Society in London:

Nothing short of English interference will avail ... [against] this deplorable state of things. ... Public opinion in Queensland is all against the Blacks.[28]

Summing up the ongoing conflict in February 1877, a correspondent to the *Cooktown Courier* stated:

This district has been settled over three years; armed police to a considerable number have been waging war with the blacks, and private individuals have been doing a good deal of shooting among them ... [and yet] we can only be secure in patches ... no man can put a reasonable limit to the bloodshed and expense that will be necessary under our present system, before we reckon on security equal to that enjoyed in central and southern Queensland.[29]

These arresting images from northern and central Queensland over a 20-year period raise questions about the nature of colonial frontiers that continue to reverberate: Was the taking and settlement of Queensland more conflictual and violent than that of other Australian colonies? And just how violent and conflictual was it?

Following the news of mass settler reprisals after the Wills massacre of 1861, the Reverend John West, Australia's foremost colonial historian, asked in mock astonishment of Queensland, "Is it a part of Her Majesty's domains?" and went on to charge that its Government was complicit in a policy of "extermination."[30] Three years later, Gideon Scott Lang told a Melbourne audience that, whereas in Queensland:

> there has always been more destruction of the blacks in occupying new country than in any other colony ... within the last few years it has been wholesale and indiscriminate and carried on with a cold blooded cruelty on the part of the whites quite unparalleled in the history of these colonies ... it is the rule and custom to arrange the black question by killing them off. This demoralization of the whites I attribute to the extreme use made of the native police.[31]

Lang did not speak as a softhearted humanitarian. In fact he had himself utilized the Native Police against the Mandandanji people when, in his capacity as "The Land Pimpernel," he had held squatting runs covering 400,000 hectares of the East Maranoa region of southwestern Queensland in the 1850s.[32] In response to any suggestion that Lang might be embroidering his case by alleging that eradication was being accomplished with "no more compunction or responsibility than if they [the Aborigines] were vermin," a British Colonial Office official ventured in January 1866:

> I believe it to be by no means easy to exaggerate the recklessness with which blacks have been destroyed (in some cases by strychnine like foxes) in Queensland. But the Home Government can but hold up its hands. There is no effectual power to interfere in their cause.[33]

Here was a striking confidential recognition, from the highest official sanctum, of Queensland's uniqueness in delivering its "special treatment" to native peoples; as well as an equally arresting admission of the Imperial Government's powerlessness to intervene since colonial self-government had been granted in 1856 and Queensland had become a separate colony in 1859.

In early 1868, in response to press reports of a Native Police massacre of unoffending Aborigines at their camp on the Morinish goldfield, inland from Rockhampton, Chesson of the Aborigines Protection Society argued that the level of official neglect and culpability concerning "barbarous outrages" was without example in the colonies. "Many of the leading journalists and public men of Australia have given utterance to strong feelings of indignation at the shocking state of things in Queensland," he concluded.[34] Yet the Colonial Office continued to register its impotence "beyond [the

Home Government] raising their voice" in verbal protest at the colony's excessive behaviour.[35]

"Putting it in plain English this is what we Queenslanders do," the editor of the *Cooktown Courier* commented a decade later: "we set the Native Police on them [the Aboriginal inhabitants] to make them 'quiet.' This is effected by massacring them indiscriminately."[36] In a series of well-researched, sensational disclosures in the *Queenslander* in mid–1880, entitled "The Way We Civilise," editor Gresley Lukin and an anonymous journalist—since identified as Carl Feilberg—concurred that settler behavior in Queensland "fell far below British standards." Of all the colonies, its editorials contended, "we alone have descended to the 'kinchen lay' of extermination ... a process which would shame us before our fellow-countrymen in every part of the British Empire." In response to fourteen editorials written in this vein, a wide range of squatters and other old pioneers wrote long, detailed accounts of witnessed or reported atrocities, virtually all agreeing, either with profound regret or brazen acceptance, that a "war of extermination" was going on.[37] Much more might have been disclosed, Feilberg contended, were it not for a prevailing climate of suppression surrounding the issue. "We have at our disposal a mass of information we cannot use," he alleged: "This ... comes from men so situated that, if it could be traced to them, they would be exposed to much annoyance, and in some cases the danger of total ruin."[38]

The dissemination of this forum in pamphlet form throughout the colonies and Great Britain led Sir Arthur Gordon, then Governor of New Zealand, to impress on Prime Minister Gladstone in April 1883 Queensland's "special unfitness" for colonial governance, and thus helped thwart the colony's imperial ambitions in Papua. Gordon referred to an amplified:

> tone of brutality and cruelty in dealing with "blacks" [in Queensland] which is very difficult for anyone who does not *know* it, as I do, to realise. I have heard men of culture and refinement ... talk not only of *wholesale* butchery ... but of the *individual* murder of natives, exactly as they would talk of a day's sport, or of having to kill some troublesome animal.[39]

Another prominent colonial historian, George W. Rusden, was also prompted by *The Way We Civilise* disclosures to mount a searing indictment of Queensland's frontier relations in his three-volume *History of Australia* (1883). Rusden was an outspoken conservative and Anglophile, highly supportive of the British imperial enterprise. Yet the compounded evidence of Aborigines "left mangled and stark on the soil of Queensland," which the *Queenslander*'s campaign disclosed, had invoked his outrage. The very "air of Queensland," he charged, "reeks with atrocities committed and condoned." The colonists there "had amply vindicated their claims to a vile existence." Yet actions by perpetrators, Government functionaries and their supporters to suppress evidence of happenings, much talked about, yet less commonly recorded, threatened to "wither" this history of excesses "out of men's knowledge unexposed."[40]

Frontier Aftermath

Rusden's fears were partially realized during the following century, as less and less was spoken about Queensland's sanguine past. Hints of dark deeds still persisted in the popular media and in private white reminiscences, as well as in the sequestered oral cultures of Aboriginal peoples themselves. In 1900, for instance, the Brisbane *Worker,* then one of the most explicitly racist journals in Australia, could still comment in passing: "We Queenslanders' ... treatment of our aboriginal races is, perhaps, the most shocking and callous on record."[41] Yet, for the most part, for around five or six decades there would be mainly obfuscation, elision, and silence on the subject.[42] For instance, in 1935, when Queensland's Chief Protector of Aborigines referred in a British publication to former "scenes of wanton slaughter," it was the Tasmanian "Black War" to which he alluded. His Queensland account concentrated instead upon a discussion of ration distributions and mission activities. In this discussion, the paramilitary Native Police were transformed conveniently into harmless "trackers."[43]

Recent academic race relations histories have tended to restore to Queensland the unenvied crown of having the most troublesome frontier story of all the Australian colonies. In 1970, Charles Rowley ventured that Queensland's pastoral expansion and "decades of attack on Aboriginal social gatherings" had dismembered these societies far more rapidly than in the Northern Territory or Western Australia.[44] Living in North Queensland from the mid-sixties first activated Henry Reynolds to face the serious history of frontier violence and racism in Australia, much as living in Southern Queensland did the same for me.[45] In his book, *An Indelible Stain?*, Reynolds asks, "Was Queensland guilty of genocide?" and answers, "There is certainly much evidence available for retrospective prosecution." He does not move towards so forceful a conclusion in the case of the other colonies.[46] Similarly, Pamela Lukin Watson concludes, based upon her study of the Channel Country: "The kill ratio was higher in Queensland than elsewhere."[47] Lorna McDonald and Gordon Reid, investigating Central Queensland, arrive at similar findings. By 1870, McDonald contends, "Central Queensland pioneering warfare had exceeded in ferocity" all other mainland regions. Reid believes that the Europeans' "terrible revenge" after Hornet Bank and Cullin-La-Ringo was of "a scale bordering on genocide." "Dispersal and killing," he writes, was "the established method. ... The killing continued until long after there was a need for it; and the hatred of blacks remained long after the killing had stopped."[48]

Younger historians such as A. Dirk Moses and Alison Palmer, who bring the theoretical apparatus of genocide studies to bear on the subject, are less tentative. Moses views Queensland's frontier as "the purest incarnation of the colonization project," because the Queensland government was the most open to implementing policies desired by settlers, and the least restrained by London. In the nineteenth century, he writes:

> the use of government terror [via the Native Mounted Police] transformed local genocidal massacres by settlers into an official state-wide policy. ... Nowhere in Australia did the objective and inherent implications of colonization become so consciously embodied.[49]

Palmer, in her recent comparative history, *Colonial Genocide*, agrees that "the role of the Queensland Government was crucial." It "actively condoned the ongoing slaughter," she writes, "and made no attempt to bring it to an end." Instead it "entertained a general, implicit policy to aid and encourage the destruction." Such devastation was "societal-led," as indicated by a wide range of private statements and actions to "exterminate" indigenes, augmented by the Native Mounted Police Corps that, by and large, functioned as "a death squad aimed at eradicating Aborigines." Cumulatively, "recurrent, piecemeal massacres" culminated in "large-scale decimation," and that is what the settlers and the state both wanted.[50]

If Queensland's history is to be freighted with such somber assessments, echoing from the nineteenth century to the twenty-first—and there is certainly cause in the accumulating stockpiles of primary data, even from exclusively non-Aboriginal sources, to give such propositions considerable weight—how do we explain all this? And how do we arrive at a reasonable appreciation of the degree of social violence that ensued?

Search for Explanation

There is much about the Queensland frontier experience that is as epic as it is gothic. Its interracial conflict spreads across a vast temporal and geographic canvas. This arguably begins between white and black as early as William Jansz's rough intervention into Wik society on Western Cape York Peninsula in 1606.[51] It petered out a little more than three hundred years later in the 1910s in roughly the same region. In September 1910, Frank Bowman, a pastoralist of Rutland Plains on the southwestern Cape, was speared by a mission Aborigine, Jimmy Inkerman of Kowanyama, following a protracted history of Aboriginal child theft, the forceful concubinage of women, and unpunished murders and floggings by Europeans in the region.[52] Inkerman was then shot and killed by James McIntyre, a stockman accompanying Bowman. Around eight years later, a man named McKenzie was apparently killed by the Kaiadilt after a shooting and raping spree on Bendinck Island in the Gulf.[53] McKenzie and others of his party had reportedly killed around eleven Aborigines in this onslaught, representing some ten percent of the Kaiadilt's small number. Native Police patrols in the Gulf Country and the Cape persisted after Federation and into the early years of World War One; but the last official investigation of a Police massacre was at Moreton in northern Cape York in 1902, after troopers shot and killed four peaceable Aboriginal men from three different tribes during a patrol.[54] Police Inspector Galbraith also reported from Normanton around this time: "the blacks are often dispersed by the station hands. Of course, such dispersals are not reported to the police."[55] These struggles occurred mainly over access to watercourses. The anthropologist John Dymock similarly records an Aboriginal massacre at Flick Yard station in the southwestern Gulf Country in 1904. Killings around the Northern Territory/Queensland border seem to have continued beyond this date. Dymock notes that Gulf Aborigines call the period of violent contact "the Wild Time," and its boundaries are fluid. "As an example," he writes, "the 'Wild Time' ended for some Aborigines on Bentinck Island (a mere forty-five miles north of Burketown) as recently as 1948! For many Aborigines the 'Wild Time' ended with their extermination."[56]

Queensland frontiers covered a vast extent of territory—a landmass of 1.73 million square kilometers, almost one quarter of the Australian total and two and one half times the size of Texas. They ranged over temperate, subtropical, and tropical zones, regions of heavy rainfall and great aridity—rainforested uplands, the "extensive mudflats" of the Gulf, "boulder-strewn highlands" of the South-East, the dry interior lowlands of the Great Artesian Basin, and "massive sand barriers," continental and reef islands, numbering more than one thousand, scattered along a coastline of more than a thousand kilometers.[57] Pervasive settlement over tens of thousands of years by scores of Aboriginal societies—numbering, it is now believed, more than two hundred thousand people— was confronted from the 1820s by permanent, largely British intrusions, which also demographically penetrated this enormous region more thoroughly than in the other larger colonies of South and Western Australia.[58] With the beginning of pastoral occupation around 1840, the frontier did not merely spread; it galloped. Even by 1859, the year of Separation (i.e., independence from New South Wales), there were already thirteen hundred squatting stations, covering one quarter of the new colony and grazing millions of sheep, and tens of thousands of cattle, pigs, and horses. In late 1862, Queensland's first Governor, George Bowen, estimated that "the tide of colonisation" was advancing by "200 miles" (320 kilometers) each year.[59] Avoiding any mention of the mayhem thereby being inflicted upon Aboriginal clans, Bowen declaimed that there was "something almost sublime" in pastoralism's "steady, silent flow."[60] Writing four years later, Queensland's Commissioner for Crown Lands, E.W. Lamb, wrote that, between 1862 and 1865, pastoral occupation in the North had now covered an area equal to that of France. "It seems a marvel," he reveled:

> that townships and homesteads would spring up on the banks of rivers, where the primeval silence and solitude was three years ago broken only by a few wandering tribes seeking a meagre subsistence along their course.[61]

From 1858, mining frontiers, notable for their large, sudden population influxes and material rapacity, began opening alongside pastoral ones. They denuded forests, commandeered watercourses, killed off the fauna, introduced few domestic animals as compensation and rarely employed Aboriginal people—a recipe for intense Aboriginal resistance and human wastage. The Palmer, Hodgkinson, Mulgrave, and Etheridge gold rushes into barely penetrated Aboriginal territories and involving many thousands of Asians as well as Europeans led to savage clashes. Noel Loos estimates that in the early 1870s, between 70 and 103 incomers were killed by Aborigines on the Palmer, and another 44 on other northern mining fields.[62] The pastoral and mining rushes, which occurred in three great waves, had monopolized most of the Queensland landmass by the late 1880s, bordering a period of some fifty years of intense dispossession. By the 1890s, the migrant population had expanded by a factor of thirteen upon its size at Separation, and the rural population had increased almost twenty-fold. Whereas this incoming society had grown from a handful of convicts and military in 1824 to around 400,000, the Aboriginal population had disastrously shrunk to around 25,000—a demographic slump of some ninety percent, due to a combination of disease, starvation, a rapidly falling birthrate, and overt violence.[63]

Frontier expansion had therefore proceeded across the widest ambit of territories and landscapes over an extensive time-frame, bringing massive disruption, via a considerable range of developmental processes—penal, pastoral, agricultural, maritime and mining. Large populations over enormous areas had been brought into conflict, and, overall, these combined populations contained the broadest racial and ethnic diversities in Australia.[64] A highly masculinist frontier also exacerbated the conflict, with male-to-female incomer ratios as high as nine to one in far western Queensland.[65] It was the only colony where pastoral, mining, maritime, and plantation frontiers were advancing simultaneously; and all this occurred as Western racist theories, grouped around polygenism and Social Darwinism, were peaking in their certitude and influence.[66] A.T. Yarwood and M.J. Knowling write of Queensland's intellectual situation as special in this regard, as respectable scientific ideas gave rise to attitudes, values, and behaviors "in their most concentrated form."[67] For instance, Dr. William Hobbs, a Social Darwinist who served as Governor Bowen's private physician while doubling as a newspaper proprietor, argued in his *Queensland Guardian* editorials in early 1861 that "no white man who shot an Aborigine, in self-defense or in sport should be exposed to trial or sentence."[68] Ideas that allowed invaded human populations to be leached of their humanity opened them simultaneously to all manner of ill treatment, without recourse to normal social and legal protection.[69] As a Ravenswood miner, David Cormack, wrote to his sister in November 1880, "I have knowen [sic] plenty of men in this Country that will shoot the poor things for Sport ... same as we used to shoot rabbits."[70]

But if scientific respectability provided succor for racial excesses, so too did Queensland legislatures, which effectively institutionalized Aboriginal clearances through the medium of the Native Police Corps. This force of up to 150 non-Aboriginal officers, utilizing around 1,000 troopers over its lifespan, performed as military units on the cutting edge of frontier expansion from May

1849, in order to suppress Indigenous resistance.[71] Andrew Markus once famously compared this force to Himmler's *Einsatzgruppen* (special action groups) in Poland during World War Two. But the Queensland force was never so large, and did not operate with the same single-minded, ruthless efficiency. On the other hand, the *Einsatzgruppen* did not operate for more than sixty years.[72] Many of the Native Police's activities were routine and non-destructive, but at its most lethal, as it was under officers like Wheeler, Fraser, Bligh, Blakeney, Carroll, Dempster, Douglas, Dutton, Fitzgerald, Johnstone, Lamond, Murray, Nicholls, O'Connor, Paschen, Uhr, and others, it cut a bloody swathe through Aboriginal communities, often wiping out whole clans, especially in Central, North, and Western Queensland.[73] Its operations peaked as Western technology transformed the gun from a weapon barely a match for the spear-thrower to a repeating rifle of mass destruction. By the early 1870s, the force were equipped with Snider carbines and by the early 1880s were using Martini-Henries.[74] Other technologies, such as the telegraph, the steamboat, and the railways were just as vital to the force's efficiency. The horse alone was not responsible for its remarkable mobility.

Despite pessimistic assertions that most Native Police records are unavailable through destruction or intense secrecy, the principal contours of their story are gradually being pieced together though a painstaking trawling of archival files, newspaper runs, and manuscript collections. Many thousands of vital documents are now coming to light, especially in the records of the Queensland Justice Department, Colonial Secretary series, Police, Attorney General, Crown Solicitor's Office, Governors, and Executive Council Papers. Broadly speaking, it appears that the force operated at its most destructive on the Cardwell to Port Douglas coastal strip, the Cairns-Cooktown-Palmer Goldfields triangle, the Gulf Country, far Western Queensland, and the Maryborough to Mackay region of Central Queensland, though their presence was painfully felt by most Aboriginal people—even on certain occasions those actually working on pastoral runs—from Brisbane to Birdsville, from Goondiwindi to Somerset.

Accumulated killings from persistent Native Police patrols, continuing from 1848 until the 1910s in the Queensland region, provided official sanction for the normalization of brutality. From Burketown in the Gulf Country of North-West Queensland, a press correspondent, "Carpentaria," reported in 1868 how Sub-Inspector D'Arcy Wentworth Uhr and his troopers had responded after a white settler and several horses had been killed. Several "mobs" had been "rounded up" and shot—the first containing "upwards of thirty"; the second, fourteen; the third, nine; and a last mob of eight. "In the latter lot," the correspondent wrote:

> there was one black who would not die after receiving eighteen or twenty bullets, but a trooper speedily put an end to his existence by smashing his skull. ... Everybody [sic] in the district is delighted with the wholesale slaughter dealt out by the native police, and thank Mr. Uhr for his energy in ridding the district of *fifty-nine* (59) myalls.[75]

In a similarly unabashed vein, Frank Hann, the lessee of Lawn Hill station in the Gulf Country, wrote to anthropologist A.W. Howitt in July 1885, disclosing that Inspector James Lamond of the Native Police had recently informed him of how his troopers had shot "over 100 blacks in three years" on that property alone.[76]

Though the Native Police were the singularly most destructive institution, private settlers, alone or in vigilante parties, undoubtedly killed many more. Possibly a ratio of two to one between settlers and the Corps may be suggested. Aborigines fought back with all the tenacity they could muster. From my research with Bill Thorpe on the Moreton Bay penal settlement, a conservative total of thirty-six whites killed and a dozen or so wounded by Aborigines between 1824 and 1839 may be suggested.[77] Researchers Peter Lawler and Frank Uhr have counted another fifty-three incomers killed by Aborigines in South East Queensland between May 1840 and October 1846.[78] The destructive impact was high, for by 1846 the total migrant population of Moreton Bay was only 960.[79] From 1842 until 1859, white deaths were contemporaneously enumerated at 250; and, by 1866, the Queensland Executive Council would minute Lord Carnarvon that "at least six hundred Englishmen [sic]" had now perished.[80] Noel Loos lists another 435 likely migrant deaths from frontier violence in North Queensland from 1867 until 1897. There were several other incomer deaths beyond this date.[81] Additional to this tentative total of 1,075, Clive Moore has recently traced Queensland's maritime frontier as it moved beyond the colonial landmass into Torres Strait, the southeast coast and eastern archipelagoes off New Guinea and eastward into the near Pacific. He has found more than 724 deaths of incomers to the north of Cape York, and in excess of 684 other foreign deaths in the Melanesian Pacific—that is, above 1,400 more newcomer deaths in 584 ascertainable frontier incidents.[82]

It must be emphasized that a total figure for non-Aboriginal casualties from frontier attacks will continue to be speculative. Numbers could arguably be inflated due to "missing" colonists being considered killed by Aborigines when they were not. On the other hand, the mortality figure could equally be an underestimate because of cases in remote areas remaining unrecorded as well as the inadequacy of present primary research. The violent deaths of stationhands may well have been underreported by their pastoral employers due to the latter's concern that frank disclosures of frontier perils might deter replacement workers from applying; and general European apathy and, indeed, callousness concerning the expendability of non-European incomers (Melanesians and Asians) may have encouraged a cavalier attitude to recording their frontier sufferings. Instead of arriving at one "rough figure," it might be more sensible to posit a reasonable "mortality range"—in this instance of say, 900 to 1,100 between 1824 and 1900. This range, moreover, represents only deaths in frontier attacks by Aborigines. Very little research has presently been done upon the number of woundings inflicted.

The indigenous death and wounding rate can only be guessed at. Contemporaries usually adopted a ten to one ratio, but Archibald Meston, who would interview members of sixty to seventy tribes, suggested in 1889 that it could have been as many as fifty to one.[83] The Reverend J.E. Tenison Woods believed in 1882 that: "Ten lives for one would, I think, be very much below the truth."[84] Several years later, ethnologist Edward Curr suggested that "fifteen to five and twenty percent" of Aborigines, Australia-wide had "fallen by the rifle," based upon a questionnaire circulated among pastoralists. If even that lower percentage were applied to the Queensland Aboriginal population, the number of violent deaths at incomer hands would easily exceed the twenty-thousand assessed by Henry Reynolds for the entire Australian frontier. A vast primary databank presently being compiled at Griffith University in Brisbane now claims to trace around ten thousand violent Aboriginal frontier deaths in Queensland with supportive documentation. That is, these deaths are no longer a matter of mathematical projection or speculation. They can be known of, it is suggested, as most things in history are known, with contingent certitude. Yet what can also be projected from this new knowledge base is that the real death rate was possibly double this number, given the impenetrable secrecy surrounding many such happenings, the frustrating bashfulness of most white sources in providing precise figures and, most significantly, the virtual absence of an Aboriginal database of contemporary witnesses that matches the European one in its detail, depth, and amplitude.[85]

The Queensland frontier was arguably one of the most violent places on earth during the global spread of Western capitalism in the nineteenth century. Many thousands in total of Aboriginal, European, Asian, and Melanesian people were killed and wounded in the process, but among the biggest casualties were veracity and justice. Behind a veneer of dismissive euphemism, mass destructive processes ground inexorably on. Despite all the slaughter, the rapes, the child theft, the floggings, and the general brutality that occurred, no Queenslander was successfully prosecuted for any crime against an Aboriginal person until 1883, when a lone Townsville man, Edward Camm, was sentenced to life for the rape of an Aboriginal child, Rosie, under ten years of age. Camm was the first European to be punished for any crime against an Aborigine in the Queensland region since 1850, nine years prior to Separation, when a soldier at Moreton Bay named William Cairns was sentenced to three years' imprisonment for wounding an Aboriginal man during a military assault on an encampment at York's Hollow. This sentence was then reduced to six months, due to Cairns's "tender age."[86] Otherwise, the tragic events of a period variously described by contemporaries as "the Great Fear," "the Wild Time," "the red, shocking years," and "a 'war' of sad ingloriousness" unfolded, challenged but unabated.[87]

Notes

1. Thanks to Robert Jensen, Murray Johnson, Jahara Rhiannon, and Bill Thorpe for help with this chapter.
2. R. Evans, "Blood Dries Quickly: Conflict Study and Australian Historiography," in John A. Moses, ed., *Historical Disciplines in Australasia: Themes, Problems and Debates,* Special Issue of the *Australian Journal of Politics and History* 41 (1995): 80–102.
3. G.V. Portus, *Australia Since 1606: A History for Young Australians* (Melbourne, 1935), 87, 151; C. Turnbull, *Black War: The Extermination of the Tasmanian Aborigines* (Melbourne, 1948).
4. R.M. Hartwell, "The Pastoral Ascendancy, 1820–50," in G. Greenwood, ed., *Australia: A Social and Political History* (Sydney, 1955), 89, 92, 95.
5. F. Moorhouse, *Days of Wine and Rage* (Ringwood, 1980), 123.
6. M. Durack, "In Search of an Australian Frontier," in J. Jones, ed., *Image of Australia,* Special Issue of *The Texas Quarterly* 2 (1962): 14–15.
7. R. Ward, *Australia* (Sydney, 1967), 26–27. Unless otherwise indicated, all italics in quotations are in the original.
8. C. Rowley, *The Destruction of Aboriginal Society* (Canberra, 1970); W.E.H. Stanner, *After the Dreaming* (Sydney, 1969); N.J.B. Plomley, *Friendly Mission:*

the Tasmanian Journals and Papers of George Augustus Robinson, 1829–1834 (Hobart, 1966).

9. R. Ward, "Introduction," in *Baal Belbora: The End of the Dancing,* ed. G. Blomfield (Sydney, 1981), xv–xvi.
10. H. Reynolds, *Frontier: Aborigines, Settlers and Land* (Sydney, 1987), 53.
11. B. Attwood, "Aboriginal History," in *Historical Disciplines,* ed. Moses, 40.
12. D. Myton, "Windschuttle's Way," *Campus Review* (23–29 January 2002): 10–11; K. Windschuttle, "The Myth of Frontier Massacres in Australian History," *Quadrant* (October 2000); R. Evans and B. Thorpe, "Indigenocide and the Massacre of Aboriginal History," *Overland* 163 (Winter 2001): 21–42; B. Thorpe, "History Clouds Windschuttle's Vision," *Campus Review* (27 February to 5 March 2002): 10–11.
13. W. Cowin, "The Impact of White Culture on the Queensland Aborigines," *Galmahra* (1950): 45–51.
14. E. Marcet, "Notice sur la partie de l'Australie récemment colonisée," *Tirée des Memoires de la Société de Géographique de Génève* 111 (Geneva, 1864), 37, 47, 52, 58–61.
15. A.J. Cutlack, "Four Years in Queensland and New South Wales," Rhodes House, Oxford University, MSS. Aust. r. 1., 1875, chapters 5 and 17, unpaginated; *Queensland Votes and Proceedings,* 1874, 34, quoted in T. Bottoms, "A History of Cairns: City of the South Pacific," Draft Manuscript, October 2000, 38.
16. Cutlack, "Four Years," chapter 4, unpaginated.
17. L. McDonald, *Rockhampton: A History of City and District* (St. Lucia, 1981), 183.
18. McDonald, *Rockhampton,* 184–85, 186–187, 188–93; G. Reid, *A Nest of Hornets: The Massacre of the Fraser Family at Hornet Bank Station, Central Queensland, 1857, and Related Events* (Melbourne, 1982), 120, 126; *Moreton Bay Courier,* 24 January 1861.
19. Reid, *Nest of Hornets,* ix, 41, 65, 119.
20. Reid, *Nest of Hornets,* chapters 5, 6, 8, and 10; McDonald, *Rockhampton,* 191–92; *Sydney Morning Herald,* 12 December 1861; A. Laurie, "The Black War in Queensland," *Royal Historical Society of Queensland Journal* 1, no. 1 (1959): 155–73.
21. *Rockhampton Bulletin,* 18 July 1865; McDonald, *Rockhampton,* 196.
22. *Rockhampton Morning Bulletin,* 3 August 1899; McDonald, *Rockhampton,* 193–94.
23. *Sydney Morning Herald,* 9 March 1873; A. Hillier, "'If You Leave Me Alone, I'll Leave You Alone': Biographical Sketches, Reports and Incidents from the Myall War of the Queensland Native Mounted Police Force, 1860–1885," unpublished MS, 156; Evans and Thorpe, "Indigenocide and the Massacre of Aboriginal History," 28.
24. Hillier, "If You Leave Me Alone," 156, 163–64; *Sydney Morning Herald,* 9 March 1871.
25. C.G. Heydon to *Sydney Morning Herald,* 15 January 1874.
26. *Journals of the Legislative Council* (Queensland), 1875, xxii, part 2, 907–9.
27. F. Johns, *John's Notable Australians: Who They Are and What They Do; Brief Biographies of Men and Women of the Commonwealth* (Melbourne, 1906), 87. Heydon was chosen in 1896 to consolidate New South Wales statute law, reviewing 1400 Acts. He was known as "the most inveterate worker who ever wore a wig." During World War One, he spoke as an avid Empire Loyalist and

a scourge of striking workers. He later became vice president of the para-military organization, The King's Men. See B. Nairn et al., eds., *Australian Dictionary of Biography*, Gil – Las, vol. 9 (Melbourne, 1983): 277.

28. J.K. Heydon, Ermington to F.W. Chesson, Aborigines Protection Society, 30 March 1874, Public Records Office (UK) Queensland, no. 6302, Co234/34, XC/A/59034.

29. *Cooktown Courier*, 21 February 1877, quoted in Bottoms, "A History of Cairns," 71–72.

30. *Sydney Morning Herald*, 12 December 1861, quoted in H. Reynolds, *An Indelible Stain? The Question of Genocide in Australia's History* (Ringwood, 2001), 127–28.

31. G.S. Lang, *The Aborigines of Australia, in their Original Condition, and in their Relations with the White Man* (Melbourne, 1865), 45–46.

32. P.J. Collins, "Goodbye Bussamarai: The Mandandanji Land–War, Southern Queensland, 1842–1852," chapters 9 and 12, unpublished MS.

33. J. Rogers, Colonial Office Minute, 29 January 1866, Public Records Office (UK), Co 234/13, 57283, 422.

34. F.W. Chesson, Aborigines Protection Society to the Duke of Buckingham, Secretary of State for the Colonies, 15 January 1868, Public Records Office (UK), Co 234/21, 57510, 153–54.

35. Colonial Office Minutes, 21 January 1867, Public Records Office (UK), Co 234/16, 57333, 282.

36. *Cooktown Courier*, 10 January 1877, quoted in Reynolds, *Indelible Stain*, 109.

37. Anon., *The Way We Civilize: Black and White; The Native Police* (Brisbane, 1880).

38. *Queenslander*, 3 July 1880.

39. R. Evans et al., *Race Relations in Colonial Queensland: A History of Exclusion, Exploitation and Extermination* (Brisbane, 1993), 78; Reynolds, *Indelible Stain*, 125, 130.

40. H. Reynolds, *This Whispering in Our Hearts* (St. Leonards, 1998), 132–34.

41. *The Worker* (Brisbane), 2 June 1900; R. Evans, "Killing Fields," *Courier Mail*, 2 June 2001.

42. Evans, "Blood Dries Quickly," 88–89.

43. J.W. Bleakley, "The Aborigines: Past and Present Treatment by the State," in *Black and White in Australia*, ed. J.S. Needham (London, 1935), 38–62.

44. C.D. Rowley, *Destruction of Aboriginal Society*, 186.

45. H. Reynolds, *Why Weren't We Told? A Personal Search for the Truth of our History* (Melbourne, 1999); R. Evans, *Fighting Word: Writing about Race* (St. Lucia, 1999).

46. Reynolds, *Indelible Stain*, 117–18.

47. P.L. Watson, *Frontier Lands and Pioneer Legends: How Pastoralists gained Karuwali Land* (Sydney, 1998), 107.

48. McDonald, *Rockhampton*, 187; Reid, *Nest of Hornets*, 138.

49. A. Dirk Moses, "An Antipodean Genocide? The Origins of the Genocidal Moment in the Colonization of Australia," *Journal of Genocide Research* 2, no. 1 (2000): 99, 102–3.

50. A. Palmer, *Colonial Genocide* (Adelaide, 2000), 19–20, 49, 58, 62, 193.

51. N.A. Loos, "Aboriginal–Dutch Relations in North Queensland, 1606–1756," *Queensland Heritage* 3, no. 1 (November 1974): 3–8.

52. B.A. Sommer, "The Bowman Incident," unpublished MS, Canberra College of Advanced Education, n.d.

53. R. Kelly and N. Evans, "The McKenzie Massacre on Bendinck Island," *Aboriginal History* 9, nos. 1–2, 44–45.

54. J. Richards, "Moreton Telegraph Station, 1902: The Native Police on Cape York Peninsula," in M. Enders and B. Dupont, eds., *Policing the Lucky Country* (Sydney, 2001), 96–106. Richards writes, "the sites of police killings have become 'special places' for indigenous people and ... firmly connected in people's memories with the intersection of history, policing and punishment" (96).

55. Inspector (and Aboriginal Protector) James Galbraith, 25 April 1901, quoted in W. Roth, *Report of the Northern Protector of Aborigines for 1902, Queensland Votes and Proceedings*, 1903, 23.

56. J. Dymock, *Nicholas River Southern Gulf of Carpentaria: Wanji and Garama Land Claim* (Canberra, 1994), 10, 44–45.

57. D. Wadley and W. King, eds., *Reef, Range and Red Dust: The Adventure Atlas of Queensland* (Brisbane, 1993), viii, 66.

58. W.J. Lines, *Taming the Great South Land: A History of the Conquest of Nature in Australia* (St Leonards, 1991), 109. Lines places the pre-contact indigenous population within the range of 750,000 to 900,000 people (10–11). Noel Butlin places it inferentially at above one million. See N. Butlin, *Our Original Aggression: Aboriginal Populations of Southeastern Australia, 1788–1888* (Sydney, 1983), 175. See also "How Many People?" in J.P. White and D.J. Mulvaney, *Australians to 1788* (Sydney, 1987), 115–17. The authors conclude "that an estimate of about 750,000 people is a reasonable one." Archibald Meston also placed Aboriginal pre-contact numbers at around 200,000 in Queensland in 1824. See A. Meston, *Geographic History of Queensland* (Brisbane, 1895), 83.

59. Palmer, *Colonial Genocide*, 87; G. Bowen to Duke of Newcastle, Dispatch 67, 3 November 1862, Queensland State Archives, Gov/23; E.W. Lamb, Crown Lands Office, 15 January 1866, Enclosure in Governor's Dispatch, no. 8, Public Records Office (UK), Co 234/15, 57333, 67–68.

60. S. Lane-Poole, ed., *Thirty Years of Colonial Government: A Selection from the Dispatches and Letters of the Right Hon. Sir George Bowen KCMG*, vol. 1 (London, 1889), 193.

61. E.W. Lamb, Crown Lands Office, 15 January 1866, Enclosure in Governor's Dispatch, no. 8, Public Records Office (UK), Co 234/15, 57333, 67–68.

62. N. Loos, *Invasion and Resistance: Aboriginal–European Relations on the North Queensland Frontier, 1861–1897* (Canberra, 1982), 62–87; Palmer, *Colonial Genocide*, 92–102.

63. J.C. Caldwell, "Population," in *Australian Historical Statistics*, ed W. Vamplew (Broadway, 1987), 26, 41; B. Davidson, "Agriculture" in *Australian Historical Statistics*, ed. W. Vamplew, 72; Palmer, *Colonial Genocide*, 114.

64. Evans et al., *Race Relations*, xvii–xviii; Evans, *Fighting Words*, 45–46.

65. Watson, *Frontier Lands*, 88.

66. Evans et al., *Race Relations*, 67–84, 241–44, 359–68.

67. A.T. Yarwood and M.J. Knowling, *Race Relations in Australia: A History* (Sydney, 1982), 192, 220–22.

68. D. Cryle, *The Press in Colonial Queensland: A Social and Political History, 1845–1875* (Brisbane, 1989), 67; *Queensland Guardian*, 14–21 February 1861.

69. J. Glover, *Humanity: A Moral History of the Twentieth Century* (London, 2001), 337–39.

70. D. Cormack, Ravenswood to A. Cormack, 24 November 1880 in "Australian Aborigines: Queensland," Mitchell Library, DOC 3167, 2, quoted in Bottoms, "A History of Cairns," 43.

71. H. Reynolds, *With the White People: The Crucial Role of Aborigines in the Exploration and Development of Australia* (Melbourne, 1990), 50; Palmer, *Colonial Genocide*, 60–61; Hillier, "If You Leave Me Alone," *passim*.

72. A. Markus, "Review of L. Skinner, *Police of the Pastoral Frontier: Native Police, 1849–59* (St. Lucia, 1975) *Labour History* 31, (November 1976) 102–3; Evans, *Fighting Words*, 39; A. Mollo, *To the Death's Head True* (London, 1982), 92–93, 106–8. See also C. Browning, *Ordinary Men* (New York, 1992).

73. See individual biographies in Hillier, "If You Leave Me Alone"; Evans, *Race Relations*, 55–56; Reynolds, *An Indelible Stain*, 99–118; Collins, *Goodbye Bussamarai*, chapters 5, 10, 12, 14, and 16; J. Richards, "Patrolling Another Northwest Frontier," unpublished paper, Law and History Conference, Hamilton, New Zealand, July 2001, 1–10.

74. Evans, *Fighting Words*, 38–39; Simon Whiley, "Eurama" to Author, 8 May 1995; M.C. O'Connell, Queensland Government House to Earl of Kimberley, Orders for Snider Rifles, 2 December 1870, 20 March 1871, 31 May 1871 and Colonial Office Minutes, Public Records Office (UK), Co234/25, XC/A 57544; Co234/26, XC/H57594; Co234/28, XC/A 575941; Extract from the Minutes of Proceedings of the Executive Council of Queensland, 9 March 1871, PRO (UK) Co234/26, XC/H57594; J. Wheeler, London to R.G.W. Herbert, 8 December 1871, PRO (UK) Co234.28, XC/A57594.

75. *Port Denison Times*, 4 July 1868; *Queenslander*, 13 June 1868.

76. Richards, "Patrolling Another Northwest Frontier," 3.

77. R. Evans, "The Mogwi Take Mi-an-jin: Race Relations and the Moreton Bay Penal Settlement, 1824–1842," in *Brisbane: The Aboriginal Presence, 1824–1860*, ed. R. Fisher, Brisbane History Group Papers, 11, 1992, 7–30; R. Evans, "To the Utmost Verge: Race and Ethnic Relations at Moreton Bay, 1799–1842," unpublished paper, presented to the Royal Historical Society of Queensland, September 2001.

78. P. Lawler and F. Uhr, "White People Killed by Aborigines in Northern Districts/Moreton Bay from 1840 to 1846," unpublished MS, September 2000, 1–2.

79. W. Ross Johnston, *Brisbane: The First Thirty Years* (Brisbane, 1988), 106.

80. Evidence of Captain John Coley to "Select Committee on Native Police," 14 May 1861, *Queensland Legislative Council Votes and Proceedings* 1861, 424–25; Governor Bowen to Carnarvon, Dispatch 61, 12 November 1866 (Enclosure 1), Queensland State Archives Gov/24. Maurice French also draws attention to Captain Wickham's listing of 174 whites killed in southeast Queensland by Aborigines between 1842 and 1853. M. French, *Conflict on the Condamine: Aborigines and the European Invasion* (Toowoomba, 1989), 112, 154.

81. Loos, *Invasion and Resistance*, 199–247. This covers Loos's list from 1867 until 1897.

82. C. Moore, "Explaining Violence," unpublished MS, 2000. Moore adds: "If German and Dutch sources were also combed, the number of violent incidents would expand considerably. Double the figures, and we may be coming close to the actual number of incidents and deaths during the early period of European contact, up until the end of the nineteenth century."

83. "Every white man murdered by blacks is represented by at least fifty blacks killed by whites." See A. Meston, "Report of the Government Scientific Expedition to the Bellenden-Ker Range (Wooroonooran) North Queensland," *Queensland Votes and Proceedings,* 1889, II, 4, 1,213. See also, Dymock, *Nicholson River,* 46. The Hon. Boyd Morehead, a future Queensland Premier, claimed in 1880 a death ratio of ten to one. See *Queensland Parliamentary Debates* xxxii (1880), 666.

84. *Queenslander,* 25 February 1882.

85. E. Curr, *The Australian Race: Its Origins, Language, Customs,* vol. 1 (Melbourne: 1886–1887), 209. At present, an extensive database of frontier violence in Queensland is in the process of being compiled within the School of Humanities, Griffith University, Brisbane, concentrating upon thorough archival research.

86. G. Highland, "Aborigines, Europeans and the Criminal Law: Two Trials at the Northern Supreme Court, Townsville in April 1888," unpublished paper, Peripheral Visions Conference, Townsville, July 1989, 29; *The Queensland Law Journal,* July 2, 1883, 136–37; *Queensland Figaro,* 14 April 1883, 241. For the comparative story of Aborigines' treatment before the law, see M. Finnane and J. McGuire, "The uses of punishment and exile: Aborigines in Colonial Australia," *Punishment and Society* (2001), 279–98: R. Evans and C. Ferrier, eds., *Radical Brisbane. An Unruly History* (Melbourne,2004), 40; For instance, almost 85 percent of those executed for rape in Queensland between 1850 and 1899 were Aboriginal men. Prior to 1850, a detainee at the Moreton Bay Penal Settlement, the convict John Smith (*Agamemnon,* 1819), was flogged for "contracting venereal disease and communicating it to a black native girl (also a child)" in September 1835. See Moreton Bay Book of Trials, 3 September 1835, Oxley Memorial Library.

87. D. Denholm, *The Colonial Australians* (Harmondsworth, 1979), 38–39, 40–42, 44–45; French, *Conflict on the Condamine,* 104; Dymock, *Nicholson River,* 44; Watson, *Frontier Land,* 89; and Palmer, *Colonial Genocide,* 133.

Chapter 7

PASSED AWAY?
The Fate of the Karuwali

Pamela Lukin Watson

What wonderful changes have taken place since those long past years!
Where are those thousands of hostile natives [i.e., *Karuwali* and neighboring societies]
who roamed the central plains of Cooper Creek in those days? Long ago the last
of those sturdy warriors passed away and few, very few, of even their
great-grandchildren are in the land of their ancestors.[1]

A ustralians have always held conflicting and changeable views about the early contacts between British settlers and the indigenous population whose land they appropriated.[2] In the last decade, controversy has mounted over whether this settlement constituted a genocide or entailed genocidal moments. In this chapter, I contend that genocide undoubtedly destroyed some, perhaps many, Aboriginal societies, an argument I illustrate by examining the fate of the *Karuwali* and neighboring societies whose "passing" is the subject of the introductory quotation. I use the United Nations Convention to define genocide and as a template to organize the evidence: the opinions of nineteenth century settler pastoralists, their families, their (white) employees, and others involved—to one extent or another—with the *Karuwali* and their neighbors.

There are three compelling reasons for this approach. The UN Convention is an international legal instrument, and its use avoids the idiosyncrasy of a personally capricious definition in which only mass death is genocide. Next, by emphasizing a composite of actions that may destroy group existence, the Convention reveals the full horror experienced by some Aboriginal groups to a degree that cannot be achieved by focusing solely on deaths by overt violence or the theft of children.[3] Finally, referring to the theoretical literature surrounding the UN Convention highlights certain features of the Australian experience and how these compare with the practices of other sovereign or settler communities.[4] But first it is necessary to know something about the victim group, the *Karuwali* people.

The *Karuwali* People

The *Karuwali* was one of a number of tribal societies living on a floodplain in far southwest Queensland, about eight hundred miles inland from the east coast of Australia.[5] The full extent of territory held by the *Karuwali* is now unknown, but together with two other populations that spoke related languages, the *Mitaka* and the *Marrula* (hereafter the *MKM* communities) they occupied about twenty-eight thousand square miles of land, an area comparable to the State of Maryland.[6] Their population numbers are similarly uncertain. One early settler claimed about three-thousand people had their hunting grounds along an eighty-two mile stretch of fertile land, some of it with permanent water holes.[7] This figure seems far higher than that normally associated with Central Australian indigenous communities, but it cannot be entirely ruled out of consideration due to the general reliability of the informant.

Until 1868, the *Karuwali* were almost completely untouched by the arrival of British settlers in Australia eighty years earlier, but that year the settler pastoralists John Costello and his brother-in-law Patrick Durack with their families and thousands of grazing stock intruded into the region, and gradually seized a contiguous sweep of more than seventeen-thousand square miles of tribal land[8]—all this without either payment or permission from the indigenous owners. From about 1872 onwards, the two settlers began profit-taking, first subdividing the land and then gradually off-loading it to speculators and pastoralists who flocked to the area once it was known to have been "opened up." Costello reputedly earned 250,000 British pounds—a vast fortune in those times.[9] Durack also recorded large profits, and so did their financial backers. By 1882, Costello and Durack had moved on, to repeat the whole process elsewhere on the edge of the ever-moving frontier.[10]

Left behind were fragmented black communities whose populations suffered severe decline due directly to the presence of settlers and the deleterious and often violent conditions and changes they introduced. Today, no *Karuwali* people live on *Karuwali* land, or in nearby towns; the local *Karuwali* ceremonies and rituals have ceased, the language is dead—indeed, its speakers disappeared before their language could be recorded. To the best of my knowledge, only a handful of individuals living today claim some *Karuwali* heritage—mixed with descent from other tribal communities and white settlers.

The Genocide of the Karuwali

Is the "passing away" of a people a genocide? According to the UN Convention, "intent to destroy" must be present in order for the claim of genocide to be established. Since the Convention does not further specify the details of intention, I follow the definition of Frank Chalk and Kurt Jonassohn: genocide is intended even if the action in question is carried out for different purposes, provided the perpetrator is likely to know that genocide is the probable or inevitable by-product of the planned action.[11]

Is it applicable in this case? There is no doubt that the British Government, in colonizing Australia, possessed a genuine wish to observe good relationships with the indigenous population. However, British ignorance of the cultural values of the population being colonized, and the resulting inherent conflicts in the situation, soon precipitated violence,[12] with the extermination of some societies, and the reduction of others to a handful of survivors.[13]

By the time John Costello and Patrick Durack began appropriating tribal land in southwest Queensland eighty years later, the potential for human disaster was widely known to police, pastoralists, and sections of the press: the influential pastoralist Charles Archer warned a select parliamentary committee in 1861 that "in the matter of kidnapping gins, [i.e., Aboriginal women] you cannot control white men ... and it is the cause of half the murders committed by the blacks upon them."[14] Frederick Walker, the first Commandant of the Native Mounted Police in Queensland, made it clear in 1852 that he found morally offensive the pastoralists' practices of first hunting blacks from creek and river frontages and thereby depriving them of food, and then shooting them for spearing cattle and stealing sheep.[15] In 1865, G.S. Lang, himself a pastoralist, noted that pastoralists had created a situation in which "every drink is at risk of their lives and [blacks] are driven to perfect desperation."[16] The ravages that venereal disease would bring to the area could have been expected, as the explorer E.J. Eyre had described in 1845 the speed and toxicity with which syphilis spread among the previously syphilis-free indigenous populations along the Murray River in South Australia.[17]

Despite Archer's forewarning, no attempts were made to find ways to prevent abduction and assault of Aboriginal women and children and to solve the problem of two competing uses for land. Settlement in southwest Queensland proceeded with the knowledge and acceptance that it would cause devastating and physically destructive changes to local indigenous communities. The "intent to destroy," as Chalk and Jonassohn define it, was part of this process of economic development and colonization. I therefore make the case in detail by examining, in turn, each of the five potentially genocidal acts listed in the UN Convention.[18]

(C)   Deliberately Inflicting on the Group Conditions of Life Calculated to Bring About Its Physical Destruction in Whole or in Part

The arrival of settler pastoralists together with their herds of cattle and flocks of sheep caused the lives of the *Karuwali* and other groups to deteriorate markedly in two major respects. The first concerned access to food and water, and the second arose from the sexual composition of the incoming settler population.

Food Supply

A preliminary report on the region by the explorer J. McKinley found that even his small herd of about two hundred expeditionary animals interfered severely with Aboriginal access to fish (the principal dietary item) in one water hole.[19] Given this, it is clear that the arrival of pastoral herds of, for example, 14,000 sheep and 700 cattle, or in another case, 90,000 sheep and 10,000 head of cattle, made a disastrous impact on indigenous food and water supplies.[20] Since almost none of the "runs" were fenced, these grazing animals wandered at will, monopolizing the creeks, streams, and water holes, and diminishing both the quantity and quality of available water. They smashed the eggs and nests of waterbirds, ruined food plants on the adjacent edges and bank, and, by close-cropping the grasses, they left little for the marsupials that formed an important part of tribal nutrition. The very presence of grazing herds and flocks disturbed the game, restricting hunting and fishing. Often, too, cattle and sheep destroyed material items used in food technology: grinding stones, fishing and bird-trapping nets, stone and wood fish-traps, snares, and hunting hides were broken under the crush of animal bodies or were trampled and smashed underfoot.

As herds and flocks increased, the countryside lost much of the variety and depth of its vegetative cover and fauna, and it became increasingly difficult for Aboriginal people to avoid malnutrition or starvation, as had happened elsewhere with pastoral settlement. Even among those working for food on pastoral properties, the diet was often severely inadequate and hunger was commonplace.[21]

Periodic dry seasons and then a crippling drought at the turn of the nineteenth century struck the area, totally denuding the already depleted countryside. The memoirs of one early pastoralist family claim that "a good many" Aborigines starved to death at Whicellow, to the east of the *MKM* border, during this drought.[22] In 1902, Harold Meston, Queensland Protector of Aborigines, made a spot-check of the area including some pastoral properties established on *Karuwali* and neighboring land.[23] He found hundreds of Aboriginal people in a starving or near-starving condition during his brief visit. These were not the only individuals in the region suffering from malnutrition or starvation, and Meston himself noted that he had not been able to visit secluded native camps in those river channels where he judged the same desperate food shortages must have existed.[24]

Rape

At the same time that the *Karuwali* and their neighbors were struggling with reduced access to food and water, indigenous societies had to accommodate themselves to an influx of white males, about 90 percent of whom may have been without sexual partners,[25] and many of whom appear to have been sexually predatory and infected with venereal disease.[26] In that remote desert area, the ratio between European men and women was eight to one. This imbalance was compounded by other factors. One was the widespread settler view of tribal people as little above the level of beasts—racist attitudes that facilitated the abuse of women and children.[27] A related component was government failure to enforce its legal obligation to protect indigenous people. Despite the fact that the latter had become British subjects under British law, and that the British Government in 1788 had instructed the first governor, Governor Arthur Phillip, to treat them as such, government agencies in southwest Queensland (as elsewhere in Australia) simply acquiesced in settler assault, abduction, and rape of black women and children.[28]

A number of local sources support this claim. In her family memoirs of 1962, Alice Duncan-Kemp cites abduction and abuse of women as one of three major causes of the violence between whites and blacks in the early days of pastoral settlement.[29] R. Thorpe, a policeman with responsibility for the Georgina River area, describes mere children being run down by stockmen on horseback and raped, and women being abducted, taken to stations for sexual purposes, and kept tied up at night to keep them from escaping.[30] A relevant aspect of these reports is that the incidents described were not one-off events, but recurring behavior, and clearly neither the police officer nor anyone else planned to take any preventative or punitive action.

While some assaults on women and children may have been motivated solely by the desire to gain access to sex, abductions had additional, economic advantages. Once separated from their community, and in despair of rescue, women and children had no alternative but grinding toil for scraps of food. In this way, white males acquired not only sexual partners but personal servants, and any children born of these encounters simply swelled the unpaid work force or could be passed on, or sometimes sold, to other whites in need of servants or sexual egress.[31]

Pastoralists found control over sexual access to black women useful in recruiting labor. Many grazing properties on or adjacent to *MKM* territory kept "stud gins" according to a local police report. H. Fischer, who seems to have been part of a sheep-shearing gang on one of these properties, Durham Downs, describes the conditions some of these women faced.[32] Aboriginal women were graded: "stud gins" were reserved for the sole use of the boss; class number two were for "colonial experience men" (that is, middle or upper-class young British males sent to the colonies to gain experience), and the third grade were for general hands. Six to eight of the most feeble toiled continuously in the sun, carting water from the creek to the shed, a distance of about three-hundred yards. After the day's work, the shearers would force sex upon the hapless women. At the end of the shearing season, many of the Aboriginal people were turned away and, Fisher thought, without any remuneration at all. Blacks seldom had the option of voluntarily leaving these and similar conditions. An agreement existed on most pastoral properties that runaway blacks would be "hunted *or* brought back." [33] The abduction of women and the establishment of "stud gins" are described in police reports, yet it is clear from their context that the police made no attempt to charge any of the perpetrators or prevent them from continuing the same behavior. Under these circumstances, the government, via the agency of the police, had become an accessory to these crimes.

(B)   Causing Serious Bodily or Mental Harm to Members of the Group

Bodily Harm

Settlers spread syphilis and gonorrhea rapidly throughout the native population of the region, hitherto free of venereal diseases. Almost certainly, far more Aboriginal people died as a result of these and other infections than from overt violence, as was the case right across Australia. Such fatalities have become a defense against accusations of genocide, because indigenous people are said to have died from "natural causes" rather than from white brutality.[34]

In fact, syphilis and gonorrhea differ markedly from other introduced diseases because their dissemination involves a very large social component, and it is this feature that justifies considering the spread of venereal infections as a genocidal act under clause (b) of the UN Convention on Genocide. Victims of influenza, smallpox, and measles have little, if any, control over the transmission of their illnesses from themselves to another, but venereal infections are sexually transmitted, and those who pass the diseases to others are almost invariably aware that they are doing so.

The dangers and consequences of infecting sexual partners were appreciated in the nineteenth century. A leading contemporary textbook written by Professor E. Keyes from Guys Hospital in London in 1881 stressed the responsibility of infected individuals to avoid contaminating others, urging complete sexual abstinence for some years after the most recent syphilitic contact.[35] The result of passing on these diseases was also generally apparent—the loathsome sores, pain, and mental decay. While arguing that syphilis was seldom fatal, Keyes noted the exception: when syphilis was introduced into populations previously totally free of the disease, syphilis became exceptionally malignant, and inhabitants died as if they suffered from a plague.

These were the effects in the region. Evidence suggests that *MKM* people were heavily contaminated by 1884. In that year, a survey among settler pastoralists conducted by a fellow pastoralist indicated that venereal disease was taking lives and probably reducing the birthrate among many tribes in the region.[36] By 1891, one settler reported that blacks living along the Diamantina were: "Fairly rotten from the loathsome diseases, some of them living skeletons and covered with erosion. When those unfortunates see a white man their cry is not as of old 'grog or tobacco' but 'medison' [medicine] in such imploring tones as would move the heart of stone." [37]

William Hume, an official with the Land Board making an inspection of areas in western Queensland, was equally moved to write to the Home Secretary in Sydney in 1898 about venereal disease in the Georgina River area and around Birdsville. Conditions were a public scandal reflecting on the good name of the colony, he declared, demanding that something be done.[38] Hume's complaint galvanized the government, and all local police in the area were ordered to report on venereal disease among blacks. These reports confirmed extensive infections everywhere, although they differed in details. For example, R. Reside, the constable at Bedourie on *MKM* land, declared that "stud gins" on local properties were generally healthy, but conditions were very bad among "walk-about blacks," a category that included former "stud gins" who were banished from properties once they contracted venereal disease from their settler patrons. Among this group, claimed the constable, most individuals were covered in venereal sores; they were hardly able to walk, and were so feeble that it was difficult for them to gather enough food to keep themselves alive.[39] In the Boulia area to the northeast of the *MKM*, venereal disease was prevalent in all Aboriginal camps, with the women the sickest, so that they were almost unable to get about, and had to depend upon others to obtain food.[40]

On the surface, this police survey of venereal disease among the Aboriginal people could imply non-genocidal intentions at one level of government. However, the survey also can be interpreted as a sop to William Hume, an influential citizen from the state capital. This seems the likelier situation because, despite the horror of the reports, the Government did nothing. No medicine was dispatched or extra food provided for those too weak to hunt for themselves; no hospital care was offered. In fact, Archibald Meston, Protector of Aborigines, added a memo to the police reports to the effect that it was useless for the government to try any temporary palliative measures, and that it was better to remove blacks entirely from their homelands and any contact with settlers. Eventually Aboriginal people were transferred to reserves under Queensland's *The Aboriginals Protection and Sale of Opium Act (1897)*.

There is some evidence that infecting others was a conscious and desired end in itself in some instances, not just a side-effect of sexual intercourse. There are two reliable local references to whites purposefully infecting native women with venereal disease; both reports describe general practices, not one-off events. Michael Costello (son of the original settler John Costello) claimed that stockmen do their very best to disease the black women.[41] Policeman Thorpe noted in an official report that a general impression existed among ignorant bushmen that the best way to rid themselves of gonorrhea, or to lessen its severity, was to infect a female with the disease. In the course of this practice, often syphilis as well as gonorrhea was transmitted, and Thorpe saw "poor young gins, mere children between eleven and fourteen, suffering from syphilis in all its stages."[42] It is impossible to estimate today the magnitude of destruction the introduction of venereal diseases wrought upon the *Karuwali* and others. But it was obviously significant enough in scale for Archibald Meston to claim in 1900 that if the number of deaths in southwest Queensland from this cause were fully known and published, "[it] would excite the horror of the nation."[43]

Equally important in terms of ethnic destruction is the extent to which venereal infections destroyed people's procreative powers and thus prevented black communities from physically reproducing themselves. There is no reliable information here. However, the sheer numbers and percentage of people infected, the fact that some individuals were contaminated before they were old enough to have opportunities to reproduce, and the reports about the lack of children and young adults in communities, all suggest that the effects on population levels among the *MKM* and other groups were very grave.

Mental Harm

Clause (B) also refers to "serious ... *mental* harm." The British aim from the beginning of settlement was to "Christianise" the indigenous population.[44] This included preventing the "barbarous" practise of initiations. But just as syphilis infections limited the power of Aboriginal societies to *physically* reproduce themselves, the prohibition on initiation ceremonies prevented the *social* reproduction of Aboriginal life. C.D. Rowley, in his book *The Destruction of Aboriginal Society*, argues that attacks on the ceremonies "could have done more to hasten the disintegration of the old Aboriginal society than all the killings."[45]

This cultural feature needs explanation. Power in indigenous societies came from control over knowledge. In Aboriginal thinking, it was the responsibility of humans to maintain the land and all it contained (including social life) as it had been since the time of the ancestral creative beings. If people disregarded these obligations, unutterable chaos would follow. Consequently, everyone had to follow sacrosanct precedents in exact and minute detail, in particular with regard to sacred paraphernalia, marriage rules, complex totemic relationships and the obligations these entailed, and ceremonial and ritual performances. A vast body of knowledge (referred to as "the Law") defined how this could best be done.[46]

This knowledge was not freely accessible; indeed, it was guarded by taboos and enforced death penalties. Knowledge could be obtained legitimately only by proceeding through a succession of initiation grades. Each of these involved periods of concentrated learning plus some degree of pain, physical mutilation, social isolation, discomfort, and fear. This system produced, incrementally, a core of leaders with great powers of endurance and self-restraint, and a deep knowledge of the laws and traditions of all aspects of their community. Because it took the best part of a lifetime to pass through all possible initiations, almost invariably those "who had the Law"—and were in a position to advise and lead others—were older people. Prevention of initiation ceremonies threatened the authority structures of tribal life, the development of future leaders, and the transfer of important social knowledge on which Aboriginal life depended.

Rowley argues that the prevention of ceremonies and ritual "probably increased the desperation of influential [Aboriginal] men and probably helped to provoke resistance on a scale resembling guerilla warfare."[47] This was the case among the *Karuwali* and their neighbors. The first violence and death on Costello and Durack properties arose when the two pastoralists set out to break the power of the senior males by encouraging younger individuals to defy them. Initiation ceremonies and white interference in tribal marriage laws appear to have been the immediate triggers. Despite warnings from their Aboriginal staff that this would bring about major confrontation, Costello persisted. One of Costello's Aboriginal servants was executed in retaliation by his fellow tribesmen, and the two pastoralists then banished blacks from local water holes and food sources. Deprived of food, blacks turned to spearing cattle or sheep, and settler anger at the loss of valuable animals led to more killing of indigenous people.[48]

This is a good example of the way that actions that appear directed solely at a community's cultural features (that is, acts that can be described as ethnocidal) can move situations closer to the genocidal. Another example of this dynamic among the *Karuwali* was the desecration of ceremonial sites by grazing animals and stockmen, nominated by one pastoralist as one of the three main causes of violence between indigenous people and settlers.[49]

(A)   Killing Members of the Group

In her family memoirs, Mary Durack asserts that by 1874 to 1875, many settlers had begun arguing openly that "Western Queensland could only be habitable for whites when the last of the blacks had been killed out—'by bullet or by bait.'"[50] Many contemporary reports and pastoral memoirs support this claim, either expressing similar intentions or describing actual events. *The Queenslander* newspaper, in its editorial, wrote of blacks being shot "because they were blacks."[51] W. Bucknell, a pastoralist from the Georgina River area, admitted candidly in the press that Aboriginal people were fired at whenever they appeared on his property.[52] Henry Dean, a settler on lower Cooper Creek, organized a military-style mounted party to clear the country of its indigenous people, and one of his stockmen wrote, "I am afraid it is now open war between the blacks and us."[53] Settlers must have killed numbers of Aborigines around the pastoral property of Morney Plains (based on seized *Karuwali* land). A letter from the manager there written sometime in the period between 1874 and 1878 argues that it was reasonable to kill blacks who camp around water holes *because* this disturbs and scatters the cattle, thus making extra work for the stockmen. The letter concludes with the reminder that neighboring properties are shooting blacks, and unless the staff at Morney Plains do so as well, the property will soon become unsafe for settlers.[54] Alice Duncan-Kemp, in her family memoirs, believes that the three-thousand people living in the vicinity of *Dangeri* Waterhole (part of the putative large population noted earlier) were gradually killed during the period between 1864 and 1894, fighting a losing battle against extermination by settlers and the Native Police Force.[55]

Durack describes the ruthlessness of one attack initiated by her great-uncle John Costello after the killing of Maloney, a white man.[56] "There were however no questions asked of the blacks as to who had committed this terrible crime or why. No arrests were made and the bodies of those shot around a camp at dawn were left to the ravages of wild dogs and birds of prey."[57] Durack continues, writing of troopers riding to kill: "To shatter the old tribes, the *Boontamurra*, the *Pita-Pita*, the *Murragon*, the *Walker-di*, the *Ngoa*, the *Murrawarri*, and the *Kalkadoon*, to leave men, women and children dead and dying on the plains, in the gullies and river beds." Durack does not make clear if these latter massacres were also the result of Maloney's death. If this was the case, then the massacres took place far from the source of the incident, which was quite possible, as a feature of some retaliatory killings was the geographic spread over which they occurred in response to a single white death.

There were a number of massacres in the country occupied by *MKM* peoples, and some of these may coincide with the statements about Aboriginal killings noted above. At least three massacres occurred in the 1870s in the southern section of *MKM* territory. Whites slaughtered Aboriginal people at Mt. Leonard Station to avenge the death of Welford, a pastoralist killed some hundreds of miles away on the Barcoo River.[58] In 1875, Conrick, a pastoralist, found the remains of about forty-two bodies with bullet wounds at Thundapurty Waterhole near Durrie.[59] Further to the west, a notorious bloodbath took place on Cooningheera Waterhole.[60] According to one report, a whole tribe—old men, women, and children—were hunted down there like wallabies and shot in revenge for the Aboriginal murder of a cook, Maconachie, who is said to have "developed a taste for the women of the local tribe."

The *MKM* group had economic, religious, and social ties to communities up and down the Diamantina, Georgina, and Cooper Creek Rivers.[61] Consequently, it was vulnerable to attack far beyond its own territories when members traveled elsewhere for ceremonies or exchange. A number of massacres occurred on those rivers that may have involved the *Karuwali* and their neighbors. There were one, possibly two, massacres at Tanbar on the western bank of the Cooper river, quite close to the eastern border of the *MKM*.[62] Welford's death, which had caused the killings at Mt. Leonard, led to more slaughter on the Barcoo River, a Cooper Creek tributary.[63] At least three other retaliatory massacres resulted from Maconochie's death, and L. Hercus, a linguist familiar with the remnant languages of the area, has suggested that these massacres were planned to coincide with major tribal ceremonies, thus maximizing the numbers who could be butchered simultaneously.[64] At Coonchere Sandhill on the lower Diamantina, more than one-hundred men, women, and children perished. Another massacre occurred east of Pandie Pandie on the same river; and the third large massacre took place at Kalidgiworra Waterhole, on the junction of the Mulligan and Georgina rivers—a place Duncan-Kemp claims was regularly visited by Aboriginal people from her family's pastoral holding on *Karuwali* land.[65]

(D)   Imposing Measures Intended to
Prevent Births Within the Group
(E)   Forcibly Transferring Children of the
Group to Another Group

The frequency of sexual disease, malnutrition, and massacres all took a toll on the fertility of Aboriginal families in the region, and consequently on the viability of particular ethnic groups like the *Karuwali*—just as was to be expected from previous contacts between settler pastoralists and the Aboriginal people whose land the former had seized. Children were also forcibly transferred from one group to another, at first by individual settlers, as discussed earlier, and later by government and institutions. Anna Haebich, writing of the Australian colonies as a whole, refers to "the presumption of colonists of their prerogative to take and keep the children and to recast their identities to fit that of their white masters."[66] At the end of the 1890s, legislation was enacted initiating formal actions that clearly fell within the parameters of clause (e). Queensland's *The Aboriginals Protection and Sale of Opium Act (1897)* empowered the Home Secretary to remove Aboriginal individuals at will to any one of a number of reserves, generally hundreds of miles from their homes. An examination of previously restricted departmental records by the historian Rosalind Kidd found that, for almost all of the twentieth century, each chief administrator of Aboriginal affairs "exercis[ed] almost total control over the lives of many thousands of Aboriginal Queenslanders, regulating freedom of movement, place of residence, employment, private savings and spending, marriage, adoption, and family cohesion."[67] As a result, families were often physically separated from one another, husbands from wives, children from parents, one sibling from another. Fragments of different tribes were herded together. Rituals and ceremonies were proscribed, use of native languages forbidden, and native beliefs ridiculed. Children were often particular targets despite the assiduous attempts of any relatives present to prevent this. Consequently, specific knowledge of country and sacred places was difficult to pass on, and children were unable to be socialized as members of the tribal groups to which their parents belonged. They remained Aboriginal in personal identity, but many lost a sense of themselves as members of specific ethnic communities like the *Karuwali*.

According to both the Duncan-Kemp and Costello memoirs, by about 1935—that is, about seventy years after British settlers arrived in the region—most of the once-thriving indigenous population of southwestern Queensland were gone. Some had been killed by native police and settlers, others died of malnutrition, exposure, and introduced diseases, many were institutionalized on missions and reserves, and a few took what they believed to be temporary shelter with other tribal societies—often to meet similar fates there. Today, a further seventy years have elapsed, and as far as I can discover, the *Karuwali* no longer exist as a viable society. The method of their "passing" accurately foreshadowed Raphael Lemkin's "composite of [five] different acts of persecution or destruction," one or more of which may cause genocide.[68]

Other Genocidal Aspects

Among current debates on the issue of genocide, one is the identity of the perpetrator. In her book *Colonial Genocide*, which compares colonial Queensland and German Southwest Africa, Alison Palmer argues that the perpetrators in Queensland were the settlers, the Native Police Force, and the Government, and there is nothing in my local study to contradict her conclusions.[69] Nevertheless, the role of the government is worth emphasizing, because it is often overlooked. Government and other authorities were linked to the majority of events that devastated the *Karuwali* and other societies. The Native Police Force that conducted many of the massacres were just as much part of the Queensland Government as were the Customs Department or the Tax Office. Archibald and Harold Meston, official Protectors of the Aborigines who initiated and controlled the transfer of Aboriginal people to reserves and missions, were government appointees. The policies that applied on reserves and missions, such as separation of parents and children, were set by government agencies or appointees.

The pastoralists, some of whom abducted and assaulted women and children and massacred entire groups of people, had legitimate status as authorities: they held government licenses that permitted them to live beyond police boundaries, and these were generally interpreted as giving pastoralists authority over their properties and the people who lived upon them.

Events that ravaged the *Karuwali* population and neighboring societies conform to several typologies of genocide. They fit Helen Fein's "developmental genocide" in which the crime eliminates a group who stand in the way of economic exploitation of resources.[70] They agree also with H. Savon's terminology based on results; as he defines it, the devastation of the *Karuwali* was a "genocide of substitution," that is, one population replaced another.[71] However, Chalk and Jonassohn's own typology is the most appropriate, as the authors' organizing principle is the motives of the perpetrators, and the pertinent category is "genocide for economic gains."[72]

Overall, almost every action that destroyed the *Karuwali* and their neighbors occurred, in part, because it made good economic sense to British settlers. The most financially satisfying of the genocidal acts was the appropriation of tribal territory and the depasturing (that is, the grazing) of cattle and sheep upon it; the profits made by Durack, Costello, and others from the sale of *Karuwali* and nearby land illustrate just how rewarding this practice was. But there were monetary gains, too, in the secondary actions that combined to ravage native society.

Removing all the indigenous people from pastoral properties was known to increase land prices and lower wages in coastal areas, and this was the expectation also in the far southwest. Failure to provide blacks with the protection of the law to which they were entitled as British citizens saved administrative costs, as letters to the editor of *The Queenslander* frankly admitted.[73] Abduction of women and children provided unpaid servants as well as sex, increased the numbers of workers through the birth of mixed-descent children, and provided pastoralists with sexual lures to attract employees. The starvation diet that blacks often received in lieu of wages lowered the running costs of properties. Finally, aggregating the remnants of southwest tribal societies and incarcerating them on coastal reserves far from their homes was, as A. Meston argued at the time, a cheaper solution than attempting to solve the social problems of hunger, illness, and dispossession in the area where they had occurred.[74]

Conclusions

Karuwali experiences during white settlement were not unique. The destruction of other Aboriginal societies as functioning entities proceeded in similar ways. The only atypical aspect of the *Karuwali* was that the ratio of settler males to settler females was even larger than it was on earlier frontiers. Otherwise, all the components that added up to produce the destruction of the *Karuwali* and surrounding societies existed elsewhere in Queensland, and probably in many other parts of Australia (with some allowances for differences in state government institutions).

The same industry faced the indigenous population wherever land was suitable for grazing sheep and cattle. Everywhere, similar if not identical conflicts arose over competing uses for land and white abuse of native women, and settlers frequently adopted the same harsh solutions as they did in the case of the *Karuwali.* Sometimes, even the same settlers were involved, because their interests and occupations took them from one geographical location to another.

At least six of the pastoralists whose appropriation of *Karuwali* and nearby territories wrought such havoc on local indigenous communities also seized Aboriginal land in other parts of Queensland, and, between them, tribal territories in every mainland Australian state except Victoria.[75] The stockmen and the shearers, the Native Police Force and the regular police, the Protectors of Aborigines, all of whom played a role in the destruction of the *Karuwali,* brought their values and behavior patterns to bear upon indigenous communities elsewhere with presumably the same results.

In addition to the continent-wide replication of components implicated in the deaths of the *Karuwali,* the results that genocide produces can be identified over much of Queensland and elsewhere. Consider the severe declines in the population of indigenous people, the disappearance of some ethnic communities, and the reduction of others to a meagre number of scattered survivors.[76] It seems valid to conclude, therefore, that a cause-and-effect relationship operated, and that many local small-scale genocides occurred across the country at the time of pastoral settlement. Certainly, the testimony is convincing enough to suggest that genocide should be suspected of having taken place in situations in which tribal societies have disappeared, and where individuals have lost critical knowledge of their specific ethnic background.

Notes

1. M. Costello, *Life of John Costello* (Sydney, 1930), 266.
2. Pamela L. Watson, *Frontier Lands and Pioneer Legends: How Pastoralists Gained Karuwali Land* (Sydney, 1998), 1–8. Attaching collective names to white and black protagonists in the colonization of Aboriginal Australia is generally unsatisfactory to sections of one group or another. In this chapter I use the word "tribe," although this term is often avoided by anthropologists due to its lack of precision. However, "tribe" has certain advantages here: con-

temporary Aboriginal people employ the expression "our old tribal people" when referring to the period following the British invasion, and "tribe" does convey a quality of life and a sense that small groups had their own identity and cultures in a way that more general terms like "Aboriginal people" do not. Using the word "settler" as a term for the British intruders aligns my chapter with the title of this book, but I acknowledge that Australia was not settled by the British but by the ancestors of present-day Aboriginal people.

3. For an example of this focus, see Robert Manne, "In Denial: The Stolen Generations and The Right," *The Australian Quarterly Essay* 1 (2000); and Anna Haebich, *Broken Circles: Fragmenting Indigenous Families, 1800–2000* (Freemantle, 2000).

4. F. Chalk, and K. Jonassohn, *The History and Sociology of Genocide: Analyses and Case Studies* (New Haven, 1990), 1–56.

5. Three big river systems, the Georgina, the Diamantina, and Cooper Creek "flow" into this plain. Much of the year the region is dry desert and the rivers only beds of sand, but almost annually the country undergoes extensive flooding. Consequently, the land swings between aridity and a copious abundance of water, plant, and animal life.

6 . J.G. Breen, "Aboriginal Languages of Western Queensland," *Linguistic Communications* 5 (1971): 1–88.

7. Alice Duncan-Kemp, *Where Strange Gods Call* (Brisbane, 1968), 26.

8. Mary Durack, *Kings in Grass Castles*, 1st ed. (London, 1959), 104–5.

9. Durack, *Kings in Grass Castles*, 187.

10. Durack, *Kings in Grass Castles*, 180, 205.

11. Chalk and Jonassohn, *History and Sociology of Genocide*, 26.

12. See A. Dirk Moses, "An Antipodean Genocide? The Origins of the Genocidal Moment in the Colonization of Australia," *Journal of Genocide Research* 2, no. 1 (2000): 89–106. This article provides a dynamic analysis that links the objective dimension of the colonial process to subjective genocidal policy development and implementation.

13. E. Curr, *The Australian Race: Its Origins, Languages, Customs*, vols. 1–4 (Melbourne, 1886/87), 209. Curr was a settler pastoralist, as were his father, son and brother: that is, he was part of the British "establishment" with no obvious reason to misrepresent the nature of settlement. During the early 1880s, Curr conducted a survey among pastoralists on the culture and living conditions of the specific Aboriginal group known to each of them. One question asked was the population number of the tribe and the cause of declining numbers if that situation existed. Curr's summary of the results was a black one: "in the bush, many tribes have disappeared, and the rest are disappearing … from fifteen to five-and-twenty per cent fall by the rifle; the tribe then submits, and diseases of European origin complete the process of extermination."

14. Cited in Raymond Evans, Kay Saunders, and Kathryn Cronin, *Exclusion, Exploitation and Extermination: Race Relations in Colonial Queensland* (Brisbane, 1975), 104.

15. Cited in D. Cryle, *The Press in Colonial Queensland* (Sydney, 1975), 15. From 1837 onwards, a number of corps of mounted Aboriginal police were formed for action on the frontiers of settlement in Australia. They were frequently led by young British males who were recent arrivals in the colony and were without any training. The Aboriginal troopers they commanded were recruited from tribes living far from the frontiers on which the recruits were to serve.

After 1859 the Queensland corps became known as the Native Mounted Police, and it was renowned for its brutality.

16. G.S. Lang, *The Aborigines of Australia and their Original Condition and in their Relations with the White Man* (Melbourne, 1986), 4.

17. E.J. Eyre, *Journals of Expeditions of Discovery into Central Australia and Overland from Adelaide to King George's Sound in the Years 1840–41* (London, 1845).

18. Chalk and Jonassohn, *History and Sociology of Genocide*, 10.

19. J. Davis, *Tracks of McKinlay across Australia* (London, 1863), 218.

20. Watson, *Frontier Lands and Pioneer Legends*, 20.

21. Evans, Saunders, and Cronin, *Exclusion, Exploitation and Extermination*, 85–107.

22. Alice Duncan-Kemp, Letters to Dr. Winterbotham, John Oxley Library (no acquisition no.), (1953).

23. The establishment of this post was originally a recommendation from a British parliamentary select committee on Aborigines in 1837. All Australian colonies had some equivalent of this position. Although the intention was to protect Aboriginal people from unfair treatment by settlers, the office soon became one of rigid control and the arbitrary enforcement of regulations. This continued in some areas right up until the 1960s and 1970s.

24. H. Meston, Letter to Home Secretary, Queensland State Archives, Col/139–44 (1902).

25. W. McPheat, "The Life and Work of John Flynn," (PhD Thesis, University of Queensland, 1964), 42. Flynn was a medical doctor in Central Australia at the turn of the nineteenth and twentieth centuries. He conducted an informal survey of (white) male to female ratios in remote desert areas and found it to be eight to one.

26. R.C. Thorpe, Letter submitted to The Select Committee on Aborigines Bill, South Australian Parliamentary Papers 77 (1898), 113–14. There is no firm data on how many settlers had venereal disease. The first research on the incidence of the disease in Australia appears to have been undertaken only during World War I when army medical authorities discovered that 25 percent of all young men called up at that time were inflicted with venereal disease. In other evidence, Professor Keyes of Guys Hospital, London, found that gonorrhoea was particularly common among respectable men in 1881. See E. Keyes, *The Venereal Diseases* (London, 1881). Keyes was referring to the British population; however, many early settlers—very probably most—in southwest Queensland were British. The economic historian Noel Butlin in *Our Original Aggression* (Sydney, 1983) argued that syphilis and gonorrhoea were "prominent" in the First Fleet. It is generally accepted that venereal disease was absent from Aboriginal Australia, although proving a negative is always difficult. Certainly many settlers and nineteenth-century medical doctors believed that settlers themselves had introduced venereal disease into a "naive" indigenous population. See Watson, *Frontier Lands and Pioneer Legends* for a fuller discussion of this issue.

27. Evans, Saunders, and Cronin, *Exclusion, Exploitation and Extermination*, 67–84.

28. Evans, Saunders, and Cronin, *Exclusion, Exploitation and Extermination*, 25.

29. A. Duncan-Kemp, *Our Channel Country* (Sydney, 1962), 136–37.

30. Thorpe, Letter submitted to the Select Committee on Aborigines Bill, 113–14.

31. H. Fisher, Letter to Archibald Meston, Protector of Aborigines, Queensland State Archives Col/139–44 (1900).

32. Fisher, Letter to Archibald Meston.

33. Archibald Meston, Aboriginals West of the Warrego, Report to the Home Secretary. Queensland State Archives, Col/139–144 (1900). Emphasis added.

34. G. Blainey, "Racists and Racism," *Courier Mail* (Brisbane) 15 May 1995. In this newspaper article, Blainey argued that in the *Mabo* judgment of 1992, some judges of the High Court of Australia were racist in claiming settlers had completely obliterated Aboriginal people in their environment. Blainey asserted that disease—not settler violence—was the main killer of Aboriginal people in those areas.

35. Keyes, *The Venereal Disease.*

36. Curr, *Australian Race* 2: 18–39, 374–75.

37. Evans, Saunders, and Cronin, *Exclusion, Exploitation and Extermination,* 99.

38. W. Hume, Letter to the Home Secretary, Queensland State Archives, Col/139–144 (1898).

39. R. Reside, Letter to Inspector Brannelly, Queensland State Archives, Col/139–144 (1898).

40. J. McNamara, Letter to Inspector Brannelly, Queensland State Archives, Col/139–144 (1898).

41. Cited in Evans, Saunders and Cronin, *Exclusion, Exploitation and Extermination,* 388.

42. R. Thorpe, Letter submitted to the Select Committee on Aborigines Bill, 113.

43. A. Meston, Western Aborigines at Durundur, Report to the Home Secretary, Queensland State Archives, Col/139–144 (1900). Raymond Evans also refers to the ravages of syphilis among Queensland blacks, asserting that the facts of the terrible story were deliberately smothered. See Evans, Saunders, and Cronin, *Exclusion, Exploitation and Extermination,* 99.

44. C. Rowley, *The Destruction of Aboriginal Society* (Harmondsworth, 1972), 19.

45. Rowley, *The Destruction of Aboriginal Society,* 42.

46. See E. Kolig, "An Obituary for Ritual Power," in *Aboriginal Power in Australian Society,* ed. Michael Power (Brisbane, 1982), 18–24.

47. Rowley, *Destruction of Aboriginal Society,* 169.

48. Durack, *Kings in Grass Castles,* 113.

49. Duncan-Kemp, *Our Channel Country.*

50. Durack, *Kings in Grass Castles,* 137–39.

51. *The Queenslander,* Editorial commissioned by the editor, Gresley Lukin, 1880.

52. W. Bucknell, "Leichhardt's Lost Expedition," *Science of Man* 2 (1899): 190–91.

53. G. Farwell, *Land of Mirage: By Camel through the Inland* (Sydney, 1983), 143.

54. H. Perry, *Pioneering: The Life of the Hon. R.M. Collins, M.L.C.* (Brisbane, 1923), 180.

55. Duncan-Kemp, *Where Strange Gods Call* (Brisbane 1968), 26.

56. Durack states that Maloney offended Aboriginal people by hiding behind trees and firing at them in the hope of astonishing them with his "white man magic." The indigenous people tolerated this for a while until Maloney "playfully" shot one of their dogs, the cultural equivalent of which would have been killing a pastoralist's horse. Maloney's body was found a few days later in a creek. See Durack, *Kings in Grass Castles,* 137–39.

57. Durack, *Kings in Grass Castles,* 137–39.

58. D. Huggonson, "Cecil 'Ngaka' Ebsworth: Wangkumara Man of the Corner Country," *Royal Historical Society of Queensland* 14 (1990): 113–16.
59. K. Willey, *The Drovers* (Melbourne, 1982).
60. Farwell, *Land of Mirage*, 132.
61. W.E. Roth, *Ethnological Studies among the North-West-Central Queensland Aborigines*, 1 (1897), 117–38.
62. N. Watton, "Where Rivers Feed a Creek," *Australian Shooters Journal* (July 1989): 34–35.
63. Durack, *Kings in Grass Castles*, 139.
64. L. Hercus, "Glimpses of the Karangura," *Records of the South Australian Museum* 25 (1991): 139–59.
65. Duncan-Kemp, *Where Strange Gods Call*, 51.
66. A. Haebich, *Broken Circles: Fragmenting Indigenous Families, 1800–2000* (Fremantle, 2000), 66.
67. Rosalind Kidd, *The Way We Civilise: Aboriginal Affairs—The Untold Story* (Brisbane, 1997), 345–49.
68. Chalk and Jonassohn, *The History and Sociology of Genocide*, 10.
69. Alison Palmer, *Colonial Genocide* (Hindmarsh, 2000), 192–93.
70. H. Fein, "Scenarios of Genocide: Models and Critical Responses," in *Toward the Understanding and Prevention of Genocide*, ed. I. Charny (London, 1984), 184.
71. Herve Savan, cited in Chalk and Jonassohn, *The History and Sociology of Genocide*.
72. Chalk and Jonassohn, *The History and Sociology of Genocide*, 29.
73. *The Queenslander,* Letters to the editor, 15 May and 17 July (1880).
74. A. Meston, Letter to the Home Secretary, July, Queensland State Archives, Col/139–44 (1901).
75. These were Patrick Durack, John Costello, Vincent Dowling, Robert Collins, De Burg Persse, and Oscar de Satge.
76. See endnote 13 from Curr, *The Australian Race*, 209.

Chapter 8

PUNITIVE EXPEDITIONS AND MASSACRES

Gippsland, Colorado, and the Question of Genocide

Paul R. Bartrop

Genocide, Massacre, and "Genocidal Massacre"

In 1988, Leo Kuper, one of the pioneers of the academic study of genocide, provided an insight into why the destruction of native peoples hitherto had been so easily dismissed in discussions of genocidal phenomena:

> [M]uch colonization proceeded without genocidal conflict ... But the effects of colonial settlement were quite variable, dependent on a variety of factors, such as the number of settlers, the forms of the colonizing economy and competition for productive resources, policies of the colonizing power, and attitudes to intermarriage or concubinage ...
>
> [S]ome of the annihilations of indigenous peoples arose not so much by deliberate act, but in the course of what may be described as a genocidal process: massacres, appropriation of land, introduction of diseases, and arduous conditions of labor.[1]

Kuper was not denying a relationship between colonization and genocide, but rather urging caution in the way that relationship was articulated. Indeed, he allowed that colonization, particularly

Notes for this section begin on page 211.

by European countries, acted as "a major source of genocide against indigenous groups."[2] We therefore need to address the relationship between colonial massacres and genocide, ask whether Kuper's "genocidal processes" are analogous with genocide outright and, if not, what the implications could mean for the historical understanding of genocide of indigenous peoples.

One initial answer could be that the definition of genocide is decisive, but this is not very helpful. Many definitions have been offered since Raphael Lemkin first coined the term in 1944, but only one—that of the United Nations Convention on the Prevention and Punishment of the Crime of Genocide (1948)—carries any weight under international law. The Convention was to a large degree drafted by Lemkin himself, though substantial amendments at the committee stage changed his intentions considerably. The main areas of contention in the final document, both then and now, are located in Article 2 of the Convention:

> [G]enocide means any of the following acts committed with intent to destroy, in whole or in part, a national, ethnical, racial, or religious group, as such:
>
> (a) Killing members of the group;
> (b) Causing serious bodily or mental harm to members of the group;
> (c) Deliberately inflicting on the group conditions of life calculated to bring about its physical destruction in whole or in part;
> (d) Imposing measures intended to prevent births within the group;
> (e) Forcibly transferring children of the group to another group.

This Article has a number of features. First, for a successful charge of genocide to be brought, the notion of *intent* on the part of the perpetrators must be proven. Second, destruction can be "in whole" or "in part," though just how many individuals constitute "in part" is not spelled out. Third, only four groups are listed as acceptable targets for genocide. People persecuted as a result of political affiliation, social origin, or sexual preference, for example, are not covered by the United Nations instrument. Finally, killing is not the only means to commit a genocide; four other activities, in which lives are not necessarily taken, also constitute genocide.[3]

The term genocide is a neologism of relatively recent origin that has come into common usage; it is a major social problem afflicting modern civilization; it is an academic area of study; and it is one of the defining features of our time. But it is, above all, a crime—for some, the crime of crimes.[4] Its criminal nature must be emphasized. It is, by the United Nations definition, a criminal act; either it is this or it is nothing. Genocide is not a relative moral value and, as an activity subject to sanction, adherence to its legal delineation requires the strictest fidelity.

Moreover, the fact that many commentators consider the definition embodied in the Genocide Convention incomplete (I count myself among them) has no bearing on its legal application.[5] Therefore, according to international law, while genocide can involve many things, it is the recognized intent to do these things that really matters. An act either is genocide according to the law of nations, or it is not genocide at all. If the quest to understand genocide is to be more than just an abstract scholarly enterprise, we must face one essential fact: it is *only* through the United Nations or its agencies that the countries of the world will ever apply themselves seriously to the question of confronting genocide.[6]

What are the implications for massacres of indigenous peoples on the frontiers of colonial settlement? Wrestling with a way to classify the notion of massacre in 1999, British scholar Mark Levene considered the concept in the following way:

> A massacre is when a group of animals or people lacking in self-defence, at least at that given moment, are killed—usually by another group ... who have the physical means, the power, with which to undertake the killing without physical danger to themselves. A massacre is unquestionably a one-sided affair and those slaughtered are usually perceived of as victims ... Massacre implies an event which takes place in a limited, though not defined geographical arena, as well as in a limited, though again not clearly defined time period.[7]

Such a description is important if we are to draw a clear line between massacre and genocide. There are three considerations: (a) the extent to which a murderous attack by one group against another is an isolated event or part of a total campaign the intention of which is the destruction of every member of that group regardless of where they may be located; (b) whether the attack is part of a coordinated series of actions that are replicated elsewhere; and (c) whether, given these considerations, the attack was committed by the state (or a state-sanctioned proxy) as an act of policy—that is, that the attack was within the law as determined by the governing authorities of the locality in which the action took place. When these three criteria have been met, we might conclude that we are able legitimately to discuss genocide; without them, we are talking about another form of atrocity such as, for example, mass murder—a crime punishable under the law of the land.

To accommodate massacres of small groups in which few (or none) were left alive, Leo Kuper introduced the term "genocidal massacre." As he saw it, these were instances "expressed characteristically in the annihilation of a section of a group—men, women and children, as for example in the wiping out of whole villages." He saw a need to develop such a concept "because the genocidal massacre has some of the elements of genocide." In adding this category to the study of genocide, he was aware also of "the almost insuperable problem of precision in classification" that already existed when he was writing.[8] The term massacre, for Kuper, is a useful addition to the demarcation of what is and is not genocide, as it can convey understanding to a limited instance of murderous destruction that might not otherwise encompass genocide in its fullest sense.

Moreover, the question of who carries out these massacres is of importance when arriving at an appreciation of what can be considered genocide. The role of the state as the primary actor in a genocide scenario has been debated by a number of scholars, and a resolution is crucial when tackling the question of genocidal massacres of indigenous peoples under colonialism. Alison Palmer, for example, has argued that "it is not necessary for the state to be the *only* perpetrator," but notes at the same time that "it is difficult to think of a case of either colonial genocide or modern genocide more generally in which the destruction was carried out by a non-state perpetrator alone."[9] In order to bring a more critical dimension to this observation, she then develops a model in which she distinguishes:

> between genocides in which the main perpetrator is (a) the state, (b) the state and others (civilians, military, and so on), or (c) others (with the tacit support of the state). With this qualification, the definition of genocide need not stipulate that the state is the perpetrator, but can allow for the varieties in the relations between different perpetrators.[10]

Here, Palmer recognizes that the state has a role to play in any act that can be termed genocide, regardless of its degree of involvement.

Others, notably Irving Louis Horowitz, have been more forthright. Genocide is "a structural and systematic destruction of innocent people by a state bureaucratic apparatus,"[11] and must be conducted "with the approval of, if not direct intervention by, the state apparatus."[12] Australian scholar Tony Barta would reject Horowitz's position, instead preferring to advance what he sees as "a conception of genocide which embraces *relations* of destruction and removes from the word the emphasis on policy and intention which brought it into being."[13] These "relations of destruction" were played out in the devastation of Aboriginal society accompanying the European settlement of Australia. For Barta, the nature of colonial society itself was genocidal, and genocide took place without either a declaration of intent or the overt involvement of the state. Genocide entailed the relationship between the settlers and the Aborigines. A genocidal society is thus one where "the whole bureaucratic apparatus might officially be directed to protect innocent people," but a target population "is nevertheless subject to remorseless pressures of destruction inherent in the very nature of society."[14]

Opposing this view, Henry Reynolds has explained that the localized nature of the destruction makes it difficult to draw any general conclusions about the nature of colonial society:

> There was no central direction or control of the conflict, no policy-making body, no overall strategy, no chain of command. Every squatter [i.e. land-owning pastoralist]—and sometimes every group of neighbouring squatters—had to decide in isolation how to deal with the local clans; how much violence was required and when the Aborigines could be let in to live on the station. *It is virtually impossible to decide if there was a general intention to destroy hostile Aboriginal groups or whether violence was used with the end of achieving dominance over, rather than exterminating, the tribes in question.*[15]

Discussing this further, Reynolds continues, *contra* Barta, that it is just as difficult to pin down a genocidal impulse running through colonial society:

> In a situation where the government was not involved, how is it possible to judge the situation beyond saying that some colonists clearly were advocates and perhaps practitioners of extermination? What percentage of a population's involvement is required before the society itself can be considered to be genocidal? There were no organisations of extirpationists, no societies with genocide as their avowed objective, no institutional structures to further the cause. The most we can say is that in some parts of the colony, public opinion at least tolerated the killing of Aborigines in a sweeping and indiscriminate fashion and that witnesses were not forthcoming with evidence that would have facilitated prosecution.[16]

While Barta's thesis provides a convenient means to explain the destruction of Aboriginal society, it has been challenged further by Canadian genocide scholar Frank Chalk, who questions whether there have been "any cases in which the energetic efforts of an entire government to rescue a group were overcome by the anonymous pressures of society."[17] For Chalk, as for Horowitz, genocide is primarily a crime of state. A society might harbor genocidal ambitions, but until the state directs and sanctions them, genocide cannot be said to exist. Killings by private individuals or groups are murder, not genocide, a view more faithful to the implicit meaning of genocidal responsibility in the United Nations Convention.[18] In order to reach an understanding of which massacres of indigenous peoples count as genocide under the United Nations Genocide Convention, this chapter examines two instances of indigenous destruction in the nineteenth century.

Warrigal Creek, Gippsland, 1843

The first considers an incident that took place at Warrigal Creek, in the Gippsland district of the British-Australian colony of Port Phillip (now Victoria) in 1843. Here, local pastoralists led by squatter Angus McMillan carried out a massacre of Aborigines belonging to the local Kurnai people. In a major study of the region, Australian historian Don Watson has described this massacre and others like it as "acts of genocide" to be distinguished from "isolated acts in the seizure of land by force."[19] Do these claims stand up to close scrutiny?

In 1843, Gippsland, occupying the eastern third of the colony, was still a wild frontier territory for Europeans. While it has proven difficult if not impossible to arrive at an accurate approximation of the Aboriginal population of the region at the time of the first European contact, a figure of nearly three thousand has been the most carefully constructed estimate in recent times.[20] It was only around 1839 that the first white explorers arrived, and in December of 1840 pastoral runs were established by the Macalister family at Boisdale and by their stock overseer Angus McMillan at Bushy Park. The region was landlocked; the first settlers were "frontiersmen in a wilderness area that was effectively isolated from the rest of the colony by mountains, rugged bush and long distances."[21] Law and order existed solely in name, as Crown Lands Commissioner Charles Tyers only arrived in the area in late 1843. As might be expected, he did not dispense justice impartially, and favored the landowners.[22] His major problems centered around two fundamental issues: having to establish order in European society on the one hand, and attempting to reduce disorder between Aborigines and settlers on the other.[23] Neither was an easy task, as the forces at his disposal initially were little more than "a handful of convicts and a bullock-driver," which, as one scholar has observed satirically, "scarcely deserve the name of a border police force."[24] Other than the kind of regular policing expected in any European social environment, Gippsland's need for some sort of law and order was principally founded on the problems to be found in Aboriginal-European relations. The fact that Tyers did not arrive until four years after the commencement of white settlement had a disastrous impact on the future direction of the relationship.

The major obstacle to a healthy interaction lay in the cattle-based pastoralism of the settlers. The Europeans, keen to establish large runs with little inconvenience, simply took over tracts of Aboriginal land and set their cattle to grazing. The Kurnai, forced to compete for the right to utilize land that had been theirs for millennia, faced the European invasion with resolute determination, spearing cattle and stockhands alike in their attempts to get the whites to leave. Such actions only led to white countermeasures, and in escalating rounds of action and reaction the degree of animosity became increasingly violent. No official force was available, either to placate the Aborigines or to curb settler excesses, which became more intense with each Aboriginal attempt at countering the white invasion.

It was in this context that the incident leading directly to Gippsland's most bloody massacre took place. In June 1843, one Ronald (in some accounts, Donald) Macalister, a nephew of the same Lachlan Macalister who had underwritten the establishment of the first cattle runs, was murdered by Aborigines near Port Albert, on the central Gippsland coast. There were conflicting interpretations as to why the murder occurred; one had it that a white stockhand (perhaps young Macalister) had thrown a shovelful of hot ashes onto the feet of an Aboriginal man; another was that some drunken herdsmen had murdered a number of Aborigines as a "diversion" from their usual routine. Whatever the reason, there was no doubting that Macalister was killed, and that his death had been a reprisal for an earlier injustice.

In response to Macalister's death, Angus McMillan took matters into his own hands and spread the word that he had decided to assemble a posse for the purpose of tracking down and killing those responsible. The initiative was not entirely his alone; Lachlan Macalister, then in Sydney, worked with McMillan behind the scenes.[25] Through the two men's efforts the posse, an irregular pack of cattle owners, stockmen, and other whites in the Gippsland vicinity, took shape under the official-sounding name of the Highland Brigade.[26] Prior to setting out, McMillan warned the party of about twenty that their mission had to be carried out in utmost secrecy.[27] A blood oath was sworn never to divulge the truth of the acts they were about to commit, for it was well known that in December 1838 seven white men had been hanged for the murder of twenty-eight Aborigines at Myall Creek, New South Wales. As one historian has written, a consequence of Myall Creek was that "murders of Aborigines did not so much decline as become more secret,"[28] and the McMillan-directed killings at Warrigal Creek certainly fitted into this category. It was "a secrecy so binding that the true facts of the massacre died with the perpetrators and their victims."[29]

A 1940 account by William Hoddinot, the son of an early pioneer in the district, outlined what transpired:

> Everyman [sic] who could find a gun or a horse went after the blacks, and came up with them around a large waterhole which was surrounded by the whites. They killed the blacks as long as their ammunition lasted. Many escaped into the bush. Others sought cover in the waterhole, but often, as one raised his head for breath, he was shot. More than a hundred of the blacks were killed.[30]

A more recent narrative, pieced together from the fragments of a number of accounts, has added more substance to Hoddinot's outline:

> The posse found a large group of Aborigines camped beside a waterhole on Warrigal Creek. Their intention was to avenge the death of Donald Macalister. No hostages were to be taken; no member of the group was to survive.
>
> McMillan gave the instruction to surround the camp. The posse split. Some men rode upstream; others downstream. In twenty minutes the camp was surrounded. McMillan gave the order and simultaneously, from every direction, the men opened fire.
>
> The Aborigines attempted to escape. Some raced into the scrub, only to be met by stockmen who gunned them down. Others jumped into the water hole. McMillan and his men positioned themselves around the water hole "and, as fast as they put their heads up for breath, they were shot until the water was red with blood."[31]

Though more colorful than Hoddinot's, this account retains the essential contours of the story, adding that "the massacre lasted less than half an hour," and that for the next few hours the killers "did a careful mopping-up operation," with the bodies of those they had killed "thrown into the waterhole." Years later, "the bones of some of the victims would be found" in this place.[32]

The killing did not stop at Warrigal Creek; in subsequent days "the posse moved through the area leaving a trail of bodies and blood. They killed at every opportunity."[33] In subsequent years, Gippsland became one large killing field, prompting one settler to write in 1846 that at least 450 Aborigines were murdered in the region:

> No wild beast of the forest was ever hunted down with such unsparing perseverance as they are. Men, women and children are shot wherever they can be met with. Some excuse might be found for shooting the men by those who are actually getting their cattle speared, but what can they urge in their excuse who shoot the women and children I cannot conceive. I have protested against it at every station I have been in Gippsland, in the strongest language, but *these things are kept very secret as the penalty would certainly be hanging.*[34]

Though by this stage the Aborigines had become overrun by the advance of white settlement, this did not mean an end either to the conflict or the killing, though the massacre at Warrigal Creek remained the largest single killing ground. The number of those slaughtered is impossible to determine with any accuracy, but if the figure of 150 is generally accepted as accurate, the bloodbath at Warrigal Creek was the biggest known massacre in Australian history.[35] By the time the Kurnai had finally been crushed, as one scholar sees it, "the whole of the Gippsland area had been won by violence"; quite simply, the settlers "just killed and killed and killed."[36]

For Peter Gardner, the historian who has done the most to bring the details of Warrigal Creek to light, the massacre "is probably one of the most important events in pre-gold Australian history"; in his view, it represents nothing less than a keystone event in the story of intercommunal relations in southeastern Australia, after which all future racism can be explained.[37] After Warrigal Creek, the frequency of massacres, rapes, and casual killings was "so normal, so commonplace, they barely deserved discussion."[38]

The massacre's other legacy, of course, with which Australia is still trying to come to terms, stems from the culture of silence that accompanied it—a culture that enables denialism to surface and deflect attention from issues such as reconciliation, inclusive nation-building, and the yet to be resolved matter of an official apology from the federal government to the Aboriginal people on behalf of all Australians.

The vast majority of Aboriginal killings in Gippsland, both before and after Warrigal Creek, were committed by private individuals acting in a private capacity. An official presence, as noted above, arrived only with the appearance of Commissioner Tyers in 1843. By the late 1850s, the number of Aborigines living in Gippsland had been slashed—according to one estimate, to under a hundred,[39] and to another, to 126—in the space of fifteen years.[40]

It is therefore more than appropriate that we should ask whether the destruction of Gippsland's Kurnai was a genocide. The United Nations Genocide Convention, it will be recalled, is absolute in its stipulation that genocide takes place when certain acts are committed "with intent to destroy" specifically identified groups "in whole or in part." There can be no doubt that the Aborigines of Gippsland could be classified as one of these groups; but was their destruction accomplished as the result of an intention to destroy them? If measured by the settlers' murderous standards, unquestionably the answer would be yes; but their standards cannot be applied, owing to the existence of a higher authority in the land that proscribed their actions and worked (sometimes resolutely, sometimes not) to nullify their behavior. It is that authority, the colonial government, that must be assessed when bringing the charge of genocide, because it was the ultimate legal arbiter of right and wrong throughout the land. And there is no evidence that demonstrates the government sought the destruction of the Gippsland Aborigines, devised policies for such destruction, conspired with those who did, or aided those who were trying to achieve it. The implementation of a policy of genocide in this case is not a charge that can be laid at the feet of the colonial government, despite the rhetoric of many who have since tried to do so. When measured by the standards of the Genocide Convention, the charge cannot stand.

Of course, this fact in no way mitigates the horror and tragedy of what happened. The effective eradication of a population took place in Gippsland, and white settlement was responsible. The Kurnai and other Aborigines suffered a population collapse at devastating speed. The magnitude of that disintegration was a human catastrophe, and must never be forgotten as an example of what can happen when the well-being of one group of humans is placed above that of another. Nothing can ever exonerate those, such as Angus McMillan, who engaged in the practice of brutal, bloody, and frequent murder.

Other definitions of genocide would contend it was a genocide, but according to international law the case is relatively straightforward. The government did not pursue a policy intended to destroy the Kurnai. Myall Creek had shown that the law regarded the killing of Aborigines to be a capital crime. At the time of the massacre, government authority in the form of troopers or officials was in fact absent, rendering the execution of *any* policies, good or bad, impossible. But this does not mean the *influence* of the law was unfelt or nonexistent. In her excellent study of Aboriginal-white relations in Victoria's Western District at the same time as the events being related were taking place in Gippsland, Jan Critchett has shown quite clearly that the power of the state—although "a rather abstract concept" to those without experience of it—nevertheless:

> has reality embodied in the local police, the local courts of justice and beyond them the more prestigious courts which deal with serious crimes. Beyond the police and the law courts is a body of law which can be appealed to either to condemn or protect the individual citizen. The law has its cases of precedence handed down from generation to generation. It has its representatives who protect the individual, those that put the case against him or her, and the Judge who has to guide the jury of citizens who in serious cases decide the verdict. All the actors have a role to play, a role established over hundreds of years.[41]

Clearly, an Aboriginal society that had rested for tens of thousands of years on a different system of social norms and sanctions could not be expected to appreciate these things in the abstract; but, as Critchett explains, the settlers could. The earliest pioneers arrived in the Western District as in Gippsland "ahead of law enforcement officers and courts of justice," which were "distant though not totally powerless, *for the settlers knew of the law and the power of the state.*"[42] This is a crucial point in any discussion of law in the absence of the state. The settlers *knew*; despite the fact that massacres such as Warrigal Creek took place before the formal arrival of the forces of the state, those committing atrocities were aware that they were breaking the law, and were fearful of the consequences of their actions. In Gippsland, this translated directly to Angus McMillan's insistence that his posse swear an oath of secrecy, which in turn conditioned the culture of silence that followed in all subsequent outrages.

Those who murdered the Kurnai at Warrigal Creek and elsewhere were murderers according to the law. That their murderous acts led in large part to the demise of the Kurnai does not diminish those acts' criminal nature, neither then nor now. And if the perpetrators had been caught, tried, and found guilty for their crimes, the law would have had no option, in light of Myall Creek, but to have called for their execution.

This is not to suggest that the colonial authorities were zealous in their pursuit of those who murdered Aborigines. For those in government with an interest in the matter—and this was a variable that did not apply in every situation—the pursuit, capture, and conviction of those responsible for such murders was next to impossible most of the time. Myall Creek, well-known throughout the colony in the years after 1838, would prove to be the exception rather than the rule. The conspiracy of silence following the Myall Creek executions made it extremely difficult to obtain evidence and, as R.H.W. Reece has concluded, "even on the rare occasions when whites admitted killing Aborigines there was still no guarantee that they could be indicted" owing to a lack of evidence.[43] By way of illustration, he shows how one representative instance, in the colony's Western District in 1840, left the authorities frustrated at their impotence. An anonymous colonist, writing to Secretary of State for the Colonies Lord John Russell in London, noted that:

> In this Colony, the Murder of a Native is punished severely if it can be proved against anyone. But the only effect of this Law is to make the Settlers cautious of telling when they do shoot the Blacks. It is quite certain that numbers of them are shot. Their bodies are buried and nothing more is heard of the matter.
>
> A short time ago, a party of 38 natives stole several hundred sheep from an outstation near Portland Bay. When the Proprietors' [shep]herds, who lived at another place, heard of it, they set off in pursuit of the Blacks, and, out of the 38, murdered 36 and left their bodies collected in a heap. This is perfectly known in Melbourne, but it is extremely hard to get sufficient proof.[44]

While investigations were made (and it is instructive to note that the anonymous letter-writer had no hesitation in using the word "murder" to describe what had happened), the case was not developed owing to a lack of adequate testimony. The most unfortunate aspect of this was that the period following the Myall Creek massacre saw "a genuine, although ill-informed, attempt to bring Aboriginal-white relations under the framework of the law."[45] The events at Portland Bay belied this effort, as did those in Gippsland soon thereafter. In the following years, authorized force and violence became more of the norm, as the state did its best to remove Aborigines from pastoral runs and break up the essential underpinnings of traditional Aboriginal society. Even then, however, in Gippsland—conditions varied throughout the century and across the continent—the intention was not a state-driven policy of genocide, at least as it would be viewed by the Genocide Convention.[46]

Sand Creek, Colorado, 1864

To appreciate the crucial role of the state when trying to arrive at a determination for or against genocide in colonial settings, we may contrast the Warrigal Creek massacre with another that took place two decades later across the Pacific. In the Colorado Territory of the United States, on 29 November 1864, Colonel John M. Chivington, commanding the Third Colorado Volunteer Cavalry Regiment, led an attack against a Cheyenne village under Chief Black Kettle. Here, those doing the killing had been given clear instructions, worked out in advance and communicated unequivocally. Like Gippsland in 1843, Colorado in 1864 was, in the words of David E. Stannard, "the quintessence of the frontier west."[47] Incidents between Indians and white settlers, as in Gippsland, resulted in escalating rounds of violence, but unlike in Gippsland the settlers were able to cloak their attacks in the legitimacy of organized military force. The period 1861 to 1865 was a time of bloody civil war for the United States, and its soldiers in the western part of the country were recalled for active duty against the Confederacy, their places being taken by militia forces raised in the territory itself. Actions against the Indians were henceforth undertaken by uniformed volunteers, that is, local men acting under orders from the territorial government. As one historian has viewed it, many of these citizen soldiers were frontiersmen with a deep contempt for Native Americans. One of these detachments fired shells into a Sioux camp for artillery practice.[48] Despite such wanton violence and the refusal of the Indian bands to be cowed, by the early 1860s some measure of accord had arrived in the form of limited peace treaties agreed upon, including with the southern Cheyenne chiefs Black Kettle and White Antelope, who had acceded to white demands for the cession of a substantial area of land near Denver.

> The other Cheyenne chiefs, however, rejected it (something which, as autonomous band leaders, they were perfectly entitled to do), and in the spring and summer of 1864, hoping for a pretext to take the land by force, members of the Colorado militia launched a series of indiscriminate raids against Cheyenne camps. They were commanded by Colonel John Chivington, a Methodist preacher and rabid Indian-hater who was notorious for publicly advocating the murder of Native American children on the grounds that "nits make Lice."[49]

Chivington did not just hate Native Americans; he was obsessed by them. In spring 1864, prior to leaving on a military expedition to track down a group accused of stealing settler-owned cattle, he issued an order "to kill every Cheyenne they found and take no prisoners."[50] The Third Colorado Volunteers and their commanding officer were, in reality, made for each other; and the government of the Colorado Territory after all had established the unit "exclusively for the purpose of killing Cheyennes, Arapahos and any other native people they might encounter over a 100 day period."[51] The volunteers themselves were keen to carry out their mandate. They included "a large number of rowdies and toughs recruited from the mining camps and Denver saloons, and they sought action and the notoriety they would gain if they smashed the Indians before their hundred day enlistment period expired."[52]

When Chivington ordered that the Third Colorado kill all the Cheyenne, a regular US army major commanding Fort Lyon, Edward Wynkoop, invited Black Kettle and White Antelope to bring their people closer to the fort for their protection; Chivington, in turn, arranged for Wynkoop to be replaced "on the grounds that he was too 'conciliatory.'"[53] Wynkoop's replacement, Major Scott Anthony, "encouraged the Indians to remain near the post, in order—there is no doubt of this—to have them available for a massacre."[54] If Chivington was to use his Third Colorado Volunteers for the purpose they were intended, he would need a pool of likely victims close at hand; the hundred days' muster for which the troops had signed on would run out before the end of 1864, and the episode with Major Wynkoop had already taken up a good deal of September.

The area in which the Cheyenne were to be protected was about forty miles to the northeast of Fort Lyon on a nearly-dry watercourse named Sand Creek. The Indians, numbering over two hundred men and five hundred women and children, had been required to surrender any weapons they possessed, and accept what Ward Churchill has described as "de facto internment status."[55] They were thoroughly defenseless.

Chivington decided to wipe out the Indians encamped at Sand Creek. His men, having signed on to become Indian fighters, had not seen much action and were being looked on with derision by the people of Colorado as nothing but paper heroes. After a forced march in a blizzard, the Third Colorado arrived at Fort Lyon on 27 November 1864 determined to press home the attack. As one account has recorded:

> Several officers remonstrated, declaring that the Cheyennes had been led to understand that they were prisoners of war. Chivington responded, as one of the protesters recalled, that "he believed it to be right and honorable to use any means under God's heaven to kill Indi-

ans that would kill women and children, and 'damn any man that was
in sympathy with the Indians.'"[56]

Having his way, Chivington then led his men off towards Sand
Creek. Surrounding the camp before dawn on the morning of 29
November, the Third Colorado's assault group, comprising some
seven hundred men and four howitzers, took the Native Americans
by complete surprise. Black Kettle pleaded with his people to keep
calm, and hoisted both an American flag and a white flag of truce
above his quarters. As the Cheyenne realized what was happening,
the troops opened fire. The ensuing massacre was so horrific that
some of Chivington's own men would later turn evidence against
him for allowing such abhorrent acts to take place. The soldiers
were indiscriminate in their killing, as an interpreter, John Smith,
later testified:

> [the Indians] were scalped, their brains knocked out; the men used their
> knives, ripped open women, clubbed little children, knocked them in
> the head with their guns, beat their brains out, mutilated their bodies in
> every sense of the word.[57]

Major Anthony wrote later that "We, of course, took no prisoners";[58] it was obvious to everyone at the scene that this would be
a total annihilation. Not only was mutilation ubiquitous; all prisoners captured were summarily executed as soon as they surrendered. Angie Debo has shown how one lieutenant "killed and
scalped three women and five children who had surrendered and
were screaming for mercy; a little girl was shot down as she came
out of a sand pit with a white flag on a stick; mothers and babes in
arms were killed together."[59] The massacre continued for some five
miles beyond the Sand Creek campsite as the soldiers, many of
whom were drunk on liquor or bloodlust, pursued those who had
run away. When Chivington and the Third Colorado returned to
Denver they exhibited more than a hundred scalps,[60] the gruesome
booty of a death toll that may have numbered up to two hundred[61]—of whom two-thirds were women and children, and nine
were chiefs. Black Kettle, alone of all the so-called "peace chiefs,"
escaped, but he was killed in a later massacre.[62]

The Sand Creek massacre did not see an end to Cheyenne resistance to white encroachment, for by the end of December 1864,
Black Kettle and other survivors had been able to spread word of
what had happened to allied Indian nations on the Great Plains.
Sioux, Arapaho, and Cheyenne united to try to avenge Sand Creek
and keep the murderous white destroyers at bay, but as subsequent

developments demonstrate, they were unsuccessful. The American Civil War ended in 1865, regular US troops returned to the west, and the conquest of the Indians became a foregone conclusion. One last massacre—of Big Foot and his Sioux at Wounded Knee, in December 1890—would see the whites' military triumph complete.

Was the massacre of the Cheyenne at Sand Creek a genocide? The actions of Colonel Chivington and the Third Colorado Volunteers were not only publicly explicit; they were eagerly advertised, with malice before the event and triumph after it. Moreover, these actions were committed by a military force raised by the government of the region for the express purpose of killing every Cheyenne on whom it could lay its hands. Chivington's orders came from the Governor of Colorado, and were endorsed by a popular clamor throughout the territory. Far from breaking the law, Chivington was carrying it out—and this was not confined to the territorial government. When a later investigation into the massacre was conducted by the United States Congress, not only was it found that the people of Colorado endorsed Chivington's attack, but no action was taken against him at the Federal level for murder or exceeding his orders. Four decades later, President Theodore Roosevelt called the Sand Creek massacre "as righteous and beneficial a deed as ever took place on the frontier."[63]

Sand Creek was clearly a genocidal massacre undertaken as part of a larger campaign of genocide against the Cheyenne and Arapaho, in which the objective was that none would remain alive. There was to be no possibility of women sold into slavery, or of children taken away and raised with a different identity (though this, too, would constitute genocide according to Article 2 [e] of the Genocide Convention). It was, in its purest form, an act committed with intent to destroy, in whole or in part, a national (or ethnic, or racial) group, through a deliberate policy of killing its members. The Genocide Convention's very terms provide an explicit frame of reference in which Sand Creek can be understood.

Warrigal Creek and Sand Creek: Conclusions

Both Warrigal Creek in Gippsland and Sand Creek in Colorado were undoubtedly genocidal massacres in the sense intended by Leo Kuper. Both justified themselves by reference to a need to punish their victims for the latest violation of a nonexistent peace, and both brought an overwhelming use of modern firepower to bear against people who were undefended noncombatants. Yet here the similarities end. Those who committed the Gippsland atrocities, though alone on the frontier, could not assume that they could kill Aborigines with impunity, despite the fact that the legal system with jurisdiction over the region had not yet become manifest there. Were it to catch up with them, it would become immediately obvious that they were acting outside of it in pursuing their murderous plans. They did not practise genocide, they committed murder, and placed themselves beyond the law in doing so.

An argument could also be put that they were committing a form of what would later become known as ethnic cleansing, but this too is not strictly genocide as recognized by the Genocide Convention. Although this can take us into even murkier definitional areas than genocide does, for current purposes the definition offered by Norman M. Naimark more than suffices:

> The intention of ethnic cleansing is to remove a people and often all traces of them from a concrete territory. The goal, in other words, is to get rid of the "alien" ... group and to seize control of the territory they had formerly inhabited.[64]

While we must again be alert to the dangers of generalization, applying the contemporary notion of ethnic cleansing to the nineteenth century experience of Gippsland's Aborigines—and undoubtedly many others—could well open up new areas of exploration for those seeking to understand colonial expansion and Aboriginal destruction. Those who brought death and devastation to the people at Sand Creek, by contrast, were enforcing the law's decree, and in doing so were carrying out policies instituted by a genocidal administration.

Neither of the perpetrators were really concerned about "punishing" their victims, as each said they were. When all was said and done, Warrigal Creek and Sand Creek were really grubby land grabs premised on the assumption that the only way to acquire title was to utterly extirpate the traditional owners. One went outside the law to do so, secretly like a murderous robber using the cover of darkness; the other used a law that had been crafted for the purpose of theft by those who had the most to gain from its realization. This difference really embodies the fundamental parting of the ways between the two massacres. Sand Creek took place with the full sanction of the state, which acted as the major force in fomenting genocide against the target population; Warrigal Creek happened because some in society saw a need to annihilate the target population, notwithstanding the fact that it was murder (a fact underscored by the oath of secrecy sworn by those who carried it out). No imaginative reassessments of the meaning of genocide can alter its legal realities, and it must again be emphasized that regardless of the myriad other definitions that have been composed by numerous scholars around the world, it is only the definition embodied in the United Nations Convention that is of relevance when seeking to bring a successful charge against a perpetrator.

In the long term, of course, none of this mattered to those who were the victims; but it makes a great deal of difference to those who remain, to those who seek some acknowledgment of past wrongs, to those with a commitment to seeing that the story is told accurately, and to those who would try to know how the term genocide should properly be employed—and when, according to those with the legal competence to do something about it, it should not.

Notes

1. Leo Kuper, "Other Selected Cases of Genocide and Genocidal Massacres: Types of Genocide," in *Genocide: A Critical Bibliographical Review*, ed. Israel W. Charny (London, 1988), 156.
2. Kuper, "Other Selected Cases." There clearly was "an affinity between colonialism and genocide," but it needed "much qualification"; Leo Kuper, *Genocide: Its Political Use in the Twentieth Century* (Harmondsworth, 1981), 45.
3. A number of works have discussed the values and shortcomings of the UN Genocide Convention. As a starting point, see Jennifer Balint, "United Nations Convention on Genocide," in *Encyclopedia of Genocide*, vol. 2, ed. Israel W. Charny (Santa Barbara, 1999), 575–77; see also an analysis of the legal issues involved in defining the groups affected by the Genocide Convention in William A. Schabas, *Genocide in International Law: The Crime of Crimes* (Cambridge, 2000), 109–50.
4. This term, currently gaining ground among many jurists and scholars, was first employed in the trial judgment of former Rwandan Prime Minister Jean Kambanda; see United Nations, International Criminal Tribunal for Rwanda, The Prosecutor v. Jean Kambanda (case No. ICTR 97–23–S), joint judgment of Kama (P), Aspegren and Pillay JJ, 4 September 1998.
5. My own definition of genocide is at variance with that of the United Nations, though in a court of law it would not be counted as either meaningful or relevant. For the record, however, it is worth noting that I consider genocide along the following lines: Genocide is a deliberate policy, authorized and intended by an officially sanctioned body, of physical destruction of a target group, and the eradication of the foundations of its identity as a group.
6. While my view might not attract widespread agreement, it is nonetheless supported by the opinion of Leo Kuper, whose view is as straightforward as it is

unequivocal: "I shall follow the definition of genocide given in the Convention. This is not to say that I agree with this definition. On the contrary, I believe a major omission to be in the exclusion of political groups from the list of groups protected. ... However, I do not think it helpful to create new definitions of genocide, when there is an internationally recognized definition and a Genocide Convention which might become the basis for some effective action, however limited the underlying conception." See Kuper, *Genocide*, 39.

7. Mark Levene, "Introduction," in *The Massacre in History*, ed. Mark Levene and Penny Roberts (New York, 1999), 5–6.

8. Kuper, *Genocide*, 10.

9. Alison Palmer, *Colonial Genocide* (Adelaide, 2000), 195. Italics in the original.

10. Palmer, *Colonial Genocide*.

11. Irving Louis Horowitz, *Taking Lives: Genocide and State Power*, 5th edition revised (New Brunswick, New Jersey, 2002), 23.

12. Horowitz, *Taking Lives*, 14.

13. Tony Barta, "Relations of Genocide: Land and Lives in the Colonization of Australia," in *Genocide and the Modern Age: Etiology and Case Studies of Mass Death*, ed. Michael N. Dobkowski and Isidor Walliman (New York, 1987), 238 (emphasis in the original).

14. Barta, "Relations of Genocide," 238–40.

15. Henry Reynolds, *An Indelible Stain? The Question of Genocide in Australia's History* (Melbourne, 2001), 97 (emphasis mine).

16. Reynolds, *An Indelible Stain?*, 96.

17. Frank Chalk, "Definitions of Genocide and their Implications for Prediction and Prevention," *Holocaust and Genocide Studies* 4, no. 2 (1989): 156–57.

18. Chalk, "Definitions of Genocide," 158. See a discussion on the important committee debate surrounding the drafting of Article IV of the United Nations Convention in Schabas, *Genocide in International Law*, 419–21. The matter was put in a strikingly different way during the 1930s, when the Chassidic rabbi of the Hungarian town of Berbest asked simply, "When a person is a murderer, the state will arrest and punish him; but when the state is the murderer, who will arrest and punish it?" (David Weiss Halivni, *The Book and the Sword: A Life of Learning in the Shadow of Destruction* [New York, 1996], 51.) Resolving the Berbester Rebbe's question, of course, was precisely what the United Nations Genocide Convention set out to achieve.

19. Don Watson, *Caledonia Australis: Scottish Highlanders on the Frontier of Australia* (Sydney, 1984), 169.

20. P.D. Gardner, *Gippsland Massacres: The Destruction of the Kurnai Tribes, 1800–1860* (Melbourne, 1993), 24.

21. Gardner, *Gipplsland Massacres*, 14.

22. Bruce Elder, *Blood on the Wattle: Massacres and Maltreatment of Australian Aborigines since 1788* (Sydney, 1988), 88–89.

23. Marie Fels, *Good Men and True: The Aboriginal Police of the Port Phillip District, 1837–1853* (Melbourne, 1988), 175.

24. Fels, *Good Men and True*, 174.

25. Michael Cannon, *Black Land, White Land* (Melbourne, 1993), 171.

26. Cannoon, *Black Land, White Land*.

27. Elder, *Blood on the Wattle*, 87.

28. Malcolm D. Prentis, *A Study in Black and White: The Aborigines in Australian History*, 2nd edition (Sydney, 1988), 70.

29. Elder, *Blood on the Wattle*, 87.

30. P.D. Gardner, *Our Founding Murdering Father: Angus McMillan and the Kurnai Tribe of Gippsland, 1839–1865* (Ensay, Victoria, 1990), 41.
31. Elder, *Blood on the Wattle*, 87. The words quoted by Elder were written in 1925 by a local who used the pseudonym "Gippslander"; one theory is that this person was the same William Hoddinot whose 1940 account is referred to above. See Gardner, *Our Founding Murdering Father*, 39.
32. Elder, *Blood on the Wattle*, 87.
33. Elder, *Blood on the Wattle*, 88.
34. R.H.W. Reece, *Aborigines and Colonists: Aborigines and Colonial Society in New South Wales in the 1830s and 1840s* (Sydney, 1974), 197 (emphasis mine).
35. Robert Murray, "What *Really* Happened to the Koories?," *Quadrant* 40, no. 11 (1996): 18.
36. Elder, *Blood on the Wattle*, 97.
37. Gardner, *Gippsland Massacres*, 57.
38. Elder, *Blood on the Wattle*, 97.
39. Murray, "What *Really* Happened to the Kooris?," 18.
40. Elder, *Blood on the Wattle*, 99.
41. Jan Critchett, *A "Distant Field of Murder": Western District Frontiers, 1834–1848* (Melbourne, 1990), 157.
42. Critchett, *A "Distant Field of Murder"* (emphasis mine)
43. Reece, *Aborigines and Colonists*, 191.
44. Reece, *Aborigines and Colonists*, 191–92.
45. Reece, *Aborigines and Colonists*, 214.
46. If there is debate concerning the question of genocide in colonial Australia, there can in my view be no doubt whatsoever that one series of actions in the twentieth century fits the Genocide Convention perfectly. It relates to the forced removal of children of part-Aboriginal descent from their parents and subsequent placement in a non-Aboriginal environment for the express purpose of "breeding out the color." In this regard, see my arguments in Paul R. Bartrop, "The Holocaust, the Aborigines, and the Bureaucracy of Destruction: An Australian Dimension of Genocide," *Journal of Genocide Research* 3, no. 1 (2001): 75–87.
47. David E. Stannard, *American Holocaust: The Conquest of the New World* (New York, 1992), 129.
48. James Wilson, *The Earth Shall Weep: A History of Native America* (London, 1998), 272.
49. Wilson, *The Earth Shall Weep*, 273.
50. Angie Debo, *A History of the Indians of the United States* (London, 1995), 191.
51. Ward Churchill, *A Little Matter of Genocide: Holocaust and Denial in the Americas, 1492 to the Present* (San Francisco, 1997), 228.
52. Robert M. Utley and Wilcomb E. Washburn, *Indian Wars* (Boston, 1977), 206.
53. Wilson, *The Earth Shall Weep*, 273.
54. Debo, *A History*, 194.
55. Churchill, *A Little Matter of Genocide*, 231.
56. Utley and Washburn, *Indian Wars*, 207.
57. Utley and Washburn, *Indian Wars*.
58. Debo, *A History*, 195.
59. Debo, *A History*, 195.

60. Debo, *A History,* 195.
61. Wilson, *The Earth Shall Weep,* 274.
62. David E. Stannard has compiled a number of eyewitness accounts of the Sand Creek massacre, many of them from soldiers who had themselves been directly involved. These accounts make for gruesome reading. See Stannard, *American Holocaust,* 132–33.
63. Stannard, *American Holocaust,* 134.
64. Norman M. Naimark, *Fires of Hatred: Ethnic Cleansing in Twentieth Century Europe* (Cambridge, Mass., 2001), 3.

– Section III –

Stolen Indigenous Children

Chapter 9

ABORIGINAL CHILD REMOVAL AND THE QUESTION OF GENOCIDE, 1900–1940

Robert Manne

Bringing Them Home, the findings of the federal government inquiry into the removal of thousands of Aboriginal children from their mothers, families, and communities in the first two-thirds of the twentieth century, was published in 1997. It argued that the Commonwealth government and the governments of several Australian states were guilty of the crime of genocide. The basic argument was straightforward. According to the United Nations Convention on the Prevention and Punishment of the Crime of Genocide, ratified by Australia in 1949, genocide is defined as the intentional destruction of a racial, religious, national, or ethnic group. Not only does the convention make it clear that genocide can be committed without killing, for example, by the use of methods to prevent births, it also explicitly mentions the forcible removal of the children of a group as one means by which the crime may occur. In *Bringing Them Home,* it is argued that the idea of the crime of genocide was introduced into international law by a resolution of the United Nations in December 1946. From that date, the argument continues, with the forcible removal of Aboriginal children, the Commonwealth government and the government of the states were engaged in unambiguously genocidal acts.[1]

Following the publication of *Bringing Them Home*, a small number of scholars prominent in the field of indigenous history and politics offered broad support for the position it had argued on the question of genocide.[2] One of these scholars, Robert van Krieken, saw the policy and practice of Aboriginal child removal, both before and after the Second World War, as a clear instance both of "cultural genocide" and of the barbarous face of the "civilising process" when set within a colonial frame.[3] In general, however, the genocide conclusion of *Bringing Them Home* was treated by the Australian government, by the popular media, and by the right-wing intelligentsia with levity and derisive contempt.[4] Nor was such an attitude restricted to the right. One of Australia's most admired liberal historians, Inga Clendinnen, the author of *Reading the Holocaust*, described the argument about genocide and Aboriginal child removal as nothing less than "a moral, intellectual and ... political disaster."[5]

Between the supporters and opponents of the genocide conclusion of *Bringing Them Home*, a third position has emerged, one that distinguishes between the prewar ideas about the biological absorption of mixed-descent Aborigines and postwar ideas about the possibility of their assimilation.[6] In chapter 12 of this volume, Russell McGregor argues persuasively that the charge of genocide with regard to Aboriginal child removal in the post-Second World War era, when Aboriginal policy was driven by the ambition for the social and cultural assimilation of the indigenous population of Australia, is misconceived. It is the purpose of the present chapter to assess whether claims about the genocidal character of Aboriginal child removal in the era before the Second World War are more soundly based. I am not concerned with the legal dimension of the problem—that is to say, whether genocide could be said to have been committed, and in particular whether it could be said to have been committed by nonmurderous means, like sterilization or child removal, before the crime entered international law. This chapter is concerned exclusively with those dimensions of the problem that can best be called historical and conceptual.

No author has taken us more swiftly and directly to the heart of the idea of genocide than Hannah Arendt in the epilogue to *Eichmann in Jerusalem*. At Nuremberg, certain Nazi defendants had been charged with what were called "crimes against humanity." Arendt argued that the genocide was, precisely, a crime committed against "humanity," or against what one of the French prosecutors at Nuremberg had called "the human status." She explained what she meant in the following words:

> It was when the Nazi regime declared that the German people not only were unwilling to have any Jews in Germany but wished to make the entire Jewish people disappear from the face of the earth that the new crime, the crime against humanity—in the sense of a crime "against the human status"—appeared. Expulsion and genocide, though both are international offences, must remain distinct; the former is an offence against fellow-nations, whereas the latter is an attack upon human diversity as such, that is, upon a characteristic of the "human status" without which the very words "mankind" or "humanity" would be devoid of meaning.[7]

At the conclusion of this chapter, Arendt composed the speech she would have liked the court at Jerusalem to have addressed to Adolf Eichmann. It included the following words:

> And just as you supported and carried out a policy of not wanting to share the earth with the Jewish people and the people of a number of other nations—as though you and your superiors had any right to determine who should and should not inhabit the world—we find that no one, that is, no member of the human race, can be expected to want to share the earth with you.[8]

In April 1937, the Aboriginal administrators of the states and the Commonwealth government met together in Canberra. It was generally agreed by those present that the "full-blood" or "tribal" Aborigines were destined eventually to become extinct no matter what policy might be adopted. A more important problem was the future of the so-called "half-caste"—the Aborigines of mixed descent—whose numbers were growing rapidly. After lengthy debate, the meeting voted unanimously in favor of the following motion, proposed by the Native Administrator from Western Australia, A.O. Neville:

> That this conference believes that the destiny of the natives of aboriginal origin, but not of the full-blood, lies in their ultimate absorption by the people of the Commonwealth and it therefore recommends that all efforts be directed to that end.[9]

In arguing for this motion, Neville asked the delegates assembled at Canberra the following question: "Are we going to have a population of 1,000,000 blacks in the Commonwealth, or are we going to merge them into our white community and eventually forget that there ever were any aborigines in Australia?"[10]

In order to grasp the genocidal implications of Neville's question from what one might call the Arendtian point of view, readers need only replace the words "blacks" and "Aborigine" with the word "Jew" in this passage and then imagine Neville's question being addressed in 1937 to a meeting of administrators that had assembled not in Canberra, but Berlin to discuss not Australia's Aboriginal problem, but Germany's Jewish one.

It is the purpose of this chapter to trace the administrative and intellectual road that led to the proposal for the elimination of Australia's Aboriginal population at the Canberra conference of April 1937.

Half-Caste Child Removal in Frontier Society

Around 1900, an almost identical thought occurred to the chief protectors of Aborigines in the different Australian colonies (or states after 1 January 1901) who were charged with responsibilities for the welfare of the eighty thousand or so Aborigines who had survived the nineteenth century dispossession. These were concentrated in the remote or frontier regions of northern Queensland, the north of Western Australia, the Northern Territory, and the desert regions of Central Australia. As a result of the frequency of sexual relations between Aboriginal women and European (or more occasionally Asian or Pacific Island) men, a discomfiting new racial type had emerged, the so-called "half-caste." The protectors, almost certainly independently of each other, came to believe that it was of greatest significance that the "problem" of the half-caste child be taken in hand.

In 1899, the Chief Protector in Western Australia, Henry Prinsep, issued the following warning in his annual report to parliament:

> The intercourse between the races is leading to a considerable increase of half-castes. Many of them find their way into the missions, but a far greater number are probably reared in native camps, without any sort of education, except a vicious one. Each half-caste, so brought up, is a menace to the future moral safety of the community.[11]

One year later, the Government Medical Officer and Protector of Aborigines in the Northern Territory (at the time an administrative district of South Australia) Dr. Frederick Goldsmith wrote officially along almost identical lines:

> Between Port Darwin and Katherine are over sixty half-caste children of various ages, and I would strongly urge that as soon as possible provi-

sion be made that they can be removed from their surroundings and educated, so that ultimately they may be useful members of society, and not—as too often happens when allowed to run wild in the blacks' camp—become a source of danger to the community.[12]

At this time, such warnings fell on deaf ears. Neither Prinsep in Western Australia nor Goldsmith in the Northern Territory possessed the legal powers to remove half-caste or Aboriginal children from their mothers or their communities at will. By contrast, the newly appointed Northern Protector of Aborigines in Queensland, the eminent anthropologist, teacher, doctor, and humanitarian Walter Roth, did. According to the old Aboriginal Act of 1865, the police in Queensland were able to bring any Aboriginal or half-caste child before a magistrates' court, to charge them with being neglected simply on the evidence that their mother was an Aborigine. They would then be transferred to a reformatory or what was called, at the time, an Industrial School. Moreover, according to the new Aboriginal Act of 1897, the Protectors were able to remove, under warrant from the Home Minister, any Aboriginal or half-caste Aboriginal adult or child to any location in the state.

Armed with these legal powers, in the years between 1900 and 1905, Roth was responsible for the removal of 167 half-caste children, chiefly to the Christian missions at Yarrabah and Mapoon in the north and, later, after he became Chief Protector for all Queensland, to Deebing Creek, near Ipswich, in the south.[13] Because of this work, Roth has rightly been named as the "author" of half-caste child removal policy in Australia.[14]

There can be little doubt that conspicuous cruelty was involved in the removal of these half-caste children. There exists in the Queensland state archives poignant evidence of the terrible suffering experienced by both Aboriginal mothers and children at the hands of Roth, suffering that left him quite unmoved.[15] There is also evidence that very many of those who were removed to the missions yearned for years thereafter to return home. In 1911, when a Minister of the Queensland government visited Yarrabah, he invited the inmates to tell him of any complaints. "Of all those who came up not one voiced any grievance, they one and all said they wanted to return to their people."[16]

Yet acts of cruelty are not, of course, evidence of genocidal intent. In his voluminous monthly and annual reports to his Minister and the Queensland parliament, Roth's intentions in the removal of the half-caste children become clear. Dr. Roth removed the children, in part, because he believed the conditions in and around the Aboriginal camps spoke of such human degradation that they were altogether unsuitable for any half-European child; in part because he was certain, as he once put it, that unless removed from the camps the girls would almost certainly all become prostitutes and the boys cattle thieves; and, in part, because he believed that, if unremoved, the half-caste children were likely to be exploited, especially in the maritime and pastoral industries, by unscrupulous European employers.[17]

In 1904, Dr. Roth was invited by the government in Western Australia to conduct a Royal Commission into the condition of the natives in the north of the state. Everywhere he went, he asked about those he customarily called the half-caste "waifs and strays." Everywhere he was told the same story. The situation of these children was a menace to society. Nonetheless, because of the inadequacy of the law nothing could be done. Unless permission for the removal of a half-caste child was given by the mother or Aboriginal parents, the Chief Protector had no power to remove any Aboriginal or half-caste child to a Western Australian mission, like the one run by the Benedictines at New Norcia or the Pallotines at Beagle Bay.[18]

In 1904, following the Roth report, Western Australia's first comprehensive Act concerning Aborigines was passed. In one of its provisions, the Chief Protector became guardian of all Aboriginal and half-caste children up to the age of sixteen. Although the legal situation with regard to Aboriginal child removal was not completely clear until certain amending legislation of 1911, which made it explicit that the Chief Protector's guardianship overrode the rights of the mother to her illegitimate child, for some time it appeared as if there was no legal impediment to the collection of the half-castes.[19]

The most enthusiastic West Australian child removalist in these early days was James Isdell, the former pastoralist and parliamentarian, who was appointed traveling protector for the north in 1907. On 13 November 1908, Isdell wrote from the Fitzroy River district to the Chief Protector, Charles Gale. "I consider it a great scandal to allow any of these half-caste girls to remain with the natives."[20] On 15 January 1909, Gale issued Isdell with the authority to "collect all half-caste boys and girls" and to transport them to Beagle Bay.[21] Isdell expressed his gratitude: "It should have been done years ago."[22] By May 1909, he was able to report from Wyndham that the entire East Kimberley region had been "cleaned up."[23]

Isdell was aware that sentimentalists from the south sometimes wrote letters to newspapers "detailing the cruelty and harrowing grief of the mothers." He regarded such complaints as nonsensical.

"Let them visit and reside for a while" in one of the native camps and see for themselves "the open indecency and immorality and hear the vile conversations ordinarily carried on which these young children see, listen to, and repeat." Isdell did not believe that the Aboriginal mother felt the forcible removal of her child more deeply then did a bitch the loss of a pup. "I would not hesitate," he wrote, "to separate any half-caste from its Aboriginal mother, no matter how frantic momentary grief might be at the time. They soon forget their offspring."[24] "All Aboriginal women," he explained in letters to Gale "are prostitutes at heart" and all Aborigines "dirty, filthy, immoral."[25]

When A.O. Neville, a young English-born public servant, was appointed Chief Protector in 1915, the practice of Aboriginal child removal in Western Australia was already well-entrenched. The state archives, if read closely, reveal a great deal about the half-caste removal system elaborated by Neville after 1915 as Chief Protector. Under this system, the preferred minimum age for removal was six. Because of the question of sexual intercourse and reproduction, the removal of girls from the Aboriginal camps was considered more urgent than the removal of boys. In the removal work, Neville always worked closely with the police. He expected to be notified by them of all half-caste children found in their districts. Removals occurred without any need to refer the matter to the courts, because of gender, age, degree of acculturation to the Aboriginal world, above all racial caste, and not because of suspected, let alone proven, parental or maternal neglect. Neville preferred to remove children for education and re-socialization to the Government-run settlements—Carrolup in the southwest before its closure in 1922 and Moore River Native Settlement after 1917—rather than to the Christian missions, with whom relations were frequently poor. If it was not the case that Neville was able to remove all half-caste children to the settlements during the period of his early protectorship, by far the most important constraints were the meagreness of his budget and the very substantial costs involved in transporting and provisioning children from the north to Moore River, and the fact that, according to a legal judgment of 1922, children born of two half-caste parents were not themselves Aborigines according to the relevant Act. Although the precise number of half-caste child removals in these early days most likely will never be known, in correspondence with the Commissioner of Police as early as 1919 Neville referred to "hundreds of cases" of Aboriginal child removal that had occurred, presumably over the last ten to fifteen years.[26]

Despite Dr. Frederick Goldsmith's 1900 recommendation, half-caste child removal did not begin in the Northern Territory until responsibility for its administration had been transferred from South Australia to the Commonwealth in 1911. While a proposal for the collection of half-caste children was made by the first Commonwealth Chief Protector, Dr. Herbert Basedow, who lasted in this post barely a month, the policy was not implemented until 1913–1914. Small numbers of half-caste children began to be transferred, for the purpose of basic education, to an iron shed in Alice Springs known as the Bungalow, and to a school at the Kahlin Compound in Darwin.[27]

In the Northern Territory, half-caste child removal soon took on a rather different character from the scheme pioneered by Dr. Roth in north Queensland before 1905 or developed by Neville in Western Australia after 1915. It had been Roth's practice to send half-caste children, sometimes with their mothers, to state-supported Christian missions to which both full-blood and half-caste Aborigines had also been removed. The children were expected to remain at these missions for their entire lives. In Western Australia, the half-caste children removed by Neville to the state-run institution at Moore River were housed in a separate compound, which was part of a general-purpose Aboriginal camp for indigent Aborigines or for those who had proved troublesome to the authorities, and sometimes for the mothers of the half-castes in the compound. Neville hoped to prepare the inmates in the compound for work in the European world as manual laborers or station hands if they were boys, and as cheap domestic servants, for which there was an insatiable demand, if they were girls.

The half-caste removal policy in the Northern Territory resembled Western Australia and not Queensland in its aspiration to prepare inmates for participation in the European world. It was singular, however, in the ferocity of its determination to segregate the half-caste children from all contact with full-blood Aborigines. It was in the interest of maintaining such segregation that all the half-caste children in Darwin were moved in 1923 from Kahlin Compound to a suburban house at nearby Myilly Point.[28] And it was in the interest of such segregation that the inmates of the half-caste home at Alice Springs were forbidden during the early 1930s even to pray together in the same church with full-blood Aborigines.[29]

Despite the theoretical ambition of preparing their children for participation in the European world by elevating the children to the standards of whites, in reality the conditions in the Territory's half-caste homes were genuinely scandalous, even according to the far-from-exacting expectations of the time. It is difficult to believe, but nonetheless true, that by 1928 seventy-six half-caste children were housed in the small three-bedroom cottage in Darwin at Myilly Point.[30] Moreover, almost everyone who visited the Bungalow at Alice Springs was appalled by the primitive and unhygienic conditions, the overcrowding and unbearable heat. That such conditions could exist in a Christian country made the blood of one Protestant minister who visited the Bungalow in 1929 "boil."[31]

The half-caste child removal system in the Territory had one final feature that made it distinct. Although in the early days, because of sexual fears and financial stringency, a clear preference was shown for the collection of girls rather than boys, by the late 1920s the Territory's administrators made it clear in policy statements that their ambition was universal, that is to say, that they aspired to collect and institutionalize each and every half-caste child. Although their aspiration was never completely realized, by the mid–1930s more than half of the Territory's identified half-caste children were housed in one of the special-purpose institutions run by the state.[32]

The Administrators' World View in the 1930s

The system of half-caste child removal, as it had developed by the late 1920s in Queensland, Western Australia, and the Northern Territory, was deeply paternalistic in its blithe indifference to the wishes of the Aborigines and its certainty that only the administrators knew what was for the best. It was racist in its most fundamental assumption, namely, that it was unconscionable to allow "part-European" children to grow up in what was commonly regarded as the filthy, immoral, superstitious, and degraded Aboriginal world. For the human beings whose lives were frequently shattered by these policies—for both the Aboriginal mothers and the children—the policy was also exceedingly cruel. Yet, scrutinized from the point of view of the intentions of the administrators, the removal policies were not yet genocidal in any recognizable sense. It would have astonished the early administrators to have been told that their half-caste child removal practices were driven by an intention to destroy the Aborigines. It was only when the policy and practice of child removal was resituated by administrators and intellectuals into a more general framework as part of a supposed solution to the problem of the half-caste—that is to say, when the administrators began to make plans for the elimination of the half-castes and to see in child removal one instrument by which this purpose could be achieved—that the genocidal dimension of Aboriginal child removal emerged. In order to understand how these administrators came, in Arendt's words, to believe that they had "the right to determine who should and should not inhabit the world," a brief sketch of certain features of their mindset in the 1930s is required.

At this time, Aboriginal administrators, like most Australians, still believed that the full-blood Aborigine was unlikely to survive. The "doomed race" theory, as it has been called, was grounded, in part at least, in nineteenth century scientific thought. As early as 1846, in his influential Oxford lectures, Herman Merivale argued that for aboriginal peoples "the mere contact of Europeans is fatal in some unknown manner." Such views were commonplace among Australian scientists, especially those influenced by Darwinism. By 1890, for example, it was axiomatic for the vice-president of the Royal Society of Tasmania to say that "following the law of evolution and survival of the fittest, the inferior races of mankind must give place to the highest type of man."[33] That the Aborigines were a dying race seemed to be demonstrated in the statistical data that showed that of the three hundred thousand Aborigines whom the professor of anthropology at the University of Sydney, A.R. Radcliffe-Brown, had authoritatively estimated to have been alive when the British arrived in 1788, only a little over sixty thousand full-bloods had, by 1930, survived.[34] Yet the doomed race theory penetrated deep into popular consciousness as well, embedded in the national imagination through the almost universally known story of the supposed entire extinction of the Tasmanian Aborigines.

While administrators felt obliged to accept that the full-blooded Aborigines were destined to die out as a consequence of contact with a superior civilization as a kind of melancholy scientific fact, by the early 1930s their minds were far more actively exercised by a demographic problem of an altogether different kind—the seemingly inexorable rise in the number of half-castes. In 1901, at the birth of the Commonwealth, there were fewer than eight thousand half-castes in Australia; by the early 1930s, more than twenty thousand. Most alarming by now were indigenous population trends in the oldest region of European settlement, New South Wales. By 1930, half-castes here outnumbered full-bloods eight to one. Fifty years earlier there had been twice as many full-bloods as half-castes in New South Wales.[35]

There were a number of reasons why the "rise of the half-caste" caused both the Aboriginal Protectors and the general public deep concern. In part, because of a racial essentialism that was almost beyond question, half-castes seemed to represent a grotesque race, somehow outside nature, and the product of sin. In 1927, a Perth newspaper warned about the possibility of three races in Australia—"white, black and the pathetic sinister third race which is neither."[36] Theories about the quality of these hybrids varied. Some believed that half-castes inherited the vices of both black and white but the virtues of neither race; some that their European ancestry made half-castes more intelligent and educable than full-bloods. Many Australians believed that the half-castes were by nature indolent but fecund. Many were convinced that if the half-caste population was allowed to grow, Australia would eventually be confronted by a serious racial problem, of the kind faced by the United States or South Africa. Some believed that unless the problem of the half-caste was solved, the White Australia ideal—the most powerful consensual political value of the young Commonwealth—would be fatally compromised.[37]

What, then, was to be done? On one occasion in 1934, a senior government official, William Gall, the Under-Secretary at the Home Department in Queensland, argued that the only feasible solution was the sterilization of all half-castes. Sterilization, however, had no serious support, probably because it was not a policy tradition in Great Britain.[38] Far more significant, as we shall see, was another proposed solution—the biological absorption into the white of the half-caste population through a state-engineered program of encouraged miscegenation.

By 1890, as Warwick Anderson has shown in a recent monograph, *The Cultivation of Whiteness,* an anthropological consensus based on the work of eminent scientists like T.H. Huxley in Britain and Hermann Klaatsch in Germany, had formed around the view that the continental Australian Aborigines (but not the extinct island Tasmanians) were unrelated to the "Negroes" but were in fact "primitive" or "dark" Caucasians, the remote racial ancestors of contemporary Europeans. Among Australian anthropologists, this theory led to the suggestion of some basic racial affinity between the British settlers and the Aborigines. Moreover, according to those like Professor Cleland and Dr. Herbert Basedow of South Australia and Dr. Raphael Cilento of Queensland, who propagated the Caucasian school of thought, in the interbreeding of Europeans and Aborigines no racial "atavism," that is to say no, embarrassing "throwback" to the Aboriginal side, had ever been observed. These views were embraced by some of the Protectors who were convinced that a state-sponsored program for "breeding

out the color," if pursued over several generations, offered the most
practical solution to the pressing problem of the half-caste.[39]

Dr. Cecil Cook: Breeding Out the Color

Among the leading Aboriginal administrators, the earliest enthusi-
ast for the program of "breeding out the color" of the half-caste
seems to have been the young tropical medicine specialist Dr. Cecil
Cook, who in 1927, at the age of twenty-nine, was appointed Chief
Medical Officer and Chief Protector of Aborigines in the Northern
Territory.[40] In June 1929, Cook wrote of the advisability of keeping
quadroon children in the Territory, rather than sending them south,
so they would be available for involvement in the program of
"breeding out the color."[41] Cook would maintain consistent support for such a program until his enforced retirement from the
Chief Protectorship in the Territory in 1939.

Concerning the problem of the half-castes, Dr. Cook's thinking
went like this. By the late 1920s, the Territory contained approximately twenty thousand full-blood Aborigines, fewer than three
thousand Europeans (mainly male), more than eight hundred half-
castes, and a little over seven hundred so-called "colored aliens,"
i.e., Chinese, Malays, Pacific Islanders, and so on. One demographic nightmare that haunted Cook throughout his Chief Protectorship was the arrival of a time when a majority of low-grade
colored hybrids would overwhelm the European population in the
Territory and destroy the prospects for the implanting of a White
Australian civilization in the north.

Cook's fears began with the differential breeding rates of Europeans and half-castes in the Territory. In a memorandum of July
1932 entitled "The Half-Caste Problem," he expressed his central
concern: "Whereas the white population declines by 1% annually
the Half-Caste population increases by 2%. In a matter of 15 or 20
years Half-Castes will have reproduced sufficiently to become a
predominant part of the local population."[42]

Dr. Cook's anxieties regarding half-caste males focused on the
questions of race and economics. If a population of low-grade half-
castes expanded, the Territory would be faced by two equally
unpalatable alternatives. If unemployed, the half-castes would
"provide a profitable field for revolutionary agitators," thereby
threatening social order and civil peace. If employed as cheap labor,
they would steal all new jobs from the whites and take "control of
the labour market."[43]

Concerning half-caste females, Dr. Cook's predominating nightmare focused not on economics and the labor market, but on questions of reproduction and sex. He was anxious not only about the problem of sexual intercourse between Aboriginal women and European men in the outback, as were almost all his contemporaries, but even more about the problem of the uncontrolled interbreeding around Darwin of half-caste females, especially with colored alien males. In April 1931, in an angry letter to the Secretary of the Society for the Protection of Native Races, Cook gave voice to his deepest racial fears with considerable eloquence:

> In the Territory ... the preponderance of coloured races, the prominence of coloured alien blood and the scarcity of white females to mate with the white male population, creates a position of incalculable future menace to purity of race in tropical Australia, and the Federal Government must so regulate its Territories that the multiplication of multicolour humanity by the mating of Half-caste with alien coloured blood shall be reduced to a minimum.

Cook believed that because of the problem of half-caste female racial interbreeding, "the future of this country may very well be doomed to disaster."[44]

What, then, was to be done? The first step to be taken for both half-caste males and females was collection during infancy from native camps and removal to one of the state-run institutions—at Alice Springs, Darwin and, after 1931, Pine Creek. At these homes, the half-caste children were to receive a rudimentary education, whose fundamental purpose was, in the official words of the policy, "elevation to the standards of the white."[45] Cook inherited this policy but pursued it with a greater rigor than before.

Following their common education, Dr. Cook's plans for the half-caste males and females of the Territory diverged. For at least some of the boys, he planned a future in the cattle industry. By 1930, against great trade union and pastoralist opposition, Cook was responsible for the passage of a regulation that obliged pastoralists to take on at least one half-caste apprentice on equal terms and conditions with white labor for every six Aborigines they employed on rations.[46] Concerning the half-caste males not employed in the cattle industry, he hoped that the requirement to compete on equal terms with white labor would drive a large number away from the Territory and towards "centres of denser white population where they would be competent to take work on the same basis as white men, thereby reducing the coloured population of the Territory and very appreciably diminishing the coloured birthrate."[47]

For the half-caste girls, Dr. Cook had plans of a rather different kind. One of the greatest problems in the Territory was the imbalance in the numbers of European males and females. By elevating the half-caste girls to white standards, Cook hoped to create a supply of females of a quality suitable for marriage to Territory men. Cook's policy for the encouragement of intermarriage of half-caste girls to European men was intended to serve three purposes simultaneously—to reduce the number of European-Aboriginal half-castes by satisfying in marriages the sexual needs of European men; to reduce the number of alien-half-caste hybrids by providing suitable husbands for half-caste females; and, most importantly of all, to help solve the Territory's growing half-caste problem by gradually breeding out the color of the blacks. Shifting half-caste males out of the Territory and marrying half-caste females to whites seemed to Cook "the only method by which the future of this country can be safeguarded in the absence of such radical methods as sterilisation of the unfit and legalized abortion."

By far the most notorious dimension of Dr. Cook's proposed solution to the problem of the half-caste was his marriage scheme. Many Australians regarded any suggestion of miscegenation with a kind of primal dread. Many believed marriages between half-caste girls and low-grade European men (for who else would marry them?) were certain to end in tragedy.[48] Many, unconvinced of the Caucasian theory of Aboriginal origins to which Dr. Cook adhered, were concerned about "throwbacks" to the Aboriginal side. Throughout the 1930s, moreover, rumors circulated that suggested that Cook was forcing half-caste girls to marry whites against their will or, alternatively, using improper means—like offers of government jobs—to induce European men to take half-caste wives.[49] On occasion, such stories even spread abroad. In June 1933, England's *Daily Herald* published a report about Cook's marriage scheme under the headline, "Bonus Offered for Marrying Half-Castes," and the subhead, "Plan to Breed Out Black Strain." So alarmed was the Australian High Commissioner, Stanley Bruce, on the publication of this story, that he sent an urgent cable to the Prime Minister, Joe Lyons, to find out whether or not the report was true.[50]

Although rooted in his fears about the Territory's future, Dr. Cook had ambitions to extend his program for the breeding out of color, in general, and for the total prohibition of all marriages between half-caste and colored aliens, in particular, in the States of Queensland and Western Australia as well. On 7 February 1933, he put such a proposal to his superiors in the Department of the Interior in Canberra:

In the Territory the mating of aborigines with any person other than an aboriginal is prohibited. The mating of coloured aliens with any female of part-Aboriginal blood is also prohibited. Every endeavour is being made to breed out the colour by elevating female half-castes to white standard with a view to their absorption by mating into the white population. The adoption of a similar policy throughout the Commonwealth is, in my opinion, a matter of vital importance.[51]

Within the Department of the Interior, Cook's proposal received support. Its Secretary, J.A. Carrodus, suggested that Cook's recommendation might, with profit, be brought before the next meeting of the state premiers scheduled for June.[52] On 25 May 1933, Carrodus wrote a memorandum for the Conference setting out the Commonwealth's view: "The policy of the Government is to encourage the marriage of half-castes with whites or half-castes, the object being to 'breed out' the colour as far as possible. Permission is not granted for coloured persons and Asiatics to marry half-caste women."[53]

Dr. Cook's proposal was placed on the agenda for discussion at the Premiers' Conference. However, at the last minute it was withdrawn, almost certainly because of strong opposition from the government of Queensland. The secretary of the Conference wrote to the Department of the Interior, explaining that it had been decided that this matter would best be dealt with in correspondence between the Commonwealth and the governments of the states most concerned, Queensland and Western Australia. The archives do not reveal whether this correspondence was pursued.[54]

It is clear that among senior public servants in the Department of the Interior, doubts about the practicality, but not the morality, of Dr. Cook's scheme existed.[55] Nonetheless, it is also clear that from the early 1930s until Dr. Cook's retirement in 1939, the Commonwealth government supported the policy for the breeding out of the color of those half-castes in the Territory under its control.[56]

A.O. Neville's Absorption Plan

On the day the Premiers' Conference of June 1933 convened, supposedly to discuss as one item a national policy for breeding out the color of the Aborigines, the Chief Protector in Western Australia, A.O. Neville, issued an official statement to the press expressing his support for the Commonwealth government's scheme:

The Australian aborigines [Neville's statement read], are of Caucasian stock and related to us. ... They are not "negrito." This means that with their intermarriage with whites, the whites will gradually predominate over the black.

The decision made by the Commonwealth Government to adopt as definite policy the encouragement of marriages of white men and half-caste women with a view to raising the standard of mixed blood to that of whites, is nothing new in this State. I have foreseen it for years, and sponsored it as the only outcome of the position.

The blacks will have to go white. It is exemplified in the quarter-castes, and by the gradual absorption of the native Australian black race by white. I have noticed no throw-backs in such cases hitherto.[57]

Over this policy for the biological absorption of the Aborigine, there was probably stronger popular and political support in Western Australia than existed in any other territory or state. In the month after Neville's press statement, the *West Australian* published an article by an anonymous author who called himself "Physicus." The article argued for "the application of Mendelianism" as the "only solution to the problem of the half-caste." It urged "the mating of the half-caste with the quadroon and octoroon, so that the confirmed infiltration of white blood will finally stamp out the black colour that, when all is said and done, is what we really object to."[58] In fashionable circles in Perth the "Physicus" solution to the problem of the Aborigines seems to have had a considerable impact.[59]

In August 1933, as a result of serious humanitarian concerns raised in London about the treatment of Aborigines in the West, a proposal for another Royal Commission into the condition of the natives was put to the Western Australian parliament. One of its principal sponsors, Frank Wise, quoted not only Neville's 7 June statement but also, extensively and approvingly, from the recent article of "Physicus." Just as the behavior of the whites, Wise argued, was responsible for the appearance of the half-caste, "so should we be responsible for his disappearance." Wise told the parliament that after having given the matter considerable thought "Physicus" recommended "the breeding out process entirely." Nor did Wise misunderstand what such a program involved. "This writer is advocating the ultimate extinction, by scientific means, of the half-caste."[60]

As it happens, "Physicus," or Dr. Cecil Bryan, made an appearance at the subsequent Moseley Royal Commission. He spoke for several hours. Bryan told the Commission that, contrary to popular opinion, the blacks were not dying out. Australia had to choose "between the setting up of a black population in our so-called White Australia or a policy of miscegenation." Between blacks and whites the "colour bar" was unbridgeable. Moreover, among both blacks and whites, there was no human type more utterly despised than the half-caste. In his wisdom, Bryan understood that it was "the greatest wish of the half-caste ... to shed the last remnant of his colour and become wholly white."

> I am come to this Royal Commission to ask that steps be taken to breed out the half-caste, not in a moment but in a few generations, and not by force but by science, goodwill and common sense. ... The position really resolves itself down to this: We can mate half-caste to half-caste and perpetuate a mongrel breed; we can let the half-caste marry into the black fold, a retrograde, foolish and dangerous step to allow; or we can, as I urge to be done, slowly absorb the half-caste into our own white ranks.

To achieve this end, Dr. Bryan suggested for the half-castes, quadroons, and octoroons a policy not of "force" but of what he called "proximity."[61]

The man who was charged with responsibility for implementing Aboriginal policy in Western Australia, A.O. Neville, had given the problem of the half-caste considerably greater thought than Dr. Bryan or, most likely, any other Australian of his time. Neville had been involved in aboriginal administration for almost twenty years. He administered, moreover, a vast state. In the underdeveloped north, where full-blood aborigines outnumbered half-castes several times, conditions resembled those in the Northern Territory confronting Dr. Cook. In the more developed south, where there were now very few full-bloods but a large and growing number of half-castes, they more closely resembled the demographic situation of New South Wales.[62]

For the full-blood Aborigines of the north and centre of the state, Neville felt great anthropological curiosity, a revulsion for certain "barbaric" traditional practices, but also a genuine cultural respect.[63] Although not entirely consistent on this question, on balance he held the still conventional view that eventually the full-blood Aborigine was certain to die out, his descendants more and more coming to resemble the degenerate and pathetic human types now encountered in the south. For southern half-castes, Neville felt little but moral contempt and cultural despair.

> Camplife as it exists [he explained to Moseley] is bringing them lower and lower. They hardly bother to put up any shelter nowadays, perhaps only a few branches thrown together, and they live like that year in and year out, gambling and, where possible, drinking, and doing many other things they ought not to. Immorality is growing, the old tribal

laws have broken down, and there is nothing to check the young men and young women. Girls at tender years are being seduced. These young men and girls are unemployed all day and are rapidly becoming unemployable ... incest is about and youthful depravity is general.[64]

Such people had "to be protected against themselves whether they like it or not. ... The sore spot requires the application of the surgeon's knife for the good of the patient, and probably against the patient's will."[65]

Neville knew what needed to be done. In order to save the quadroons or those of even lesser Aboriginal blood from growing up as "white natives," in 1932 he had encouraged the Anglican nun Sister Kate Clutterbuck to establish Australia's first special-purpose quadroon home. Sister Kate's, as it was called, was reserved for the upbringing of children born of half-caste mothers and European fathers or those of even lesser Aboriginal blood, although to Neville's annoyance, from time to time Sister Kate admitted children of a darker hue.[66] The purpose of the institution was to sever completely the connection between these children and the Aboriginal world. On one occasion, the home was advised to "dispose" discreetly of letters sent to the children by Aboriginal family members and to inhibit contact between the children and their own native mothers, especially the mothers of the nonrespectable kind.[67] Neville pursued his quadroon children with such determination that in 1938 two scientists conducting a half-caste survey discovered that West Australian mothers of quadroons were unwilling to supply them with information "owing to Neville's policy of seizing all children" and dispatching them to Sister Kate's.[68]

Since 1917, Neville had been removing half-caste children, especially from the north, to the Moore River Native Settlement. He made it clear, however, at the Moseley Royal Commission that he would have liked to remove all half-caste children, including those from what he regarded as the dismal Aboriginal communities in the south. Institutions like Moore River, he argued, "succeed above all in bridging the gulf between the black and the white. They teach discipline, and imbue the natives with self-respect." He looked forward to the time when "all half-caste children shall be educated and trained" in places like this.[69] His proposed solution to the problem of the half-caste had three elements—comprehensive child separation; reeducation and resocialization in government-run settlements and institutions; and encouraged miscegenation on the female side for the purpose of breeding out the color. Standing in the way of the success of this solution were, however, two main obstacles—lack of financial resource and lack of legal power.

Throughout his career, Neville was frustrated by the miserliness of every Western Australian government he served. Somewhat unusually for a public servant within a Westminster system, he became an open advocate for a more generous Aboriginal vote, producing telling figures showing that per capita expenditure on Aborigines in Western Australia was considerably lower than in any other state, and that inside Western Australia per capita expenditure on inmates at Moore River was lower than in any non-Aboriginal institution. On the financial front, Neville's advocacy completely failed. At the time he appeared at the Moseley Royal Commission, the Aboriginal budget was slightly lower than it had been when he was appointed Chief Protector in 1915.[70]

On the legal front, Neville did not fail. Before the amendments to the Aborigines Act of 1936, Neville was not able to prohibit by law, as he desired, the association of quadroons with those of greater Aboriginal blood, and he had limited powers to control Aboriginal marriages. While guardian of all Aboriginal and half-caste children, he was obliged to relinquish control when these children reached the age of sixteen. Moreover, because his guardianship did not extend under the 1911 amendment to the 1905 Act to the legitimate children of half-caste mothers, and because a court in 1922 had found that the child of two half-caste parents was not a half-caste under the Act, there were very large numbers of half-caste children in the state who were beyond his control. Neville gained the powers he wanted in the 1936 amendments to the Aborigines Act. The Native Administrator, as the former Chief Protector was to be called, was now guardian of all "native" children up to the age of twenty-one. He had the power to approve or disapprove of all "native" marriages. He also had the power to take legal action against quadroons who associated with blacks.[71] The amended Aborigines Act is perhaps the most illiberal piece of legislation passed by any parliament in the history of Australia. Although he still lacked the financial resources he needed, A.O. Neville now at least possessed the legal powers he required for the implementation of his long-range plans.

The Canberra Conference, April 1937

In April 1937, administrators of Aboriginal policy from the Northern Territory and each of the states (with the exception of Tasmania) met for the first time since the formation of the Commonwealth to discuss matters of common concern. The most important issue at the conference was the problem of the half-caste.

Discussions on this question were initiated by the only academic present, the anthropologist J.B. Cleland of South Australia. Professor Cleland argued that a "very unfortunate situation would arise if a large half-caste population breeding within themselves eventually arose in any of the Australian states." There was, he thought, "only one satisfactory solution, and that is the ultimate absorption of these people into the white population." He proposed Commonwealth support for a scientific study to determine whether or not the half-caste would always "prove to be a grown-up child" or whether he could be absorbed.[72]

Neville followed Cleland. His purpose was to explain to the conference how in Western Australia the absorption objective was to be achieved. The legislation that had passed through the last session of the Western Australian parliament, he explained, was based upon the understanding that "the aborigines of Australia sprang from the same stock as we did ourselves; that is to say that they are not negroid but give evidence of Caucasian origin." Absorption was both a biological and a cultural process. To prevent "the return of those half-castes who are nearly white to the black," he had taken control over "native" marriages. "Under this law no half-caste need be allowed to marry a full-blooded aboriginal if it is possible to avoid it." Education and resocialization of the half-caste in state-run institutions was even more important if absorption was to be accomplished. "To achieve this end, however, we must have charge of the children at the age of six years." Neville explained how the quarter-caste children in Western Australia were removed to a special institution to be brought up as whites and how the half-caste children who were sent to Moore River were placed in a compound kept separate from the aboriginal camp. "At first," he informed the delegates, "the mothers tried to entice the children back to the camps but that difficulty is now being overcome." Such institutions were what Neville called the "clearing stations for the future members of the race."

Neville analyzed the demographic dimension of the half-caste problem in the following way. Conditions in the north of the state resembled conditions in the southwest of fifty years ago, and in the north-centre the conditions of twenty-five years before. In the southwest, there were only 1,419 natives in 1901; now there were six thousand (mainly half-castes); within twenty-five years, there might be as many as fifteen thousand. It was the primary duty of the conference to decide upon a long-term solution to Australia's growing half-caste problem. For his part, he could see no objection to what he called "the ultimate absorption into our own race of the whole of the existing native race."[73] With the partial exception of the delegate from Queensland, the Chief Protector, J.W. Bleakley, who opposed all idea of encouraged miscegenation and who, insofar as he thought of absorption at all thought of it as a purely socio-cultural process, the other delegates were of similar mind.[74]

Dr. Cook spoke after Neville. He raised the question of the destiny of the full-blood. In the Territory, where full-bloods heavily outnumbered both Europeans and half-castes, policy-makers, he claimed, faced a terrible dilemma where humanity pulled in one direction and self-interest in the other:

> If aborigines are protected physically and morally, before long there will be in the Northern Territory, a black race ... multiplying at a rate far in excess of the whites. If we leave them alone, they will die, and we still have no problem, apart from dealing with those pangs of conscience, which must attend the passing of a dying race. If, on the other hand, we protect them with the elaborate methods of protection which every conscientious protector would adopt, we shall raise another problem which may become a serious one from a national viewpoint, for we shall have in the Northern Territory, and possibly in north-western Australia also a large black population which may drive out the white.

Dr. Cook argued that the only escape from his dilemma was for the "speedy" absorption of the full-blood Aboriginal population, as well as the half-caste one, into the white.[75]

Neville thought Dr. Cook's view about the chance of full-blood survival wrong. "No matter what we do," he argued, "they will die."[76] Professor Cleland also disagreed, not so much with Cook's prognosis as with the drift of the discussion towards public advocacy of the absorption of the full-blood:

> I would not like an idea to get abroad that there is any suggestion of a deliberate attempt on the part of the Conference to hurry up the detribalization of the full-bloods. There are sentimental and scientific reasons why such a course would be very unwise ... they are unique and one of the wonders of the world.

The Secretary of the Department of the Interior, J.A. Carrodus, sympathized with Cleland's concern. In the interest of avoiding pointless controversy it would be best to pass a resolution advocating only the absorption of the half-caste. For after all, as he pointed out, "ultimately if history is repeated, the full-bloods will become half-castes."[77]

The balance of opinion at the April 1937 conference on the question of the future of the Aborigine can best be summarized as

follows. The Aborigines could and should be absorbed, both culturally and biologically, into the white population. In the short-
term, absorption policy would concentrate solely on the half-castes.
Eventually, the full-bloods would, most likely, become extinct. The
half-caste descendants of the current full-blood population would,
however, also have to be absorbed. This whole process would take
fifty years or more. After this time, in Neville's words, everyone
would be able "to forget that there were ever any aborigines in
Australia." The conference had produced a long-term plan for the
elimination of the Aboriginal people.

Conclusions

There are two main reasons why the description of the 1930s
absorption plans as genocide has been resisted. In popular understanding, genocide is associated exclusively with acts of mass state
violence. The administrators advocating absorption did not advocate violence as a solution to the Aboriginal problem; all would
have been genuinely outraged by any such suggestion. None even
seriously supported what William Gall in Queensland once advocated, namely a general program of half-caste sterilisation. The
methods involved in the absorption policy were limited to child
removal, institutionalization, and marriage control. Although it is
clear, both legally and conceptually, that genocide can be planned
and executed without the use of violence, because of the powerful
historical associations that have gathered around the world, for
many the description of absorption plans as genocide remains stub-
bornly counterintuitive.

There was, too, always something impractical, indeed fanciful,
about the absorption plans. Although both Cook and Neville possessed the determination and the legal power to pursue their
absorption dreams, neither possessed even remotely the financial
resources, the bureaucratic machinery or, in the vast regions they
administered, the kind of social control in depth that they needed if
their schemes were to have any prospect of success. Because of the
fantastical nature of the absorption policy, "genocidal thoughts"
and "genocidal plans" are more adequate descriptors of what they
were implicated in than "genocidal crimes."

Absorption as a policy for the solution of Australia's Aboriginal problem was always intimately associated with the administrations of Neville in Western Australia and Cook in the Northern
Territory. The administrative will to pursue these plans did not sur-

vive Cook's virtual removal from his post in 1939 and Neville's retirement one year later.[78] It is generally agreed that Aboriginal policy received little serious government attention during the Second World War. When attention returned after the war, it was in a post-Nazi intellectual climate in which general understanding had developed about where racial-engineering policies might lead. The new proposal for the long-term solution of the Aboriginal problem was economic, social, and cultural assimilation. Even though under assimilation Aboriginal children continued to be removed, and in larger numbers than before, this should not disguise the fact that assimilation and absorption were, as policies, conceptually distinct. To put it briefly, assimilation was a policy for all Aborigines, not merely those of mixed descent, from which the racial-biological element of the absorption policy had been erased.

Notes

1. Human Rights and Equal Opportunity Commission, *Bringing Them Home: Report of the National Inquiry into the Separation of Aboriginal and Torres Strait Islander Children from their Families* (Sydney, 1997), 270–75.
2. For example, Colin Tatz, "Genocide in Australia," *Australian Institute of Aboriginal Studies Research Discussion Paper,* no. 8 (Canberra, 1999); Anna Haebich, *Broken Circles: Fragmenting Indigenous Families, 1800–2000* (Fremantle, 2000).
3. Robert van Krieken, "The Barbarism of Civilization: Cultural Genocide and the 'Stolen Generations,'" *British Journal of Sociology* 50, no. 2 (1999): 297–315.
4. Ron Brunton, *Betraying the Victims,* Institute of Public Affairs Backgrounder (Melbourne, 1998); Ron Brunton, "Genocide, the 'Stolen Generations' and the 'Unconceived Generations,'" *Quadrant* 42, no. 5 (May 1998): 19–24; "Submission 36, Minister for Aboriginal and Torres Strait Islander Affairs" to Senate Legal and Constitutional References Committee Inquiry into the Federal Government's Implementation of Recommendations Made by the Human Rights and Equal Opportunity Commission in *Bringing Them Home,* 29–32. For a general analysis of the response of Australian conservatism to *Bringing Them Home,* see Robert Manne, "In Denial: The Stolen Generations and the Right," *Australian Quarterly Essay* issue 1 (2001): 1–113.
5. Inga Clendinnen, "First Contact," *Australian's Review of Books,* 9 May 2001.
6. Robert Manne, *The Way We Live Now* (Melbourne, 1998), 15–41; Raimond Gaita, *A Common Humanity* (Melbourne, 1999), 107–30; Henry Reynolds, *An Indelible Stain? The Question of Genocide in Australia's History* (Melbourne, 2001), 139–54.

7. Hannah Arendt, *Eichmann in Jerusalem: A Report on the Banality of Evil* (New York, 1965), 268–69.
8. Arendt, *Eichmann in Jerusalem*, 279.
9. Commonwealth of Australia, *Aboriginal Welfare: Initial Conference of Commonwealth and State Aboriginal Authorities* (Canberra, 1937), 21.
10. Ibid., 11.
11. State Records Office of Western Australia (hereafter SROWA), AN1/1 ACC 495/1899.
12. National Archives of Australia, Northern Territory (hereafter NAA NT), *Government Administrators Report* (1900), 15.
13. Queensland Parliament, Parliamentary Papers, *Annual Report of the Chief Protector of Aboriginals for 1905* (Brisbane, 1906), 12.
14. Australian Institute of Aboriginal and Torres Strait Islander Studies, *The Encyclopædia of Aboriginal Australia*, vol. 2, ed. David Horton (Canberra, 1994), 995–96.
15. Robert Manne, "Days of Healing/Memories of Shame," in *The Best Australian Essays, 1999*, ed. Peter Craven (Melbourne, 1999), 374–77; Anna Haebich, *Broken Circles*, 289–92.
16. "A Journal of the events of the Ministerial visit to Yarrabah," Queensland State Archives (hereafter QSA), A/69486/1910/11/3550, 5.
17. The reference to prostitutes and cattle thieves is found in *Annual Report of the Northern Protector for Aboriginals for 1901*.
18. *Royal Commission on the Condition of the Natives, Report and Recommendations* (Perth, 1905), 25-26. In 1902 a list of half-caste children in Western Australia was compiled by the Office of the Chief Protector of Aborigines. Beside the names of a number of these children were comments like: "But mothers will not give up" or "But parents will not give up." SROWA AN1/2 ACC 255 412/02, Table F.
19. On 22 September 1909, C.F. Gale, the Chief Protector of Aborigines, wrote to the Inspector of Police, Coolgardie: "Unfortunately my guardianship does not override parental authority and therefore I am unable to take these children away, unless the parents give their consent. ... I am endeavouring to have the Aborigines Act amended during the present session, with a view to giving me the power to take charge of half-caste children irrespective of the wishes of the parents." SROWA AN1/3 ACC 652 1303/09. The amending legislation Gale relied upon was eventually passed in January 1911.
20. James Isdell to C.F. Gale, 13 November 1908, SROWA AN1/3 ACC 652 1433/09.
21. C.F. Gale to James Isdell, 15 January 1909, SROWA AN1/3 ACC 652 1433/09.
22. James Isdell to C.F. Gale, Report of the Travelling Protector, 1909, SROWA AN1/3 ACC 652 213/09.
23. James Isdell to C.F. Gale, 6 May 1909, SROWA AN1/3 ACC 652 1433/09.
24. James Isdell to C.F. Gale, Report of the Travelling Protector, 1909, SROWA AN1/3 ACC 652 213/09.
25. James Isdell to C.F. Gale, 31 August 1909, SROWA AN1/3 ACC 652 1433/09; James Isdell to C.F. Gale, 18 December 1909, SROWA AN1/3 ACC 652 1433/09.
26. The most important files are SROWA AN1/4 ACC 653 16/20 and SROWA AN1/4 ACC 653 343/25.

27. *Report of the Administrator,* National Archives of Australia, Australian Capital Territory (hereafter NAA ACT), CRS A1/15, 11/18824; the Parliament of the Commonwealth of Australia, Northern Territory of Australia, 1913 and 1914–1915, NAA NT.

28. NAA ACT CRS A 659/1, 39/1/15580.

29. NAA ACT CRS A1/15, 33/4488.

30. *The Aboriginals and Half-Castes of Central Australia and North Australia,* Report by J.W. Bleakley, Chief Protector of Aboriginals, Queensland, 1928, the Parliament of the Commonwealth of Australia (Melbourne, 1929), 14.

31. "Extract from a letter dated July 31st 1929, written by the Rev. W.M. Davies, Rector of Port Lincoln, who visited Alice Springs in July 1929," NAA ACT CRS, A461/7, F300/1.

32. *Report on the Administration of the Northern Territory for Year 1937–38,* the Parliament of the Commonwealth of Australia (Canberra, 1939), 25–26. According to the census for year ended 30 June 1938 there were 406 half-caste children in the Northern Territory of which at least 210 were in the half-caste homes at Darwin and Alice Springs.

33. Russell McGregor, *Imagined Destinies: Aboriginal Australians and the Doomed Race Theory, 1880–1939* (Melbourne, 1997), 14, 48–49.

34. A.R. Radcliffe-Brown, "Former numbers and distribution of the Australian Aborigines," *Australian Yearbook* (Melbourne, 1930), 23, 687–96. L.R. Smith, *The Aboriginal Population of Australia,* (Canberra, 1980), 199.

35. L.R. Smith, *The Aboriginal Population of Australia,* 98–99, 199.

36. Cited in Pat Jacobs, *Mister Neville* (Fremantle, 1990), 160.

37. See chapter four in this volume by Raymond Evans.

38. William Gall, Memorandum, *Aboriginal Protection Acts Queensland, 1859–1934,* QSA A/8725. "The problem then is, what is to become of the half-castes on the different settlements, more especially as it must be admitted that side by side with the white race they will be undesirables. ... Inferior races will have to go and, in my opinion, Governments sooner or later, will have seriously to consider the question of sterilization of the half-caste." As far as I am aware there is no evidence that any other administrator suggested a sterilization solution to the problem of the half-caste, although on one occasion Dr. Cook, the Chief Protector in the Northern Territory, did suggest the sterilization of half-caste "mental defectives." This suggestion was rejected by the Minister of the Interior. An official argued, in part, that "while sterilisation is permitted by law in most of the states of the United States of America and some European countries, no similar legislation has been passed in any of the Australian States or in England." See NAA ACT CRS A1/15 33/3589. Dr. Cook's memorandum was submitted on 30 March 1933. The response of the Ministry of the Interior, which included a report from the Director-General of Health, was written on 4 July 1933.

39. Warwick Anderson, *The Cultivation of Whiteness: Science, Health and Racial Destiny in Australia* (Melbourne, 2002), chaps. 7–8.

40. For a detailed study of Dr. Cook's period as Chief Protector, see Tony Austin, *Never Trust a Government Man: Northern Territory Aboriginal Policy, 1911–1939* (Darwin, 1997), chaps. 5–11.

41. Memorandum, Dr. Cecil Cook, 11 June 1929, NAA ACT CRS A431/1 46/3026.

42. Memorandum, Dr. Cecil Cook, 23 July 1932, NAA ACT CRS A1/15 33/479.

43. Ibid.

44. Dr. Cecil Cook to Reverend W. Morley, 28 April 1931, NAA ACT CRS A1/1 36/6595.
45. Annual Report, Northern Territory Administration, 1932, NAA NT, 8.
46. NAA ACT CRS A1/15 33/479.
47. Dr. Cecil Cook Memorandum, 23 July 1932, NAA ACT CRS A1/15 33/479, 5.
48. Many letters on these themes appeared in the *Northern Standard* of Darwin, NAA ACT CRS A659/1 40/1/408. Dr. Cook summarized the objections to his marriage proposals in his memorandum of 27 June 1933. See "Marriages of Half-Castes," NAA ACT CRS A659/1 40/1/408.
49. On 28 June 1934 Mr. Holloway aired some of these rumours in a speech in the House of Representatives, NAA ACT CRS A659/1 40/1/408.
50. "Bonus Offered for Marrying Half-Castes," *Daily Herald*, 8 June 1933, NAA ACT CRS A659/1 40/1/408. Rt. Hon. S.M. Bruce to Mr. Lyons, Prime Minister, 8 June 1933, NAA ACT CRS A461/7 A300/1, pt. 1.
51. Memorandum of Dr. Cecil Cook, "Permission to Marry Aborigines," 7 February 1933, NAA ACT CRS A659/1 40/1/408.
52. Memorandum by J.A. Carrodus, 27 February 1933, NAA ACT CRS A461/7 300/1, pt. 1.
53. Memorandum, "Intermarriage of Other Races with Aboriginals," 25 May 1933, NAA ACT CRS A 461/7 A300/1, pt. 1.
54. The opposition of the Queensland Government to Dr. Cook's marriage scheme was in the report of the *Daily Herald*, 8 June 1933. The Secretary to the Premier's Conference, G. Whiteford, informed the Department of the Interior on 15 June 1933, NAA ACT CRS A461/7 A300/1, pt. 1.
55. On 3 November 1933, H.C. Brown argued that "I have perused Dr. Cook's report and whilst I am of the opinion that, theoretically, his suggestion would be quite good, in practice I think it would prove to be unsound." The Minister of the Interior, J.O. Perkins, however, minuted on Brown's memorandum: "Present policy to continue." See NAA ACT CRS A659/1 40/1/408.
56. On 12 September 1938 the South African Minister of External Affairs requested information from the Australian government about Australian legislation "prohibiting marriages between White persons and Negroes, Mulattos, Mongolians and Indians." In his memorandum of 19 December 1938, J.A. Carrodus appended, for information, a copy of Dr. Cook's memorandum of 27 June 1933, which set out the case for the policy of "breeding out the color." See NAA ACT CRS A659/1 40/1/408.
57. B.T. Haynes et al., *W. A. Aborigines, 1622–1972* (Fremantle, 1972), 57–58.
58. *West Australian*, 22 July 1933.
59. Paul Hasluck, *Shades of Darkness: Aboriginal Affairs, 1925–1965* (Melbourne, 1988), 29–30. See also the biography of A.O. Neville: Pat Jacobs, *Mister Neville*, 208–9, 236–38.
60. Western Australian Parliamentary Debates, Legislative Assembly, 30 August 1933, 652–55.
61. H.D. Moseley, Commissioner, *Report of Evidence*, Royal Commission to Investigate, Report, and Advise upon Matters in Relation to the Condition and Treatment of Aborigines, 22 March 1934, 346 ff.
62. See Jacobs, *Mister Neville*. For a study of Neville's administration in the southwest, see Anna Haebich, *For Their Own Good: Aborigines and Government in the South West of Western Australia* (Perth, 1988) and her chapter in this volume.

63. See Jacobs, *Mister Neville*, passim. See also A.O. Neville, "Contributory Causes of Aboriginal Depopulation in Western Australia," *Mankind*, vol. 14, no. 1 (1948), 3–13.
64. Moseley, *Report of Evidence*, Royal Commission, 12 March 1934, 13.
65. A.O. Neville, "Notes for Royal Commission," SROWA AN1/7 ACC 933 333/33 vol. 2.
66. A.O. Neville, Memorandum, 15 June 1939, SROWA AN1/7 ACC 933 240/34: "Sister Kate has children at her Home that the Department does not wish her to have, because they cannot be classed as quarter-caste and in fact are natives in law, and should be at a fully native institution, and I have suggested that she should relinquish the care of these, but she is not agreeable."
67. Letter from F. Bray to Sister Kate, 6 May 1941, SROWA AN1/7 ACC 933 305/38: "I should be glad if you would discourage all correspondence from bush or camp natives, including letters from mothers who live as camp or bush natives. Some mothers live according to white standards ... they should be allowed to write now and again to their children ... I think you should exercise control over all other correspondence and dispose of it suitably."
68. Warwick Anderson, *The Cultivation of Whiteness*, 229.
69. H.D. Moseley, Record of Evidence, Royal Commission, 34, 89.
70. Jacobs, *Mister Neville*, 227–28, 231–32.
71. Neville's explanation of the amendments to the Aborigines Act which passed through the Western Australian parliament can be found in A.O. Neville to H.A. Barrenger, Department of the Interior, Canberra, 11 May 1937, NAA NT F1/332651.
72. *Aboriginal Welfare: Initial Conference of Commonwealth and State Aboriginal Authorities* Commonwealth of Australia (Canberra, 1937), 10.
73. Ibid., 10–12, 16–17, 20–21.
74. Ibid., Bleakley, 6–10, 12, 18–20. McLean of South Australia: "It appears essential to merge these people into the white race," 15; Pettitt of New South Wales: "The crux of this problem is the adoption of some means of merging the half-castes into the general community," 15; Bailey of Victoria: "The intention behind the establishment of the Lake Tyers camp was the training of half-castes to enable their absorption into the general community," 12.
75. Ibid., 13–14.
76. Ibid., 16.
77. Ibid., 21.
78. Dr. Cook was replaced by E.W.P. Chinnery as Native Administrator in the Northern Territory. In 1939–1940 Chinnery planned to transfer the half-caste children in the state-run homes to Christian island missions and had no interest in the Cook policy of "breeding out the color." Nor did the Minister of the Interior at the time of Cook's forced resignation, John McEwen, or his most influential outside adviser, Professor A.P. Elkin, whose key place in the transition from the policy of absorption to assimilation is discussed briefly by Russell McGregor in this volume. There is no detailed study of Aboriginal administration in Western Australia after the retirement of A.O. Neville in 1940. See Neville's book, *Australia's Coloured Minority: Its Place in the Community* (Sydney, 1947), written during the Second World War but published after Neville put the case for the national implementation of the absorption resolution at the Canberra 1937 Conference. This book is best regarded as absorption's last hurrah.

Chapter 10

"UNTIL THE LAST DROP OF GOOD BLOOD"

The Kidnapping of "Racially Valuable"
Children and Nazi Racial Policy in
Occupied Eastern Europe

Isabel Heinemann
Translated by Andrew H. Beattie

In 1943, Lucie Bergner, a twelve-year-old Polish girl, was force-fully removed from the house of her grandmother, who had brought her up in Posen, and taken to an SS children's home in Kalisz in the Warthegau. There she learned German, and was pre-pared for her adoption by a German foster family. A year later, she became the foster daughter of a Baden-Würtemberg farming family whose two sons had been killed at war. After 1945, she decided to remain with her foster parents and did not return to Posen.[1]

Such stories of the removal and adoption of non-German chil-dren by German authorities occurred thousands of times under National Socialism, and only in a small minority of cases were the results as benign for the affected children as in the case of Lucie Bergner. Kidnappings and forced adoptions by German foster par-ents played an important role in Nazi occupation policy, especially in the second half of the war. The purpose was the forced German-ization *(Zwangsgermanisierung)* of "racially valuable" *(gutrassig)* children of parents "of foreign nationality" *(fremdvölkisch)*, espe-

Notes for this section begin on page 259.

cially from Eastern Europe, who were to provide the German people *(Volk)* with a fresh supply of "good blood." The program was the responsibility of the SS, the elite National Socialist order under Heinrich Himmler. It was rooted in Nazi racial ideology, and particularly in Himmler's desire to foster and strengthen the German Volk by providing it with every "last drop of good blood" that these children were regarded as possessing.[2]

National Socialist Racial Ideology and the Germanization of the East

The National Socialist regime was founded on two central premises. The first was the belief in the superiority of the so-called "Nordic" race that Nazi ideologues regarded as consisting mainly of the Germans and the Scandinavian peoples, believed to be "related by descent" *(stammesverwandt)*. The second was the idea that the German Volk—on the basis of its racial value and its cultural achievements—was entitled to more "living space" *(Lebensraum)* in Eastern Europe. The means of gaining this "living space in the East" was violent warfare, which led initially to considerable German territorial advances. From the Baltic to the Black Sea and from the Atlantic to the Don River, in 1941 to 1942, Europe was under German rule, and the Nazis developed wide-ranging plans to transform and resettle Europe's population, for example in the "General Plan East" of 1942 and the "General Settlement Plan" of 1942 to 1943.[3] In the Nazi state, the "protection of German blood" from racial impurities was to be guaranteed by a series of racial laws from the early 1930s, by the persecution and the murder of disabled and psychologically disturbed people in the so-called "Euthanasia Program," and by the persecution and mass murder of Europe's Jews.[4] At the same time, the regime carried out an overtly racist policy, forcefully subjecting a range of "deviant" groups to persecutory measures that were justified with their supposed "racial inferiority."[5]

With the onset of war and the German conquests in Europe, these racial policies were applied to the non-German civil populations of the occupied territories. European Jews became the target of the most ambitious measures; there was to be no place for them in Europe under German leadership.[6] But the non-Jewish populations of these regions also became the victims of racially-motivated coercive measures, from dispossession and resettlement to deportation and mass murder. This was part of the process of "German-

izing" the conquered areas with which Hitler had commissioned his
Reich Leader of the SS (RFSS), Heinrich Himmler, in October 1939.
As the new "Reich Commissioner for the Strengthening of Germandom" (RKFDV), Himmler was responsible not just for settling
Germans in the newly conquered territories (at first the annexed
west of Poland), but also for selecting and annihilating those elements that supposedly posed a danger to the process of Germanization. In effect, Himmler had a license to expel and to murder.[7]
Thus by 1939, the SS was already a key institution of Nazi racial
policy, a position that it was to expand in the following years.

The basis of this racial Germanization policy and the most
important criterion for the treatment of people was their "racial
value," which was determined pedantically in individual cases by an
anthropological examination, and was registered on the so-called
"race card." This registration of the German and non-German population according to racial criteria was the responsibility of racial
experts from the SS Race and Settlement Main Office (RuSHA).[8]
True to the conception of the SS as an elite Nordic order, they had
already developed a procedure of racial selection for SS candidates
and their wives in the mid–1930s, and after 1939 this was also
applied to the population of the occupied territories. Through millions of examinations, they sought to determine who, on account of
his or her "racial value," was to be considered "German" and was
thus to be included in the policy of Germanization. For the purpose
of selection, the SS experts tested 21 physical traits, such as eye and
hair color and height, as well as racial, anthropologically-significant
characteristics like "head shape," "formation of eye wrinkles," and
"cheek height."[9] On the basis of these tests, people were divided
into four racial categories (RuS I to RuS IV). Only the members of
the first two groups were regarded as being "predominantly
Nordic" *(überwiegend nordisch und fälisch)* and thus of "good
blood" who met the criteria for providing a "desired population
increase" for the German Volk.[10] The "racially undesirable" people,
by contrast, were forcefully resettled in order to make land and
housing available for Germans, were exploited as slave laborers, or
were murdered in work, concentration, and extermination camps.

The "racially valuable" children of "parents of foreign nation-
alities," who are the subject of this chapter, had a special place in
this scheme. Within the general "Germanization policy," Himmler
and the SS deliberately targeted the policy at children in order to
weaken what, according to Himmler's logic, were the "blood foundations" of the peoples under German occupation. This aim was
recognized by the American investigators at the Nuremberg Mili-

tary Tribunal, and was the basis for the charge of "Kidnapping of children of foreign Nationality" at the eighth Nuremberg trial against those responsible for the criminal population and settlement policies in Europe. The prosecution interpreted the practice as a genocidal measure whose purpose was the biological-physical destruction of the peoples under German occupation.[11] The accused were representatives of the following SS organizations: firstly, members of the RKFDV Main Staff Office who on Himmler's instructions had ordered the registration and forced removal of the "racially valuable" children; secondly, the race experts from the RuSHA responsible for the selection of the children; thirdly, staff of the Ethnic German Central Office (VoMi) who had brought the children into the camps and oversaw them there; and, fourthly, representatives of the SS association "Lebensborn" (Well of Life) responsible for assigning the supposed orphans to German families.

Himmler had already made unmistakably clear in his memorandum "Some thoughts on the treatment of people of foreign nationality in the East" of May 1940—a secret program for the planned forced Germanization measures in Poland—that his plans for the treatment of Poles within the General Government in Poland included the systematic exploitation of "racially high quality people capable of re-Germanization" *(rassisch hochwertige Wiedereindeutschungsfähige)* for the German cause.[12] For this purpose, "an annual sorting of all children in the General Government aged between six and ten into those with good blood and those with valueless blood" was to occur. The former would be brought to Germany. Either the parents would accompany them and become "loyal citizens of the state," or their children would be simply taken away: "they will then probably not produce any more children, so that the danger that this subhuman people of the East would become dangerous to us through having such people of good blood as a leadership class ceases to exist."[13]

This theory was put into practice, and tens of thousands of children from occupied Poland were removed from their families or taken from orphanages during the war and assigned to German foster families.[14] This "child-stealing" *(Kinderraub)* by the SS also occurred in Bohemia and Moravia, Belorussia, the Ukraine, and Slovenia. Precise figures on the "forced Germanization" of children are not available, but a rough estimate would be at least fifty thousand cases in South Eastern Europe, Poland, and the Soviet Union.[15]

A number of questions arise in investigating the SS's forced Germanization policy in the context of the Nazi occupation of Europe: was the "hunt for good blood" and for "racially valuable

children," in particular as directed by Himmler in occupied
Europe, part of a coherent program of forced Germanization, or
rather an accidental by-product of Nazi occupation policy? What
significance did the racist child-stealing have within wider Germanization efforts? To what extent is there evidence for the
assumption made by the prosecutors in Nuremberg that the policy
against "children of foreign nationality" constituted a genocidal
act against the enemy nations?

In this chapter, three groups of children who were targeted for
Germanization are differentiated: firstly, the children declared to be
"German orphans" who had been raised by non-German parents;
secondly, children whose parents had been killed as "partisans" or
concentration camp prisoners; and, thirdly, children of German soldiers and foreign mothers. These groups will be considered separately, before the final section concludes by considering the
genocidal character of the policy against children.

"German Orphans"

The search for supposed "German orphans" in Polish homes and
Polish foster families began in the Warthegau.[16] The SS alleged that
the Poles had previously systematically brought all orphans of parents of German nationality as "foundlings" into Polish orphanages
and Polish foster families. In order to locate and Germanize the
children, the RKFDV urged the Reich Governor, the health offices,
Lebensborn, and the RuSHA to concerted action:

> First, all children in formerly Polish orphanages are to be gone over *[sic]*
> and accommodated. After completion of this action, the children who
> live with Polish foster parents are examined. In order to avoid any
> unsettling of the Polish foster parents, it is to be expressed as far as pos-
> sible to the Polish foster parents at this examination that the children
> are to be brought to holiday camps *(Schulfreiplätze)* or vacation homes
> *(Erholungsheime)*.[17]

That it was by no means a voluntary decision of the foster parents to send their children to Germany is demonstrated by a further
passage of the same RKFDV order: "The foster children are <u>not</u> to
be removed from Germanizable families" *(eindeutschungsfähige
Familien)*. Thus, they could be removed from other Polish families.
The "process" actually worked as follows: the offices for youth
registered the children, the Reich Governor charged the Łódź/Litz-
mannstadt RuSHA branch with the racial examination, and the

health offices medically examined those children found to be "Germanizable," who were then brought to a central children's home in Brockau in the Gostingen district in the Warthegau. There they were observed for six weeks and subjected to a "character evaluation" by the staff. Lebensborn then took over the children; the two- to six-year-olds were taken for adoption by SS families, the six- to twelve-year-olds to "German home schools," that is, Nazi education homes *(Erziehungsheime)*. After this, "for the first time children [were] available on request by 1 April 1942." At least 300 children, and probably many more, had been examined in the Warthegau by this point.[18] A few months later, the head of the RuSHA "Re-Germanization" *(Wiedereindeutschung)* department, SS First Lieutenant Georg Harders, reported on the "Germanization" of Polish orphans:

> At this time, the Germanizable children are being removed from the Polish orphanages, and if appropriate after a character assessment, they are brought for several weeks in a children's home (Brockau) for Germanization. A similar regulation is planned for the Warthegau and for the Gau Upper Silesia. A home for children is also to be built for the Gau Danzig-West Prussia. One is also planned for Upper Silesia.[19]

In the Warthegau, in addition to the home in Brockau, there was also a home for children in Puschkau in the Posen district, and a third came into existence at the beginning of 1943 in Kalisz.[20] The latter had its own police registry office, which made it impossible for the families to determine their children's current location.[21] The true date of birth of children who were assigned by Lebensborn to foster families was often not given. Instead, they were described as two or three years older, which produced doubts about their age among some foster parents.[22]

Slavomir Grodomski Paczesny, born in 1931 in Łódź, was a "racially valuable child." According to his statement to the court in Nuremberg, he was taken away from his family in 1942, and brought at first to a home for children in Łódź, where he was racially examined and photographed.[23] After a period, he was taken to the home in Kalisz where he spent six months and received lessons in German. His name was changed to Karl Grohmann and he was taken to Salzburg, where he was assigned to a foster family. Because he spoke Polish with Serbian prisoners of war, he was moved to another family. Only after the war was he able to return to his family in Łódź.[24]

But it was not just in the occupied West of Poland that children were violently torn from their families, examined by race experts, and taken to Germany. It was just as common in the General Government in Poland and in the occupied territories of the Soviet Union. Himmler charged the head of Lebensborn, Guntram Pflaum, with the custodianship of "racially valuable" children of German nationality in the USSR in summer 1941.[25] Thereupon Pflaum established a home for children in the Belorussian town of Bobruisk where he collected "racially valuable" children. Just as with the Polish children, these children who were to be sent to Germany for adoption were by no means all orphans. If one considers that the thirty to forty children in this home generally spent several months there before being sent on to families, one can assume that during the existence of this home in Bobruisk from the summer of 1942 until the autumn of 1943, a relatively "modest" total of between one hundred and two hundred children were sent to Germany.[26] It cannot be ruled out that there were other similar institutions in the occupied Soviet Union.[27]

In the Ukraine, the SS selected "parentless children" *(elternlose Kinder)*. Here the Security Service (SD) collected them in camps and notified the Ukraine Race and Settlement leader, who then had them subjected to a racial selection process.[28] This procedure was completely in accordance with Himmler's wishes. In a programmatic speech before the police chiefs of the SS Higher Section "South Russia," the RFSS had announced:

> Our task is to pick out what is racially valuable. We will take it to Germany, send it to a German school, and those who are even better qualified will come to a German Home School or a Napola [elite Nazi boarding schools], so that the boy grows up from the beginning as a conscious bearer of his blood and as a conscious citizen of the greater Germanic Reich and is not brought up as a Ukrainian national. No one need have any concerns that in carrying out this selection the SS might ruin the blood of the German Volk. We only take those who are really racially valuable.[29]

This "program" became especially significant between 1942 and 1944 in the context of the increasingly intensely fought war against the civil population in the occupied regions, which was legitimized as a "struggle against gangs" or "fighting partisans." The SS forced the "racially valuable" children of killed or imprisoned alleged partisans in their thousands into homes in the Reich or sent them to German families.

The Forced Germanization of "Partisan Children"

Without doubt, the best-known examples of the children, whose parents who were killed in "antipartisan actions" or imprisoned in concentration camps, kidnapped by the SS, are those of Lidice. In an act of reprisal for the assassination of the RSHA chief and Reich Protector of Bohemia and Moravia, Reinhard Heydrich, in Prague on 27 May 1942, the SS reduced the Czech village of Lidice to rubble.[30] The 199 male inhabitants were shot immediately and the 184 women were brought to the Ravensbrück concentration camp.[31] A total of 88 children aged between one and fifteen years were taken by train to the collection camp of the so-called Central Office for Resettlers (*Umwandererzentralstelle*, UWZ) of the Security Police in Łódź/Litzmannstadt.[32] Representatives of the Bohemia and Moravia RuSHA branch had already selected three children as "Germanizable" in Lidice. Seven children under one year old, who were deemed too young for a racial examination, were sent to a children's home in Prague. In Łódź, the director of the RuSHA branch, Walter Dongus, selected seven "racially suitable" (*rassisch tauglich*) children from the total of eighty-eight for "Re-Germanization" (*Wiedereindeutschung*), and they were taken to the home in Puschkau, given German names, and sent to foster families.

The head of the UWZ in Łódź, Hermann Krumey, asked the RSHA in Berlin by telex what was to happen to the remaining eighty-one unwanted children. He assumed that "special treatment" (*Sonderbehandlung*), i.e., their murder, was intended. On 13 June 1942, eighty-eight Czech children without parents as a result of the action arrived in Litzmannstadt from the municipality of Lidice:

> As a further decision about the stay of the children has not been made, I request instructions on this matter. I notified IV B4 about the transfer of the children in the assumption that their special treatment is intended. In the meantime the RuSHA has removed seven re-Germanizable (*rückdeutschungsfähige*) children.[33]

The eighty-one remaining children were then transferred to the Łódź state police office that had them taken to the nearby Chełmno extermination camp, where they were murdered.[34]

Fourteen days after Lidice, the township Lezaky in the Chrudim region was destroyed and its inhabitants killed.[35] Again the RuSHA, represented by its Bohemia and Moravia branch in Prague, was at the scene participating in the selection of "racially valuable children."[36] A few days after the annihilation of Lezaky, the RuSHA branch leader in Prague, SS Captain Preuß, sent the UWZ chief Hermann Krumey twelve "non-re-Germanizable children for further handling" *(Nichtwiedereindeutschungsfähige)*. They had come to Łódź from "the actions in Lidice and Lezaky." In the same transport were six "re-Germanizable" children from the Protectorate "who were destined for the Gau children's home in Brokau and are to be sent there from the Litzmannstadt branch."[37]

One of the twelve "unwanted children" in the second transport came from Lidice, the rest from Lezaky. They were handed over to the Gestapo in Łódź on 25 July 1942 and sent like the others to Chełmno.[38] The statements of the responsible nurse and doctor in the UWZ camp in Łódź confirm the practice indicated above: the children from Lidice and Lezaky were divided into "re-Germanizable" and "undesirable population increase," a few (thirteen in total) were sent to children's homes in the Warthegau, while most (ninety-three in total) were murdered in the gas car station in Chełmno.[39]

Some of the Czech children who were classified as "Germanizable," were taken to German foster families, and therefore survived, testified before the Nuremberg Tribunal. Maria Hanfova described how—then aged twelve—she was brought with the other children to Łódź, was selected, and finally was taken to the children's home in Puschkau in the Warthegau. There she was named Maria Hanff, and had to learn German and work. She reported that "They told us that we would become Germans; that we would probably never come back to Czechoslovakia; that we would become Germans." A German family in Dessau adopted her and called her Magda Richter. She joined the Hitler Youth, went to a German school, and was only able to return to her relatives in Czechoslovakia at the end of 1945.[40]

The children of Lidice and Lezaky were not the only "re-Germanizable partisans' children" who came under German control. There are indications that other children were also transported to Germany from the Protectorate.[41] Further children whose parents had been assassinated originated from Slovenia, the General Government in Poland, and Croatia—as three further examples will demonstrate.

In Upper Carnolia and Lower Styria in today's Slovenia, the antipartisan measure "Enzian" in summer 1942 cost numerous victims. Himmler's order for action and the corresponding execution order of 25 June 1942 had called for use of the same practice as had been used in Bohemia and Moravia: the men were to be shot, the women taken to concentration camps, and the "racially valuable children" Germanized.[42] Basically, in "areas sympathetic to gangs" the whole civil population, "which was almost entirely connected with the rebels either voluntarily or by force," was arrested.[43] The RuSHA representative in the SS Higher Section "Alpenland," SS Major Heinrich Obersteiner and his colleague Georg Albert Rödel, undertook the racial examination of the arrested families.[44] Here, too, the purpose was the removal of "racially valuable children," as the Salzburg police chief, Ernst Rösener, reported to Berlin:

> The families are racially evaluated and the children are taken away from their parents after the assessment of the latter. The children are to be brought to the Old Reich and placed in the charge of the Reich Leader according to instructions still to come.[45]

The racially selected children from Lower Styria were taken to the home in Frohnleiten;[46] the children from Upper Carnolia were still in "heavily overcrowded reception camps" in mid-September 1942, in St. Veit, in particular.[47] Lebensborn representatives, VoMi, the Security Police, and SS Major Obersteiner from the RuSHA conferred about the imminent transfer of these children—aged between six months and twelve years—to the Munich Lebensborn center.[48] In February 1943, approximately 600 children from Upper Carnolia and Lower Styria were in the custodianship of VoMi in Bayreuth. Lebensborn prepared the adoption of the younger children (up to ten years of age).[49] Another document confirms that by January 1943 the 260 children from Lower Styria, whose parents had been shot as partisans, were in the charge of Lebensborn.[50] Thus, in total, at least 860 Slovenian children were in the hands of the SS at the beginning of 1943: 260 being looked after by Lebensborn and 600 more with VoMi, who were expected to be assigned by Lebensborn to German families for adoption. It cannot be ruled out that the actual numbers were far greater.[51]

Mathias Potucnik was such a child of Slovenian parents; he was transferred in 1943 at the age of two from the Lebensborn Kohren-Sahlis home to a German foster family. His foster parents were told that he was an orphan. The foster father, Otto Übe, testified in Nuremberg in 1947 that the child was "blond and blue-eyed" and its background and nationality had been examined. His natural father turned up after the war, having been imprisoned in a concentration camp. His mother had died in German custody.[52]

The same practice was applied in the General Government in Poland as in the occupied western Polish territories. The children of parents of "German descent" who did not want to be added to the

"German People's List (DVL)," the register of people of German nationality in the conquered territories, and who were thus sent to a concentration camp, were removed from their parents and taken to Germany.[53] The Head of the RuSHA, Otto Hofmann, had informed his staff in early 1942 that Himmler planned "to take away the children of Germanizable Poles who cause particular difficulties, ... These children are to be accommodated in special homes, etc. The Reich Leader expects a special educational effect from such a measure."[54] A few days later, the RFSS himself announced a corresponding order on the treatment of unruly "Germanizable Poles" and candidates for the "German People's List," which prescribed imprisonment in a concentration camp and the removal of children as possible means of coercion.[55]

What is more, real or supposed orphans were transferred from the General Government to the Warthegau. Dr. Josef Rembacz, who was "evacuated" out of the Zamość region in the Lublin district in 1942 and was the Polish camp doctor in the "re-Germanizables" camp in Łódź from the autumn 1943, said before the district court in Łódź: "I know of children from various orphanages who went through racial examinations, not just from Łódź, but from the General Government."[56]

At the same time, in the course of the resettlement measures and fighting of partisans in the Zamość region, "gang children of good blood," i.e., children whose parents were in the Majdanek concentration camp or were forced to perform slave labor, were taken to the Old Reich for "Germanization."[57] The Polish historian Czesław Madajczyk estimates that at least 4,500 children were forcibly removed from the area. This figure is based of the list of 29 transports that left the Lublin district between 7 July and 25 August 1943, and gives the bare minimum.[58]

A further example shows how closely the war against the civil population of the occupied and contested areas was ideologically and practically connected with the racial selection of "partisan children" who had become parentless. In May 1944, Himmler gave SS Lieutenant General Arthur Phleps, the commander of the 7th SS Volunteer Mountain Division "Prince Eugen," which was engaged in a bitter suppression of "partisans" in Croatia, the instruction "to seize parentless youths in the Balkans" and bring them to the Reich. The RFSS wanted to educate these "orphaned youths" as a "type of new soldiers" *(Janitscharen)*, "so that, when order and stability have returned, we can give the boys and girls of the relevant states back as respectable people, *while the Reich has in them loyal followers of the Führer and future soldiers and soldier women of the old defensive border (Wehrgrenze) of the Reich."*[59] Himmler demanded a monthly report from the division commander on the number of children collected. The RuSHA received the task of racially examining these children and youths.[60] Even if the plan did not get much further—the Red Army wiped the division out in October 1944—the principle of Himmler's racial thinking and the approach of the SS race experts is nevertheless quite clearly indicated in this case. In areas "endangered by partisans," where the SS, the army, and the police murdered unrelentingly and suppressed the civil population, as in Lidice, Slovenia, Zamość, and Croatia, children became the object of SS attention. They were captured, collected, and sorted, and the "good blood" was taken for adoption by German families or transferred to SS Home Schools *(Heimschulen)*.[61] Those who were "undesirable" were murdered or left to their fate. Himmler himself had discussed this ideological program on many occasions, and laid claim to the "children of good blood" of the enemy peoples.[62] In a speech in October 1943, when the war could no longer be won, he made the connection between the kidnapping of the foreign children and youths and the partisan war against the civilian population of the occupied territories clear. His motto was "Either we win the good blood that we can use and fit in with us or ... we exterminate this blood."[63]

"Children of German Soldiers"

A third group that the SS hoped would help "foster and maintain the racially valuable genetic make-up" were children born of German soldiers and foreign mothers. At first it was the children of "Germanic mothers," especially of Norwegian and Dutch women, who attracted attention.[64] These children were believed to be racially superior per se to children of Russian or Polish mothers, for example. Consequently, with this group the racial experts only had to perform the "eradication of the unbearable" *(der Untragbaren)*, as the RuSHA chief Hofmann informed his staff in the Hague.[65] This selection praxis functioned particularly well in Norway, as the police chief Wilhelm Redieß set great store on having the soldiers' children checked by RuSHA specialists and, what is more, the RuSHA and Lebensborn tried together to move the Norwegian mothers to resettle in Germany.[66]

Thus by the end of the war, thousands of children from Norway and the Netherlands went through the SS aptitude tests and were looked after by Lebensborn or National Socialist Welfare (NSV).

Many then went to Germany either alone or with their mothers.[67] It is important to note that the mothers, as "members of the Germanic peoples" *(Angehörige eines germanischen Volkstums)*, were able to marry the German fathers. Furthermore, the SS, Lebensborn, and the NSV generally did not take their children away against their will as was the case in the East.[68] This different treatment reflected the more moderate occupation policy in the North and the West corresponding on an ideological level with the dogma of the superior "Germanic" blood of these women and children.

But the children of Russian women and German soldiers soon found the interest of the SS, as they were after all 50 percent "of German descent." Himmler estimated that there were approximately one million children of German soldiers in the occupied territories of the Soviet Union alone, and planned their concentration and selection:[69]

> These children would constitute an unheard-of increase—quantitatively and above all racially-qualitatively—for the Russian people, which is today experiencing a significant loss of blood. The Führer therefore let me know yesterday—I am still to receive the precise authority and instruction—that we, the SS, are to determine where all these children are and that they are to be scrutinized. The racially valuable children are taken away from their mothers and brought to Germany, or, if the mothers are racially good and in order, we bring them over as well. We leave the racially poor children *(schlechtrassig)* behind.[70]

Himmler discussed the first steps with RuSHA chief Hofmann and NSV chief Hilgenfeldt in his command quarters in the Ukraine in mid–September 1942.[71] Otto Hofmann summed up the result of the discussions to the RSHA and stressed that, together with Hilgenfeldt, he had been commissioned with "carrying out the selection of the children born out of wedlock of German soldiers and their mothers." He would pass on the "racially valuable" children and their mothers to the NSV, which would then oversee their care and education.[72] Even if the planned approach was thus determined early on and here—in contrast with the procedure in the Netherlands—the NSV was heavily involved instead of Lebensborn, the result once again failed to meet the high expectations. The estimates by the army leadership and the RFSS regarding the numbers of actual soldiers' children were once again highly exaggerated: instead of the estimated million, only ten thousand to eleven thousand such children were detected.[73] How many of these were actually racially selected and (forcefully) taken into German custody must remain open for the time being. A precise total of the "soldiers' children" in Eastern and Western Europe handled by Nazi organizations is also unclear. There were probably many more than 10,000 cases.

The Significance of the Forced Germanization of Non-German Children in Nazi Occupation Policy: Part of a Genocidal Program?

The influence of SS racial ideology on Nazi occupation policy in Europe is clearly demonstrated by the fact that the kidnapped children in Eastern and Western Europe were selected fundamentally on the basis of their perceived "racial value," irrespective of whether they were "orphans," "partisan children," or "soldiers' children." Their racial quality provided the key criterion in deciding to regard them as "desirable population increase" and include them in the macabre kidnapping and Germanization program, or to classify them as "undesirable" and leave them with their parents, abandon them to their fate, or murder them, as in the case of the Lidice children. According to Himmler's thinking and that of the SS organizations, the large numbers of forcefully removed children, mainly from Eastern and South Eastern Europe, were to ensure the German Volk a continuous influx of "desirable blood" and thus compensate for the losses of the war. On the one hand, this notion encompassed the goal of further weakening the "blood stock" of the enemy nations, while, on the other, it was founded in the idea that German society was a community of bearers of "good blood."

Himmler's inhuman prescriptions for the "weakening of the blood" of the enemy nations were not achieved to the extent intended, because insufficient children were sent to Germany (approximately fifty thousand). Nonetheless, the forced Germanization policy against children was seen as part of a genocidal program by the Nuremberg judges, and representatives of RKFDV, RuSHA and VoMi were all brought to justice.[74] The prosecutors saw the removal of children—along with "forced evacuations and resettlement of populations" and "hampering the reproduction of enemy nationals"—as a significant aspect of the "crimes against humanity" of which those responsible for the Germanization policy were accused:

> The abduction of "racially valuable" alien children was thus a part of the greater program of destroying or crippling national groups in the occupied territories, ... This was nothing more than another technique in furtherance of the basic crime of genocide and Germanization.[75]

The Nuremberg prosecutors used Raphael Lemkin's 1944 definition of genocide as a "coordinated plan of different actions aiming at the destruction of essential foundations of life of national groups, with the aim of annihilating the groups themselves." According to Lemkin, these measures could include political and social living conditions as well as biological, physical, economic, and cultural factors, so that the forced Germanization policy and kidnapping could be described as genocidal attacks on this basis.[76] A few months after the pronouncement of judgment in the eighth Nuremberg trial, Article 2 (e) of the United Nations Genocide Convention explicitly defined "forcibly transferring children of the group to another group" as a genocidal act.[77]

If one poses the question of the extent to which the SS campaign for securing "German blood" in occupied Eastern and South Eastern Europe can be described as a genocidal act in the light of recent scholarship on genocide,[78] one comes to the following conclusion: the two central criteria for genocide are fulfilled, namely intentionality and the attempted restriction or destruction of at least a part of a national group by removing or killing its offspring. This is confirmed by numerous documents—speeches and declarations by Himmler, as well as orders and reports of the persons and organizations involved in carrying out the policy. The aim of the removal of children by the SS must thus be clearly differentiated from a forceful movement of populations ("ethnic cleansing"), as the latter *can* lead to the destruction of the people who are to be moved, but is not aimed at that from the outset.[79] At the same time, it seems appropriate to use Robert Melson's term of "partial genocide," as the annihilatory intentions of the Nazis were not directed at the entirety of the Polish, Russian, Belorussian, or Slovenian peoples, but at their "racially inferior" elements.[80] Such a restriction also differentiates this policy from the total genocide aimed at the European Jews. Jewish children were murdered without differentiation; they could not end up in German children's homes and foster families, for they were never regarded as "desirable population increase." What is more, one cannot regard the policy of child removal described here as an isolated measure of the Nazis; it must be seen as part of a larger program for genocide and the transformation of Eastern and Central Eastern Europe: for the forced Germanization and ethnic reordering on racial grounds. This program had conspicuously genocidal characteristics, as the goal, evident in the different variants of the "General Plan East," to annihilate up to 31 million "foreign nationals" (excluding the Jews) makes clear.[81]

Notes

1. See the statement of Lucie Bergner before the Nuremberg Military Tribunal on 23 January 1948, in *Trials of War Criminals before the Nürnberg Military Tribunals under Control Council Law No. 10* (hereafter TWC), vol. 4, 2: 1021–28.

2. For example, on 7 September 1940 in Metz, Lorraine, Himmler had spoken to officers of the SS Adolf Hitler bodyguard unit *(SS-Leibstandarte)* of the need to have the SS "Blood Orders" take the "Nordic blood" from the other European peoples: "We must get it for ourselves and—the others cannot have any." Himmler's speech in Metz, Lorraine, 9 September 1940, 1918–PS, International Military Tribunal (hereafter IMT), *Der Prozeß gegen die Hauptkriegsverbrecher vor dem internationalen Militärgerichtshof, Nürnberg, 1947–1949*, vol. 29, 98–110.

3. See the extensive collection of documents in Czesław Madajczyk, *Vom Generalplan Ost zum Generalsiedlungsplan* (Munich, 1994); Karl-Heinz Roth, "'Generalplan Ost – Gesamtplan Ost': Forschungsstand, Quellenprobleme, neue Ergebnisse," in Mechthild Rössler and Sabine Schleiermacher, eds., *Der "Generalplan Ost": Hauptlinien der nationalsozialistischen Planungs- und Vernichtungspolitik* (Berlin, 1993), 25–117.

4. Ulrich Herbert, "Traditionen des Rassismus," in *Bürgerliche Gesellschaft in Deutschland: Historische Einblicke, Fragen, Perspektiven*, ed. Lutz Niethammer (Frankfurt am Main, 1990), 472–88; Saul Friedländer, *Das Dritte Reich und die Juden: Die Jahre der Verfolgung, 1933–1939* (Munich, 1998); Michael Burleigh and Wolfgang Wippermann, *The Racial State: Germany, 1933–1945* (Cambridge, 1991); Henry Friedlander, *The Origins of Nazi Genocide: From Euthanasia to the Final Solution* (Chapel Hill, 1995).

5. See Michael Zimmermann, *Rassenutopie und Genozid: Die nationalsozialistische "Lösung der Zigeunerfrage"* (Hamburg, 1996); Wolfgang Ayas, *"Asoziale" im Nationalsozialismus* (Stuttgart, 1985).

6. Raul Hilberg, *Die Vernichtung der europäischen Juden*, 3 vol. (Frankfurt am Main, 1997); Götz Aly, "Final Solution": *Nazi Population Policy and the Murder of the European Jews* (London and New York, 1999); Peter Longerich, *Politik der Vernichtung: Eine Gesamtdarstellung der nationalsozialistischen Judenverfolgung* (Munich, 1998).

7. "Erlaß Adolf Hitlers zur Festigung deutschen Volkstums vom 7.10.1939," in *Ursachen und Folgen: Eine Urkunden- und Dokumentensammlung zur Zeitgeschichte*, vol. 14 (Berlin, 1969), 85–86; Robert L. Koehl, *RKFDV: German Settlement and Population Policy, A History of the Reich Commission for the Strengthening of Germandom* (Cambridge, Mass., 1957).

8. Isabel Heinemann, *"Rasse, Siedlung, deutsches Blut": Das Rasse- und Siedlungshauptamt der SS und die rassenpolitische Neuordnung Europas* (Göttingen, 2003); idem, "'Another Type of Perpetrator': The SS Racial Experts and Forced Population Movements in the Occupied Regions," *Holocaust and Genocide Studies* 15, no. 3 (2001): 387–411.

9. Form of a race card of 16 December 1942, Bundesarchiv (hereafter: BA) NS 2/152, 108.

10. Decree of the RFSS of 12 September 1940 on the "Überprüfung und Aussonderung der Bevölkerung der besetzten Ostgebiete," United States Holocaust Memorial Museum (hereafter: USHMM) RG–48.005 M; Report of the Reich Security Main Office (hereafter: RSHA) on the Germanization of "racially

valuable people of foreign descent" of 19 December 1941, Archiwum Głównej Komisji Badania Zbrodni przeciwko Narodowi Polskiemu, Warszawa (hereafter: AGK) 167/38, 11–21.

11. See Indictment, Opening Statement of the Prosecution in Case Eight, TWC, IV, 2: 613, 645–62, 674–87.

12. See Heinemann, *"Rasse, Siedlung, deutsches Blut."*

13. Memorandum of the RFSS, "Einige Gedanken über die Behandlung der Fremdvölkischen im Osten" of 28 May 1940, *Ursachen und Folgen,* 14, 128–32.

14. Official Polish estimates suggest a total of 200,000 children being transported from Poland to Germany and the annexed territories for the purpose of "Germanization." But this figure seems too high, and is not borne out by the available figures about the children forcefully removed from Poland, nor those of the Polish children who were repatriated after the war. Even so, in light of the (incomplete) available material one can assume that at least 20,000 children were kidnapped in this way. For a detailed account, see Heinemann, *"Rasse, Siedlung, deutsches Blut."* The United Nations Relief and Rehabilitation Administration (UNRRA) counted a total of 3,000 Polish children in Baden-Württemberg, 660 in Bavaria and 72 in Hessen in May 1947. According to a report by the Polish Red Cross of 30 June 1950, to that date 3,404 Polish children had been repatriated from the three western zones of occupation, 83 were still awaiting repatriation, and 1,440 were awaiting the production of documents. On the figures, see Roman Hrabar, Zofia Tokarz and Jacek Wilczur, *Kinder im Krieg – Krieg gegen Kinder: Die Geschichte der polnischen Kinder, 1939-1945* (Hamburg, 1981), 241–42, 333–35.

15. In addition to my estimation of 20,000 Polish children, there were approximately the same number of children from the Soviet Union (including the alleged "children of German soldiers"), and a further 10,000 from Western and South Eastern Europe. According to Polish estimates, there were still 6,000 children from Eastern Europe in Schleswig-Holstein in 1949 and more than 7,000 from Western and Northern Europe in Lower Saxony. See Hrabar et al., *Kinder im Krieg,* 240, 334.

16. A relevant recommendation of 18 June 1941 from Himmler to Gau leader Greiser is BA NS 19/2621. Cf. Peter Witte et al. (eds.), *Der Dienstkalender Heinrich Himmlers 1941–42* (Hamburg, 1999), 166.

17. Order No. 67/1 of the RKFDV, sgd. SS Major General Greifelt, on the Germanization of children from Polish families and from formerly Polish orphanages of 19 February 1942, BA NS 2/58, 102–6.

18. See the letter of SS Colonel Creutz of the RKFDV of 12 August 1941 to the Reich Governor in the Warthegau, NO–3074.

19. Overview of the work of the Department C 2 (Re-Germanization) of the RuSHA, sgd. SS First Lieutenant Harders, of 25 September 1942, BA NS 2/89, 25–36.

20. According to information of the head of the Department III in the Gau Administration in Posen, in total there were more than 20 such children's homes for German children and "children of German descent" in the Warthegau. Testimony of the witness Dr. Bartels in Nuremberg on 20 January 1948, TWC, IV, 2: 1,047. The home in Kalisch had room for 50 to 60 children, that in Puschkau for about 70, and that in Brockau was smaller still. Georg Lilienthal, *Der "Lebensborn e.V.": Ein Instrument nationalsozialistischer Rassenpolitik* (Mainz, 1985), 221. Witness statement by Maria Hanfova of 30 October

1947, TWC, 4, 2: 1035.

21. See the letter of 10 October 1942 from the Reich Minister of the Interior, sgd. p.p. Bader, to the Reich Governor in Posen, NO–2793.

22. See the letter of 16 July 1943 from SS Major Tesch of the Lebensborn adoption office to the head doctor of Lebensborn, SS Colonel Dr. Ebner about four instances of doubt about "Germanized children." Their years of birth were given as 1935 or 1936, but they seemed much younger to their foster parents, NO–1371.

23. That home had room for 40 children. It was in Kopernika Street in Lódz, in the camp complex of the Central Office for Resettlement (UWZ) of the Security Police.

24. Statement of Slavomir Grodomski Paczesny in Nuremberg on 6 November 1947, TWC, 4, 2: 1002–6.

25. "Beauftragung Pflaums durch den RFSS vom 11.7.1941 und Erweiterung seines Auftrages 'auf die gesamten besetzten Gebiete der europäischen UdSSR' am 16.8.1941," Berlin Document Center, SS-Officer Files (hereafter BDC) Guntram Pflaum.

26. Activity Statement of the RuSHA representative with the Higher SS and Police Leader (hereafter HSSPF) Central Russia, SS Major Buchs, of 19 July 1942, BA NS 2/91, 95–96. Statement by the head doctor of the Bobruisk SS military hospital, Willibald Zwirner, of 19 June 1947, NO–5223, quoted by Christian Gerlach, *Kalkulierte Morde: Die deutsche Wirtschafts- und Vernichtungspolitik in Weißrußland 1941 bis 1944* (Hamburg, 1999), 1082.

27. See Himmler's comments in a speech of 16 September 1942 in his headquarters in Hegewald to the South Russia police chiefs (SSPF) about the ideal character of the handling of children in Bobruisk, BA NS 19/4009, 141.

28. That was the outcome of a meeting between the staff leader in the Race and Settlement department in South Russia, SS Captain Bauer, and the Commander of the Security Police (hereafter BdS) in Kiev in October 1942. See Bauer's report of 25 October 1942, BA NS 2/81, 2–5.

29. Speech by the RFSS to the South Russia SSPF of 16 September 1942 in Hegewald, BA NS 19/4009, 128–78. Napola were National-Political Educational Institutes—elite Nazi schools.

30. Heydrich died on 4 June 1942 as a result of the assassination. In revenge, Hitler ordered Lidice's destruction on 9 June 1942, the day of Heydrich's burial. On 24 June the village Lezàky was also destroyed and its inhabitants killed or arrested.

31. Report of June 1942 from the Reich Protector, sgd. Daluege, to Martin Bormann about the assassination of SS Lieutenant General Heydrich. Slightly different figures (179 men and 198 women) are given by a report of 12 June 1942 by BdS Horst Böhme to the Office of the Reich Protector about the punitive measures against Lidice in the Kladno district. See Václav Král, *Die Deutschen in der Tschechoslowakei 1933–1947: Dokumentensammlung* (Prague, 1964), 480–81, 486–89.

32. The UWZ was actually responsible for the deportation of Jews and the expulsion of the Polish population in the Germanization process. See Aly, *Endlösung*. The head of the Litzmannstadt UWZ branch, Hermann Krumey, was informed by a telex from the RuSHA of 12 June 1942, sgd. Franz Pichler, about the arrival of the children. See the comments in the decision to cease proceedings *(Einstellungsbeschluss)* of the Frankfurt public attorney's office of 9

December 1976, Zentrale Stelle der Landesjustizverwaltungen (hereafter: ZSt.) 501 AR 1184/67, vol. II, 922d.

33. Secret telex of the head of the UWZ Litzmannstadt, Krumey, via the Gestapo Office Litzmannstadt to the RSHA, department 4 B 4, attention SS Colonel Dr. Ehlich, concerning the transfer of 88 Czech children on 22 June 1942, BDC Hermann Krumey.

34. This conclusion is also reached in the decision to cease proceedings of the Frankfurt public attorney's office of 9 December 1976, ZSt. 501 AR 1184/67, vol. 2, 992d.

35. "33 adults (men and women) were shot. The children were passed on to German officers." Report of June 1942 from the Reich Protector, sgd. Daluege, to Martin Bormann about the assassination of SS Lieutenant General Heydrich, in Král, *Die Deutschen in der Tschechoslowakei,* 486–89.

36. See the letter from the managing director of the Bohemia and Moravia RuSHA branch, SS Captain Wettern, to the RKFDV, attention SS Lieutenant Colonel Fischer, with the request for immediate provision of 2000 litres of gas, as the branch's fuel provisions had been exhausted by the "actions" of Lidice and Lezaky, IMT, vol. 39, Dok. 060(9)–USSR, 365.

37. Letter of July 1942 from SS Captain Wettern to the head of the Litzmannstadt UWZ about "non-re-Germanizable children from the Protectorate Bohemia and Moravia," BDC Hermann Krumey.

38. Decision to cease proceedings of the Frankfurt public attorney's office of 9 December 1976, ZSt. 501 AR 1184/67, vol. 2, 992d. However, the decision describes the murder of the children in Chełmno as unprovable.

39. Statement of camp doctor Dr. Jan Zielina of 12 November 1947 in Cieszyn; statement of nurse Julia Makowska of 11 October 1946 before the district court in Łódź, ZSt. 501 AR 1184/67. See also the statement of the responsible section head of the Gau administration, Dr. Bartels, in Nuremberg on 20 January 1948, TWC, 4, 2: 1047.

40. Witness statement by Maria Hanfova on 30 October 1947, TWC, 4, 2: 1033–38, here 1036.

41. See for example the statement of the camp nurse, Julia Makowska, of 11 October 1946, who testified that other transports with Czech children also arrived in the "race camp" in Litzmannstadt, ZSt. 501 AR 1184/67.

42. Secret instruction of 25 June 1942 from the RFSS to carry out action against partisans and other bandits in Upper Carnolia and Lower Styria, NO–681. See also the Special Order No. 1 of the Commander of the Alpenland Police *(Ordnungspolizei Alpenland),* Veldes Office, sgd. Brigadier general Brenner, of 19 July 1942, regarding the punitive measures against the population sympathetic to the gangs, Tone Ferenc, *Quellen zur nationalsozialistischen Entnationalisierungspolitik in Slowenien, 1941–1945* (Maribor, 1980), 463–64.

43. Report of 8 August 1942 from HSSPF Alpenland, Erwin Rösener, to RHSA chief Otto Hofmann after the beginning of the "action" about Race and Settlement work in the Alpenland region, BA NS 2/81, 48–49.

44. This task was already set down in Himmler's order of 25 June 1942. Himmler had demanded a separate establishment of the "racial value" of the "gang children." See also the letter of 14 September 1942 from the RKFDV at the HSSPF in the Defence District *(Wehrkreis)* 18, sgd. p.p. SS Major Heinrich Obersteiner, to the VoMi about the transportation of the bandit children from Upper Carnolia and Lower Styria to the Old Reich, NO–3019, in Ferenc, *Entnationalisierungspolitik,* 492–93.

45. See the report of 8 August 1942 from the HSSPF Alpenland, Ernst Rösener, to the head of the RuSHA, Hofmann, about the work of the RuSHA in the Higher Division Alpenland, BA NS 2/81, 48–49.
46. A total of 430 children were brought to this collection camp in this transport. See the report of 17 August 1942 from Anna Rath of the German Red Cross about the first transport of children to Frohnleiten on 10 August 1942, in Ferenc, *Entnationalisierungspolitik,* 485–86. A second transport in mid–August brought more children to Frohnleiten.
47. Letter of 14 September 1942 from the RFKDV at the HSSPF in Defensive District 15, sgd. p.p. SS Major Heinrich Obersteiner, to the VoMi about the transfer of bandit children from Upper Carnolia and Lower Styria to the Old Reich, NO–3019, in Ferenc, *Entnationalisierungspolitik,* 492–93. The Lebensborn representative, Inge Viermetz, visited this camp and spoke with the aptitude assessor Rödel, whom she believed to be the leader of the camp, statement of Inge Viermetz in Nuremberg on 28 January and 2 February 1948, TWC, 4, 2: 1064–70.
48. See the question of 5 September 1942 from SS Colonel Creutz of the RKFDV to the Vomi regarding the accommodation of children of shot criminals from Upper Carnolia and Lower Styria, NO–5304. Report of the Gau Vomi leadership, sgd. SS Colonel Maier Kaibitsch, to the representative of the RKFDV at the HSSPF in Defensive District WVIII regarding the "children of the justicized" *[sic (Justifizierten)]* from Upper Carnolia. According to a calculation in Ferenc, between 1942 and 1944 circa 4,200 relatives of "partisans" were forced from Upper Carnolia via the camp Zwischenwässern into the Old Reich, but it is unclear how many of them were children. See Ferenc, *Entnationalisierungspolitik,* 489, 520–22.
49. Note of 10 February 1943 for SS Major Brückner on the treatment of settlers *(Absiedler)* from the Upper Carnolia, prepared by SS First Lieutenant Klingsporn of VoMi, NO–5201. Enquiry of 19 July 1943 from the Lebensborn board, sgd. p.p. Dr. Tesch, concerning the transfer of children from the Upper Carnolia and Lower Styria to the Old Reich, in Ferenc, *Entnationalisierungspolitik,* 615. Tesch inquired whether children who were older than 12 years should also be looked after by Lebensborn.
50. According to Tone Ferenc, these children were in the VoMi camps in Coburg, Seligenporten, Kastel bei Amberg, Markt-Eisenstein and Metten-Himmelberg, all in the Gau Bayrische Ostmark. Letter of 14 January 1943 from the Reich Youth Leader representative at the RFKDV to VoMi regarding the handling of various youths. Response of 19 January 1943 from SS Major Brückner. Both in Ferenc, *Entnationalisierungspolitik,* 565–66.
51. Lilienthal's estimation, that Lebensborn had already taken approximately 20 Slovenian children in its "Alpenland" home in Oberweis, thus seems to be clearly too low. See Lilienthal, *Lebensborn,* 227.
52. Testimony of Otto Übe, the foster father of Mathias Potucnik, before the Nuremberg Tribunal on 4 November 1047, in TWC, 4, 2: 1060–63.
53. Bruno Wasser cites a relevant letter from a district councillor *(Landrat)* of 15 July 1942, in Wasser, *Himmlers Raumplanung im Osten: der Generalplan Ost in Polen 1940–1944* (Berlin, 1993), 263.
54. Letter of 12 February 1942 from RuSHA chief Hofmann to the head of the Race Office, SS Colonel Schultz, BA NS 2/89, 112.
55. Decree of the RFSS, head of the German Police, and RKFDV, sgd. Himmler, of 16 February 1942 about the treatment of persons listed in section 4 of the Ger-

man People's List. USHMM RG–15007, 113. Himmler ordered that re-Germanization could also be achieved "by use of measures of force by the state police" (i.e., detention in a concentration camp) and recommended the removal of children as a possible sanction.

56. Dr. Josef Rembacz was himself "evacuated" out of Skierbisczowo in the Zamość district, where he had worked in the health office, in October 1942 and was regarded as "racially valuable." Until December 1942 he worked as the camp doctor in the resettlement camp in Zamość before being sent as the camp doctor to the RuSHA camp in Litzmannstadt. From February 1944 he was the camp doctor in the UWZ resettlement camp. Testimony of Dr. Josef Rembacz before the district court in Łódź on 25 April 1946, NO–5266.

57. On resettlement from the Zamość district in the Lublin region, see Wasser, *Himmler's Raumplanung*; Czesław Madajczyk, *Zamojscyzna-Sonderlaboratorium-SS: Zbiór dokumentów polskich I niemieckich z okresu okupacji hitlerowskiej*, 2. vols. (Warsaw, 1979).

58. Madajczyk, *Zamojscyzna-Sonderlaboratorium-SS*, 14–15; Hrabar et al., *Kinder im Krieg*, 224.

59. Secret order from Himmler to SS Lieutenant General Phleps of 20 May 1944, NO–2218; note for the files by the head of the personal staff of the RFSS, SS Colonel Brandt, about an instruction from Himmler of 20 May 1944, italicization as underlining in original, NO–4000. See the corresponding letter from Himmler to the head of the SS Main Office, Gottlob Berger, of 14 July 1944, NO–3998.

60. Telex of 12 September 1944 from Lieutenant Colonel Grothmann, chief adjutant of the RFSS, to the General Commander of the 5th SS Mountain Corps, regarding the handling of the parentless Balkan youths, NO–3997: "Reich Leader SS has instructed the Race and Settlement Main Office SS to take over the youths from the operational area of the 7th SS Volunteer Mountain Division 'Prinz Eugen,' who were captured by the 5th SS Mountain Corps."

61. The idea of returning the "orphaned youths of the Balkans," as expressed by Himmler, was however new and was perhaps due to the state of the war. The SS had certainly not considered eventually returning the Polish, Slovenian, and Czech youths to their countries of origin.

62. See the already cited programmatic speech in Hegewald on 16 September 1942, BA NS 19/4009, 128–78.

63. Speech of the RFSS in Bad Schachen on 14 October 1943, L–70. IMT, vol. 37, 498–523. There are numerous further examples of Himmler's fearful attempts to deny all enemy peoples every last drop of "Nordic blood" and thus to weaken the German Reich's potential opponents.

64. An order by the Führer of 28 July 1942 regulated the care of these children: Order about the care of children of members of the German Army in the occupied territories, RGBl I, 1942, 488. It was at first limited to the children of German soldiers and Norwegian and Dutch mothers.

65. The head of the RuSHA, Hoffmann, to the Race and Settlement leader at the HSSPF North-West in the Hague, SS Major Herbert Aust, of 29 January 1943 about the instruction to care for the children of members of the German Army in the occupied territories, BA NS 2/57, 87–91.

66. Telex from RuSHA chief Hofmann to HSSPF North Major General Rediess of 29 July 1941, BA NS 2/78, 221. Since 1941 there was an office in the RuSHA Family Office *(Sippenamt)* for Norwegian women who were looked after by Lebensborn. It was to facilitate the arrival of (racially examined) Norwegian

women who were prepared to relocate to Germany. See the plan of the structure of the RuSHA offices of 5 September 1944, BA NS 2/103, 1–11. Cf. the two-year activity report for the Main Section 4 in the Family Office *(Sippenamt)*, sgd. Dreier, of 3 October 1941, BA NS 2/57, 87–91.

67. In his study of Lebensborn, Georg Lilienthal reckons with a total of 6,000 children who were born in Lebensborn homes in Norway and at least 200 other children who were brought to the Reich from Norway. Lebensborn ran at least six maternity homes and three homes for children in Norway. The deputy leader of Lebensborn in Oslo, Ernst Ragaller, maintained after the war that ca. 2,000 Norwegian women and their children had gone to Germany. The figures for the Netherlands are less clear. In its "Gelderland" home Lebensborn had only a few children. It cannot be stated with any certainty here how many of the more than 1,000 German-Dutch children in the care of NSV actually left the Netherlands for Germany. Sworn statement by Ernst Ragallers of 28 July 1947, cited by Lilienthal, *Lebensborn*, 178, 190, 243, 258; letter of 17 November 1942 from RuSHA chief Hofmann to Herbert Aust, BA NS 2/82, 112.

68. Lilienthal, however, questions, given the criminal Germanization measures in the East, the extent to which the mothers "agreed" to Lebensborn taking ca. 200 to 250 children to Germany for adoption, Lilienthal, *Lebensborn*, 179. Here, too, this figure is the minimum. These children were taken without their mothers and were intended for adoption by Germany families, and thus should not be confused with the Norwegian children who were taken to Germany by the RuSHA with their mothers.

69. The Commander of the 2nd Armored Army, General Schmidt, reckoned at this time with 1.5 million children. See *Dienstkalender*, 548. Report of Himmler's speech to the police chiefs of 16 September 1942, in "Inspection tour of the Ukraine (South Russia)," BA NS 2/82, 221.

70. Himmler's speech to the HSSPF South Russia in Hegewald on 16 September 1942, BA NS 18/4009, 137–38.

71. Such discussions took place on 13 and 14 September 1942 at the Field HQ at Winniza, *Dienstkalender*, 548–50.

72. Letter of 23 October 1943 from the chief of the RuSHA, Hofmann, to the RSHA regarding the care of children of members of the Germany Army in the occupied territories, BA NS 2/71, 24–25. See the Decree of the Führer about the care of illegitimate Germany children in the occupied territories of 11 October 1943.

73. Christian Gerlach gives the figure of 10,000 children in the Reich Commissariat Ukraine, and only 500 in the Reich Commissariat Ostland including the General District of White Ruthenia, Gerlach, *Kalkulierte Morde*, 1081.

74. See the Indictment and Opening Statement of the Prosecution in Case Eight of the Nürnberg Military Trials, TWC, 4, 2: 610, 613, 650, 674–87; Opinion and Judgement, TWC, 5, 1: 102–8, 152–54.

75. Opening Statement of the Prosecution in Case Eight of the Nürnberg Military Trials, TWC, vol. 4, 2: 675, 687.

76. Raphael Lemkin, *Axis Rule in Occupied Europe: Laws of Occupation, Analysis of Government, Proposals for Redress* (Washington, 1944), 79–90.

77. UN Convention on the Prevention and Punishment of the Crime of Genocide of 9 December 1948.

78. Robert Melson, *Revolution and Genocide: On the Origins of the Armenian Genocide and the Holocaust* (Chicago, 1992); Stig Förster and Gerhard Hirschfeld, eds., *Genozid in der modernen Geschichte* (Münster, 1999); Nor-

man Naimark, *Fires of Hatred: Ethnic Cleansing in Twentieth Century Europe* (Cambridge, Mass., 2001).

79. See Naimark, *Fires of Hatred,* 2–5, 15.
80. Melson, *Revolution and Genocide,* 26.
81. See Erhard Wetzel, "Stellungnahme und Gedanken zum Generalplan Ost des Reichsführers SS vom 27.4.1942," in Madajczyk, *Generalplan Ost,* 50–81.

Chapter 11

"CLEARING THE WHEAT BELT"
Erasing the Indigenous Presence in the Southwest of Western Australia

Anna Haebich

Incremental Genocide

The collaboration of white settlers and the state to erase the presence of Indigenous people from the southwest of Western Australia between 1900 and 1940 provides an especially interesting case study of what recent contributions to the theoretical literature have called "unintended genocide," "societal genocide," or "indigenocide" by a "genocidal society" and its "relations of genocide."[1] By these accounts, mass Indigenous death and cultural effacement in colonial situations can be accounted for by the incremental and often unintended consequences of settler expansion and governmental neglect as much as by the explicit intention to kill as state policy. Adherents of the United Nations definition of genocide will object that the requirement of a genocidal intention cannot be defined away to suit the purposes of historians who want colonial governments to be held responsible for the catastrophe that befell the Indigenous inhabitants. The answer to this objection is that insisting on premeditation and planning ignores the fact that government intentions evolve over time as policy-makers, faced with changing circumstances, head in directions they had not foreseen.

Notes for this section begin on page 287.

Moreover, policy does not develop in a vacuum, but is driven by state interaction with society; in the colonial context, with rapacious settlers who incessantly lobby state authorities to expel or otherwise "deal" with the Indigenous presence in their midst.[2]

In reconstructing this radicalization process, it is worth revisiting Raphael Lemkin's adumbration of the means by which occupied populations can be subjugated. This approach also shifts the focus of study from overt forms of killing to strategies of dealing with unwanted populations that, acting together, can have genocidal effects. The treatment of Aboriginal people in "settled" Australia in the early twentieth century emerges as a rich site for further analysis and comparative discussion of the question of colonial genocide.

Lemkin's view of genocide was shaped by his study of the networks of laws, regulations, and administrations imposed by the colonizing regimes of the Axis Powers—Germany, Italy, Hungary, Bulgaria, and Rumania—and their puppet regimes on subjugated peoples in occupied Europe during the Second World War.[3] In *Axis Rule in Occupied Europe,* published in 1944, Lemkin provided the following definition of genocide:

> Generally speaking, genocide does not necessarily mean the immediate destruction of a nation, except when accomplished by mass killings of all members of a nation. It is intended rather to signify a co-ordinated plan of different actions aiming at the destruction of essential foundations of the life of national groups themselves. The objectives of such a plan would be the disintegration of the political and social institutions, of culture, language, national feelings, religion and the economic existence of national groups, and the destruction of the personal security, liberty, health, dignity, and even the lives of individuals belonging to such groups.[4]

These legal and administrative "techniques of genocide" directed at "national groups" suggest the multiplicity of ways in which human groups can be destroyed apart from outright killing, and have yet to be applied systematically to an Australian case study.[5] The "drastic methods" employed and their intended outcome of "destruction of essential foundations of the life" of human groups go much further than the goals and aims of forced assimilation. They constitute a mix of genocidal cultural and biological measures. Lemkin grouped these techniques into the following "fields":[6]

- Economic: land, resources and wealth are confiscated and transferred to members of the invading nations, local economic institutions are destroyed and economic development is crippled. In the process the oppressed group is impoverished and deprived of "the elemental means of existence" and its living standards are reduced to the point where it becomes so preoccupied with survival that it is unable to meet "cultural-spiritual" obligations and to maintain traditional ways of living and thinking. These conditions are exacerbated by measures limiting entry to occupations and the right to engage in trade. Forced deportation of workers undermines traditional working arrangements, disrupts family life and adversely affects the health of workers.[7] The unequal treatment of targeted groups encourages ideas of human inequality and racial superiority.

- Political: local institutions of self-government are destroyed and replaced by imposed systems of administration that act to further the interests of the occupying forces.

- Social: social cohesion is undermined through the abolition of local social systems and the imposition of laws that are "bereft of moral content and of respect for human rights" and that act as a means of "administrative coercion" to benefit the objectives of the occupying forces.[8] Spiritual resources are weakened through the removal or killing of elements that provide leadership and resistance.

- Culture: local cultural institutions and activities including languages and all forms of creative expression are prohibited. Systems of education are destroyed and replaced by instruction directed at producing workers for introduced industries.

- Biological: depopulation is promoted through measures to decrease the birth-rate, for example, controls over marriage, separation of males and females through deportation and gross undernourishment of parents. Measures such as subsidies and tax concessions for large families are introduced to encourage increase in the invading population. Procreation with local populations is encouraged and special care is provided for offspring.

- Physical existence: discriminatory and unequal food rationing, severely reduce quality of diet and deprivation of basic nutrients cause physical debilitation and death. This is exacerbated by inadequate shelter and clothing, overcrowded living conditions, limits on freedom of movement and transportation in severe climatic conditions. This can culminate in mass killings of specific groups, intellectuals and resistance leaders.

- Religion: religious practices are prohibited and institutions undermined, particularly through education of children in other religious traditions.
- Moral: "spiritual resistance" is weakened by creating an "atmosphere of moral debasement" that diverts thinking from "moral and national thinking" and substituting "cheap individual pleasure" [sexual immorality, alcoholism, gambling etc.] for "collective feelings and ideals."[9]

As we will see, there are many parallels with what transpired in the southwest of Western Australia in the first half of the twentieth century, where instances from all of Lemkin's fields of "techniques of genocide"—economic, political, social, cultural, biological, physical, religious, and moral—can be identified. To be sure, there is a significant difference in the degree to which the actions were a deliberately "coordinated plan" of government, as Lemkin insisted reflected genocide. Here they constituted a cobbled-together process of collaboration between state and settlers, both determined to advance their interests by erasing the Aboriginal presence from the region. The state, thwarted in its effort to achieve this outcome through more benign measures, and faced by settlers' relentless demands, resorted to increasingly radical solutions over the years. In essence, frustration drove policy, creating conditions that undermined Aboriginal cultural and social life and threatened their very survival—an outcome that settlers observed, but did not care to remedy. This was not so much a matter of deliberate and conscious genocidal intent. Rather, it reflected what Tony Barta has referred to as the "inevitable rather than intentional" consequences of "genocidal relations" set in train by the appropriation of Aboriginal land and resources for settlement and economic development, which left Aboriginal people subject to "remorseless pressures of destruction" and that rendered "coexistence impossible."[10]

The Setting

The first three decades of the twentieth century brought dramatic environmental, demographic, and social changes to the southwest region of Western Australia. Vast areas of bush "wilderness" and sprawling pastoral properties in the region were carved up into thousands of small family farms as part of an ambitious state-directed program of agricultural development. Attracted by offers of generous land grants and financial assistance, prospective farmers—many of them unemployed miners stranded in the west after the 1890s gold rushes—streamed onto the land. By the 1920s, the region had been transformed into a prosperous wheat growing area accommodating thousands of new settlers whose needs were serviced by networks of towns, roads, and railways spread out across the landscape.

Initially, politicians and settlers alike gave little thought to the impact of these changes on Aboriginal inhabitants of the region. Indeed, it was widely believed that they had all but died out, reflecting public perceptions at the time of Aborigines as a "doomed race."[11] White settlement certainly had a drastic impact on the estimated original Aboriginal population of 6,000 in the south, although this decline was most pronounced in coastal areas of concentrated white settlement. Despite the white encroachment, a sizable population had survived in the inland areas now designated for agricultural development. In 1901, the Western Australian Census counted 1,200 Aborigines in the area, the majority of mixed descent, and noted that the population was increasing.[12] They lived in the bush in family groups, following patterns of life that combined traditional ways and adaptations to white settlement. An official tour of inspection in 1902 reported that families were leading a vigorous life, working and camping on pastoral stations (that is, ranches), or living and hunting in the bush.[13]

This second frontier of development was devastating for the Aboriginal people. Like the populations in occupied Europe described by Lemkin, they were forced off their land, and denied access to its resources, and their economic independence was destroyed, leaving them impoverished outcasts. Only a few were granted farms, and then under special conditions that created insurmountable financial problems and doomed their efforts to failure.[14] The only available employment was clearing or seasonal farm work, and families had to camp where they could on pockets of uncleared bush or on their employer's land. With severe drought conditions from 1911 and decreasing demand for their labor, most were forced to seek refuge in camps on the fringes of the new towns, where they came under the control of imposed systems of administration and law that acted against their interests, and progressively undermined their way of life.

The Aborigines Department was charged with the duty of the "protection and care" of Indigenous people, and in theory it was to provide for all their welfare and health needs, as well as education for their children. In practice, however, its duty of care became a form of "dole and control," as it issued meager rations to "deserving" cases and enforced the restrictive provisions of the *Aborigines Act 1905,* acting through police officers at the local level. The 1905 Act controlled virtually every aspect of Aboriginal lives—with whom they could associate, where they could live and work, and their earnings, personal property, family life, marriage, and sexual contacts—and allowed for their removal to institutions where they could be detained indefinitely.[15] Fines and imprisonment awaited those who dared not to comply with its provisions. Such was the virtually totalitarian control vested in the so-called Chief Protector of Aborigines.

The Evolution of Policy from Below

Between 1911 and 1914, the Aboriginal population in the town of Katanning in the far southwest increased from 40 to over 200, and in Moora, to the north of Perth, numbers grew from 60 to 240. Conditions in the town camps quickly deteriorated. There were no proper shelters, no sanitary or rubbish services, no fresh water, no work, and only meager rations of flour, tea, and sugar for the elderly and dependent mothers and their children, issued by the police on behalf of the Aborigines Department. The tragic toll on Aboriginal families in Katanning was evident in the litany of sickness and death recorded in the personal correspondence of missionary Annie Lock. In April and May 1914 she noted that:

> there has been much sickness, and several deaths. One week a child died, and the following week the mother passed away ... A young man passed away leaving a wife and four children. ... We have had two deaths ... a little boy nine years old ... the other, an old man.[16]

The abject poverty in the camps was compounded by the hostility of town residents to the unanticipated and unwanted Aboriginal presence in their midst. The locals were imbued with beliefs and anxieties about race mixing that were reinforced by conditions in the camps. In particular, they feared physical and moral contagion from proximity to people of mixed descent who were believed to have "inherited the vices of both races." While some residents evinced sympathy for the Aborigines' plight, they were more concerned about their own health and safety. To this end, the towns enforced strict "caste barriers"—some backed by legal sanctions—which also denied Aborigines access to town services such as hospitals. An editorial in the *Great Southern Herald* in 1909 expressed the potent mix of racism and stated paternalistic concern circulating in the towns:

> KATANNING is just now swarming with aborigines ... No right-think-ing townsman or townswoman can fail to pity these remnants of a dying race, or to show them any possible kindness. Especially will right-minded people desire that something could be done for the little black children. ... But none the less clearly must it be recognized that it is bad for both whites and blacks that these aboriginals should lounge about the town.[17]

Simmering tensions erupted in a wave of racist hysteria that spread throughout the wheat belt, with devastating consequences for Aboriginal people. The catalyst was the enrolment of Aborigi-nal children in local state schools. White parents demanded their immediate expulsion. A letter in the *West Australian* newspaper in 1912 expressed the view that "intermingling" in the schools would encourage "the future mothers and fathers of this State in the belief that there [were] no differences between the races."[18] Parents in the town of Mt. Barker complained to the Minister for Education in 1914 that the children were a "horrible menace to the health and morals of young Australians."[19] The issue escalated into demands for Aboriginal families to be driven out of the towns altogether. Politicians and government officials were bombarded with peti-tions, deputations, and letters insisting on the permanent segrega-tion of the families in farming settlements distant from the towns. Local activists threatened public "indignation meetings" and inquiries "instituted in the British parliament" if the government failed to take immediate action.[20]

By 1915, tempers in the towns were at breaking point. Early in the year, a Moora resident threatened in a letter to the *Truth* news-paper to do "a bit of rifle practice" at the town camp. Referring to a recent event in war-torn Europe, the correspondent claimed that this would "cause a sensation ... as big as the forcing of the Dard-anelles [in Turkey]."[21] When residents demanded that Moora be declared a "prohibited area" for Aborigines, and authorities in the surrounding districts refused to accommodate them, the Aborigines were left with nowhere to go.[22] They wrote to the government ask-ing, "How we going to live on rock and water? We will be camels directly," but Katanning residents did not wait for the Minister's reply.[23] They took matters into their own hands, expelling Aborig-ines from the town by marching them under police escort to an iso-lated camping site and leaving them to fend for themselves.

The Aboriginal people had no base to represent their interests. The extent to which their society had been undermined by white settlement was evident in the failure of their efforts in Katanning in 1914 to enforce a system of order in the camps based on traditional authority structures. A range of laws denied them the right to participate as citizens in state institutions, and their personal freedoms were severely restricted under the 1905 Act. Rather than representing its charges, the Aborigines Department bowed to political and public pressure to protect white interests at their expense. The official policy of "protection" was replaced by policies of enforced segregation and assimilation, as the occasion demanded.

No one contemplated the idea of enforcing acceptance of Aboriginal families in the towns. The establishment of a system of segregated schools and other services in the towns was deemed to be too expensive and unacceptable to town residents. Nothing came of discussions between officials and local authorities concerning alternative camping sites. Finally, in 1914, Aboriginal children were expelled from the schools under a provision in the *Education Act 1893* authorizing the exclusion of children deemed to be "injurious" to the health, welfare, and morality of other pupils. This practice continued into the late 1940s, thereby denying generations of Aboriginal children the right to a state education. In 1915, in the face of mounting public agitation and a severely reduced majority in the November 1914 elections, the government finally endorsed the white residents' proposal to clear Aborigines from the town camps and to intern them in segregated settlements.

Over the years, the Department collaborated with settlers by using its powers under the 1905 Act to remove Aboriginal adults to institutions in order to clear the way for white settlement and economic development. Dispossessed Aboriginal families were left to survive in bleak conditions that would never have been tolerated for other residents of the wheat belt. To break the continuity of Aboriginal ways of life and their connection to the land, powers of guardianship in the 1905 Act were used to remove children and to rear them in institutions in isolation from their families. Although officials claimed to be acting in the interests of Aboriginal welfare, their actions strongly resembled Lemkin's "technologies of genocide" in their inevitable corrosion of Indigenous political, social, and cultural life and their ability to survive. In particular, the treatment of the children, rather than saving them, as official rhetoric of the time maintained, constituted a form of cultural genocide intended to destroy the "cultural unit."[24]

A discernible official policy had finally emerged. Rather than solving the problem of white-black coexistence, this Apartheid-like "solution" laid the basis for continuing race conflict and division, and created conditions that threatened the cultural and physical survival of the Aboriginal people.

The Escalation: A.O. Neville and "Biological Absorption"

A determined new Chief Protector of Aborigines, A.O. Neville (1874–1954), was appointed to introduce administrative solutions that would protect white interests, fit with the provisions of the 1905 Act, and reflect models of welfare and institutional care deemed suitable for Aboriginal people—all within a shoestring budget. He began by setting up an administrative regime based on strict economy and efficiency and the implementation of the Department's extensive powers and controls over Aboriginal people, with particular attention to the wheat belt. The focus of the administration was the establishment and operation of two native settlements—Carrolup near Katanning and Moore River near Moora, opened in 1915 and 1918 respectively—to contain Aboriginal people forcibly removed from the town camps. Aboriginal "welfare"—rations, shelter, and medical attention—and schooling were centralized in these settlements, providing an economical solution for the care of the elderly, the sick, dependent mothers, and children.[25] Neville envisaged that they would become self-sufficient agricultural farms. There was no possibility of accommodating all Aboriginal people—because of limited funds—and officials believed that "able-bodied" men should earn their own keep, especially with the renewed demand for their labor following the outbreak of war in 1914, even when this meant long-term separation from their families.

The settlements were intended to act as "clearing houses," a term that had powerful resonances with the popular phrase "clearing the wheat belt." While the older generations at the settlements gradually passed away, the young people would be trained to begin new lives in the wider community. Neville's optimistic calculation that after two or three generations, the settlements would have served their purpose and could be closed down contrasted with settlements and missions in other parts of Australia that were intended to become "permanent homes" for their Aboriginal residents.[26] His vision also differed from practice in Canada, where children forcibly removed to residential schools were expected to return to their families on completion of their schooling and to live out their lives on the reservations.[27]

This imagined outcome reflected pervasive beliefs in the "doomed race" theory for the so-called "full-blood" Aborigines, and in the potential of children of "mixed race" to become "civilized." Social Darwinian theory underlay the conviction that, in the "struggle for survival of the fittest," "Stone Age" Aboriginal people were "doomed to extinction" and that this was a natural and inevitable outcome that human agency could not prevent. All that could be done was to "smooth the dying pillow" by providing minimal care in the form of rations and shelter. Such views were the basis of the department's policy of Aboriginal "protection," summarized by a parliamentarian during debate on the *Aborigines Bill* in 1905: "all we can do is to protect them as far as possible and leave nature to do the rest. It is a case of the survival of the fittest but let the fittest do their best."[28]

The Aborigines' "mixed race" children were variously believed to have inherited the best or the worst of both races: either way, they were susceptible to education and training and in need of the controlling influence of institutional life. It was generally accepted that the government had a particular duty to ensure that children who were "half-British" were not left to grow up as "vagrants and coloureds" in the camps.[29] The children's training would equip them to become menial domestic and farm workers living in the wider community under the control of the Aborigines Department. The success of these regimes was predicated on the children's permanent separation from their families and their way of life. Neville was convinced that "until the children [were] taken ... and trained apart from their parents no real progress towards assimilation [was] to be expected."[30]

Using the full force of the law, Neville began to clear the town camps and to build up the settlement populations, tearing families apart in the process. By 1919, there were 150 Aboriginal "inmates"[31] at Carrolup—sixty of them children. The closure of town depots and the centralizing of rations in the settlements had the intended effect of reducing the department's ration bill; it decreased by 1,180 pounds between 1915 and 1919, and numbers on rations fell from 379 to 188.[32] As might be expected, many families fiercely resisted relocation, leaving town at the slightest hint of action by police or an Aborigines Department official. Settlement inmates also resisted the new order. In 1916, following repeated escapes and refusal to work, regulations were introduced granting sweeping powers to discipline "inmates" and to force them to work or attend the settlement schools as directed.

In his 1919 Annual Report, Neville wrote proudly of the "success" of his "sociological experiment," asserting that "in the light of experience already gained," he was "satisfied that the ... settlement system [was] the only solution to the native question."[33] Yet conditions at the settlements belied the reality of his claims. The shoestring budget provided for their development was reflected in substandard facilities and services. To save costs, some buildings were erected using recycled materials from disbanded institutions, including a former venereal "hospital" for Aboriginal patients. Poor quality land and equipment dashed any hopes that the settlements would become self-sufficient farms.

Living conditions for the children were deplorable, and contrasted with even the spartan conditions for white children in institutions. Funding for their keep averaged ten pence a week per child, compared to a minimum of seven shillings per week for white children. In contrast to institutions for white children, there were no regular inspections of conditions and no official regulations setting standards for their diet, living quarters, medical and dental care, schooling, or training.[34] They were crowded together in dormitories in the "compound" under the supervision of white staff, and survived on a diet described by a visiting official to Carrolup in 1920 as "Dickensian."[35] Untrained teachers taught them in overcrowded classrooms, their vocational training consisted of backbreaking work and endless chores, and corporal punishment and even solitary confinement were a regular occurrence. Forbidden to speak Aboriginal languages or to practice their customs, Aborigines learned to speak English and were instructed in Christianity. Adults lived separately from the children in makeshift shelters in the settlement camp. While "able-bodied" men and women worked on settlement buildings and roads, the rest spent their days in enforced idleness. There was little that the untrained staff could do to staunch the ravages of disease, despair, and death that swept through the settlements.

Conditions deteriorated further following the decision, taken in 1922 against the advice of Neville, who was then working for the Department of the North West, to close Carrolup, transfer inmates to Moore River, and open the land up for soldier settlement. Despite protests at this further dislocation from their families and homes, the entire community was rounded up, marched to Katanning under police escort, and forced onto the train for Moore River.[36] The department's 1923 Annual Report proudly announced that the move had resulted in savings of over 2,000 pounds. Yet the decision would prove shortsighted. Moore River was the only settlement in the south with an average population of 250, far exceeding its original target of 100 inmates. With sustained overcrowding and overuse of facilities, the already substandard conditions deteriorated further, and in 1925 buildings were reported to be verminous and in desperate need of repair. In 1924, the Superintendent at Moore River described it as "a stupid piece of cruelty ... the misguided action of amateurs, in the name of economy. ...

Worse still the cruelty was inflicted and no economy was
achieved."[37] At the same time, expenditure increased as the wors-
ening economic situation forced Aborigines into Moore River, and
by 1929 it had reached the original combined levels of spending on
both settlements.[38]

Unintended Consequences

Conditions at the settlements made the "doomed race" theory a
chilling reality, yet this could not be blamed on "nature" or
"progress." Poor health, disease, high levels of maternal, infant and
child mortality, and shortened life expectancy were the norm.
Adults lived out their days and died there. Births were kept to a
minimum by the long periods of separation of couples as women
remained at the settlement while their men worked on farms outside. Meanwhile, a steady stream of young women sent out to work
as domestic servants were returned to the settlement pregnant to
white men. In some instances, these men were their employers.
Despite stated official aims, the settlements were not preparing the
children for an assimilated life on the outside. Instead, they were
creating institutionalized adults who were suited to a passive life in
the settlements, but ill-equipped for independent living. Their
schooling and training confined them to a narrow niche of menial
work; nor could they expect to find acceptance in a hostile white
community. As adults, they could claim none of the rights of civil,
political, and social citizenship enjoyed by other Australians, since
they had to live under the control of the Aborigines Department. In
contradiction to official intentions, most made the settlements their
home, thereby creating enduring institutionalized communities
rather than "clearing houses." Given the well-publicized failure of
nineteenth century Aboriginal settlements and missions, and
orphanages and reformatories for white children, this was hardly a
surprising outcome.

Aboriginal families who remained "on the outside" also lived
in very difficult circumstances. They faced the continual threat of
relocation under the 1905 Act, which allowed for their removal to
the settlements for virtually any reason by police, under ministerial
warrant. They had no right of appeal against the decision, and once
there they could be detained indefinitely. This policy constituted a
powerful tool of behavior control. Families sought to render themselves invisible in the local landscape to avoid racist outbursts from
local whites and attracting the attention of authorities that could

lead to immediate removal. Strategies such as hiding children in the bush sometimes prevented their forced removal from their families. These children were reared within their family networks, thereby ensuring continuity of Aboriginal ways, but such strategies were undermined as further land clearing forced families back into town camps. In contrast to Neville's earlier policies, the Aborigines Department, in consultation with local authorities, created a number of small camping reserves for their use. Most were located outside the town boundaries on unwanted land adjacent to rubbish and sanitary disposal depots, and they were kept under close police surveillance. This practice was common across Australia from colonial times into the mid-twentieth century as a way of dealing with dispossessed Aboriginal people.[39] Gypsies in Europe were similarly forced into municipally administered camps during the early twentieth century in Europe, on the pretext that this would prevent crime.[40] The Aborigines' fragile economic independence was also threatened by competition for limited seasonal farm work from Italian migrants who arrived in the area during the 1920s, and the Aborigines Department's insistence that employers take out permits and pay fees to employ Aboriginal workers. With welfare centralized in the settlements (Moore River only from 1922) and police resentful of any approaches for help, families could only turn to each other in difficult times.

Extermination by Neglect

Conditions in the camps during the 1920s promised another way of clearing Aborigines from the wheat belt. Families lived in tents and huts made out of flattened kerosene tins, wheat bags, and bush timber, and slept on mattresses of rushes covered with bags. Their health needs were ignored; the Department's annual expenditure on medical services for the entire state averaged only two hundred pounds; and most hospitals and doctors refused to treat Aboriginal patients, which contributed to high levels of maternal and infant mortality. Instead, they were instructed to travel to the grandiosely named "Midlands District Hospital." Opened at Moore River in 1929, it consisted of a single ward accommodating male and female patients, including women in labor and patients with communicable diseases such as syphilis. These conditions, the long distances involved, and fear of permanent detention ensured that few women voluntarily went there. Nonetheless, numbers of Aborigines outside the settlements continued to increase, suggesting a process of population recovery, despite these difficulties. Anthropologist Diane Barwick noted a similar increase in Aboriginal populations in Victoria during the early twentieth century, attributable to high fertility rates due to early marriage and remarriage, early initial child bearing extending into middle age, and a positive desire for children.[41] Of course, these gains were dampened by a low average life expectancy of forty years and alarming levels of infant and child mortality. Between 1881 and 1925, a third of Aboriginal babies and children died. The large number of dependent children in the camps in Western Australia—they made up 44 percent of the population at the end of the 1920s—signaled a further problem for wage earners struggling to support their families.

White residents of the wheat belt were not unaware of the Aborigines' situation. The settlements were part of the local landscape, linked to towns by their reliance on the services of police, doctors, employers, and businesses, and the townspeople's prurient interest in events there. Local newspapers also kept them informed. The *Great Southern Herald* told its readers in 1920 about the eighty-five children living in the dormitories at Carrolup.[42] Two years earlier it had reported how the Superintendent had chained a girl by her neck to a bed for three days to prevent her from absconding.[43] In 1922, the *Southern Districts Advocate* published an eyewitness report that children transferred from Carrolup to Moore River spent their days carrying "bags full of gravel for long distances from the pits to the camp to make footpaths" instead of attending school.[44] Conditions in the local camps were obvious to casual observers. However, rather than insisting on improvements, white residents reiterated their demands that the Aboriginal "menace" be swept from their districts. Once removed, the fate of the families, while known to many townspeople, was no longer their responsibility or concern. This willful blindness was evident in events in Moora in 1922 following complaints about unhygienic conditions and unruly behavior on the town reserve. The Aborigines Department responded by canceling the reserve and expelling the families from the town. Although they were ordered to move to Moore River, most fled into the surrounding districts, where they struggled to survive without work or rations.[45]

Despite the creation of a "near-White" Australian landscape in the southwest, race remained an ever-present threat in the minds of local white residents. During the Depression years of the early 1930s the wheat belt was once again gripped by racist hysteria. The Aborigines' growing visibility in the towns and the escalating poverty in their camps were the catalysts for renewed demands for their immediate removal. Alarmist press reports of a dramatic growth in the state's "mixed-race" population fanned fears of racial violence, and prompted calls for the introduction of measures to prevent any further increase in their numbers. Between 1930 and 1934, over 600 articles and letters about the "Aboriginal problem" appeared in the Perth press and, between June and August in 1933 alone, the government received 150 public representations concerning the situation of Aborigines in the south. While some expressed sympathy for the Aborigines' plight, few could see any further than increased segregation and punitive control.[46] These complaints reflected a more general climate of dissatisfaction with existing Aboriginal policies, which culminated in the appointment in 1934 of the Moseley Royal Commission to report on "matters relating to the condition and treatment of Aborigines" in Western Australia.[47]

The Aborigines' visibility reflected, in part, the doubling of their population from 1,200 in 1900 to 2,500 by the mid-1930s—although this was hardly the number reported in the press. The situation owed more to their precarious economic position in a rural economy devastated by the combined effects of the economic depression, bungled government agricultural planning, and serious droughts. Between 1926 and 1932 the number of Aborigines receiving rations in the town camps grew from 29 to 892.[48] The families' desperate conditions prompted Neville to write in his 1931 Annual Report that "no section of the community has suffered more from the effects of the financial depression."[49] Yet, in the same year, as part of a general cost-cutting exercise necessitated by mounting economic difficulties, the government ordered a twenty percent reduction in the Aborigines Department's annual grant, and two years later it fell to its lowest level in eight years— 27,238 pounds. The department was forced to cut expenditure on welfare. The meat issue was stopped altogether in most towns, and flour, tea, and sugar were reduced. Rations were valued at only two shillings and tuppence a week per person, less than a third of the "sustenance" allowance provided for white workers.

Police were instructed to issue rations only to the "most deserving," and some added their own rules of eligibility, refusing to assist men who, in their opinion, were not working hard enough or who had previous convictions under the 1905 Act.[50] Between 1930 and 1934, only 750 blankets were distributed. In 1931, 160 pounds— 0.06 percent of the department's annual budget—was spent on medical care. Nothing was done to improve conditions in the camps. In 1934, Neville told the Moseley Royal Commission that

chronic malnutrition had weakened the Aborigines' "powers of
resistance to disease" and had left them susceptible to epidemics of
respiratory, stomach, bowel, eye, skin, and other infectious diseases.[51] Despite this alarming disclosure, Aboriginal objections that
the level of relief provided by the Department was a "miserable pit-
tance" and "totally inadequate" went unheeded.[52]

Faced by the demands of white residents and conditions in the
camps, Neville looked to increased legislative controls and expansion of the settlement scheme to resolve the situation. In 1929, he
succeeded in having a Bill to amend the 1905 Act placed before
Parliament. In introducing the Bill, the Honorary Minister, W.H.
Kitson, stated that its major aim was to enable the Aborigines
Department to deal effectively with the "half-caste problem" in the
south, in particular, by extending its application to virtually all people of Aboriginal descent. The Bill was defeated—not in the interests of Aboriginal rights, but by critics of Neville opposed to any
further increase in his powers. At the same time Neville pushed for
the reopening of Carrolup. Although Cabinet approved the proposal, the decision was reversed following objections from Katanning residents that adjoining properties would be devalued, the
safety of white women and children would be compromised, and
that the area was too cold and wet for Aborigines.

This opposition left relocation to Moore River as the only
option. But the settlement was already seriously overcrowded, and
conditions were even worse than in the town camps. At the height
of the depression the settlement accommodated over five hundred
people—one third of them children—with inmates funded at the
rate of 3 shillings a week, a fifth of the scale for prisoners at Fremantle Gaol.[53] The same epidemics of disease that were ravaging
the camps had spread through the settlement, and in 1931 alone
there were nine deaths. In 1934, the Moseley Royal Commission
described Moore River as a "woeful spectacle," and a medical
report on the children in the same year reported alarming levels of
disease and physical defects directly attributable to poor diet and
hygiene.[54] Attempted escapes escalated, and in 1932 there was a
mass outbreak of twenty-eight young people. In the same year, the
land around the settlement was declared a "prohibited area," so
that escapees now faced terms of up to six months' imprisonment
in Fremantle Gaol.

Given such conditions, it is hardly surprising that families refused
to move to Moore River. Many capitulated only when their rations
were cut off and they were starving. Direct police action was used in
1933 to force the entire Northam camp to move there. It was no

coincidence that this was an election year and the town was in the Premier's electorate. Parents also defied official efforts to remove their children. Some were aware of a court ruling that children of "half-caste" parents did not come under the 1905 Act and could not be legally removed by the department.[55] Nonetheless, Neville continued to enforce such removals, exceeding his legal powers in the process.[56] Growing scrutiny of the department by the Native Union, an all-Aboriginal organization based in the south, and white activists such as Mary Bennett, threatened public exposure of such practices.[57]

A Eugenic Solution?

Thwarted at all turns, Neville looked to radical new eugenic inspired solutions to deal with the problem in the south. His counterpart in the Northern Territory, Dr. Cecil Cook, was also moving in this direction.[58] Such solutions were already on the agenda in other areas of government in Western Australia. In 1929, Parliament debated and narrowly rejected legislation authorizing the sterilization of certain criminals and the identification and permanent institutionalization of "mental defectives." Recent scientific and anthropological research held out the promise that, through an alliance of science and government, Aboriginal racial characteristics could be "bred out" through intermarriage between "half-castes," lighter castes, and whites over several generations. Essentially, Neville's vision, which he outlined in a series of articles in the Perth press in 1930, was a program of biological and social engineering designed to make "black go white."[59] The gradual predominance of "white over black," Neville argued, was a "natural outcome." This view was endorsed in an anonymous letter to the *West Australian* in 1933, which claimed that the "half-caste" was "merely a passing phase, an incident in history ... a natural transmutation in what we know as cultural evolution."[60] Directed at Aborigines of mixed descent—Neville remained convinced that Aborigines of full descent were doomed to extinction—this policy of biological absorption was predicated on the wholesale removal and institutionalization of "mixed race" children.

To the existing practices of social engineering, it added a new, sinister dimension of biological engineering based on state controls over Aboriginal sexual reproduction. Reared in government institutions to be white, young adults would be directed into state-approved marriages with progressively lighter "castes" or whites. Marriage and sexual contact between lighter and darker "skins" would be prohibited by law. In this way, Aboriginal physical features would be bred out, and the specter of Aboriginality would be permanently erased from the wheat belt. Dr. Cecil Bryan, a Perth medical practitioner, suggested to the 1934 Moseley Royal Commission that "half-castes" actually desired such an outcome:

> The greatest wish of the half-caste is to shed the last remnant of his colour and become wholly white. That is impossible. ... But it is not impossible for his children, and next to making himself white the dearest wish of the half-caste is to see his children white so they can receive a fairer deal.[61]

Contrary to such expectations, this was not what Aboriginal witnesses told the Commission. They pleaded for an end to government intervention in their lives, for release from the "stigma" of the *Aborigines Act 1905,* and for the right to live together with their families in "their own way," free from the threat of removal to Moore River settlement.[62]

Despite these protests and some public discussion of more enlightened policies of social assimilation, Neville's draconian vision won the day, and the policy of biological absorption was enshrined in the new *Aborigines Act Amendment (Native Administration Act) 1936.* In the following year, Neville persuaded the inaugural federal conference of heads of state and territory departments of Aboriginal affairs in Canberra to endorse the following resolution:

> That this Conference believes that the destiny of the native of Aboriginal origin, but not the full-blood, lies in their ultimate absorption by the people of the Commonwealth and it therefore recommends that all efforts be directed to that end.[63]

Neville's "ultimate solution" was a genocidal plan that meets the terms of the UN Convention on Genocide, including the thorny issue of "intent to destroy, in whole or in part, a national, ethnical, or racial or religious group."[64] The policy represented the culmination of over twenty years of conflict in the south. Given what Neville described as the "inherent and ineradicable" racism in the region, state and settler determination to push ahead with agricultural development at any cost, the lack of resources and political will to deal equitably with Aboriginal people, and mounting official and public frustration, this final outcome was perhaps inevitable.

The policy did not require drastic new provisions or a major outlay of funding; rather, it built on and refined existing measures in the 1905 Act. Powers of guardianship over Aboriginal children were extended, controls over sexual contact and marriage were increased, and measures to prevent contacts between "quarter-castes" and other Aborigines were introduced. The institutional base was already in place. Sister Kate's Quarter Caste Children's Home, opened in 1933, had begun the process of grooming "near-white children" for absorption into the white community.[65] They lived in cottages at the Home in isolation from their families, attended the local school and, as a former resident recalled, "our Aboriginality was never mentioned."[66] Children were identified for placement on the basis of whiteness by police officers in the towns and by staff at Moore River. Neville told a meeting of federal and state authorities in 1937 that many of the children were the off-spring of Moore River trainees:

> Our policy is to send them out into the white community, and if the girl comes back pregnant our rule is to keep her for two years. The child is then taken away from the mother and sometimes never sees her again. Thus these children grow up as whites, knowing nothing of their own environment. At the expiration of the period of two years the mother goes back to service. So that it really doesn't matter if she has half a dozen children.[67]

Children who did not fit Neville's standards of whiteness continued to live at Moore River.

Despite recommendations by the Moseley Royal Commission that the settlement should be restructured or closed down, only piecemeal improvements were made. A further recommendation that town camps should be abolished and Aborigines transferred to localized community farming settlements on arable land was also overlooked. Nothing was done to relieve the misery in the camps, although police controls were dramatically increased. In 1939, Neville sought funding to redevelop Carrolup as a centralized settlement with the capacity to accommodate one thousand Aborigines from the south. When Carrolup was finally reopened in 1940, it was only able to cater for five hundred people and conditions there simply duplicated the appalling institutional setting of Moore River.

Neville's vision of biological absorption was short-lived. He retired in 1940, and subsequent public exposure of Nazi eugenics-based race atrocities undermined support for the policy. Nevertheless, his determination to "make black go white" remained practice at Sister Kate's into the late 1940s, and it left a painful legacy for the children who inadvertently became part of this experiment in social and biological engineering.

Conclusion

This chapter is a case study of radicalizing intentions and inevitable but largely unintended outcomes. It documents the path of a society driven by hunger for land, commitment to ruthless economic development, and discriminatory relations of race that could only bring destruction for Aboriginal people caught up in its wake. This was indeed, in Tony Barta's term, a "genocidal society." In their efforts to deal with Aboriginal people trapped in their midst, the state and settlers resorted over time to strategies that mirrored the "techniques of genocide" in the various fields listed by Lemkin: economic, political, social, cultural, biological, physical, religious, and moral. The jumbled mix of policies of protection, segregation, assimilation, and biological absorption had the effect of striking at the "essential foundations of the life" of Aboriginal people, at the heart of their ability to survive culturally and physically. Responsibility for this outcome rested with settlers and the state collaborating to protect and further their own interests, while they claimed to be acting to help Aboriginal people.

This was not a "coordinated plan" of genocide. It was a set of bungled outcomes resulting from persistent demands by settlers to erase the Aboriginal presence from the region through seemingly benign measures, and of government responses based on expediency, ruthless economy, neglect, and entrenched racism. Mounting frustrations in achieving their goals pushed officials to adopt increasingly drastic measures that culminated in the genocidal policy of biological absorption. That Aborigines survived was due in large part to their strong family networks of support and a culture of resistance expressed in a dogged determination to remain together on their land. Government parsimony and official inertia also prevented the necessary investment of sustained high levels of energy, time, finance, and manpower.

Notes

1. Yves Ternon, "Reflections on Genocide," in *Minority Peoples in the Age of Nation States*, ed. G. Chaliand (London, 1989), 126–48; Alison Palmer, *Colonial Genocide* (Adelaide, 2000); Raymond Evans and Bill Thorpe, "The Massacre of Aboriginal History," *Overland* 163 (2001): 21–40; Tony Barta, "Relations of Genocide: Land and Lives in the Colonization of Australia," in *Genocide and the Modern Age*, ed. Isidor Wallimann and Michael N. Dobkowski (Westport, Conn., 1987), 237–52.
2. For an example of this approach, see A. Dirk Moses, "An Antipodean Genocide? The Origin of the Genocide Moment in the Colonization of Australia," *Journal of Genocide Research* 2:1 (2000): 89–105.
3. R. Lemkin, *Axis Rule in Occupied Europe: Laws of Occupation Analysis of Government Proposals for Redress* (New York, 1973 [1944]), ix.
4. Lemkin, *Axis Rule*, 79.
5. To be sure, historians have identified some of these techniques at work, but not in the context of Lemkin's definition. For Queensland, see R. Kidd, *The Way We Civilise Aboriginal Affairs: The Untold Story* (Brisbane, 1997); for New South Wales, see H. Goodall, *From Invasion to Embassy: Land and Aboriginal Politics in New South Wales from 1780 to 1972* (Sydney, 1996).
6. This list draws on Lemkin's discussion in *Axis Rule*, ix–xv, 82–90.
7. Lemkin, *Axis Rule*, xi.
8. Lemkin, *Axis Rule*, x.
9. Lemkin, *Axis Rule*, 90.
10. Barta, "Relations of Genocide," 239, 240, 247.
11. R. McGregor, *Imagined Destinies: Aboriginal Australians and the Doomed Race Theory, 1880–1939* (Melbourne, 1997).
12. Western Australian Government, *Census of Western Australia* (Perth, 1901).
13. Western Australian Government, *Reports on Stations Visited by the Travelling Inspector of Aborigines* (Perth, 1903).
14. For further details, see A. Haebich, *For Their Own Good: Aborigines and Government in the South West of Western Australia, 1900–1940*, 2nd ed. (Nedlands, Western Australia, 1992), 28–35.
15. For further discussion of the *Aborigines Act 1905*, see Haebich, *For Their Own Good*, 83–88.
16. Personal correspondence of Annie Lock in C. Bishop, "'A Woman Missionary Living amongst Naked Blacks': Annie Lock, 1876–1943" (MA Thesis, Australian National University, 1991), 118; cited in Haebich, *Broken Circles*, 254.
17. *Great Southern Herald*, 24/4/1909.
18. *West Australian*, 28/5/1912; cited in Haebich, *For Their Own Good*, 138.
19. *Southern Districts Advocate*, 28/3/14.
20. Personal correspondence of Lock in Bishop "A Woman Missionary," 118; cited in Haebich, *Broken Circles*, 254.
21. *Truth*, 4/9/1915; cited in Haebich, *For Their Own Good*, 144.
22. Under the *Aborigines Act 1905*, towns could be declared "prohibited areas" and unemployed Aborigines who entered these areas without permission could be prosecuted.
23. State Records Office, Western Australia, Colonial Secretary's Office, 213/1921; cited in Haebich, *For Their Own Good*, 144.

24. See Russell McGregor's chapter at 304f. for further discussion of the relevance
    of the concept of "cultural genocide" in the Australian context.
25. T. Rowse, *White Flour, White Power: From Rations to Citizenship* (Mel-
    bourne, 1998) provides a detailed analysis of the ubiquitous practice of the
    rationing of goods to Indigenous people as an instrument of colonial govern-
    ment in Australia.
26. For example, Wybalenna Aboriginal settlement (1833–1847) on Flinders
    Island in Bass Strait was intended to become "home to a permanent popula-
    tion"; see Reynolds, *Indelible Stain?*, 82. Settlements and missions set up in
    Queensland during the early decades of the twentieth century were also meant
    to become "permanent home[s]" where residents could "live happily free from
    all contact with the white race "; see Archibald Meston, 1897, cited in Hae-
    bich, *Broken Circles*, 169.
27. A. Armitage, *Comparing the Policy of Aboriginal Assimilation: Australia,
    Canada, and New Zealand* (Vancouver, 1995).
28. Western Australian Government, *Parliamentary Debates* (Perth, 1905), vol. 5,
    433; cited in Haebich, *For Their Own Good*, 80.
29. Western Australian Government, *Aborigines Department Annual Report*
    (Perth, 1901), 3.
30. A.O. Neville, *Australia's Coloured Minority: Its Place in the Community* (Syd-
    ney, 1947), 176.
31. This was the official term used to refer to Aboriginal residents at the settle-
    ments.
32. Western Australian Government, *Aborigines Department Annual Report*
    (Perth, 1915); *Aborigines Department Annual Report* (Perth, 1919).
33. *Aborigines Department Annual Report* (Perth, 1919), 11.
34. Haebich, *Broken Circles*, 227. Their meager rations consisted of meat, flour,
    tea, sugar and a weekly stick of tobacco.
35. State Records Office of Western Australia, 993/169/1927.
36. See Haebich, *For Their Own Good*, 194–99.
37. Cited in Haebich, *For Their Own Good*, 196.
38. Haebich, *For Their Own Good*, 199; *Aborigines Department Annual Reports*
    (Perth, 1923, 1929).
39. See for example, Goodall, *From Invasion to Embassy.*
40. I. Fonseca, *Bury Me Standing: The Gypsies and their Journey* (London, 1996),
    254–71.
41. D. Barwick, "Changes in the Aboriginal population of Victoria, 1867–1966,"
    eds. D. Mulvaney and J. Golson, *Aboriginal Man and Environment in Aus-
    tralia* (Canberra, 1971), 288-315.
42. *Great Southern Herald*, 12/6/1920.
43. *Great Southern Herald*, 6/7/1918.
44. *Southern Districts Advocate*, 4/9/1922.
45. Haebich, *For Their Own Good*, 233.
46. Haebich, *For Their Own Good*, 315.
47. Western Australian Government, "Report of the Royal Commissioner
    Appointed to Investigate, Report and Advise Upon Matters in Relation to the
    Conditions and Treatment of Aborigines," *Western Australia, Votes and Pro-
    ceedings*, 2 (Perth, 1935).
48. Statistics are from the *Aborigines Department Annual Reports* (Perth, 1926,
    1930, 1931, 1932).
49. *Aborigines Department Annual Report* (Perth, 1931), 2.

50. Haebich, *For Their Own Good*, 289–90.
51. Haebich, *For Their Own Good*, 288, 295.
52. State Records Office of Western Australia, Aborigines Department A213/1927. Cited in Haebich, *For Their Own Good*, 289.
53. Haebich, *For Their Own Good*, 310.
54. Haebich, *For Their Own Good*, 311, 340.
55. Haebich, *For Their Own Good*, 267.
56. Cited in Western Australian Government, *Parliamentary Debates* (Perth 1936), 2, 167–8.
57. Aboriginal leader William Harris established the Native Union in 1926. The Union was one of several Aboriginal protest organizations to emerge in southern Australia during the 1920s and 1930s. In 1928 Harris led the first deputation of Aborigines to meet with a Western Australia Premier. They demanded exemption from the 1905 Act, and they attacked removals to Moore River and conditions at the settlement. (Haebich, *For Their Own Good*, 274.) Mary Bennett was associated with women's organizations and missions in Western Australia. Her allegations in the British press of conditions of slavery in employment in Western Australia and of abusive treatment of women and the breaking up of Aboriginal families contributed to the government's decision to appoint the Moseley Royal Commission in 1934 (Haebich, *Broken Circles*, 329–35).
58. T. Austin, "Cecil Cook, scientific thought and 'half castes' in the Northern Territory, 1927–1939," *Aboriginal History* 14, no.1 (1990), 104–22.
59. *West Australian*, 18/4/1930, 19/4/1930; *Daily News* 8/6/1930. See Haebich, *For Their Own Good*, 316–18 and 350–51 and Haebich, *Broken Circles*, 270–76 for a more detailed discussion of the policy.
60. Cited in Haebich, *For Their Own Good*, 319.
61. Cited in Haebich, *Broken Circles*, 275.
62. Cited in Haebich, *Broken Circles*, 276–77.
63. Cited in Haebich, *Broken Circles*, 279.
64. R. Manne, "The Stolen Generations," in his *The Way We Live Now* (Melbourne, 1998), 15–41. See also his chapter in this volume.
65. Sister Kate Clutterbuck, who established the Home with Neville's support, was a British-born Anglican nun. The Home was located in Perth. In the 1950s it was taken over by the Methodist Church and it is now an Aboriginal-run agency. (For a more detailed discussion of Sister Kate's Children's Home, see Haebich, *Broken Circles*, 280–87 and V. Whittington, *Sister Kate: A Life Dedicated to Children in Need of Care* (Perth, 1999).
66. Cited in Haebich, *Broken Circles*, 285.
67. Cited in Aboriginal Legal Service of Western Australia, *Telling Our Story: A Report by the Aboriginal Legal Service (Inc.) on the Removal of Aboriginal Children from their Families in Western Australia* (Perth, 1995), 173.

Chapter 12

GOVERNANCE, NOT GENOCIDE
Aboriginal Assimilation in the Postwar Era

Russell McGregor

Introduction

This chapter contests recent characterizations of post–1945 Aboriginal assimilation policies as genocidal.[1] Far from seeking elimination of the Aborigines, these policies of sociocultural assimilation were the first in more than a century to seriously envisage Aboriginal survival, to seek to ensure survival, and to prescribe strategies predicated upon their survival. Precisely because it envisaged Aboriginal survival, the postwar state turned more resolutely to their governance. Of course, Aborigines had earlier been governed, but now their governance would be both normative and normalized. As part of the project of governance in a modern liberal national polity, Aborigines were expected, or compelled, to adhere to and internalize the social norms and cultural competencies of the national community. To inculcate these norms and competencies, Aborigines were subjected to various tutelary and educative regimes. Under these, many of the old controls and restrictions remained in place, being gradually lifted only when Aboriginal persons proved themselves, to the satisfaction of officialdom, capable of exercising the rights and privileges of citizenship. In the assimilationist era, roughly the twenty-five years after 1945, the state sought to assert control over the processes of social and cultural change in Aboriginal Australia, to produce Aboriginal citizens who, like other (ideal) citizens, could be governed consensually through their fidelity to the norms and values of the national community.[2] Assimilation, I argue, was a project of governance, not of elimination, and analyses that mistake the latter for the former seriously misdiagnose the policy.

Some would call this replacement of indigenous with Western sociocultural norms "cultural genocide."[3] But cultural genocide was specifically excluded from the ambit of the 1948 UN Genocide Convention.[4] The majority of delegates to the Convention agreed—rightly in my view—that destruction of a group's culture was morally distinct from deliberately destroying the group itself, and that "cultural genocide" was too vague and diffuse a concept to be included in the UN definition. To endorse their restrictions on the term "genocide" is not to condone the cultural destruction wrought by Aboriginal assimilation policy, or, more generally, the culturally destructive impulses of modern nation-building. It is simply to recognize that if the concept of "genocide" is allowed to float free of the notion of physical destruction of a group, its potential applicability becomes so vast as to lose all moral and conceptual coherence.

Assertions of the genocidal intent of postwar assimilation have focused on the practice of removing Aboriginal children from their families, aligning this with Article II(e) of the UN Genocide Convention, which lists "forcibly transferring children of the group to another group" as an act constituting genocide if "committed with intent to destroy, in whole or in part, a national, ethnical, racial or religious group as such."[5] In the first section of this chapter, I provide a brief critique of the most influential work arguing this line, the Human Rights and Equal Opportunity Commission's *Bringing Them Home* report on the separation of Aboriginal and Torres Strait Islander children from their families. That report, published in 1997, provided a powerful exposé of the trauma and tragedy inflicted on the indigenous by settler Australians. It sparked an intense and often acrimonious public controversy, much of it centering on the report's assertion of the genocidal intentions of Aboriginal child removals. The greater part of this chapter, however, deals not with child removal but with assimilation policy more generally, since, as the *Bringing Them Home* report acknowledges, the intentions of such acts can be assessed only in the context of the policy frameworks within which they were conducted. The second section of this chapter draws attention to important distinctions, neglected by the *Bringing Them Home* report, between the prewar policy of biological absorption and the postwar policy of sociocultural assimilation. (Henceforth, I use the terms "absorption" and "assimilation" without the qualifying adjectives to designate these policy options.) In the third section, I discuss the extent to which the assimilationist state was prepared to permit the persistence of Aboriginality, moving in the fourth to argue that the concept of "cultural genocide" is unhelpful in advancing our understanding of the policy. Finally, I return to the issue of child removal, suggesting that in the assimilation era this practice was driven by reformist rather than exterminatory intentions.

Bringing Them Home and Genocide

The *Bringing Them Home* report adopted a legalistic stance, attempting to demonstrate that Aboriginal child removals constituted genocide within the terms of the 1948 UN Convention. On several counts, its arguments are seriously flawed. The report assumes that its category of "forcible removals" equates with the Convention's "forcibly transferring children." Yet the report acknowledges that its term "forcible removals" includes temporary separations for purposes of schooling, removals "on the ground of protecting the child from injury, abuse or neglect," and removals "to receive medical treatment."[6] This extraordinarily wide conception of "forcible removal" has drawn criticism from both defenders and detractors of the report.[7] Making the category of "forcible removal" so wide may have been necessary for the inquiry's purposes in revealing the tragic consequences of child removal. But it also means that the inquiry's "forcible removal" category is not straightforwardly interchangeable with the UN Convention's forcible transfer category, which at the very least implies permanent transfer, and beyond that, transfer with specific destructive intent.

   Bringing Them Home muddles its discussion of destructive intent by mistakenly assuming that the UN Convention covers instances of purely cultural destruction.[8] The "forcibly transferring children" clause was introduced into the debates leading up to the drafting of the Convention under the rubric of "cultural genocide," but was included in the final Convention, after "cultural genocide" had been rejected, on the understanding that it could be a means of physical genocide. The UN delegates accepted that forced child transfers could have "serious physical and biological consequences ... the transfer of children from their group to an alien one being construed as an act resembling compulsory measures to prevent reproduction, or in other words, to prevent the biological survival of a human group."[9] To come within the ambit of the UN Convention, forcible child transfers must be carried out with the intention of physically destroying the target group. Were child removals in Australia ever carried out with this intention? The answer, unfortunately, is yes. In the programs of systematic absorption pursued in some Australian jurisdictions in the interwar years, mixed-descent children were taken from their families as the first step in a process that, via reproductive management, would culminate in the physical demise of the entire Aboriginal race.[10]

Absorption was framed within the longstanding assumption that "full-blood" Aborigines were fated inevitably to extinction. As A.O. Neville, Western Australia's Commissioner of Native Affairs and Australia's most enthusiastic exponent of absorption, explained at the 1937 Conference of Commonwealth and State Aboriginal Authorities, the "full-bloods" constituted a "problem ... which will eventually solve itself [since] no matter what we do, they will die out."[11] Aborigines of mixed descent, by contrast, were multiplying rapidly, posing a problem that, according to absorptionists, must be tackled by "breeding out their color" to transform their descendants physically into white Australians.[12] Some scholars have suggested that these programs of "breeding out the color" persisted into the postwar period.[13] I can find no evidence for these claims. Perhaps they stem from the fact that assimilationists freely acknowledged that miscegenation was a likely accompaniment of assimilation. But miscegenation is a likely accompaniment of any policy other than total segregation, and legitimizing miscegenation must be clearly distinguished from programs seeking to engineer miscegenation to the predetermined outcome of effacing one of the groups involved. Interwar absorption did seek to engineer this outcome; postwar assimilation did not.

The *Bringing Them Home* report does acknowledge that Aboriginal policy changed around the time of the Second World War, from absorption to assimilation, but treats this policy change as inconsequential, a misjudgment that seriously weakens the report's arguments on genocide.[14] The report assumes a consistency of intent behind child removals, and ultimately behind Aboriginal policy in general, for the entire first seventy years of the twentieth century. But this consistency of intent can be neither assumed, nor inferred from the fact that certain practices, notably child removal, continued throughout the period (and before, and after). Assimilation inherited from earlier policy eras a vast ensemble of practices, laws, administrative arrangements, assumptions, and outlooks. Policy shifts do not usually dispense entirely with earlier practices and procedures, but modify and adapt them to new purposes. The significance of the shift from absorption to assimilation is too often neglected or underrated, not just in the *Bringing Them Home* report but in Australian historiography more generally. The following section attempts a corrective.

Absorption and Assimilation

Symptomatic of the tendency to conflate absorption with assimilation, it has been claimed that the foundations of a national assimilation policy were laid at the 1937 Conference of Commonwealth and State Aboriginal Authorities.[15] In fact, the 1937 Conference represented the high-water point of official endorsement of absorption, and from that point the tide rapidly ebbed. When Commonwealth-State conferences on Aboriginal affairs were resumed after the war, in 1948, the preoccupations of the 1937 conference delegates—the dangers posed by a rapidly increasing "half-caste" population and the necessary remedy of regulating their reproduction—did not rate a mention.[16] Nor were these matters raised at subsequent conferences, the most notable of which was in 1951 when the newly-appointed Commonwealth Minister for Territories, Paul Hasluck, assumed national political leadership of the assimilationist cause, placing emphasis squarely on citizenship as its paramount objective.[17] At these conferences, and more generally throughout postwar assimilationist discourse, a distinction continued to be made between "full-bloods" and "mixed-bloods," the latter being commonly considered more ready for assimilation. But now this was to be achieved not by erasing their color but by remodeling their social lives. As for "full-bloods," the assumption of inevitable extinction expressed by delegates at the 1937 conference was replaced by a presumption that they shared the destiny of "mixed-bloods": citizenship of the nation.

The first instalment of assimilation policy, with explicit reference to citizenship as the goal for all Aboriginal people, came two years after the 1937 conference, in the "New Deal for Aborigines" drafted by the anthropologist Professor A.P. Elkin, John McEwen, Minister for the Interior, and his departmental secretary J.A. Carrodus.[18] Elkin, who could justly be regarded as the leading mid-century theorist of Aboriginal assimilation, distinguished sharply between the assimilation he espoused and the absorption he deplored.[19] C.D. Rowley, in his pioneering study of settler-indigenous relations published in 1971, recognized that it was the "New Deal," not the 1937 Conference, that laid "the foundation of the assimilation policy" implemented after the war. In the context of its times, he observed, the "New Deal" was "epoch-making," because "it formulated a long-term objective for policy that was other than some kind of social engineering for the disappearance of the race into the white majority. The objective was a positive one, envisaging a common citizenship, without postulating genetic changes."[20] Rowley also pointed out that in the postwar era many Australians, including some in official capacities, continued to confuse assimilation with absorption, and persisted in viewing assimilation as "a means of disappearance of the Aborigines."[21] These confusions and continuities raise more questions than can be addressed here. However, my argument concerns state policies rather than popular attitudes. Neither absorption nor assimilation necessarily commanded strong public support; both were doubtless widely misunderstood, even at times by those charged with their implementation. The point remains that around the 1940s the Australian state(s) moved from a policy framework in which the demise of the Aboriginal race was assumed (and sometimes deliberately engineered) to one that assumed its survival.

Underlining this policy shift, official statements on the growth of the Aboriginal population changed dramatically. After the war, not only did "mixed-blood" numbers continue to increase, but the "full-blood" population began to rise just as steeply.[22] Far from deploring this in the manner of prewar absorptionists, assimilationists applauded the demographic turnaround, even claiming it as a positive consequence of their own policy. A 1958 report of the Commonwealth Department of the Interior stated: "That this policy [assimilation] is likely to be successful is encouraged by the fact that for the first time since white settlement the aboriginal population is on the increase."[23] A year earlier, Howard Beale, Commonwealth Minister for Supply and Defence Production, had asserted that the Aboriginal population in the Northern Territory was "increasing, and increasing for one reason—the humane administration which has been given to the aborigines by the present Minister for Territories (Mr. Hasluck) and by this Government."[24] Hasluck himself noted that the "population of the aboriginal race is growing" at "a higher rate of natural increase than the general population of Australia," suggesting that this indicated the rightness of his policies.[25] A.P. Elkin claimed that the assimilationist measures adopted in the 1940s and 1950s had not only halted "the hitherto inexorable decline in population of the Aborigines" but had resulted in their numbers "increasing ... at a greater rate than the natural increase rate of the non-aboriginal population."[26] Whether there really was any causal connection between the implementation of assimilation and the rapid increase in the Aboriginal population is immaterial to my argument, although it bears noting that assimilationists regarded the health, hygiene, and nutritional reforms they instituted as intrinsic parts of the assimilation package, essential for raising Aborigines to a physical as well as cultural level commensurate with that of white people.[27] Whatever the causes of Aboriginal population increase, the fact that it could be taken as a measure of assimilation's success is incompatible with genocidal intent.

It is, however, entirely consistent with one of assimilation's original aspirations: averting extinction. Since the early nineteenth century, when the doctrine of inevitable Aboriginal extinction took root, a minority had argued to the contrary that survival was possible, though only by the "uplift" of the Aborigines to "civilization." In the interwar years, this minority view gained in credibility as earlier dogmas of race were discredited and the universalism of an Enlightenment vision of progress was reasserted.[28] In 1932, A.P. Elkin explained that:

> The position demands that if he [the Aborigine] is to survive, he must pass with great rapidity from the food gathering stage of complete dependence on nature, and from the socio-mystical organization of tribal life, to a stage in which nature is exploited and in which mechanization and economics control the outlook on nature and society.[29]

Prominent Aboriginal activist and Secretary of the Australian Aborigines' League, William Cooper, made the point more straightforwardly, demanding "an official policy of uplift" to allow Aborigines "to rise to the full standard of European culture"; only by this means was it possible to "stop the rot and save the race."[30] In these various interwar renditions, by Aboriginal as well as non-Aboriginal lobbyists, assimilation to Western sociocultural norms was represented not as a route to destruction, but as the only viable strategy for survival. Postwar assimilationists continued to insist that Aboriginal survival depended on their Westernization and modernization. Increasingly, however, emphasis shifted from ensuring survival per se to monitoring the terms of that survival; and the more assured survival seemed, the more emphasis shifted to the imperatives of citizenship. As assimilation moved from the margins to the mainstream of political discourse in the 1940s and 1950s, the older objective of survival was increasingly overshadowed by the new objective of national incorporation.

Both absorption and assimilation were doctrines of national incorporation, aspiring to the inclusion of racially-defined outgroups in the Australian nation. But each imagined the nation differently. Absorption was informed by a potently ethnic conception of nationhood whereby myths of blood kinship and of an organic coherence of descent, sentiment, and values provided the foundation-stones of the national community. Outsiders could enter that community only by mixing their "blood" with that of its members, ultimately expunging all characteristics, physical as well as cultural, which would mark their origins, history, and descent as discordant.[31] Assimilation, by contrast, was based on a more civic-orientated nationalism whereby national cohesion would be attained through shared rights and responsibilities, a common public culture, substantial consistency in values and aspirations, and the veneration of national symbols such as flag and anthem. This is not to suggest that Australian nationalism underwent a magical transformation around the time of the Second World War. Australian nationalism always contained both civic and ethnic elements. As Anthony Smith observes, this tension inheres in all nationalisms, although under certain circumstances the ethnic elements will be emphasized while other circumstances call forth an emphasis on the civic.[32] Why the emphasis in Australian nationalism shifted around mid-century is a question beyond the scope of this chapter, although extensive non-British immigration in the postwar period was probably a factor. In any event, the shift was manifested in Aboriginal policy.

The frontispiece of the Commonwealth's assimilation propaganda booklet for 1961 is exemplary of this shift. A full-page photograph depicting two mechanics, one white, one black, faces the title page bearing the words "One People" in large, bold letters.[33] Their one-peoplehood rested on no shared race or descent, a conception totally at odds with the absorptionist ideal whereby "one Australian people" could only equal "one white people." The definition of assimilation agreed to at the Native Welfare Conference in the same year—a definition widely regarded as the classic statement of postwar assimilation—is equally exemplary of civic nationhood:

> The policy of assimilation means in the view of all Australian governments that all aborigines and part-aborigines are expected eventually to attain the same manner of living as other Australians and to live as members of a single Australian community enjoying the same rights and privileges, accepting the same responsibilities, observing the same

customs and influenced by the same beliefs, hopes and loyalties as other Australians.[34]

Like other expressions of civic nationhood, assimilation as here defined demands a large measure of sociocultural conformity, and entails an intolerance of collective loyalties that might challenge the individual's commitment to the abstract community of the nation. As in other civic-orientated nationalisms, the public culture to which conformity is demanded is essentially the culture of the nation's dominant ethnic group.[35] Civic-orientated nations are not necessarily noted for their tolerance, but they do permit admission of outsiders, the price for which is typically not the complete abnegation of prior ethnic identities but their privatization and relegation to political and social inconsequence. This, as the following section will explain, was the price assimilation demanded of Aborigines.

Citizenship, Culture, Identity

Assimilation was tied to a normative concept of the citizen as an individual possessing certain prescribed competencies, values, aspirations, and sensibilities. The postwar Australian citizen was, more than ever before, a self-regulating, self-governing individual, committed to the ideal of the self-sufficient nuclear family and to the vast abstract collectivity of the nation.[36] To make Aborigines into citizens, it was assumed, required instilling in them this constellation of competencies, convictions, and commitments, remodeling their social and cultural lives into conformity with national norms and the demands of modernity. This reformation was attempted by means that were often no less authoritarian than those prevailing in the preassimilation era. As the anthropologist W.E.H. Stanner observed in 1964, assimilation was offered on terms that were "still fundamentally dictatorial."[37] Aboriginal behaviors, movements, places of residence, and employment continued to be monitored and controlled.[38] State surveillance was intense and intrusive to the point that in New South Wales, inspectors were empowered to enter Aboriginal homes and rummage through cupboards to determine whether the family income was appropriately spent. Although Aborigines did gradually acquire the civil rights and welfare entitlements of other Australians, mainly in the 1960s, the assimilationist state tended to be parsimonious and grudging in its concessions of rights, demanding prior evidence of Aboriginal "readiness" to exercise them "responsibly."[39] Rights were the reward for successful assimilation.

To exemplify the strategies and objectives of assimilation, I shall focus in this section on Commonwealth policy under the ministership of assimilation's most articulate political advocate, Paul Hasluck. In 1953, Hasluck introduced the Northern Territory *Welfare Ordinance,* arguably the most rigorously assimilationist item of legislation ever enacted in an Australian jurisdiction. It was certainly an extraordinary legislative item, for while patently an instrument of Aboriginal governance, at Hasluck's insistence it studiously avoided all reference to "Aborigines" or any other racial or ethnic identifier. Instead, it nominated its subjects "wards of the state," which became the legal status of the overwhelming majority of Northern Territory "full-blood" Aborigines when the ordinance came into operation. Hasluck was quite explicit about the reasons for his choice of terminology. The word "Aborigine" was to be avoided in legislation because the state must not extend legal recognition to any racial or ethnic group; to do so would discriminate between people on the improper grounds of racial or ethnic origins rather than on the (to him) quite proper grounds of "conduct and mode of living."[40] The term "ward" was preferable, both because it was a revocable legal status and because it embodied the notion that the majority of Aborigines were, for the time being, "in need of guardianship and tutelage," in a situation akin to that of persons "of European race who need special care—for example neglected children."[41] Not only did such language epitomize the widespread assimilationist assumption of Aboriginal incompetence, it also infantilized Aboriginal adults, presuming their need for the firm paternal guidance of the state if they were to mature into responsible citizens. Even committed assimilationists, such as Elkin, were outraged at this legislative demeaning of Aboriginal people.[42] As "wards," Aborigines were treated as a malleable mass, or perhaps rather as an ensemble of ductile individuals, able to be remolded into ideal citizens.

Hasluck's *Welfare Ordinance,* like his conception of assimilation more generally, was founded on an assumption of the inevitable dissolution of Aboriginal cultures and social structures. In his view, indigenous societies and cultures had been shattered by the impact of the West, rendering Aboriginal people "stranded individuals," bereft of social support or cultural integrity, whose only viable future lay in becoming full members of the Australian nation by adopting its mores, values, and "way of life."[43] The collision with Western civilization was unstoppable; so too was the resultant cultural dissolution. While their societies and cultures were beyond redemption, Aboriginal individuals were not. In

Hasluck's view, shared by many of his contemporaries, assimilation was primarily a matter of emancipating individuals from a decaying sociocultural heritage.[44]

For all that, Hasluck did not suggest that Aboriginal identities and heritage should be suppressed to the point of disappearance. Summing up his views on the retention of Aboriginality, he stated that assimilated Aborigines "could recall and honour their own origins and traditions (in much the same way as Scotsmen wear kilts, play bagpipes, dance reels, celebrate ancient festivals and try to preserve Gaelic)."[45] While this conception certainly expresses an attenuated notion of identity, attached to frozen bits of cultural exotica, it still implies some sense of collective membership that is envisaged as persisting through and beyond the process of assimilation. Even Hasluck's *Welfare Ordinance,* despite its draconian provisions, was compatible with the maintenance of such a circumscribed Aboriginality, for while the legislation refused to name its subjects collectively as "Aborigines," individually they were given Aboriginal names.

In 1953, R.K. McCaffery, Acting Director of Native Affairs in the Northern Territory, explained the procedures to be followed in giving Aboriginal people officially-recognized names, as required for implementation of the *Welfare Ordinance.* The "tribal" pattern of naming, he affirmed, must be superseded by the Western system of Christian names followed by a fixed family surname. He also insisted that the surname itself should be selected from the ensemble of names the Aboriginal person already possessed, preferably the local group or horde name, alternatively the totemic or subsection name. Arguing his case, McCaffery dwelt on the issue of cultural continuity:

> The surname should be chosen with definite associations with their aboriginal past giving them ties with their aboriginal heritage. This will serve also to preserve names with meaning in Territory aboriginal life.

McCaffery appreciated the connections between names and ethnic identity. He equally appreciated the connections between changed naming systems and changing social structures, observing that "the acceptance and use of a family surname will counter the normal social organization of tribal aboriginal society with its associated duties and beliefs."[46] That is, a family surname would encourage Aborigines to orient their social life primarily around the nuclear family, rather than in terms of the fluid and ever-ramifying networks of kinship characteristic of "tribal" society. Ascribing fixed family names was, among other things, an induction and invitation into the nuclear-family-orientated world of the "Australian way of life." This measure entailed no effacement of Aboriginality. Fixed family surnames such as Namatjira and Pareroultja—two examples cited by McCaffery—would be transmitted down the generations, marking their bearers unmistakably as Aborigines. Yet the meaning and significance of those names would be radically transformed. No longer signifying totemic ancestry or subsection membership or clan affiliation, the name would simply designate a family and the (hopefully incidental) fact of ethnic origins, just as former Celtic clan names (such as McCaffery) had been transformed from signifiers of social obligation and political allegiance into neutral family names, and indicators of the (largely incidental) fact of Irish or Scottish descent. Aboriginal names both preserved and privatized Aboriginal identities.

In similar vein, the Aboriginal education program set up in the Northern Territory from the late 1940s sought not to erase but to circumscribe Aboriginal identities. Educational objectives were explicitly assimilatory, schools being regarded as primary sites for the inculcation of the knowledge, norms, and behaviors requisite "for living in full citizenship as part of the Australian community."[47] By 1950, the Commonwealth Office of Education had devised a syllabus and curriculum that, with some modifications, provided the foundation for Aboriginal education for more than a decade.[48] While the syllabus placed emphasis on fitting Aboriginal children into a white Australian social, cultural, and economic environment, it also insisted that this "can be achieved only by a constant and open recognition of the worth of native culture, by the deliberate process of creating a new outlook and approach to life through the skilful distillation of all the elements of the aboriginal way of life." Teachers were instructed to cultivate in students an appreciation of the fact that "there IS a place for aboriginals in Australian life," suggesting Harold Blair, Doug Nicholls, and Albert Namatjira as appropriate role models.[49] According to the 1950 syllabus, the subject "Social Studies" deserved special attention as a means of preparing Aboriginal children "for entry into the white man's world" and for "the creation of the new intellectual, emotional and moral attitude which is essential to the continued survival of the aborigines." It also specified that through social studies the Aboriginal student should:

> learn to respect his own cultural heritage and see the assumption of the
> new way of life as a necessary progression and not as the emergence

from a shameful past.... In his every approach, therefore, the teacher
will draw out from the children the relevant essentials of their own way
of life, praise these essentials, encourage the children to discuss them,
hold up the merit of them for approval.

Covering such issues as the transition from hunting and gathering to pastoralism and farming, and the history of Australia from
"The Aborigines Before the White Men Came" to the "Life of the
Aborigines Today," social studies taught the lesson of progress.[50]
Aboriginal children were enjoined not to abandon, but to reinter-
pret, their Aboriginality, and to appreciate the benefits of aligning
it with the trajectory of Western sociocultural "progress."

Commonwealth assimilationist propaganda carried compatible
messages. The 1961 propaganda booklet affirmed that year's Native
Welfare Conference definition of assimilation (quoted above), with
its persistent reiteration of the sameness of Aboriginal and white
Australians across a range of attributes, followed by the statement:

> Assimilation does not mean that aborigines should necessarily lose their
> identity as aborigines or forgo their proper pride in this identity. It does
> not mean that aboriginal language, myths and legends, and art forms
> should be lost—there is a proper and proud place in the wider Aus-
> tralian culture for all of these.[51]

This juxtaposition of a demand for sameness and a concession
of difference recurs throughout the series of official pamphlets. The
1960 pamphlet asserted that Aborigines "must, to survive and to
prosper, learn to live as white Australians do, and to think as white
Australians do," adding that: "Assimilation does not mean that the
aborigines should lose their racial identity, or lose contact with
their arts, their crafts and their philosophy."[52] The 1963 pamphlet
defined assimilation in similar terms to the 1961 Conference,
immediately afterward stating:

> Assimilation does *not* mean that aborigines will necessarily lose their
> identity as aborigines or their pride in their aboriginal ancestry. It does
> not mean, either, that aboriginal language, arts and customs should be
> allowed to languish. These can and should enrich the whole Australian
> culture.[53]

The consistency of these juxtapositions—and they recur
throughout assimilationist literature, not merely in this series of
pamphlets—suggests that something more than confusion was
involved. Nor can the affirmations of identity and heritage be interpreted as mere sops to a growing public unease at the more coercive

aspects of assimilation. Although these were propaganda pamphlets, their tenor was not so much to justify the policy as to instruct middle-class white Australians in the appropriate demeanor to adopt toward Aboriginal people, thereby enlisting their active participation in the assimilatory project. To that extent, the propaganda was directed against what Rowley claimed to be a popular understanding of assimilation as Aboriginal disappearance.

The pamphlets themselves were quite specific, even prescriptive, about both the maintenance and the repudiation of cultural heritage. They persistently distinguished between the "best aspects" of Aboriginal culture, which could be retained, and those elements that would be "a positive hindrance to their advancement" that must be discarded. Among the latter were "extravagant sharing" of possessions, a "tendency to go on 'walkabout'," "primitive standards of hygiene" and, most of all, kinship or "tribal obligations."[54] "On the other hand," the 1960 pamphlet explained:

> [T]here are many virtues that belong to the aboriginal tribal life, many arts, and many skills, that can well be carried forward into the new life, to enrich it and to provide for the aborigines something of a link with the past and provide them with justifiable grounds for pride in their aboriginal identity ...
> The aboriginal stockman who plays his didjeridoo to entertain his mates in the drafting camp, the artisan who makes boomerangs for the tourist trade, the enterprising aboriginal man or woman who can build a small business around aboriginal arts and crafts are examples, in a small way, of the carry-through of the aboriginal tradition.
> The merit of aboriginal art is now being recognized by designers, aboriginal music and dancing have had some small recognition, and aboriginal myths and legends now form a small part of our tradition in literature. It may well be that further developments of this sort in the near future will provide aborigines with a pride and a unity that they have previously lacked.[55]

During the assimilationist era, elements of Aboriginal cultural heritage (especially aesthetic) were tolerated, even encouraged if they could be commodified and turned to profit. At the same time, in social norms, values, and behaviors Aborigines were enjoined to forsake the old and subscribe to the new, in the form of the "Australian way of life."

Cultural Genocide?

Assimilation sought to reduce Aboriginal culture to Aboriginal folklore. According to the assimilationist vision, Aboriginal people should come to think and act according to the norms of the dominant national culture, with the ultimate consequence that there would remain no distinctively Aboriginal "societal cultures," to use Will Kymlicka's useful term.[56] But this did not mean that there would remain no Aborigines. Assimilated Aborigines could still consider themselves Aboriginal, and could still cherish some residue of their cultural heritage, if only within limits determined by the state.

Was this "cultural genocide"? Attempting an answer immediately stumbles on the problem of the amorphousness of the term. Sometimes in the scholarly literature, "cultural genocide" denotes the destruction of a culture, that is, of the framework within which a human group conceives and constructs meaning, value, and purpose in social life; alternatively, it denotes the destruction of the group itself by eradicating all markers of its cultural distinctiveness. In the literature, there is persistent slippage between these two senses of the term.[57] This slippage has not been remedied by the suggestion of some scholars for use of the term "ethnocide" to cover cases of purely cultural destruction.[58] Since "genocide" and "ethnocide" are etymologically so closely akin, use of the latter term has arguably facilitated the slippage. Sharper conceptual clarity is required. A culture, in the "thick" anthropological sense, can be destroyed without destroying the group that formerly lived and thought according to that cultural framework; the group can continue to maintain existence as a group, even if its cultural heritage has been reduced to a "thin" folkloric residue.

One of the foremost exponents of the concept of "ethnocide," Pierre Clastres, puts his finger on its fundamental problem in his statement that "every State organisation is ethnocidal, ethnocide is the State's normal mode of existence."[59] To the extent that the modern national state seeks to establish and enforce a common national culture within its territory, and thereby curtails alternative local and ethnic cultures, this is quite true. But it is profoundly misleading if "ethnocide" is taken to mean total extirpation of local or minority cultures and eradication of ethnic identities. State-led nation-building has commonly entailed the suppression of local and ethnic cultures, to the point not of annihilation but of attenuation to a rather superficial repertoire of folk customs and quaint traditions. Writing of nineteenth century European nation-building, Eric Hobsbawm observes that while states demanded assimilation of minorities to the majority culture, in most cases "the major nation could cherish and foster the dialects and lesser languages within it, the historic and folkloric traditions of the lesser communities it contained, if only as proof of the range of colours on its macro-national palette."[60] In broad terms, his observation applies equally to postwar Australia.

There is now a burgeoning literature highly critical of the assimilatory impulses intrinsic to modern national state-formation.[61] Recent scholarship has emphasized the high costs of assimilation, for minority groups in general and for specific groups such as Aborigines. Advancing that scholarly critique is, in my view, both commendable and necessary. For that purpose, however, the terminology of "genocide" (with or without qualifying adjectives) and "ethnocide" obscures more than it reveals. Cultural suppressions must be critiqued as cultural suppressions, not forcibly assimilated into the category of genocide. To subsume the cultural suppressions characteristic of modern nation-building into the category "genocide" is to succumb to the fallacy identified by Helen Fein and Michael Ignatieff, whereby the connotations of the word become so expansive "that genocide becomes not only unbounded but banal, an everyday occurrence."[62]

Yet in some ways Aboriginal assimilation differed from the assimilatory processes typical of modern European national states, most of all in the intensity of state surveillance and control with which it was attempted. This distinctive feature could be attributed to various factors, though two are particularly noteworthy. The perceived cultural distance between indigenous and settler Australians—the former represented as quintessentially "primitive," the latter as paragons of modernity—rendered the forging of linkages between "them" and "us" exceptionally problematic. Secondly, and perhaps more importantly, there was the long-standing and ultimately racist assumption that Aborigines were a peculiarly incompetent people, incapable of realizing or even recognizing their own best interests. In this regard, it is apposite to return briefly to child removals in the era of assimilation.

Assimilation and Child Removal

Child removal—like much else—in the era of assimilation was mired in contradiction. As Anna Haebich observes, the "modern nuclear family was both a vehicle and goal of the assimilation project."[63] Prominent among assimilationist objectives was the Aboriginal adoption of models of family life according to the conventions of the modern suburban household. As an essential component of the "Australian way of life," that goal was intrinsic

to the ambition that "they" should live "like us." But if the goal of
the modern nuclear family was clear, what of the actual Aboriginal
family as vehicle? Haebich notes that there was dissension between
those who considered assimilation could best be attained through
removing children from their families, and those advocating its
achievement through reformation of the domestic unit as a whole,
though generally the latter voices predominated.[64] Yet child
removals not only continued, they possibly increased.[65] How could
this be, when the nuclear family was promoted more vigorously
than ever, and Aboriginal people enjoined to embrace its benefits?
It was so because the modern nuclear family was not merely normal (in the sense of being the standard domestic arrangement), but
also normative (in the sense of sustaining and perpetuating a range
of social norms considered essential for effective social functioning). When the family significantly failed to perform that normative
role, whether through poverty or neglect or abuse or adherence to
alternative norms, it became vulnerable to interventions by the
state, including the possibility of child removal. In other words, if
the family as vehicle of assimilation was judged incapable of reaching the destination of assimilation, it could and would be disas-
sembled. This is not meant as an all-encompassing explanation of
child removal in the assimilation era. Particular removals were
conducted for specific reasons. My point is that insofar as an underlying logic can be identified in postwar child removal practices, it
was reformatory rather than exterminatory.

This is borne out by the fact that in the assimilationist era,
authority to conduct Aboriginal child removals was taken from the
various Aboriginals Departments and vested in the courts. First in
New South Wales in 1940, then gradually in other jurisdictions
over the following decade, Aboriginal families became subject to
the same legal regimes as white families, and removals were conducted according to mainstream child welfare provisions.[66] As a
socially disadvantaged and economically deprived group, Aborigines were exceptionally susceptible to such welfare interventions,
and their children continued to be taken in vastly disproportionate
numbers. Some separated children were placed in special Aborig-
ines-only institutions; some had their Aboriginality deliberately
kept secret from them; some were adopted or fostered out, occasionally to other Aboriginal families. The range of destinations of
separated children was vast, but it is the intent of the separations
that is pertinent here. To the extent that child removals were now
conducted within the framework of mainstream child welfare provisions—and both the imperfection and the injustice of this must be

acknowledged—the intentions behind the removals were quite distinct from those specified by the UN Convention as genocidal.

Conclusion

Aboriginal assimilation, I contend, cannot be comprehended within the conceptual framework of genocide. Assimilation policy did not aspire to the extermination of the Aborigines, or even the effacement of Aboriginality. It sought to bring these within the ambit of state power. To that extent, it was congruent with the assimilatory strategies pursued by European national states toward their internal minorities since the early nineteenth century. Assimilation was often destructive, arrogant, and neglectful of Aboriginal desires and dignity. But in acknowledging the reformability of Aboriginal people, assimilation marked a shift from earlier policy regimes wherein the presumed non-reformability of Aborigines was held to guarantee their ultimate demise. As a reformable people, Aborigines could survive, should come to live "like us," and would be governed "like us," as members of the community of the nation. According to the assimilationist scenario, indigenous sociocultural orders would crumble, leaving a mere residue of cultural heritage and a largely privatized sense of Aboriginality, as Aboriginal people found new meaning and purpose in an overarching "Australian way of life." To point out the flaws and failures of these assumptions and aspirations is entirely apposite. To designate the intentions genocidal is to render the term conceptually and morally incoherent.

Notes

1. See for example Human Rights and Equal Opportunity Commission, *Bringing Them Home: Report of the National Inquiry into the Separation of Aboriginal and Torres Strait Islander Children from their Families* (Sydney, 1997); Q. Beresford and P. Omaji, *Our State of Mind: Racial Planning and the Stolen Generations* (Fremantle, 1998).
2. For a study of assimilation as a project of normative governance, see Tim Rowse, *White Flour, White Power: From Rations to Citizenship in Central Australia* (Cambridge, 1998).

3. See for example Robert van Krieken, "The Barbarism of Civilization: Cultural Genocide and the 'Stolen Generations'," *British Journal of Sociology* 50, no. 2 (1999): 297–315.

4. Uriel Tal, "On the study of the Holocaust and Genocide," *Yad Vashem Studies*, 8 (1979): 14–17; Johannes Morsink, "Cultural Genocide, the Universal Declaration, and Minority Rights," *Human Rights Quarterly* 21, no. 4 (1999): 1009–60.

5. Quoted in *Bringing Them Home*, 270.

6. *Bringing Them Home*, 6–11, 34.

7. Ron Brunton, "Betraying the Victims: The 'Stolen Generations' Report," *IPA Backgrounder* 10, no. 1 (1998): 3–5, 7–10 (available online at <http://www.ipa.org.au/pubs/backgrounddocs/BG10-1.html>); Hal Wootten, "Ron Brunton and Bringing Them Home," *Indigenous Law Bulletin* 4, no. 12 (1998): 6–7.

8. *Bringing Them Home*, 270–75.

9. Tal, "On the Study," 19.

10. See Robert Manne's chapter in this volume; Russell McGregor, "'Breed Out the Colour,' or the Importance of Being White," *Australian Historical Studies* 33, no. 20 (2002), 286-302.

11. *Aboriginal Welfare: Initial Conference of Commonwealth and State Aboriginal Authorities* (Canberra, 1937), 16.

12. Tony Austin, "Cecil Cook, Scientific Thought and 'Half-castes' in the Northern Territory, 1927–1939," *Aboriginal History* 14, no. 1 (1990): 104–22; Anna Haebich, *For Their Own Good: Aborigines and Government in the Southwest of Western Australia, 1900–1940* (Perth, 1988); Patricia Jacobs, "Science and Veiled Assumptions: Miscegenation in Western Australia, 1930–1937," *Australian Aboriginal Studies* no. 2 (1986): 15–23.

13. Paul Bartrop, "The Holocaust, the Aborigines, and the Bureaucracy of Destruction: An Australian Dimension of Genocide," *Journal of Genocide Research* 3, no. 1 (2001): 76, 84–85; Peter Read, *The Stolen Generations: The Removal of Aboriginal Children in New South Wales, 1883 to 1969*, NSW Ministry of Aboriginal Affairs Occasional Paper no. 1, n.d., 2.

14. Robert Manne, "In Denial: The Stolen Generations and the Right," *The Australian Quarterly Essay* no. 1 (2001): 30, 38–41.

15. See for example Stuart Macintyre, "Assimilation," in *The Oxford Companion to Australian History*, ed. G. Davison, J. Hirst, and S. Macintyre (Melbourne, 1998), 42; Patrick Wolfe, *Settler Colonialism and the Transformation of Anthropology: The Politics and Poetics of an Ethnographic Event* (London, 1999), 11; Royal Commission into Aboriginal Deaths in Custody, *National Report*, vol. 2 (Canberra, 1991), 510.

16. Conference of Commonwealth and State Aboriginal Welfare Authorities, 3 February 1948, National Archives of Australia (NAA), A431, 1951/866.

17. Commonwealth and States Conference on Native Welfare, Canberra, 3rd–4th September, 1951: Statement on Citizenship Status; and Native Welfare Council, Second Meeting, 29th September 1952: Agenda Item 1: Citizenship Status; both in National Library of Australia (NLA), Papers of Paul Hasluck, MS 5274, box 32.

18. "The Northern Territory of Australia: Commonwealth Government's Policy with Respect to Aboriginals ... February 1939," NLA typescript, Np 572.99429 McE, 1–2.

19. See for example Elkin to A.M. Brown, 30 September 1959, Papers of A.P. Elkin (EP), University of Sydney Archives, box 217, item 5/2/20; Elkin, type-

script: "The Australian Aborigines To-day," c. 1963, EP, box 109, item 1/17/53.

20. C.D. Rowley, *Outcasts in White Australia* (Canberra, 1971), 31.

21. C.D. Rowley, "Aborigines and Other Australians," *Oceania* 32, no. 4 (1962): 252, 254, 259; *Outcasts*, 383–85.

22. L.R. Smith, *The Aboriginal Population of Australia* (Canberra, 1980).

23. Ken Kennedy, Assimilation of Aboriginal Tribes, c. 1958, NAA, A452, 1958/4514.

24. Commonwealth of Australia, *Parliamentary Debates (Hansard)*, House of Representatives, vol. 15 (Canberra, 1957), 1234.

25. Hasluck, Opening Statement to the Native Welfare Conference, Darwin, 1963, NLA MS 5274, box 32.

26. A.P. Elkin, typescript: "The Australian Aborigines Today," c. 1964, NAA, A452, 1964/5746.

27. See for example C.R. Lambert, Statement on the Northern Territory Aborigine Problem, 4 April 1951, NAA, A431, 1951/866; S.T. Watsford, Health Problems in Relation to Full Bloods in the Northern Territory, 1953, NAA, A452, 1953/138.

28. Russell McGregor, *Imagined Destinies: Aboriginal Australians and the Doomed Race Theory, 1880–1939* (Melbourne, 1997).

29. A.P. Elkin, "Cultural and Racial Clash in Australia," *Morpeth Review* no. 21 (1932): 38.

30. W. Cooper to Minister for the Interior, 26 July 1938, NAA, CRS A659, 40/1/858. See also Andrew Markus, *Blood from a Stone: William Cooper and the Australian Aborigines' League* (Melbourne, 1986); R. McGregor, "Protest and Progress: Aboriginal Activism in the 1930s," *Australian Historical Studies* 25, no. 101 (1993): 555–68.

31. McGregor, "'Breed Out the Colour'."

32. Anthony Smith, *Nations and Nationalism in a Global Era* (Cambridge, 1995), 99; idem, *The Nation in History* (Hanover, 2000), 4, 25–26.

33. Commonwealth Department of Territories, *One People* (Canberra, 1961).

34. *The Policy of Assimilation: Decisions of Commonwealth and State Ministers at the Native Welfare Conference, Canberra, January 26th and 27th, 1961* (Canberra, 1961), 1. This definition follows closely the wording of an earlier definition of assimilation by Hasluck; see Hasluck to R.S. Leydin, Administrator, NT, 2 January 1952, NAA, A452, 1952/162.

35. Smith, *Global Era*, 101; Smith, *Nation in History*, 18–19; Will Kymlicka, *Multicultural Citizenship: A Liberal Theory of Minority Rights* (Oxford, 1995), 14, 24.

36. John Murphy, *Imagining the Fifties: Private Sentiment and Political Culture in Menzies' Australia* (Sydney, 2000).

37. W.E.H. Stanner, "Foreword" to *Aborigines Now: New Perspectives in the Study of Aboriginal Communities*, ed. Marie Reay (Sydney, 1964), ix.

38. Rowley, *Outcasts*; Ann McGrath, ed., *Contested Ground: Australian Aborigines under the British Crown* (Sydney, 1995).

39. Rowley, *Outcasts*, especially chapter 18; John Chesterman and Brian Galligan, *Citizens without Rights: Aborigines and Australian Citizenship* (Cambridge, 1997), chapter 6.

40. See correspondence in NAA, A452, 1952/162, especially Statement by the Minister for Territories the Hon. Paul Hasluck: Native Welfare in the Northern Territory, 6 August 1952.

41. Statement by the Minister ... 6 August 1952; also Hasluck to F.J.S. Wise, Administrator, NT, 28 July 1952; both in NAA, A452, 1952/162.
42. A.P. Elkin, typescript: Wards, not Aborigines in the Northern Territory: The Proposed Ordinance "To Provide for the Care and Assistance of Certain Persons," February 1953, EP, box 71, item 1/12/187.
43. Paul Hasluck, "Some Problems of Assimilation," ANZAAS Address, 1959; and "Are Our Aborigines Neglected?" PSA Address, 1959; both in EP, box 80, items 1/12/295 and 1/12/294. Hasluck, "A National Problem" (1950) in *Native Welfare in Australia: Speeches and Addresses by the Hon. Paul Hasluck, M.P.* (Perth, 1953), 5–12.
44. W.E.H. Stanner, "Continuity and Change among the Aborigines," (1958) in Stanner, *White Man Got No Dreaming: Essays, 1938–1973* (Canberra, 1979), 41–66; Reay, ed., *Aborigines Now*; Rowley, *Outcasts*; Rowse, *White Flour*; Rowse, "The Modesty of the State: Hasluck and the Anthropological Critics of Assimilation" in *Paul Hasluck in Australian History: Civic Personality and Public Life*, ed. T. Stannage, K. Saunders, and R. Nile (Brisbane, n.d.), 119–32.
45. Paul Hasluck, *Shades of Darkness: Aboriginal Affairs, 1925–1965* (Melbourne, 1988), 30.
46. R.K. McCaffery, Identification and Naming of Aborigines, 1953, NAA, A452, 1953/138.
47. L.R. Newby, Commonwealth Senior Education Officer, Education of Full Blood Aborigines, NAA, A452, 1953/138.
48. Commonwealth Office of Education, Provisional Syllabus for Use in Aboriginal Schools in the Northern Territory, 23 June 1950, NAA, A431, 1951/560; B.H. Watts and J.D. Gallacher, *Report on an Investigation into the Curriculum and Teaching Methods used in Aboriginal Schools in the Northern Territory* (Darwin, 1964).
49. Provisional Syllabus, NAA, A431, 1951/560. Harold Blair was a celebrated Aboriginal tenor. Albert Namatjira was an artist whose watercolor renditions of his ancestral (Arrente) lands were enormously popular in 1950s Australia. Doug Nicholls was a Church of Christ pastor and former Australian Rules footballer; his inclusion here is interesting since by 1950 he had acquired a degree of notoriety as a political activist on behalf of his people.
50. Provisional Syllabus, NAA, A431, 1951/560.
51. *One People*, 12.
52. Commonwealth Department of Territories, *The Skills of Our Aborigines* (Canberra, 1960), 23.
53. Commonwealth Department of Territories, *The Aborigines and You* (Canberra, 1963), 3 (italics in the original).
54. Commonwealth Department of Territories, *Fringe Dwellers* (Canberra, 1959), 13, 18–22; *Skills*, 30; *Aborigines and You*, 9–10.
55. *Skills*, 30–31.
56. See Will Kymlicka, *Politics in the Vernacular: Nationalism, Multiculturalism, and Citizenship* (Oxford, 2001), 25–28, 55.
57. See for example David Moshman, "Conceptual Constraints on Thinking About Genocide," *Journal of Genocide Research* 3, no. 3 (2001): 438–39, 445; Robert Hitchcock and Tara Twedt, "Physical and Cultural Genocide of Various Indigenous Peoples," in *Genocide in the Twentieth Century*, ed. S. Totten, W. Parsons, and I. Charny (New York, 1995), 485, 493.
58. Frank Chalk and Kurt Jonassohn, *The History and Sociology of Genocide* (New Haven, 1990), 23; Helen Fein, "Genocide: A Sociological Perspective,"

Current Sociology 38, no. 1 (1990): 9–10; Pierre Clastres, "On Ethnocide," *Art and Text* 28 (1988): 51–58.

59. Clastres, "On Ethnocide," 56.

60. Eric Hobsbawm, *Nations and Nationalism Since 1780: Programme, Myth, Reality* (Cambridge, 1992), 35.

61. See for example Kymlicka, *Multicultural Citizenship;* Zygmunt Bauman, *Modernity and Ambivalence* (Cambridge, 1991).

62. Fein, "Genocide," 17; Michael Ignatieff, "The Dangers of a World without Enemies: Lemkin's World," *The New Republic* (26 February 2001): 25–28.

63. Anna Haebich, *Broken Circles: Fragmenting Indigenous Families, 1800–2000* (Fremantle, 2000), 458; see also 426.

64. Haebich, *Broken Circles,* chapters 7 and 8.

65. Haebich, *Broken Circles,* 421; *Bringing Them Home,* 34. Ascertaining how many and what proportion of Aboriginal children were removed raises more problems than can be addressed here. Manne, "In Denial," 24–28, provides a good, brief discussion of these problems, suggesting that the likely proportion of removals was in the order of one in every ten Aboriginal children; this, however, was for the entire period 1900 to 1970.

66. *Bringing Them Home,* 33; Haebich, *Broken Circles,* chapter 7.

Epilogue

NOTES ON THE HISTORY OF
ABORIGINAL POPULATION
OF AUSTRALIA

Tim Rowse

Introduction

Nobody knows how many people lived on the territory now known as "Australia" in the late eighteenth century, when people from the British Isles began the process of colonization.[1] After reviewing all the estimates, and discussing their reasoning, John Mulvaney has recently suggested 750,000.[2] For many years (from 1930 to the mid 1980s), scholarly opinion had fixed on the figure of 300,000—the minimum estimated by anthropologist Radcliffe-Brown in 1930.[3] This estimate did not take sufficient account of the impact of diseases that decimated Aborigines from the late eighteenth century until just after the First World War. Nor did the Radcliffe Brown estimate appreciate what archaeologists have discovered—that parts of the Murray-Darling Basin were capable of sustaining populations more dense than those encountered by twentieth century anthropologists in northern and central Australia.

Between Radcliffe-Brown's and Mulvaney's estimate is the official 2001 Census count of 410,003 indigenous Australians. If we use

Radcliffe-Brown's estimate, we can tell a story of indigenous expansion between 1788 to 2001. If we use Mulvaney's, the story is, at first sight, one of decline. Though I accept Mulvaney's figure, I do not tell a simple story of decline. Rather, the history of the indigenous Australian population is one of decline and recovery. At least part of that "recovery" story, however, has to concern a change in the definition of those counted as indigenous Australians.[4]

Demographic Pessimism

Throughout the nineteenth century and until the 1930s, the consensus among thoughtful (and less thoughtful) colonists was that the Australian Aborigines were a "doomed race." They would "fade away" until the continent was populated only by people of European origin. In the many versions of the "doomed race" idea we can see a variety of explanations for Aborigines' demise.

William Thomas, the assistant Protector of Aborigines (1838-49) and guardian of Aborigines in the counties of Bourke, Mornington and Evelyn (1850-60) in the Port Phillip Protectorate, was one of the first observers to try to be systematic in his understanding of the decline in Aborigines' numbers. He recorded births and deaths in the Yarra and Westernport area over the eleven years 1839-49. Eighteen of his nineteen attributed causes of recorded deaths were "violent," and some deaths were by execution. Even so, Thomas could comment that "the Almighty only knows the Cause [of the depopulation] … they have not diminished through ill-usage. Their dissipated habits have, I may say, been their executioners."[5] His contemporary William Westgarth wrote in less bewildered vein in 1846.

> The causes of this gradual extinction appear to be tolerably ascertained; their own mutual wars; their hostile encounters with the whites; the diseases and vices of European society, unusually destructive in their effects, from irregularity in the mode of life, and the want of proper medical treatment; the common practice of infanticide; and, more remotely, perhaps, by the gradual disappearance of various animals used as food, and of other sources of their support.[6]

In his study of the colonists' opinions about Aborigines' dwindling population, Russell McGregor found many explanations from the 1830s to the 1930s. Aborigines were dying out because of their contact with Asian peoples, because their culture was fragile, because of their susceptibility to diseases, because of their fondness for drugs and alcohol and other "vices of civilization," because of their primitive inability to adapt to their changing circumstances, because they had sexual intercourse with people of other races (thus catching diseases that limited fertility), because their sexual contact with other races led to a proliferation of hybrid children, because their self-appointed guardians (such as missionaries) had neither the knowledge nor the resources to care properly for them, and because of their violent encounters with both colonists and other Aborigines. And of course ... Divine Providence.

It was difficult for the colonists to be detached when puzzling over the falling numbers of Aborigines. The imminent extinction of the colonized was bound to provoke their anxieties and encourage their complacencies. In particular, much of this tradition of demographic explanation exhibits uneasiness about the contribution made by the colonists' violence and neglect. McGregor writes that "in Australia scientific treatment of the mechanisms of extinction was at best perfunctory."[7] However, there was no doubt among responsible colonists that Aborigines were doomed to extinction. One of the assumptions that made that prognosis plausible was that hybrids—the issue of sexual unions between Aborigines and other races—were not "Aborigines." The extinction thesis was most confidently put forward when "Aborigine" was equated with "full-blood." Our story of the recovery of the Aboriginal population is based partly on the contemporary preference for defining indigenous Australians more broadly.

Enumeration and Estimation Histories

One of the effects of the early and continuing belief that Aborigines were a doomed race was that governments did little to enumerate them. In New South Wales, some Aborigines were included in Censuses of 1871 and 1881, and they were fully enumerated in that Colony from 1891. From 1882 to 1941, the government of this Colony/State made an annual Census of Aborigines, with the help of police. In Victoria, there were Census estimates from 1836 and Protection Board estimates from 1860. Queensland did not estimate its Aboriginal and Torres Strait Islander population until 1881, and Smith advises us not to rely on Queensland figures from the nineteenth century. He makes the same critical comment about the South Australian efforts to count Aborigines in 1851, 1861, 1866, 1871, 1876, and 1891. In Western Australia in the nineteenth century, there were no reliable enumerations of Aborigines across the State. As recently as 1961, officials in this State were so uncertain of the reach of their enumeration that they added an estimated 2000 Aborigines who were not yet in administrative contact with white society. In Tasmania, there were four Census estimates of Aborigines before the first post-federation Census of 1901—in 1847, 1857, 1881, and 1891.[8]

When the colonists claimed nationhood in the Australian federation of 1901, it became possible to discuss a "national" enumeration of indigenous Australians. However, the Constitution of the Commonwealth of Australia included a Section (127) directing that "aboriginal natives shall not be counted" when "reckoning the numbers of the people of the Commonwealth, or of a State or any part of the Commonwealth." The Section was deleted by referendum in May 1967. Commonwealth authorities responsible for the nation's statistics interpreted this Section as forbidding them from including "full-blood" Aborigines in published tables from the Census.[9] In the Census of 1901, before there was a Commonwealth statistical authority, the States' practices differed. Some (Victoria and Tasmania) counted all people and made a separate count of "aborigines and other races" that could be deducted from "all people" if and when that was appropriate. South Australia (which until 1910 included the Northern Territory) counted Aborigines, but never included them in the total count. Queensland defined its "total population" so as to exclude a number of categories of "aliens" (such as "wandering Aborigines" and "half-castes"). However, for administrative purposes, the State government still made an effort to count separately these excluded people. In New South Wales and Western Australia, in 1901, Aborigines were excluded from the total count (though these two States differed in their definition of "Aborigines").

In subsequent Commonwealth Censuses—1911, 1921, 1933, 1947, 1954, and 1966, the Western Australian practice became standard. That is,

- Aborigines were enumerated if they were accessible to ordinary enumeration procedures;
- All those not enumerated were assumed to be "full bloods" and their number was estimated;
- The general Census population included "half-castes" (but not "full bloods");
- The Commonwealth published separate figures on "full bloods" and on "half-castes."

The practical effects of this model were that the Commonwealth became complacent about developing its enumeration procedures.[10] In 1911, some 20,000 persons enumerated in 1901 were
not enumerated because they were not in "the vicinity of settlements"; and New South Wales, having enumerated all its Aborigines in 1901, fell back to estimating eleven per cent of them in
1911. Not until 1966 did the Commonwealth claim that it had
fully enumerated Aborigines. Their confidence, at this point, rested
on the officials' impression (and hope) that all Aborigines, even in
the most remote parts of the continent, were now in regular contact
with a settlement or a mission. Each State or Territory ascended to
this moment of confidence (100 per cent enumeration of its indigenous population) at a different time: New South Wales in 1901,
and again in 1921 and again in 1947; Victoria and Tasmania in
1901, the ACT in 1921, Queensland and South Australia in 1961,
Western Australia and the Northern Territory in 1966.

The Commonwealth's failure to enumerate "full bloods" had
another effect on its practice. Whether they were enumerated or
estimated, "full bloods" were to be excluded from all tabulations of
the Australian population. There were defects in this approach
from the point of view of States that had nonetheless to try to *gov-
ern* Aborigines, so the Commonwealth initiated an annual Census,
in cooperation with State authorities, in which only Aborigines
were enumerated, from 1924 to 1944. As well, in the 1921, 1933,
1947, 1954, and 1966 Censuses, the Commonwealth and State
government cooperated in order to estimate the total number of
Aborigines in each State and their 'caste' and their sex.

The different treatment of "half-castes" (their inclusion in the
general Census population) rested on a popular and official view
that "half-castes" were on their way to being "absorbed" into the
general population. However, the Commonwealth and the six
States lacked a clear, shared definition of the category "half-caste."
Some "half-castes" were included in the Commonwealth's special
figures on "half-castes"; others would have been counted as Europeans if local information made available to Census collectors
deemed them to be "less than half" castes.

The Torres Strait Islanders were not consistently counted as a
separate population. In 1933, they were counted as "Aborigines,"
in 1947 as "Polynesians." In 1971, for the first time, the Commonwealth allowed those filling in the Census the option to nomi-
nate themselves as Torres Strait Islanders. In 1996, the Census
introduced a new category: people of mixed Aboriginal and Torres
Strait Islander descent.

Some Narratives of Depopulation and Recovery

The population history of Australian Aborigines can be divided into phases beginning in 1788. The first phase was "depopulation." It has long been acknowledged that diseases took a frightful toll.[11] Butlin has reminded us of some lethal characteristics of diseases brought to Australia. They characteristically cause high mortality in populations not previously exposed to them. They could spread beyond the limits of white occupation and, in particular, smallpox could spread by contagion, not only by close association and respiratory infection. They could kill at all ages. And they attacked women's reproductive capacity: syphilis limited women's ability to produce live children, and gonorrhoea limited conception. In combination, the smallpox and the two venereal diseases rapidly depopulated the southeast of Australia.[12] Lest "disease" be understood as "the hand of God," Smith has suggested that "lack of biological adaptation was only one and often a minor factor." Aboriginal vulnerability to exotic microbes was increased by the social and ecological changes brought by new colonial practices of land use and by the confinement of the remnant population.

Smith suggests a likely sequence of disease effects. There would have been a sharp drop in the birth rate, and a rise in the death rate, from their pre-European levels of perhaps 40 per thousand each. Mortality probably continued to rise, especially among women, reaching a peak if and when a very few of the fittest ages survived. Fertility probably bottomed rapidly and then recovered slowly, in the main merely contributing immediately to mortality through almost total infant mortality. The first colonial censuses probably took a snapshot of the Aboriginal population at this low point. They showed very high ratios of males to females among both children and adults, and a very small proportion of children. That this was a moment of "bottoming out" is suggested, Smith argues, by the fact that each succeeding cohort showed a slightly more balanced sex composition, and each succeeding census reveals at least no lower, and in general and slightly higher, proportion of children.[13]

Butlin has developed a more complex—if hypothetical—model of this low point in the Aboriginal population. He estimated that from 1788 to 1850 the Aboriginal population in New South Wales and Victoria fell by 80 per cent. Using WHO data from India as a guide to the likely age structure of those affected by smallpox, he estimated the shape and size of the population surviving the first two smallpox epidemics (1789 and 1829-31). He estimated also the impact of other diseases such as influenza and venereal diseases. It is a feature of Butlin's argument that Aborigines were probably not deprived by colonists of the natural resources on which they relied. At the moment when resource competition with colonists would have posed a challenge to a people unaffected by disease, the proportion of the 1788 Aboriginal population was probably down to 50-60 per cent (1805 in New South Wales) and 25-30 per cent (1830 in Victoria). In Butlin's model, when Europeans first met Aborigines in many parts of southeast Australia their population was already below the numbers that could have been and had been supported by the natural resources of the region. Thus "whites faced black when their populations were dramatically destabilised, were no longer optimal and when there was large scale excess capacity available to blacks."[14] While it is possible that the colonists' taking of resources was not in itself an important cause of Aboriginal mortality, there is no doubt that disputes over resources occasioned violence—an undoubted cause of mortality. Another historian of Aborigines' experience of smallpox, Rosemary Campbell, conjectures that the disease so decimated Aborigines that it precluded their effective resistance to the colonists.[15]

Butlin's speculative model of the impact of disease does not go beyond 1850. Some time after that, the Aboriginal population stabilised and began to recover. Smith estimates that Aboriginal populations in southeast Australia probably stabilised by about 1880, through a combination of increased fertility and lower mortality. In the third phase, the Aboriginal populations began to grow. The information for dating the beginning of this growth is patchy, but Smith estimates that it started in the period 1890s to 1920s.[16]

Why did the Aboriginal population start to grow? The answers to this question are as likely to be politically sensitive as the answers to the question: why did it decline? Were the welfare efforts of concerned colonists—in governments and churches—effective in reversing the effects of disease and violence?

Because the Census began to give indirect evidence of the births and deaths of all indigenous Australians only two thirds of the way through the twentieth century, no comprehensive account of this recovery is possible. However, the births and deaths of one local population—those associated with the Point McLeay Mission (Raukkan) in South Australia—were recorded from 1870 to 1964. In 1870, there were 271 Aboriginal people at Raukkan. Social scientist Fay Gale found reliable information about the birth, fertility, and death of 2336 persons who were subsequently associated with that mission. She calculated the birth rate and the death rate among these people for 19 (five-yearly) periods. From 1870 to 1894, the population declined because death rates were higher than birth rates. She infers that this decline continued a trend that had begun when Aborigines first came into contact with colonists, around 1838. From 1895, the birth rate rose. More and more of the births were the result of sex between an Aboriginal and a non-Aboriginal person, but the Raukkan people deemed these babies to be no less "Aboriginal" for that. (Some commentators, regarding only "full bloods" as "true Aborigines," could still maintain that the "race" was "doomed"). Though epidemics of respiratory illness threatened this population recovery between 1905 and 1909, birth rates continued to exceed death rates, as the death rate slowly declined. This population recovery accelerated between 1910 and 1940, and continued in the period 1940 to 1964. Though the birth rate declined after 1940, so too did the death rate. Eventually population pressure encouraged a steady stream of migration away from Raukkan.[17]

What changes in Aboriginal life caused the recovery (from 1895) and what factors have sustained this recovery? Gale mentions white interventions that probably caused the mortality rate to fall: reduced contact with non-Aborigines (other than those sanctioned by mission authorities) and medical attention to reduce the very high rates of infant and child mortality. After the high toll on the first generation of people exposed to new diseases, the immediately following generations would have "acquired immunity" to "European" diseases. Gale suggests as a reason for the late nineteenth century rise in fertility the increasing proportion of "mixed bloods" and the Aborigines' adjustment to a changed way of life. That adjustment may also have contributed to reducing mortality, Gale implies, when she speculates that to be sedentary on a settlement was, for the first generation that attempted it, an unhealthy way of life.[18]

Gale's study does not discuss farming at Raukkan. Did it not secure the supply of nutritious food, and provide many with exercise? When she mentions economic factors it is rather to make the point that the Raukkan population was resilient in the face of one of the twentieth century's demographic shocks. The Depression of the 1930s did not slow the growth of the Raukkan population as it slowed growth of the Australian population (to less than one per cent per year, in the 1930s). For Aborigines, the Depression presented no greater material hardship than periods of general prosperity, Gale explains. Not until the Second World War (when Aborigines experienced unprecedented employment opportunities away from Raukkan) did the population trends among Raukkan folk parallel the Australia-wide trends.

Gale's history of those associated with Raukkan suggests that some colonial institutions that set Aborigines apart and subjected them to what we now consider to be illiberal and stigmatising custody also contributed to reversing the destruction of the Aboriginal population. Other studies point in the same direction. The Commonwealth government included Western Desert people in its welfare administration during the Second World War, opening ration depots at Haasts Bluff (1941) and Areyonga (1943). The birth rates and death rates of those in contact with Haasts Bluff in 1946-50 and 1957-9, reported by Jeremy Long, a public servant then responsible for looking after Haasts Bluff residents, show an increase in birth rates and a decrease in death rates. Long's suggested causes were: an improving diet, access to medical care, and acquired immunities to disease. Moreover, the assurance of a food supply in one place had relaxed one of the restraints on fertility. In the hunter gatherer economy, it had been difficult to support children if they were less than four years apart, but now "the reasons for limiting family size no longer hold good, and infant mortality has been reduced, especially at the crucial weaning period, when, in the bush, malnutrition was the normal condition." Gordon Briscoe's account of Western Australia's and Queensland's Aboriginal population data from 1900 to 1940, paying particular attention to sex ratio and age structure, concludes that these States' missions and settlements did more good than harm to the mortality and morbidity rates of those whom they sequestered. Peterson and Taylor's analysis of Tiwi population data from 1929 to 1996 suggests a sequence of different effects of government and mission intervention. A poorly resourced mission at first made the people less healthy in inducing them to be more sedentary. Sustained growth began soon after Second World War, probably the effect of a new hospital (1946) on infant mortality. However, the mission became overcrowded, and infant mortality rose. Meanwhile Tiwi fertility remained high by Australian standards. The Tiwi population grew consistently from the mid 1970s, when they got access to cash welfare benefits. Infant mortality rates seem to have been affected by the quality of medical care, housing and sanitation, and by levels of cash income and infrastructure funding. The viability of the Tiwi population, once it was incited to become more sedentary and centralised, has been largely determined by the quality and quantity of church and government support.[19]

Factors Sustaining "Recovery"

To what extent can the recovery of the Aboriginal population be explained by the changing definition of the "Aboriginal population" and by the improved coverage of government efforts at enumeration? There is no doubt that definitions and coverage have changed, as Smith summarises:

> Initially, Aborigines enumerated were those in employment, on settlements or in contact, often including numbers of people of mixed descent; those excluded were tribal people not in regular contact, presumably mostly of full Aboriginal descent. With the development of restrictive legislation [starting in Victoria in 1886], people of mixed descent were progressively excluded from, or voluntarily left, the identified or official Aboriginal population. At the same time tribal ("full-blood") people were being attracted or confined to institutional settlements or being overtaken by the frontier of settlement, and hence included in population statistics. Finally, in recent times, with the "full-blood" people now fully identified and enumerated [that is, by 1966], the combination of changing policies and changing identifications has resulted in large numbers of "part-Aboriginal" people previously excluded from the Aboriginal population moving back into it.[20]

In the "doomed race" theory, it was only the "full bloods" that were imagined to be dying out. How have these "full bloods" fared in the twentieth century? One statistical series allows an answer to that question. Using the best estimates of the five mainland States and the Commonwealth, but excluding the Western Australian government's estimates of "full bloods" not in contact with any administration, we can see a decline followed by a recovery in "full blood" numbers between 1921 and 1966 (the last Commonwealth Census using the classification "full-blood"). From 52,738 in 1921, their numbers sank to a low of 39,415 in 1954, recovering to 53,390 by 1966.[21] This recovery is possibly exaggerated by the imprecision of the term "full-blood" and the likelihood that some Aborigines, proud of their heritage and resenting the classificatory zeal of governments, presented themselves as "full bloods," whatever the details of their ancestry.

If we abandon the "doomed race" theory's fixation on "full bloods" in order to recognise as "Aboriginal" those of mixed descent who identify as "Aboriginal", then the recovery of the total Aboriginal populations was much steeper and began earlier. According to the States and Territories estimates—not to be confused with the Commonwealth Censuses—between 1921 and 1944 this (full-blood plus others) total remained almost static (falling slightly from 67,918 to 67,886). From 1944 to 1966, however, it grew to 130,207. Another way to describe this trend in the "full-blood plus other" Aboriginal population is to say that in 1921 the ratio of "full bloods" to other "castes" was about 4 to 1; by 1966 that ratio was 2 to 3. In short, the recovery of the Aboriginal population since the middle of the twentieth century is due to a small extent to a rise in the numbers of enumerated and estimated "full bloods" (as administrative coverage improved), and to a large extent to the rise in the enumerated and estimated "others" as official and popular attitudes favoured considering "mixed descent" people as part of the total "Aboriginal" population. We know that large numbers of Aboriginal children were taken from their natural parents and brought up in foster homes and in institutions. This was especially likely to happen to those classed as "half-castes." However, we do not have systematic data about how this process affected their subsequent classification by officials or their self-identification, where that was relevant to enumeration. Although, in theory, many such children were being pushed out of the legally-defined Aboriginal milieux through adoption, there were lots of ways for them to pass back into the milieux of the dark people (whether or not they ever re-discovered their family of origin) and thus to be enumerated once more as "Aborigines."

After the 1966 Census, the enumeration of indigenous Australians ceased to make distinctions of "caste." From 1971, the Bureau of Census and Statistics established a new approach that minimized officials' influence on the enumeration of "race" and maximized the impact of respondents' discretion. "In consultation with persons and organizations concerned with Aboriginal affairs, the Bureau decided to abandon the 'biological' or 'genealogical' concept of race in favor of an entirely social or self-identification concept."[22] That is, all respondents to the Census were asked to choose whether they were to be recorded as Aboriginal, Torres Strait Islander, European or "other." The indigenous totals in the Censuses since 1966 have been:

1966	101,978
1971	115,953
1981	159,897
1986	227,645
1991	265,458
1996	352,970
2001	410,003[23]

Demographers have been puzzled by the high rate of increase in the indigenous population in the last third of the twentieth century. Does it reflect high rates of indigenous Australian women's fertility? In her analysis of the Raukkan birth and death data in the mid 1960s, Gale put fertility in the long-term perspective of colonial history. "Fertility declined for many years after the initial white contact. Then, as the percentage numbers of mixed-bloods increased, and Aborigines adjusted to a changed way of life, fertility rose to unprecedented levels. Then slowly it began to decline again, although it remained considerably higher than the fertility of the average Australian woman."[24] Gale explained the declining fertility of people associated with Raukkan as the result of moving to the city and living like white people (that is, with small family/households considered the norm With urbanisation, Aboriginal women became more interested in family planning and in non-Aboriginal partners. As Aboriginal women overcame their social isolation within the state's welfare institutions, Gale suggested, their fertility would fall. Whether that is the reason for the falling fertility of indigenous women remains an open question. However, there has undoubtedly been a steady and nationwide trend for indigenous Australian women to give birth to fewer children. Gray's 1997 estimates of Aboriginal and Torres Strait Islander women's fertility showed it to have declined steadily over the forty years to 1996, and quite sharply within the fifteen years from 1966 to 1981.[25] When Taylor reproduced these estimates, he pointed out that the current Total Fertility Rate of 2.7 represents a fall of about 50 per cent in indigenous women's fertility since 1970.[26] Recently, Kinfu and Taylor have concluded from 2001 Census data that the total fertility rate for indigenous women "has reached, or may even now be below, replacement level." [27]

Notwithstanding this trend, there has been extraordinary growth of the Aboriginal population. Demographers offer three explanations. First, it is likely that public attitudes have encouraged many people who might once have "passed" as "White" to identify as Aboriginal. Second, the indigenous death rate has fallen in the second half of the twentieth century. (However, it is currently a matter of political anguish in Australia that Aboriginal mortality remains higher than for "all Australians," and the downward trend of Aboriginal mortality "flattened out" in the 1990s.)[28] Third, the Aboriginal population is being boosted by the recruitment of spouses from the non-indigenous population. That is, when Aboriginal men or women take a non-Aboriginal partner, they mostly regard their offspring as "Aboriginal," and so these children are counted as Aboriginal in the Census. About one third of "indigenous births" are now to non-indigenous women who have taken indigenous partners. Gray illustrates the significance of "out-marriage" as a stimulus to indigenous population growth.

> If an Aboriginal man and an Aboriginal woman each have two children, and the man and woman are married to each other, then the next generation has exactly the same size as the parents' generation. But if each is married to a non-Aboriginal person, the number of children is four and the next generation is twice as large.[29]

This tendency to out-marriage might well be—as Gale suggested—one of the factors influencing Aboriginal women to have fewer babies (that is, conforming to the long-standing tendency among non-indigenous Australians to form small families). However, at the same time, the tendency to out-marriage is now the main source of growth in the indigenous population. "Even if indigenous women achieve replacement level fertility, the additional contribution of indigenous births to non-indigenous mothers will continue to boost indigenous population growth far above the level achieved by the rest of the population."[30]

This trend has an interesting long-term consequence. "Eventually virtually all people with Australian-born parents will have indigenous descent, however dilute."[31] We have no sound basis for predicting what proportion of these "dilute" indigenous Australians will choose to identify as "Aboriginal" or as "Torres Strait Islander." However, there is no doubt that the indigenous Australian population, assumed until the 1930s to be headed for extinction, has bounced back and will continue to grow.

Notes

1. A. Gray, "Demographic and Social History," in The Encyclopedia of the Australian People, ed. J. Jupp, Part II, "Indigenous Australians" (Melbourne and Cambridge, 2001), 88-93.
2. J. Mulvaney "Difficult to found an opinion: 1788 Aboriginal population estimates," in The Aboriginal Population Revisited: 70,000 Years to the Present, ed. G. Briscoe and L. Smith (Aboriginal History Monograph, vol. 10, 2002), 1-8.
3. A.R. Radcliffe-Brown, "Former numbers and distribution of the Australian Aborigines," Official Yearbook of the Commonwealth 23, 671-96.

4. On the question of definition, see J. McCorquodale, "The legal classification of race in Australia," *Aboriginal History* 10 (1986): 7-24.

5. Cited by L. Smith, *The Aboriginal Population of Australia* (Canberra, 1980), 227.

6. Cited by R. McGregor, *Imagined Destinies: Aboriginal Australians and the Doomed Race Theory, 1880-1939* (Melbourne, 1997), 14.

7. McGregor, *Imagined Destinies,* 52.

8. Smith, *Aboriginal Population,* chapter seven.

9. Whether the authors of the Constitution intended this effect is doubtful. See G. Sawer, "The Australian Constitution and the Australian Aborigine," *Federal Law Review* 2, no. 1 (1966): 17-36; Smith, *Aboriginal Problem,* 20-23.

10. Smith, *Aboriginal Problem,* 29-35.

11. A. Grenfell Price, *White Settlers and Native Peoples* (Melbourne, 1950), 117-21. This book was substantially written in the late 1930s.

12. I draw heavily on N.G. Butlin, *Our Original Aggression* (Sydney, 1983).

13. Smith, *Aboriginal Population,* 228f.

14. Butlin, *Our Original Aggression,* 57.

15. J. Campbell, *Invisible Invaders: Smallpox and other Diseases in Aboriginal Australia 1780-1880* (Melbourne, 2002).

16. Smith, *Aboriginal Population* 229-33.

17. F. Gale, "A Changing Aboriginal Population," in *Settlement and Encounter: Geographical Studies Presented to Sir Grenfell Price,* ed. F. Gale and G. Lawton (Melbourne and Oxford, 1969), 65-88.

18. Gale, "Changing Aboriginal Population," 82.

19. This paragraph draws on J.P.M. Long, "Change in an Aboriginal community in Central Australia," in *Diprotodon to Detribalisation,* ed. A.R. Pilling and R.A. Waterman (East Lansing, 1970), 318-332; G. Briscoe, *Counting, Health and Identity: A History of Aboriginal Health and Demography in Western Australia and Queensland* (Canberra, 2003); and N. Peterson and J. Taylor, "Demographic Transition in a Hunter-Gatherer Population: The Tiwi Case, 1929-96," *Australian Aboriginal Studies* no. 1 (1998): 11-27.

20. Smith, *Aboriginal Population,* 55.

21. I draw here on Smith, *Aboriginal Population,* Table 8.1.3, 201-3, a table that excludes the ACT and Tasmania.

22 Smith, *Aboriginal Population,* 44.

23. The reader will note a large difference between the 1966 Census total and the 1966 combined estimate of all States and Territories (save ACT and Tasmania) cited earlier. Len Smith (per comm) advises that the larger 1966 figure is the more soundly-based.

24. Gale, "Changing Aboriginal Population," 82.

25. A. Gray, "The Explosion of Aboriginality: Components of Indigenous Population Growth 1991–6," CAEPR Discussion Paper 142,1997, Table 1.

26. J. Taylor, "Transformations of the Indigenous population: Recent and future trends." CAEPR Discussion Paper 194, 2000, 5.

27. J. Kinfu and J. Taylor, "Estimating the Components of Indigenous Population Change, 1996-2001," CAEPR Discussion Paper 240, 2002, 15.

28. A. Gray, "The Future History of Aboriginal Families," *The Aboriginal Population Revisited,* ed. G. Briscoe and L. Smith, 109-131, 123.

29. Gray, "Future History of Aboriginal Families," 129.

30. Gray, "Future History of Aboriginal Families," 118.

31. Gray, "Future History of Aboriginal Families," 118.